MAN IN ISOLATION & CONFINEMENT

MAN IN ISOLATION & CONFINEMENT

JOHN RASMUSSEN
editor

AldineTransaction
A Division of Transaction Publishers
New Brunswick (U.S.A.) and London (U.K.)

First paperback printing 2008
Copyright © 1973 by Transaction Publishers.

This book is printed on acid-free paper that meets the American National Standard for Permanence of Paper for Printed Library Materials.

Library of Congress Catalog Number: 2007027151
ISBN: 978-0-202-36145-1
Printed in the United States of America

Library of Congress Cataloging-in-Publication Data

Rasmussen, John.
    Man in isolation and confinement / John Rasmussen, editor.
        p. cm.
    Originally published: Chicago : Aldine Pub. Co., 1973.
    Includes bibliographical references and index.
    ISBN 978-0-202-36415-1 (acid-free paper)
    1. Social isolation. I. Rasmussen, John E.

HM1131.M35   2007
302.5'45—dc22   2007027151

Contents

Preface

The chapters of this volume constitute a substantial expansion and revision of papers presented at a Symposium on Man in Isolation and/or Enclosed Space, sponsored by the NATO Science Committee Advisory Group on Human Factors and held in Rome, Italy, 20–24 October 1969. In every case, developments in the field subsequent to the symposium have been included.

The major contributions to research on human behavior in isolation and confinement have been made in a relatively limited number of laboratories and by surprisingly few leaders in the field. As much of the research in this area has been based on team approaches to the same experimental populations, an effort has been made to omit overlap in content wherever possible. However, this cannot fully be achieved without destroying the logical thrust or conceptual foundation upon which the various authors base their own position and research. Each author has been permitted the freedom of describing and interpreting the basic experimental or field situations under which his data were collected, as well as the results of this study, in his own fashion. Thus, by design, several of the same major studies are described more than once in the volume.

Carefully selected investigators, who over the years have become internationally known authorities, were invited to make major presentations in the particular area of their expertise at the symposium. Three 45-minute to 1-hour papers, each representing an interrelated and logical unit, were presented each day. Each paper was followed by a 15-minute formal discussion and a 30-minute break. Formal papers often fail however to meet the need for the type of individual exchange of information and ideas which is so necessary in scientific communication. Accordingly, 2½ hours at the end of the day were devoted to a workshop where the three major speakers were available for informal discussion with the conference participants. The last day of the symposium was devoted to synthesizing the week's effort.

The program originally was planned to include a distinguished European psychologist, not necessarily working in the area of isolation, as the discussant for each major presentation. This goal was only partially achieved; last minute changes left us without formal discussants for several papers. But the quality and significance of the formal discussants' presentations were such as to rank their contribution on a par with the major papers. It is on this basis that Professor Fraisse and Madame de Montmollin were requested to expand their discussions into chapters for this volume. Drs. Bouvier, Nuttin, and Fokkema were asked to combine their presentations to form another chapter. Unfortunately, previous commitments and geographical separation made this unpractical.

The area of sensory deprivation was covered in two papers. Professor Zubek covered general development of the field and primarily considered North American research. Professor Bonaiuto reviewed work in this area from his and other European laboratories. Because of other pressures on his time, Dr. Bonaiuto was unable to prepare his manuscript for publication. The volume suffers, therefore, from the absence of this important contribution.

The afternoon workshops proved to be so lively that it frequently became difficult to close the discussion at the end of the day, even though the free discussions were carried out in three languages with all of the translation difficulties expected under such circumstances. Because of the monumental task of transcribing and editing the approximately 20 hours of multilingual discussion, no attempt was made to include in this volume the rather stimulating and exciting conclusions that grew out of the workshop experience.

The idea of an international conference on problems of man in isolation originated with the Advisory Group on Human Factors, which invited me to organize the program and serve as the symposium director. As is the case of any international meeing, arrangements for the symposium were complex. The Associate Director, Professor Paulo Bonaiuto of the Institute of Psychology, Bologna University, Bologna, Italy, worked with tireless dedication both in development of the program and in supervising the administrative arrangements, housing, and registration in Rome. In this effort Professor Bonaiuto was most admirably assisted by three colleagues at Bologna, Drs. M. Renna, R. Naldi, and S. Salvagni. It is not possible to acknowledge all of the psychologists who participated in development and shaping of the symposium program and this book. However, in terms of actual time devoted to this task, Drs. I. Altman, P. D. Nelson, and W. L. Wilkins deserve a special vote of thanks. Mr. M. A. G. Knight, of the Scientific Affairs Division, NATO, occupied a particularly important role in providing advice and guidance with regard to NATO Science Committee policies, as well as in solving several administrative and financial crises that arose in connection with the symposium. The excellent meeting and simultaneous translation facilities of the Italian National Research Council were made available through the courtesy and cooperation of Senator Professor Antonio Bonadies, the Italian Undersecretary of State for Coordination of Research and Technology, and Professor Amedeo Giacomini of the Italian National Research Council.

Finally, a word of thanks and appreciation must be extended to Miss Christina Nesbitt, ONR, London; Mrs. Betty Saunders, Bureau of Medicine and Surgery, Navy Department, Washington, D.C.; and Mrs. Nadene Ped, my present secretary, for their dedicated and efficient assistance in organizing the symposium and in preparing as well as editing this manuscript.

Man
in
Isolation
and
Confinement

John E. Rasmussen, *Director of the Battelle Human Affairs Research Centers in Seattle, received his Ph.D. in psychology from American University in 1961. A career Navy Medical Service Corps officer, he had assignments that included serving as Head of the Clinical Psychology Program; Director of the Behavioral Science Department, Navy Medical Research Institute; Head, Neuropsychiatric Section, Research Division, Bureau of Medicine and Surgery; and Liaison Scientist in Psychology, Office of Naval Research, London. At the time of his retirement as a Captain in 1969, he was serving as Assistant to the Chief of Naval Development for Medical and Allied Sciences. While in the Navy he was actively involved both in the research and the operational aspects of the Navy's Antarctic, underwater, and fallout shelter programs. He is a Fellow of the American Psychological Association, the American Association for the Advancement of Science, and the Royal Society of Medicine.*

1

Introduction

JOHN E. RASMUSSEN

Although man has lived and worked under conditions of isolation and confinement for many centuries, only recently has there been any major, sustained, *scientific* interest in problems of human adjustment to such conditions. A few years ago the study of small crew interaction was not considered sufficiently important to be included in planning projected requirements for research to support United States manned spaceflight. Nevertheless, the last two decades, and particularly the last 10 years, have seen a tremendous growth in large-scale research programs concerned with isolation and confinement. What has stimulated such an intensive interest in these problem areas during recent years, and why has the research effort been so much more heavily concentrated in Canada and the United States than in Europe?

At the risk of oversimplification, several major influences may be postulated as responsible for development and maintenance of interest in these research problem areas: the concern with "brainwashing" that arose from the Korean war; the advances in engineering technology that made it possible to sustain life in exotic environments; the wide publicity given to early research findings and the glamour of pioneering isolation programs; and the continued quest for a fundamental understanding of human behavior. Hebb's (Bexton, Heron, & Scott, 1954) pioneering work in sensory deprivation initially was stimulated by a concern of the Canadian government about the problem of brainwashing.

It may be legitimate to speculate, however, as to whether this area of research would have attracted as much attention as it did among experimental and theoretical psychologists if Hebb's rather dramatic initial findings had not been extended, elaborated, and above all widely publicized by Vernon in his early Princeton studies (Vernon & McGill, 1957; Vernon, McGill, & Schiffman, 1958). The attention drawn by the spectacular and dramatic nature of these findings quite possibly had a significant part in stimulating the development of long-term and continuing systematic investigation of sensory deprivation as well as of group behavior under conditions of isolation and confinement.

While there was some limited, although significant, early work on small groups in isolation, the beginning of the major programmatic and systematic efforts in this area of social psychology well may be traced to an incident that occurred in connection with the 1957 International Geophysical Year program. Again, drama rather than science per se may have been responsible for stimulation of a major research area. Would a major research program have been undertaken had an individual in the United States Antarctic team not developed a florid and highly disruptive schizophrenic illness while totally isolated with a small group of men in the middle of the long winter night? As in the case of sensory deprivation, research was stimulated for very pragmatic reasons; officials responsible for administration of the Antarctic programs encouraged systematic study and made funds available in the hope of precluding future incidents of disruptive behavior in their program. The advent of space flight, as well as the experiments in underwater living made possible by the discovery of saturation diving, have given additional major impetus to research on small groups in isolation.

The circumstances and technological advances leading to our present-day space and Antarctic programs have created a set of conditions that had not previously been encountered as man lived and worked in isolation. As discussed elsewhere (Rasmussen & Haythorn, 1963), it is possible that this particular set of conditions also has contributed to the rapid expansion of research activity on behavior in isolation and confinement. Thus, for the first time man faced situations involving a unique combination of (1) prolonged total isolation in a sensory-poor environment, (2) intensive, enforced interaction between members of small groups, (3) total interdependence of all individuals for group survival, (4) total impossibility of removing an ineffective crew member, and (5) sustained demands for vigilance and reaching rapid and often irrevocable decisions. In addition, major financial and ideological commitments are made on a nationwide basis to the accomplishment of the mission. The flurry of concern with organization and management of fallout shelters in the late 1950s and early 1960s also undoubtedly sparked interest in this area.

While military problems and the evolution of technology initially may have stimulated scientific interest and investigation, the effort appears to have been sustained by a desire on the part of psychologists and others to understand human behavior and the nature of man's interaction with his environment. For example, present-day sensory deprivation work continues, even though public concern with brainwashing is no longer great enough to provide the impetus for systematic investigation. Likewise, much of the work on small groups in isolation is motivated by a concern with adding to man's fundamental knowledge of human behavior. Some of the major recent developments in social psychology, both in terms of content and methodology, have arisen out of the study of small groups in confinement. This book attempts to explore these contributions.

Several major factors appear to be responsible for the greater emphasis on research in isolation and confinement in North America than in Europe. Such research is extremely costly; few professional groups anywhere in the world, including North America, can afford to equip laboratories and logistically support research programs without considerable impetus from institutions and organizations wishing to apply the results of these efforts. Certainly most of the funds have come from military and space program sources. This is beginning to change. Fortunately, there is a growing interest on the part of European behavioral scientists in this problem area, as witnessed by the fact that the symposium upon which this book is based was initially proposed by our Italian colleagues.

The terms *isolation* and *confinement,* as well as *natural* and *artificial* groups, will be used in a very broad sense throughout this book. Without attempting to provide rigorous definitions, it may be well to briefly explore the implications of these concepts as an introduction to the chapters that follow. At the most gross level of description, isolation might be considered primarily a psychological concept and confinement primarily a physical concept. Isolation is seen as a reduction in level of normal sensory and social input without necessarily involving a limitation in physical space or freedom of movement. While there are obvious physical aspects to the concept of isolation (most people would agree that a castaway on a desert island is isolated), the psychological implications of the concept rest primarily with the individual's own perception of and emotional response to his physical environment. It is possible, therefore, to conceive of an old person in a large city as being far more isolated than a lighthouse keeper or a solitary trapper in the Canadian wilderness.

Confinement means different things to different people. As used in this volume, the term generally connotes a limitation in amount of physical space and/or a restraint on actual physical movement. Isolation may or may not involve physical confinement. Likewise, a situation perceived as confining by one person may be perceived differently by others.

The understanding and prediction of behavior under isolation or confined conditions cannot be accomplished solely on the basis of the above dimensions. Two additional issues must be considered—the individual, and the group or segment of society in which he is functioning at the time. In this book a distinction has been made between *artificial* and *natural* groups. One again encounters problems of definition and taxonomy. As generally used in this volume, the term *natural group* refers to groups of individuals functioning in their natural work or social environment rather than in a laboratory or a simulated situation.

A third issue, which is methodological in nature, is introduced as one begins the systematic study of man under conditions of isolation and confinement. This is the very nature of the situations involved in the study, ranging from highly controlled, experimental laboratory studies, to unobtrusive observation in a naturalistic environment. Thus, the least sophisticated framework under which one might conceptualize studies in isolation and confinement includes consideration of three major issues.

This book represents the first attempt to cover the total spectrum of isolation and confinement in one volume. The chapters are arranged so as to begin with study of the individual, proceed through artificial and natural groups, and conclude with broad ecological and taxonomic considerations. With one exception, Dr. Wilkins's summary, the chapters may be grouped into three overlapping units as indicated below.

Individual	*Group*	*Social Systems and Taxonomy*
Chap. 2: Classical sensory deprivation Chap. 3: The individual in underground cave studies Chap. 4: The individual in natural settings	Chap. 5: The individual in artificial group experiments Chap. 6: Field studies of groups under indirect observation Chap. 7: Field studies of groups under direct observation	Chap. 8: Controlled laboratory studies of artificial groups Chaps. 9, 10: The ecology of groups in enclosed space Chap. 11: The taxonomy of man in enclosed space

The first three chapters focus primarily on the individual. Professor Zubek's chapter deals with sensory deprivation, a condition of maximum environmental artificiality combined with maximum freedom of the investigator to experimentally manipulate both the environment and his subjects. The chapter by Professor Fraisse on cave studies represents an example of study focused on individuals under artificial field conditions which, at the same time, permit moderate experimental manipulation.

The situation studied by Fraisse represents an interesting and logical extension of the classical sensory-deprivation work. These experiments well may be considered classics in the study of time perception. Professor Haggard has concerned himself with the study of individual development in natural isolated groups and an enviromental setting where the problems of unobtrusive measures become paramount. This work, which is at the opposite end of the continuum from sensory deprivation, is undertaken without manipulation of either environment or subjects; and, quite obviously, there is no artificiality of environment.

The next three chapters are concerned with field research. There is little difference in artificiality of environment but some difference in the extent to which experimental conditions can be manipulated. Beyond this, there is a highly significant difference in methodological problems; direct observation is not possible in the Antarctic, where it is possible in undersea experiments. The Antarctic and underwater exploration programs of the past decade have provided previously unequaled opportunities for the systematic study of human behavior of small groups under real life conditions of isolation and confinement. Fortunately, full advantage has been taken of these situations. For example, Dr. Gunderson's chapter focuses on almost 15 years of research concerned with individual behavior in the isolation of Antarctica. Dr. Nelson approaches the same program from the standpoint of the group. Dr. Radloff presents a detailed consideration of a most unique field research situation—the Sealab and Tektite projects, where the small group is under direct observation while in meaningful real-world isolation.

The third set of chapters is concerned with broader and more general issues of isolation and confinement. Professors Haythorn and Altman have advanced bold theoretical formulations on the basis of their highly controlled laboratory studies of isolation and confinement. Dr. Haythorn is concerned with a highly artificial laboratory environment that permits extensive manipulation of the entire environmental context, although the severity and control of conditions does not reach that of sensory deprivation. His chapter is concerned with group rather than individual behavior.

The other three chapters in this section constitute the broadest treatment of the entire problem area, with Professor Altman's chapter on the ecology of isolation cutting across all of the preceding contributions. Madame de Montmollin's chapter provides an interesting and cogent extension of Dr. Altman's theoretical position.

Finally, one cannot intelligently cope with this broad problem area as a whole without considering questions of taxonomy addressed by Professor Sells. Dr. Sells has drawn heavily from U.S. Air Force sponsored studies in the Arctic and the American space program. At the same time, his own research goals have necessitated a broad look at the entire area of isolation and confinement in an effort to order data and findings into a meaningful conceptual framework.

Dr. Wilkins has undertaken the task of integrating, synthesizing, and critically examining the preceding chapters, both from the point of view of a behavioral scientist who has been involved in research in isolation and confinement since its early days, and from the standpoint of methodology. Each author has made his own individual contribution to this ill-defined and complex research area, as well as identifying future challenges. Dr. Wilkins explores a number of philosophical issues which permeate this research area by raising cogent and penetrating questions. In attempting to answer some of his own questions, he skillfully synthesizes the material of the preceding chapters and integrates the contents of this volume with the mainstream of human behavior.

Thus, while the separate chapters focus on problems of individual and group isolation and confinement from different prespectives, they all contribute to the overriding theme of the volume—that increased understanding of an important social issue depends on a spectrum of conceptual and methodological strategy, and on an interplay between what has been termed "basic" and "applied" research.

REFERENCES

Bexton, W. H., Heron, W., & Scott, T. H. 1954. Effects of decreased variation in the sensory environment. *Canad. J. Psychol.* 8:70–6.

Rasmussen, J. E., & Haythorn, W. W. 1963. Selection and environmental considerations arising from enforced confinement of small groups. *Proceedings, 2nd Manned Space Flight Meeting, AIAA,* 114–9.

Vernon, J. A., & McGill, T. E. 1957. The effect of sensory deprivation upon rote learning. *Amer. J. Psychol.* 70:637.

Vernon, J. A., McGill, T. E., & Schiffman, H. 1958. Visual hallucinations during perceptual isolation. *Canad. J. Psychol.* 12:31.

John P. Zubek *is Research Professor of Psychology and Director of the Sensory Deprivation Laboratory at the University of Manitoba in Winnipeg, Canada. After receiving his Ph.D. from Johns Hopkins University in 1950, he joined the staff of McGill University. In 1953 he went to the University of Manitoba as Head of the Department of Psychology, a position he held until 1961. In 1958, he initiated a large-scale program of research on the behavioral and physiological effects of sensory deprivation which has continued to the present time. He has published five books, including* Sensory Deprivation: Fifteen Years of Research, *and more than 50 journal articles on sensory isolation and confinement.*

Zubek discusses some of the historical influences that led to the world-wide experimental interest in sensory deprivation, as well as the various techniques that have been devised to achieve sensory restriction. He then presents a critical review of the main findings, particularly those derived from the exposure of human subjects to prolonged periods of sensory isolation and confinement. These results are described and evaluated under the following headings: subjective and questionnaire-elicited phenomena; cognitive functioning; susceptibility to persuasion or influence; stimulus-seeking behavior; sensory and perceptual-motor effects; biochemical and physiological changes; isolation tolerance and its prediction; counteracting the effects of isolation; recent research on the relative effects of confinement; social isolation and sensory restriction; and the main theories that have been advanced to explain the experimental findings. In addition, Zubek offers numerous suggestions and ideas for future research in this area of investigation.

2

Behavioral and Physiological Effects of Prolonged Sensory and Perceptual Deprivation: A Review

JOHN P. ZUBEK

Introduction

During the past 15 years considerable experimental interest has been shown in the behavioral and physiological effects resulting from the exposure of human subjects to a reduction in the level and variability of visual, auditory, and tactual-kinesthetic stimulation. The attempts to achieve such a reduction in environmental stimulation are commonly referred to by such terms as *sensory isolation, sensory deprivation,* and *perceptual deprivation.* Although interest in this field has had a long history (see Brownfield, 1965 and Solomon et al., 1957, for experiences of solitary sailors, Arctic and Antarctic explorers, prison inmates, mystics in seclusion, etc.), the first experimental work began in 1951 at McGill University, Montreal, under the direction of Professor D. O. Hebb (Bexton, Heron, & Scott, 1954). Its purpose was to further our understanding of the mechanisms underlying "brainwashing" (a term first employed during the Korean War), and of the lapses of attention noted under monotonous environmental conditions, such as watching a radar screen.

The results of this research were startling. The subjects, who were paid to do nothing except lie in a semisoundproofed cubicle for several days and wear translucent goggles and listen to a constant masking sound of low intensity, reported a variety of unusual subjective phenomena, such as vivid and highly structured hallucinations, delusions, and gross changes in the appearance of the perceptual environment upon emerging

The preparation of this review article has been supported by Grant 9425-08, Defense Research Board, Canada, and Grant APA-290, National Research Council, Canada.

9

from isolation. In addition to these introspective reports, objective test data were obtained that indicated an increased susceptibility to propaganda material, impairments in cognitive and perceptual functioning, and a progressive slowing of occipital alpha frequencies with increasing duration of isolation.

These dramatic results, together with three other post-World War II developments, soon excited considerable scientific interest in the effects of isolation (see Suedfeld, 1969a for historical background). The first postwar development involved the highly publicized "confessions" extracted by Communist interrogators (for example, the Cardinal Mindzenty case). What little information was available suggested that the results were obtained by techniques that often included solitary confinement and the deliberate improverishment of the prisoner's perceptual environment (Brownfield, 1965). Drugs and physical torture were apparently not used.

The second development was the arrival of the space age in October 1957. The crew members of a space vehicle not only have to function in very restricted quarters under relatively monotonous conditions, but also, more importantly, they are subjected to prolonged separation from their accustomed environment. Other technological advances, as reflected in increased use of submarines, isolated radar and meteorological stations in the Arctic and Antarctic, and of automated equipment in general, also provided considerable impetus to the initiation and development of research programs dealing with reactions to restricted sensory and social environments.

The final source of interest in this topic resulted from certain advances in neurophysiology, particularly the research on the reticular activating system, which is important in producing a general state of "arousal" or alertness in the organism. Since this alerting action appeared to be dependent upon the organism's exposure to a constantly changing sensory input, behavioral experiments employing conditions of either constant, nonvarying sensory stimuli, or a lack of sensory stimuli were required as possible tests of these neurophysiological findings. As a result of the converging influence of these various developments, experimental studies similar to those at McGill were initiated in numerous institutions, not only in North America but also in England, the Netherlands, Italy, Czechoslovakia, and Japan.

A survey of the experimental literature, which at present numbers well over a thousand publications (for comprehensive bibliographies see Svab & Gross, 1966; Weinstein et al., 1968; Zubek, 1969a), reveals wide differences in the quality of the studies, ranging from carefully designed experiments employing precise psychophysical measures to vaguely formulated studies with a handful of subjects, no controls, and relying entirely on oral reports from the subject unchecked for their reliability. Large differences also exist in the duration of the deprivation periods, ranging from a few minutes to 2 weeks. In this chapter, no attempt will be made to survey this voluminous literature in its entirety, since six books (Brownfield, 1965; de Ajuriaguerra, 1965; Schultz, 1965; Solomon et al., 1961; Vernon, 1963; Zubek, 1969a) and numerous review articles and chapters in edited books have dealt with it (for example Brownfield, 1964; Cameron et al., 1961; Fiske, 1961; Frankenhaeuser, 1968; Kenna, 1962; Kubzansky, 1961; Okuma, 1962; Riesen, 1966; Shurley, 1968; Svorad, 1960; Zubek, 1964a). My aim will be selective. First, emphasis will be placed almost exclusively upon well-controlled laboratory experiments that have employed human subjects individually exposed to *prolonged* periods of isolation. Little attention will be paid to the numerous short-duration studies of less than 1 day, since some doubts exist as to whether many of the reported effects are due to reduced sensory input (Cameron et al., 1961; Jackson & Pollard, 1962), and since the majority of these brief-duration studies are only of limited usefulness in furthering our knowledge about man in enclosed space. Second, this chapter will be devoted largely to a survey of the North American and Japanese literature, with only limited attention to the scanty European research.

Experimental Procedures

In surveying the literature on sensory restriction, one is struck not only by the variety of procedures and techniques that have been employed to reduce the level and variability of environmental stimulation (see Rossi, 1969), but even more so by the innumerable terms used to describe this experimental condition (see Brownfield, 1965, for a list of 25 terms). For the purposes of this chapter, however, a widely used, broad classification (Kubzansky, 1961) involving a differentiation between sensory deprivation (SD) and perceptual deprivation (PD) will be employed.

In the SD condition, efforts are made to reduce sensory stimulation to as low a level as possible. This is usually accomplished by the use of a dark, soundproofed chamber in which the subject, wearing gauntlet-type gloves, is instructed to lie quietly on a cot or mattress. Earplugs or earmuffs may be used to reduce further the level of sensory stimulation. Communication between subject and experimenter is kept to a minimum, thus reducing social stimulation. An even more severe procedure to produce "total" deprivation is the water-immersion technique (Lilly, 1956; Shurley, 1963, 1968) in which the subject, wearing nothing but an opaque mask, is immersed in a large tank of slowly flowing water (94° F) and instructed to inhibit all movements. Because of its severity, this procedure can only be used for short-term deprivation experiments. Maximum endurance is approximately 8 hours (Shurley, 1968). Although both of these procedures may attempt to totally eliminate all sensory stimulation this, of course, is not possible since some stimulation is invariably present as a result of imperfect soundproofing, tactual stimuli, and cardiac and respiratory sounds emanating from the subject himself. They do, however, provide as low a level of sensory input as is humanly possible.

In the PD condition, on the other hand, an attempt is made to reduce the patterning and meaningful organization of sensory stimulation while maintaining its level near normal. This is the McGill procedure. The subject typically lies on a cot in a chamber wearing gloves and translucent goggles, which permit diffuse light but eliminate all pattern vision. A masking sound, usually white noise, or less commonly the hum of a fan, is directed into both ears. The intensity of the light and noise is maintained at a constant level. A less widely used variation of the PD procedure, employed for durations of less than a day, involves placing the subject in a polio tank respirator and exposing him to the repetitive drone of a motor and a visual environment restricted to the front of the respirator and the blank surface of an overhead screen (Mendelson et al., 1961). It can be seen, therefore, that PD involves a higher level of sensory input

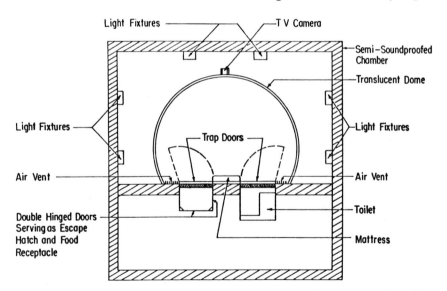

FIGURE 2.1 *This uniquely constructed isolation chamber, equipped with a closed circuit TV system, permits long-term studies (up to 2 weeks) to be carried out on either sensory or perceptual deprivation. A double trap-door arrangement makes it possible to administer food and a variety of tests with no direct contact with the isolated subject.* (Reprinted, with modifications, by permission from J. P. Zubeck, W. Sansom, & A. Prysiazniuk, 1960, *Canad. J. Phychol.* 14:233–43.)

than SD, but the stimulation is largely devoid of any meaningful organization. Figure 2.1 shows a cross-section of the University of Manitoba isolation chamber which, though it has been used primarily for studies on PD, can also, with a slight modification, be employed for experiments on SD. Using this chamber, Zubek and his associates have confined subjects for durations ranging from 1 to 14 days.

In addition to these two main types of procedures, which attempt to reduce the overall level and variability of stimulation from several sense modalities, my associates and I (Aftanas & Zubek 1963a 1963b, 1964; Zubek, Flye, & Aftanas, 1964; Zubek, Flye, & Willows, 1964) have more recently conducted a series of studies in which these procedures have been applied to only one modality—the restriction of visual input alone (darkness vs unpatterned stimulation)— or the restriction of tactile stimulation over a small circumscribed area of the skin (no stimulation vs constant pressure).

In order to present a more coherent overview of the research literature in this field, the differentiation between SD and PD as outlined above will be employed throughout the remainder of this chapter. This division is of considerable importance since these two experimental conditions are not always equivalent in either their physiological or behavioral effects (Zubek, 1964a).

Subjective Phenomena

APPEARANCE OF EXTERNAL ENVIRONMENT

One of the dramatic findings of the McGill studies was the presence of gross disturbances in the appearance of the perceptual environment (Bexton, Heron, & Scott, 1954; Doane et al., 1959). The subjects, after emerging from several days of PD, reported a variety of unusual experiences, such as movements of the visual field, changes in shape and size of objects, "exaggerated contrast, hyper-saturation and luminosity of colors, pronounced positive and negative after-images, accentuated or diminished depth of perception, and distortions of human faces. All of the effects described were obtained with both monocular and binocular vision, but were more marked binocularly" (Doane et al., 1959, p. 213). These phenomena usually disappeared in about half an hour. The aftereffects of 6 days of PD (Heron, Doane, & Scott, 1956) were even more "profound and prolonged" than those observed in the earlier shorter duration experiments: "the wall bulged towards me and went back; the experimenter looked short then he suddenly got taller, then he closed up again; the whole room is undulating, swirling; things don't stay put; people appear rouged" (p. 15). Some of these perceptual distortions were still present 24 hours later, in all three experimental subjects.

The presence of these unusual and pronounced subjective phenomena has not, unfortunately, been confirmed in subsequent research at other laboratories. For example, Vernon and Hoffman (1956) questioned four subjects, after 2 days of SD, specifically about difficulty in focusing, increased saturation of colors, and lack of three-dimensional depth perception, and reported negative findings for all three phenomena. Numerous investigators in various countries have also failed to observe these gross perceptual changes, regardless of the duration or type of deprivation condition employed—8 hours of PD (Schwitzgebel, 1962), 2 days of PD (Arnhoff, Leon, & Brownfield, 1962), 3 and 4 days of SD (Myers et al., 1966; Weinstein et al., 1967), 4 hours to 7 days of SD (Levy, Ruff, & Thaler, 1959; Ruff & Levy, 1959), and PD "for as long as you can take it" (Smith & Lewty, 1959). Negative results have also been reported from the Manitoba laboratory after a week of either SD or PD (Zubek et al., 1961, 1962). Furthermore, no gross perceptual distortions or disturbances have been observed even after 14 days of PD (Zubek, 1964b; Zubek, Welch, & Saunders, 1963) or after 7 days of PD with no test intrusions and no communication with the subject (Zubek, 1964c). In addition to these studies, others of varying duration could be cited in which no specific mention is made of the presence of postisolation perceptual distortions. If they had occurred to any noticeable degree, they would undoubtedly have been reported.

The overwhelming weight of experimental evidence, therefore, indicates that conditions of reduced sensory input, regardless of duration or severity, do not produce a disruption in the structural organization or appearance of the subject's perceptual environment, a finding contrary to that reported initially by the McGill laboratory. A satisfactory explanation of these contradictory results still remains, after many years, as one of the main unresolved problems in the deprivation literature. Although it has been demonstrated that numerous variables can influence the results of deprivation experiments (see Zuckerman, 1969a, for a detailed review), it is doubtful whether the operation of any *one* variable can account for the discrepancy between the McGill results and those reported from numerous other laboratories. A more likely possibility is that the unusual McGill phenomena were produced by some unique interaction of several variables of a procedural, personality, or motivational nature. Whether this unique set of conditions will ever be discovered is debatable.

HALLUCINATORY ACTIVITY

An even more dramatic aspect of the McGill studies (Bexton, Heron, & Scott, 1954; Doane, 1955; Heron, 1961; Heron, Doane, & Scott, 1956) was the report that various hallucinatorylike phenomena, similar in some respects to those described for mescal intoxication, were experienced by virtually all of their subjects during several days of PD. These phenomena were largely visual and ranged in complexity from meaningless flashes of light, dots, or geometric forms to meaningful integrated scenes of a picturelike nature, such as people, scenery, bizarre architecture, and so forth. Approximately two-thirds of the subjects experienced the simple visual sensations and one-third the more complex, meaningful phenomena. These "images" were often quite vivid, generally involved movement, could be scanned, and could not be terminated at will. The subjects, it is interesting to note, were surprised by these unusual experiences. This is an important point "because it bears on the set hypothesis which attempts to explain these phenomena as being due to expectation or experimental suggestion. Neither experimenters nor subjects in this first experiment expected the phenomena which appeared" (Zuckerman, 1969b, p. 95). Furthermore, the incidence of these visual sensations was much higher than that reported in subsequent studies when more publicity was given to the phenomena.

The presence of these symptoms, apparently similar to those observed in certain psychotic and drug-induced states, excited the interest of investigators, particularly clinically-oriented groups, since it appeared that a new experimental approach to the study of various abnormal or pathological states that had long resisted scientific analysis had been discovered. But in fact, the subsequent research work has generated more problems than it has solved.

Undoubtedly the most comprehensive review of the literature on hallucinatory activity during SD and PD (Zuckerman, 1969b) is an updated version of an earlier article published by Zuckerman and Cohen (1964). In attempting to cope with the problem of differences in terminology, Zuckerman and Cohen decided to substitute for *hallucinations* or *images* Murphy, Myers, and Smith's (1963) operational term *reported visual sensations* (RVSs). Furthermore, since the RVSs may vary in degree of structure and meaningfulness from flashes of light to complex integrated scenes, they advocated the grouping of these phenomena into two categories based primarily on their meaningfulness: Type A (flashes of light, dots, and geometric forms, for example) which may include simple idioretinal responses or illusions, and Type B (meaningful objects, people, scenes, and so forth) which seem to signify a greater cortical involvement. According to this system, the term *hallucination* should only be applied to the Type B phenomena. Since this classificatory system has been well received, it will be employed throughout this discussion.

A review of the extensive literature on this topic reveals that one of the main areas of controversy concerns the frequency of occurrence of RVSs. In general, the *majority* of the long-term studies, employing durations of 1 to 16 days, have reported either a total absence or a rare occurrence of both types of RVS phenomena (see, for example, Arnhoff, Leon, & Brownfield, 1962; Cameron et al., 1961; Gendreau et al., 1968; Kokubun & Ohyama, 1965; Ruff, Levy, & Thaler, 1961; Smith & Lewty, 1959; Vernon, Marton, & Peterson, 1961; Zubek, 1964b, 1964c; Zubek et al., 1962). These studies represent laboratory research conducted in Canada, the U.S., England, and Japan. On the other hand, the preponderance of the short-duration studies, employing deprivation periods ranging from 1 to 12 hours, have reported a fairly high incidence of RVSs Cohen et al., 1959; Davis, McCourt, & Solomon, 1960; Davis et al., 1961; Freedman & Greenblatt, 1960; Goldberger & Holt, 1958; Holt & Goldberger, 1961; Jackson & Kelly, 1962; Persky et al., 1966; Pollard, Uhr, & Jackson, 1963; Shurley, 1962; Zuckerman, Levine, & Biase, 1964; Zuckerman et al., 1962, 1966, 1968). According to Zuckerman and Cohen's (1964) survey of these studies, the median percentage of subjects reporting Type A RVSs is 43 per cent; for Type B RVSs the median is 19 per cent—figures somewhat lower than those reported in the early McGill studies.

In attempting to reconcile these two sets of apparently divergent results, Zuckerman (1969b) has suggested that Type A RVSs must undoubtedly have occurred in the long-duration studies but "either were not asked for by the interviewer or were not reported for other reasons. Although the methods are not thoroughly described in many of these reports, it would appear that spontaneous reporting of imagery was not encouraged by the experimenters in any of these experiments. Most of them apparently relied on post-isolation inquiries. A spontaneous visual sensation may be "remembered" more vividly by a subject in isolation for 1 hour than one in for a day or a week" (p. 108).

A second possible explanation of these divergent results may pertain to differences in the degree of stringency of the criteria for determining the presence or absence of hallucinatory activity. In the series of long-duration studies conducted by Vernon and Zubek at the Princeton and Manitoba laboratories, respectively, a visual experience in order to qualify as a hallucination had to possess an "out-thereness" quality, be capable of being scanned or attended to selectively, its appearance and disappearance had to be independent of the subject's volition, and the subject, at least at the beginning, had to be convinced of its reality (Suedfeld & Vernon, 1964; Zubek et al., 1962). If such stringent or even partially stringent criteria, which represent an adaptation of Guiraud's (1937) system, were employed in the other long-duration studies (unfortunately, no mention of criteria is made), an almost total absence of hallucinatory activity might be expected. But since none of the short-duration studies have employed these tough criteria, relying largely on what the subjects "saw before their eyes," the presence of a high incidence of hallucinatorylike phenomena is not surprising. In this connection, it is interesting to note that Myers and his colleagues, who did not employ the Vernon-Zubek criteria, reported a considerable amount of RVSs in a series of *long-duration* experiments involving periods of up to 4 days of SD (Murphy, Myers, & Smith, 1963; Myers et al., 1966).

Further evidence for the crucial importance of differences in criteria is provided in two recent studies. In the first, Zuckerman and Hopkins (1966) reported that 45 per cent of their subjects exposed to 1 hour of SD experienced Type A RVSs, and 18 per cent, Type B. However, they stated that few of their RVSs would have qualified as hallucinations if the Vernon-Zubek criteria had been applied.

In the second study, Schulman, Richlin, and Weinstein (1967) stated that of 71 subjects exposed to 3 days of SD, 74 per cent reported some type of RVS phenomena based on the simple criterion of verbal responses to questions on whether or not the subject "saw" such things as lights, spots, patterns, or meaningful objects. When the restriction was added that the RVSs must not be under the control of the subject, the frequency decreased to 23 per cent, and the "further restriction that the RVSs have some reality for S, at least at first, caused the RVSs to become quite infrequent" (2 per cent). In their discussion of this controversial topic, Schulman and her colleagues have concluded that "it seems clear that the confusion which has been apparent in the literature regarding both the frequency of visual hallucinations in sensory deprivation, and the nature of the hallucinations, whether true perceptual distortions or merely heightened fragments of normal imagery, is largely a function of the behavioral criterion of what constitutes an hallucinatory event. . . . There is no conflict among different experimental findings if the operational definitions of the relevant behaviors are held constant" (p. 1015). It would appear, therefore, that if future controversies are to be avoided, investigators should provide a detailed specification of the criteria being employed in their experiments.

In discussing the question of the actual incidence of RVS phenomena, many of the early investigators have overlooked the fact that various hallucinatorylike experiences, similar to those reported in the SD and PD literature, can occur even under relatively normal environmental conditions. For example, subjects exposed to 10 to 30 minutes of darkness (Myers & Murphy, 1962; Myers, Murphy, & Smith, 1961; Ziskind & Augsburg, 1962), or just lying quietly in an ordinary room with no restriction of sensory input (Zubek et al., 1962), have frequently reported RVSs of varying degrees of complexity. In view of these findings, it is imperative that future investigators establish a base line of "normally" occurring RVSs against which the deprivation phenomena can be evaluated. If this had been done in the earlier research, a much lower incidence of *SD-related* RVS phenomena would undoubtedly have been reported.

A second problem that has attracted considerable research is the determination of the relevant variables that can influence both the incidence and complexity of RVSs. According to Zuckerman (1969b), some of these variables are: type of procedure (SD or PD), deprivation duration, degree of motor activity, sex, intelligence, age, personality characteristics of the volunteers, level of arousal during RVSs, experimental set, prior knowledge about possible results, and method of reporting RVSs (continuous vs retrospective). Although most of this literature has produced conflicting results, certain general findings have emerged (Zuckerman, 1969b). First, the SD condition tends to produce a lower incidence of both types of RVSs than does the PD condition. Second, RVSs typically show a progression from the simple Type A to the more complex B phenomena. Third, there is some indication that only the Type A RVSs are vulnerable to the influence of experimental sets contained in the instructions given to the subjects. Fourth, most studies involving concurrent recording of EEG activity and spontaneous reporting of RVSs indicate that "they typically occur in states of high or medium arousal, even when such states are not preceded by periods of sleep" (p. 124).

The final problem concerns the degree to which the deprivation-elicited RVSs are similar to psychotic and drug-induced hallucinations (see, for example, Bliss & Clark, 1962; Cohen, Silverman, & Shmavonian, 1962; Lawes, 1963). The present status of this question has been well summarized by Zuckerman (1969b), who concluded that "most psychotic hallucinations are auditory, while auditory hallucinations of voices are rare in sensory deprivation experiments. RVSs show more resemblance to drug-induced hallucinations although the latter are more colorful, vivid, and persistent. Although an occasional RVS shows the characteristics of a psychotic hallucination, such as dimensionality, belief of subject, affect arousal, and dynamic significance, most seem to be transient, impersonal phenomena of no dynamic or pathological significance" (p. 124).

OTHER TYPES OF SYMPTOMATOLOGY

Most of the early research, relying largely on subjective, introspective reports, revealed the presence of a wide range of unusual experiences during both short-term and long-term deprivation periods (see Zuckerman, 1964, for review). For example, in the McGill PD experiments (Bexton, Heron, & Scott, 1954; Scott et al., 1959) the subjects reported an inability to concentrate and think clearly, boredom, high degree of restlessness, and changes in body-image. Many of them also developed a childish sense of humor, exaggerated emotional reactions, excessive irritation by small things, annoyance with the experimenters, and, occasionally, brooding and dwelling on imaginary injustices. Similar types of symptoms have been reported in the more recent research in which the phenomena have been investigated in a more objective and quantitative fashion.

Undoubtedly the most widely used standardized instrument in this area is the Isolation Symptom Questionnaire (ISQ) developed by Myers, Murphy, and Terry (1962). This questionnaire consists of 242 items embracing a variety of feelings and reactions and covering 23 categories or content areas. Furthermore, the 242 items were so devised as to be equally applicable to both isolated and ambulatory control groups, a procedure designed to take into consideration the fact that various "unusual" experiences can occur under relatively normal environmental conditions. In these more recent studies, the ISQ is typically administered at the end of the experimental period. The isolated subjects answer the items as they applied to the period spent in the chamber, while the ambulatory controls answer the same items as they applied to the corresponding period of normal life.

Administering the ISQ at the end of 7 days of PD, Zubek and McNeill (1967) reported a significantly higher incidence, relative to ambulatory controls, of such phenomena as RVSs, complex and vivid dreams, changes in body-image, loss of contact with reality, reminiscence and vivid memories, cognitive inefficiencies, speech impairments, temporal disorientation, anxiety, hunger, and subjective restlessness. There was also a significantly higher incidence of boredom, sexual and religious preoccupation, changes in self-appraisal, and novelty and surprise in the isolated relative to the control subjects. An almost identical set of results on the ISQ, it is important to note, has been reported by Myers, Murphy, and Terry (1962) and Myers et al. (1966) in volunteers exposed to 4 days of SD. Other investigators, using modifications of the ISQ and SD durations ranging from 8 hours to 3 days, have also observed a variety of affective and cognitive disturbances (see, for example, Schulman, Richlin, & Weinstein, 1967; Zuckerman et al., 1962, 1966).

In furthering our knowledge of the nature of these phenomena, two lines of future research may prove to be fruitful. First, is the incidence of these various symptoms related to the type of deprivation condition employed? Since it has been noted earlier that RVSs tend to be less frequent during SD than during PD, it is possible that some of the other unusual experiences may also show a lower incidence during the SD condition.[1] Although both types of conditions have been employed in the various laboratories, the large differences in deprivation durations and other procedural variables make a direct comparison impossible. Second, what is the temporal course of development of these phenomena as determined by periodic testing at various intervals *during* a prolonged period of depriva-

1. In a recently completed study at the University of Manitoba, employing a 4-day period of SD and PD, no significant differences were found between these two conditions on any of the symptom categories of the ISQ. However, a definite trend was observed. On most of the categories, the incidence was lower during SD.

tion—7 days, for example? This type of study would not only indicate the minimum duration required for their appearance; it might also reveal a different temporal pattern of development for the various subjective phenomena. For example, certain symptoms might be characterized by a progressive increase in incidence with increasing duration while others might reach an asymptote after a day or two. No such longitudinal experiment has as yet been conducted. What little data is available has been derived from a handful of cross-sectional studies (see Myers, 1969, pp. 292–94), but because of large interlaboratory procedural differences no meaningful conclusions can be drawn.

Cognitive Measures

The nature and extent of the cognitive changes seems to be related, to some degree, to the type of deprivation condition employed. There are indications that disturbances of cognitive functioning are greater after prolonged periods of PD than of SD. In the original McGill studies (Bexton, Heron, & Scott, 1954; Scott et al., 1959) the administration of a battery of objective tests revealed a consistently poorer performance on measures of verbal fluency, anagrams, and various numerical tasks presented orally during several days of PD. Tests of digit span, analogies, and associative learning showed little change. No cognitive deficits were observed on postisolation administered tests. Essentially similar results were reported in a 7-day PD study by (Zubek et al., 1962). Using a battery of both orally and visually presented tests, administered during isolation, we reported a significant impairment on arithmetic problems, numerical reasoning, verbal fluency, space visualization, abstract reasoning, and recognition. No significant changes were found on digit span, rote learning, recall, and verbal reasoning, although the performance on the last two tests tended to be worse. Furthermore, an analysis of the results of the quitters (those who were unable to endure the week of isolation) revealed a pattern of intellectual deficits similar to those shown by the successful endurers.

The effects of SD seem to be less severe than those of PD. In another experiment (Zubek, Sansom, & Prysiazniuk, 1960) in which the same cognitive battery was administered during 7 days of SD, we observed that only recall and recognition of nonsense syllables were significantly impaired. A similar lack of an effect has been reported in two other studies. In the first, Weinstein et al. (1967) observed no significant impairment on tests of verbal comprehension and space visualization during 3 days of SD. In the second study, using a large sample of 34 experimental and 34 control subjects, Myers et al. (1957) administered a battery of five cognitive tests before, during, and after 3 days of SD. Although a significant impairment was observed on successive subtraction and verbal fluency, no deficits were observed on arithmetic problems, inductive reasoning (coin change-making problems), and digit span. It is important to note, however, that no significant deficits on any of the tests were observed when they were administered shortly after the termination of isolation. Such an absence of postisolation cognitive deficits has also been reported by two other groups of investigators using either an SD (Levy, Ruff, & Thaler, 1959) or PD procedure (Scott et al., 1959). This apparent discrepancy is probably due to differences in the subject's motivational state during and after deprivation. Regardless of the explanation, these results indicate that whatever cognitive decrements are present are transitory in nature and specific to the isolation environment.

Although the performance on the standard types of structured cognitive test batteries does not appear to be affected to any noticeable degree by SD, the results of certain unstructured or open-ended tasks indicate a considerable impairment. Suedfeld, Grissom, and Vernon (1964) described a TAT-like scene to subjects before and just prior to the end of 1 day of SD. Their instructions were to make up a story as detailed and elaborate as possible. The stories were tape-recorded. The results revealed that the SD group decreased the length of its story by over one-third, while the controls showed essentially no change over the same time interval. Since in this first study a preliminary intergroup difference in story length was present, Suedfeld et al. (1965) replicated the study using groups of initially matched subjects. Identical results were obtained. A further confirmation of this decrease in verbal productivity has been reported by the Japanese investigator Oyamada (1966), who also employed TAT-like cards and a 1-day deprivation period. No significant decrement, however, occurred in an 18-hour study.

Although certain cognitive abilities are impaired, others appear to be facilitated or improved by prolonged deprivation periods. The first such report was by Vernon and Hoffman (1956) who, in an exploratory study, noted a significant improvement in rote learning ability (fewer trials to reach the criterion of one errorless trial) during 2 days of SD. In an attempt at replication, Vernon and McGill (1957) employed a larger sample of subjects and a 3-day period of SD. Using both trials and the number of errors to criterion as the measure of learning ability (list of 15 adjectives), no significant differences were observed between the experimental and control groups. However, the isolated subjects were less variable in their performance, made fewer incorrect responses, had fewer fluctuation cycles (correct response followed by an incorrect response), and also obtained a better efficiency ratio. Thus, an unmistakable trend toward an improvement in rote learning was observed. Further evidence in support of this finding has been reported by Zubek, Sansom, and Prysiazniuk (1960), who noted a superior performance on rote learning at virtually all test periods during 7 days of SD. Evidence is also available indicating an improvement in immediate memory span for digits (Cohen et al., 1961; Goldberger & Holt, 1958; Myers et al., 1957; Zubek et al., 1962) and memory for meaningful material, such as recall of prose passages and drawings of common objects (Grissom, 1963, 1966; Grissom, Suedfeld, & Vernon, 1962; Suedfeld & Landon, 1970).

In addition to the type of deprivation procedure employed, another important variable involved in determining the nature of the cognitive effects is deprivation duration. There are several scattered suggestions in the literature indicating that the greatest deprivation effects appear to occur after 1 day. Beyond this "critical period" the effects tend to diminish, presumably as a result of the adaptation of the subject to the impoverished sensory environment. For example, Scott et al. (1959) reported a significant impairment on tests of verbal fluency, anagrams, and number series at the end of 1 day of PD, but no significant change thereafter. Vernon (1961) has also demonstrated that a much higher percentage of subjects show an improvement in rote learning after 1 day than after 2 or 3 days of SD.

Finally, an even more impressive bit of evidence has been presented by Suedfeld and Landon (1970) in a study in which subjects were required to recall meaningful material at intervals of 0, 12, 24, or 36 hours of SD. A curvilinear performance was observed: memorization improved, reaching an optimal performance at 24 hours, and then declined. It is interesting to note that a critical period for the appearance of certain optimal *sensory and perceptual-motor effects* also appears to be present, but at 2 days rather than at the 1-day period (Zubek, 1969b). The existence of these critical periods, which seem to have been overlooked by most investigators in this field, can probably account for some of the negative or contradictory results reported in studies employing durations falling either below or above this critical range of 1 to 2 days.

From this survey of results it is clear that certain measures of cognitive functioning are impaired, others are unaffected, while still others appear to be improved. In attempting to account for this differential pattern of results, Suedfeld (1969b) has suggested that they may be related to differences in degree of complexity or open-endedness of the cognitive tasks being employed. According to Suedfeld, a simple or closed-end task is one whose solution depends "on the use of overlearned, structured, logical steps to reach a definite clear answer," while a cognitive task may be considered complex or open-ended if "new combinations must be made, uncertain approaches tried, new material generated, on the way to an unknown, self-defined, unstructured goal" (p. 147). Applying this hypothesis to a review of the literature, Suedfeld has concluded that "highly structured performances (retention and learning) seem to be undamaged or even facilitated by SD (used in a general sense to refer to both SD and PD conditions); moderately structured ones, such as problem solving on standard IQ and other test items, reveal some deficit; while considerable impairment occurs on unstructured behaviors such as projective test performance" (p. 165). A similar hypothesis (based, however, on somewhat limited data) was advanced in 1958 by Goldberger and Holt who stated that probably any task involving "active reflection and manipulation of ideas" rather than highly overlearned sets of operations (such as arithmetic problems) or requiring passive receptivity (such as digit span, rote learning) would be most affected by sensory isolation.

Although this hypothesis presents a reasonably accurate picture of the existing results, little evidence has been provided in support of the suggestion that unstructured test performance will be severely impaired. Since only a handful of prolonged duration studies (see, for example, Oyamada, 1966; Suedfeld & Landon, 1970; Suedfeld, Grissom, & Vernon, 1964; Suedfeld et al., 1965) have employed open-ended tests (largely restricted to storytelling and Uses tests), two studies were conducted at the University of Manitoba in an attempt to determine whether performance on a variety of other types of open-ended tests will similarly be impaired.

In the first study (Fuerst & Zubek, 1968), the Guilford battery of creative thinking, consisting of 10 subtests measuring the cognitive factors of fluency, flexibility, and elaboration, was administered as a paper-and-pencil test before and at the end of 3 days of a 4-day SD or PD condition. In both conditions, no significant differences were found between the isolated and control subjects on any of the ten cognitive tests. However, in both conditions the experimental subjects performed worse on eight of the ten subtests. In view of this definite trend toward impairment, and since the negative results could be attributed to the use of a deprivation period extending beyond the critical period of 1 day, a second study (Oleson & Zubek, 1970) was conducted in which the Guilford battery was administered at the end of one day of SD. In this study, the experimental subjects performed significantly worse on only 1 of the 10 subtests (associational fluency). However, on the three other measures of the fluency factor (word, expressional, and ideational fluency) a definite trend toward poorer performance was observed. No such trends, unfortunately, were present for the flexibility and elaboration factors.

These essentially negative results obtained in the 1-day Manitoba study are puzzling, particularly in view of the severe impairments on open-ended storytelling tasks noted in the other studies, also employing a 1-day period of SD. Two possible factors may account for this apparent discrepancy. The first pertains to test duration. In the Manitoba studies the Guilford battery required a completion time of approximately 1 hour, whereas in the others single tests requiring short durations of up to 15 minutes were always employed. The use of a lengthy and diverse battery, exposing the subject to a wide range of perceptual experiences, may have masked any effects that would have been discernable under an SD condition employing a shorter period of sensory encroachment.

The second factor pertains to the use of a written versus an oral test response procedure. In the Manitoba studies the answers were written in the test booklets provided, whereas in the storytelling studies the subjects responded to the TAT-like cards by relating the stories over an intercom system. This difference in administration procedure may be an important variable, since numerous investigators have uniformly reported a considerable decrease in speech rate in isolated subjects (See Suedfeld, 1969b). This impairment of the speech process, which was not a confounding factor in the Manitoba studies, may have been partly responsible for the decrease in story length reported in the literature.

Although Suedfeld's hypothesis possesses considerable merit, further research should be directed at other experimental variables as well as at test duration and test response procedures. In addition, to substantiate this hypothesis even further it is essential that both structured and unstructured tests be employed in the same study. A small but notable beginning, in this respect, has recently been made by Suedfeld and Landon (1970) in a 36-hour SD experiment. Two types of tests were employed: a simple task requiring the recall of common objects presented on a slide, and a complex task requiring that the subject name uses for these objects. The results revealed a significant improvement on the simple task and a significant impairment on the complex, unstructured task, an excellent verification of Suedfeld's hypothesis. It remains to be seen whether other types of cognitive measures will show a similar differential effect when administered in the same experiment.

In a further extension of his hypothesis concerning the role of task complexity, Suedfeld (1969b), viewing SD as a drive-arousing (Jones, 1969) or activation-inducing (Berlyne, 1969) manipulation, has proposed a theoretical model, based on the familiar U-curve, relating level of arousal, task complexity, and cognitive performance. Applying this arousal theory to the past literature, including a series of recent studies in which an SD-financial incentive design was employed (Suedfeld, 1968; Suedfeld, Glucksberg, & Vernon, 1967; Suedfeld & Landon, 1970), he has argued that "the effects of SD on cognitive behavior are explicable by the application of the U-curve model to the various tasks used by SD researchers to measure cognitive effects" (Suedfeld, 1968, p. 306). Although one may question this conclusion because of the failure to take into serious consideration such important variables as duration and type of deprivation condition, Suedfeld's arousal model does possess the virtue of being able to account for a number of puzzling findings. If SD is viewed as a drive-inducing treatment, the drive being need for stimulation (Lilly, 1956) or for information (Jones, 1969), one can understand why the introduction of physical exercises (Zubek, 1963a) or meaningful stimuli (Rosenzweig & Gardner, 1966) during isolation can reduce the magnitude of the cognitive impairments. It also accounts for the fact that in general the cognitive deficits observed during isolation tend to be greater than those observed in the immediate post isolation period when the drive level is presumably lower.

Susceptibility to Persuasion or Influence

As with so many other phenomena, the first demonstration of an increased susceptibility to persuasive messages was reported at McGill University (Bexton, 1953; Scott et al., 1959). A group of 14 experimental subjects who were mildly sceptical about psychic phenomena were given a questionnaire dealing with attitudes toward five topics: telepathy, clairvoyance, ghosts, poltergeists, and psychic research. During several days of PD they were then subjected to a series of nine tape-recorded messages (total of 90 minutes) presenting strong one-sided arguments in favor of the existence of these phenomena, citing authorities and scientific evidence, and making derogatory remarks about nonbelievers. Of the 14 PD subjects, 9 asked to hear the recordings more than once, compared to only 2 of the 17 controls, who, incidentally, were paid extra if they requested repetitions. On the postsession questionnaire, both groups of subjects, as might be expected, showed a significant persuasion effect. However, the effect was significantly greater in the experimental group. Of the five scales comprising the questionnaire, the most pronounced change was seen in the attitudes toward ghosts, poltergeists, and clairvoyance. Additional data indicated that the isolated subjects were also more interested in the topics and considered them to be of greater importance than was the case before hearing the tapes.

In a subsequent report, Hebb (1958), commenting on these results, has presented some additional information concerning the duration of the aftereffects. "The effects of the propaganda were the only ones that showed signs of lasting well beyond the experimental period. The groups tested two weeks later were too small to establish the point definitely, in a statistical sense, but the tentative conclusions were reinforced by incidental reports from the subjects. A number of the experimental subjects, unlike the controls, went to the library to borrow books on psychical (*not* psychological) research, mind-reading, and so forth; there were spontaneous reports of being afraid of ghosts, late at night, for the first time in the subject's experience; and reports of trying to use ESP in card-playing" (p. 111).

Subsequent research at two other laboratories has not only generally verified these persuasion effects but has also indicated that their magnitude can be affected by several experimental variables. Myers, Murphy, and Smith (1963), working at HumRRO (Human Resources Research Office, Monterey, California) prepared two messages, one criticizing and the other praising a certain national group (Turks). Subsequently, they selected a group of Army volunteers who had strong attitudes toward the Turks and attempted to change their attitudes by presenting the dissonant message. During the 75-minute test period, each subject was permitted to hear, as often as he wished, a 3-minute recording about the national group. Immediately following the request period, the postpropaganda attitude measure was obtained. The results revealed that the 2-day SD subjects significantly exceeded the controls in their frequency of requests for the recordings, but, contrary to the McGill results, they showed no greater change in attitude. According to Suedfeld (1964), this negative finding can probably be attributed to the use of subjects with strong initial opinions who may have developed a resistance against the obvious attempt to manipulate their attitudes. Although an overall difference in attitude change was not found, an interaction between intelligence and treatment of borderline significance was observed: the less intelligent experimentals changed more than the less intelligent controls, while the direction between the two higher-intelligence groups was reversed.

In contrast to the HumRRO study, Suedfeld (1963, 1964), in a 1-day SD experiment, employed subjects whose initial attitudes toward the topic of the propaganda (Turkey) were neutral, and presented them a message consisting of a strong pro-Turkish argument followed by a somewhat weaker counterargument. Since this message contained both positive and negative information it *seemed* fair. Furthermore, the manipulative attempt was disguised by instructions to try to memorize the material in preparation for a recall test. According to Suedfeld, these "subtleties" had the desired effect: the experimental subjects showed a significantly greater change in the pro-Turkey direction than the controls (approximately eight times as much), and also evaluated the propaganda material more favorably. Further analysis of the data revealed that subjects who had previously been classified as conceptually simple or concrete (Schroder, Driver, & Streufert, 1967) evidenced significantly more attitude change as a result of SD than did subjects classified as complex or abstract. The concrete subjects responded to, and accepted, the stronger portion of the propaganda material, while the abstract individuals tended to weigh and combine both types of arguments, thus arriving at a more balanced opinion.

In a follow-up study, Suedfeld and Vernon (1966) required the subjects to evaluate the content of each of seven passages which presented two-sided information about Turkey. If their interpretation was that the passage was pro-Turkish they were rewarded by the presentation of the next passage; otherwise the material was repeated at 10-minute intervals until the subjects did comply. After each passage had been heard and evaluated, an attitude scale was administered. The SD condition, it was observed, increased compliance—the isolated subjects gave significantly fewer "neutral" or "anti-Turkish" evaluations of the passages. Furthermore, the abstract SD subjects were particularly compliant relative to the abstract controls and concrete SD group. According to Suedfeld and Vernon (1966), this latter finding is not surprising in view of the high information motivation of conceptually abstract individuals. Attitude change, on the other hand, exhibited a different pattern. As in the earlier study, concrete subjects changed significantly more in the pro-Turkish direction, but there was a significant interaction. While these subjects changed more in SD, relative to the control condition, the abstract SD subjects evidenced relatively little attitude change, a differential effect which may be explained by "positing that the SD situation caused less behavioral simplification in abstract than in concrete subjects" (p. 588).

Finally, a brief mention will be made of two other studies from the HumRRO laboratory, which represent a variation of the original attitude change experiment. In the first (Murphy, Smith, & Myers, 1963), a group of 2-day SD subjects were compared to controls with respect to the strength of conditioning of connotative meaning. A classical conditioning paradigm was used in which names of four national groups were paired with adjectives of either high, low, or neutral evaluative connotations. Coupling the specific CS (name of national group) with the specific list of UCS (adjectives) was counterbalanced, each nationality being "good" for one group of subjects and "bad" for another. After being told to memorize and then recall the CS-UCS pairs, the subjects had to rate the national groups on several dimensions. The isolated subjects showed significantly greater changes in connotative meaning relative to the controls. Furthermore, this difference was significantly more pronounced for the lower half of the intelligence distribution than for the upper half, a finding similar to that observed in the earlier attitude change experiment.

In the second study (Smith, Myers, & Murphy, 1963), further evidence for the importance of intelligence level was provided. Using a version of the Asch and Crutchfield type of apparatus to measure conformity to a fictitious group norm, it was observed that 2 days of SD led to greater conformity in the less intelligent half of the group, while the conforming behavior of the upper half was not affected by SD.

Although it is clear from this review of the literature that SD-PD conditions can produce an increased susceptibility to influence, little is known about the variables that may affect its magnitude and nature. In view of the positive findings of the role of intelligence level and conceptual simplicity-complexity, research is required on the possible effects of age and sex differences, birth order, instructional set, duration of isolation, and type of deprivation procedure (SD, PD, and deprivation of a single modality). Another important problem is the duration of the aftereffects. Are these aftereffects as longlasting as has been suggested in the McGill study? Further research directed at these and other related problems would not only be of theoretical significance; it would also add to our presently limited experimental knowledge of the nature of brainwashing.

Stimulus-Seeking Behavior

In an attempt to bring some theoretical order into certain of the McGill findings, Hebb (1955) introduced the concept of homeostasis. It was assumed that a person tends to seek an optimal level of stimulation and that a marked deviation from this level produces an effort to bring the system back into "balance." Since one of the primary effects of a sensory impoverished environment is to disrupt this balance, one might expect a subject in isolation to seek an increase in sensory input to restore his desired level of stimulation. A similar type of hypothesis has been suggested by Schultz (1965), who postulated a homeostatic drive mechanism for sensory variation, called *sensoristasis*. Under SD and PD conditions, Schultz predicts that the deprived organism will attempt to obtain an increased variation of sensory stimulation.

A review of the literature (see Jones, 1969, for detailed discussion) indicates considerable experimental support for the presence of stimulus-seeking behavior during isolation. In this review we will be concerned first, with those studies that provided meaningful sensory incentives for which isolated subjects were permitted to respond and, second, those studies that provided nonmeaningful or "content-free" sensory incentives.

MEANINGFUL INCENTIVES

For years there have been frequent references to stimulus craving or *stimulus-hunger* [a term first introduced by Lilly (1956)], in accounts of Arctic and Antarctic explorers, personnel at remote outposts, solitary sailors, and individuals in solitary confinement (see, for example, Bombard, 1953; Brainard, 1929; Byrd, 1938; Tiira, 1955). It was not until the McGill studies, however, that stimulus-seeking behavior was studied in an experimental setting. Bexton (1953) conducted two studies to determine whether PD subjects would listen to uninteresting or boring material consisting of a segment of a stock market report, radio soap commercials, and religious talks for children. In the first experiment this material was presented prior to PD. Although all four subjects rated the material as strongly aversive, two of them requested to hear the recordings nine times during confinement. Furthermore, the requests for the material were three times as high during the second half of the 2-to-3-day period as during the first, a finding suggestive of a drive process. In the second experiment, in which no prior familiarization with the material was provided, three of the four subjects requested a total of 53 repetitions. Additional evidence for the presence of stimulus seeking was reported by Bexton (1953) in his persuasion study, in which more requests for a repetition of propaganda material were made by the isolated than by the control subjects, a finding subsequently verified by the HumRRO laboratory (Myers, Murphy, & Smith, 1963).

Three other studies, all employing segments of stock market reports and groups of Naval enlisted men, have been conducted by Myers and his colleagues. In the first experiment (Smith & Myers, 1966), involving 1 day of SD, the subjects were allowed to respond (lever-pressing) for the stock market reports as often as they wished during a 1-hour period. Significantly more listening occurred in the isolated than in the control subjects. In the second study (Smith, Myers, & Johnson, 1967), the deprivation period was extended to 7 days. The SD subjects exhibited an increase in listening duration from the 6th through the 78th to the 150th hour of the 7-day isolation period, while the controls showed a decrease. Moreover, by the 78th hour, the experimentals had a mean listening time approximately three times as long as the controls, while by the 150th hour the SD subjects listened more than five times as much as the controls. In the third study (Smith, Myers, & Johnson, 1968), which was essentially a replication of the previous one but with some minor modifications, almost identical results were reported. The presence, in two separate 7-day experiments, of an increasing response rate over days is of particular interest since it strongly suggests a drive process associated with SD.

In contrast to this impressive evidence in favor of stimulation seeking, Gendreau et al. (1968a), using a nonlaboratory type of situation, have reported negative results. Ten volunteers from a Canadian maximum security penitentiary (federal) were placed individually in special segregation cells, isolated from the prison, for a period of 7 days. The deprivation condition consisted of a low constant level of illumination and noise (type not specified) with a fixed feeding schedule. Contrary to the typical PD procedure, no translucent goggles were worn; the subject was thus able to see his surroundings (walls, bed, and toilet). Each cell contained a stimulus box with selector switches for meaningful material ("music of popular taste") and nonmeaningful material (white light). Before and "immediately after 7 days of deprivation was finished, the deprived S was instructed to choose 5 minutes each of level of light and selected sound in decibels. Amount of selected light was measured in millilamberts and selected sound in decibels" (p. 548). A control partner, who lived a routine prison life, was tested at the same time in a similar cell.

The investigators reported that the experimental subjects sought a *lower* level of visual stimulation and about the same level of auditory stimulation as the controls. There are several variables in this study that may account for the negative finding—insufficient severity of PD relative to that of other laboratories, briefness of the test period (only 5 minutes), and questionable use of intensity as a measure of stimulus seeking. In addition, it is important to note that *both* the experimental and control volunteers had already spent a number of years confined in a maximum security prison and thus may already have become partially adapted to a restricted perceptual environment prior to participation in the experiment (see Zuckerman, 1969a, for a survey of studies on adaptation effects).

NONMEANINGFUL INCENTIVES

The bulk of the experimental evidence also indicates that deprived subjects will seek or respond to sensory incentives of a nonmeaningful nature, this term being used to include sequences of brief tones, light flashes, simple geometric figures, and so forth, of presumably low association value and with few secondary reward properties.

Contrary to their results on meaningful stimuli, Myers et al. (1966) failed to obtain evidence for stimulus seeking in a 2-day SD experiment which required that the subject respond for either a brief 500 cps tone or a comparable period of white noise during a 40-minute test period. The authors in interpreting these results have suggested that the considerable irritation and annoyance generated in most of the subjects by these specific sensory stimuli, together with their view of the test period as a "game playing" situation, may have produced the obtained results. Some support for this hypothesis was provided in their subsequent, positive studies on meaningful stimuli, in which the material was not irritating, and in which various attempts were made to remove as much potential "game playing" as possible from the experimental situation (Smith & Myers, 1966; Smith, Myers, & Johnson, 1967, 1968).

With the exception of this single study, the remaining relevant literature has clearly demonstrated the presence of stimulus seeking for nonmeaningful material. In probably the first report on this topic, Vernon and McGill (1960) showed a relationship between amount of stimulation seeking and duration of SD. Early release subjects spent significantly more time (15 times as much!) viewing a neutral pattern during the first 24 hours than did those who endured the full 3-day SD period, a finding similar to that reported subsequently by Smith, Myers, and Johnson (1967) for stock market listening.

In another study, Goldstein (1965) required subjects to press a button for either a visual (unstructured scene on card) or an auditory stimulus (a tone mixture) for 30 minutes prior to 19½ hours of SD. Relative to controls, the SD group pressed more for both types of stimuli. Furthermore, he found that visual stimulation was responded to more frequently than auditory stimulation. A similar preference for visual stimulation seeking has been observed by Zuckerman and Haber (1965) who, unlike Goldstein, made a serious attempt to insure some general psychological equivalence of the visual and auditory stimuli they employed.

A somewhat different approach to the problem was introduced by Rossi and Solomon (1964a, 1964b) in a series of studies in which subjects experiencing 3 hours of SD were permitted an instrumental response (button-pressing) which earned them "time-off" in the form of shortened total durations in the experiment, but which did not provide immediate escape or avoidance. One of their main findings was that the response rate was a significant, increasing function of the magnitude of the "time-off" rewards.

Undoubtedly the most comprehensive and methodologically impeccable series of studies have been conducted by Jones and his colleagues at the University of Pittsburgh (see Jones, 1961, 1964; Jones & McGill, 1967; Jones, Wilkinson, & Braden, 1961). In this series of experiments the subjects, after varying initial periods of SD up to 2 days, were given control of an apparatus that could be used to introduce sequences of visual or auditory stimuli as they wished throughout the remainder of the deprivation period. In addition, the stimuli that were employed were manipulated according to three dimensions—information, complexity, and fluctuation values. Because of the highly complex nature of these experiments, a study-by-study survey of the results is not possible (see Jones, 1969 for comprehensive coverage). Briefly, however, Jones's (1969) findings indicate that (1) subjects' response rates in SD are a direct linear function of the amount of prior deprivation, at least up to 2 days, (2) stimulation seeking is a drive with "information" rather than stimulus complexity or fluctuation being the primary commodity sought, and (3) "information drive is homeostatic in the sense that both relatively high and relatively low levels of stimulus information induce drive states which motivate responses serving to maintain some intermediate level of information transmission" (p. 206).

Sensory and Perceptual-Motor Effects

MEASURES OF MOTOR COORDINATION

Simple Measures. There seems little doubt that dexterity and other measures of simple eye-hand coordination are impaired by prolonged deprivation periods. At the Manitoba laboratory, an appraisal was made of such abilities as speed of cancellation of a particular number on a page of randomized numbers, placing a dot in small triangles, making two check marks in squares, and tracing a line through a maze without touching the sides. All measures showed a significant impairment, relative to both ambulatory and recumbent control groups, during a week of either SD or PD (Zubek, Sansom, & Prysiazniuk, 1960; Zubek et al., 1962). Essentially similar results were reported from HumRRO laboratory (Myers et al., 1966), in which the MacQuarrie Test of Mechanical Skills, consisting of seven subtests, was administered to a large group of subjects after 3 days of SD. Evidence of motor incoordination was also obtained at the McGill laboratory (Bexton, Heron, & Scott, 1954; Scott et al., 1959). The PD subjects were not only slower in copying a prose paragraph, but the quality of their handwriting was poorer.

Gross motor coordination, as measured by a test of rail-walking ability, is also severely impaired (Vernon, 1963; Vernon et al., 1959, 1961). In this test the subjects simply had to walk along an 18 foot wooden rail in stocking feet. Performance was measured by the time in seconds required to complete the task, administered before and after 3 days of SD. The results revealed that whereas the controls showed an improvement of 8 per cent, the experimentals not only did not improve but were on the average 42 per cent slower.

Measures of simple motor coordination can be impaired not only by SD and PD but also by social isolation alone, provided that unusually long durations are employed. Walters, Callagan, and Newman (1963) observed no significant changes on a manual dexterity test (tweezers) in a group of prison inmates isolated in cells for 4 days. However, the Soviet investigators Agadzhanian et al. (1963) reported a progressive increase in time required to trace a geometric pattern in subjects socially isolated for 60 days. The drawing time at the end of the experiment was approximately twice what it was during the first month. No changes occurred in the quality of the tracing.

Complex Measures. Performance on a mirror-tracing task can also be adversely affected, but only by an experimental period of medium duration. Vernon et al. (1959, 1961) required subjects to trace a six-pointed star, while looking at a mirror, before and after 1, 2, or 3 days of SD.

Using amount of time required to complete the task, no significant difference in performance between the experimentals and controls was observed after either the first or third day. However, a significant impairment was noted after the second day. In this same study, results similar to those for mirror-tracing were also reported for rotary pursuit performance—a significant impairment after a 2-day period but no significant changes after either a 1- or 3-day period of SD. This demonstration of a "critical period" at 2 days is of considerable importance in accounting for certain contradictory results in the literature. For example, neither Scott et al. (1959), using a mirror-tracing task, nor Weinstein et al. (1967), using a visual pursuit task, reported a significant impairment after 3 days of PD or SD, respectively. Since the tests were administered a day after the "critical period," the presence of negative results is understandable.

VISUAL MEASURES

Since an unusually broad range of visual perception measures have been employed, the relevant material has been subdivided in the following sections on the basis of the type of performance being appraised. Only measures that have received more than passing attention will be dealt with. For a comprehensive coverage of both the long-term and short-term studies, see Zubek (1969b).

Depth Perception. Although no objective measures of depth perception were used at the McGill laboratory, many subjects there commented on the two-dimensional nature of the environment. An impairment of depth perception might therefore be predicted. This prediction, however, has not been confirmed in subsequent studies. Negative results were obtained at the Manitoba laboratory after a week of either SD (Zubek et al., 1961) or PD (Zubek et al., 1962). Furthermore, depth perception was not affected even after 14 days of PD (Zubek, 1964b). The Howard Dohlman apparatus was employed in all three Manitoba studies. Finally, Vernon et al. (1961), in a study on the effect of duration, reported no change in depth perception after either 2 or 3 days of SD, but a deficit, bordering on statistical significance, after 1 day of SD. Vernon has interpreted these results as indicating that short-term deprivation "has a more deleterious effect upon depth perception ability than does longer term confinement" (p. 52). This interpretation, however, is questionable, since both Freedman and Greenblatt (1959) and Pollard, Uhr, and Jackson (1963) reported no disturbances of depth perception after an 8-hour period. On the other hand, it is possible that a "critical period" may exist between 8 and 24 hours, during which the perception of depth is adversely affected.

The Constancies. Doane et al. (1959) reported no change in shape and brightness constancy but a significant decrease in size constancy in 17 subjects who were perceptually deprived for 3 days. A similar impairment of size constancy was also reported in three subjects after 6 days of PD (Heron, Doane, & Scott, 1956). Contrary results on size constancy have been reported in a series of studies from the Manitoba laboratory. Zubek et al. (1961) observed no significant changes in 16 subjects exposed to a week of SD. Negative results were also obtained in two subsequent experiments involving: (1) 29 subjects undergoing a week of PD with periodic test intrusions (Zubek et al., 1962), and (2) 12 subjects exposed to a week of PD but with no test intrusions and no subject-experimenter communication (Zubek, 1964c). Furthermore, no significant changes in size constancy were observed in 10 subjects even after 14 days of PD (Zubek, 1964b). An analysis was also made of the performance of an additional group of 23 subjects from the four experiments, all of whom had terminated isolation prematurely after a mean period of approximately 2 days. These isolation quitters also evidenced no significant impairment. Negative results on size constancy have also been reported in four short-term studies—two recent Japanese studies employing a 1-day period of PD (Suzuki, Ueno, & Tada, 1966; Ueno & Suzuki, 1967), and two other studies using 8 hours of either SD or PD (Freedman & Greenblatt, 1959; Schwitzgebel, 1962).

From this review it is clear that the bulk of experimental evidence indicates that both depth perception and size constancy appear to be immune to conditions of reduced sensory stimulation, regardless of their duration. This conclusion, however, has to be tempered in the light of a recently published paper from the Manitoba laboratory (Zubek et al., 1969) in which the subjects were exposed to *both* PD and whole-body immobilization (except at night) for a period of 1 week. As a consequence of this unusually severe deprivation condition, both depth perception and size constancy were significantly impaired. No such effect was observed after immobilization per se. Thus, these two basic perceptual processes can be affected, but only under the most extreme conditions of deprivation.

Visual Acuity. Doane et al. (1959) appraised visual acuity by means of a horizontal row of 14 vertical black lines, with each line in the series possessing a small gap of progressively decreasing width. The lines were presented at a distance of 10 feet, and the subject was required to indicate where the gap in each line was. The experimental subjects showed an increase in visual acuity, in contrast to no change in controls who received the same test 3 days apart. Although the results only bordered on statistical significance, the McGill investigators attached considerable weight to this trend in view of the presence of a significant increase in tactual acuity in the same subjects. Unfortunately, these suggestive results have not been supported by three studies using certain standardized and more accurate measures of visual acuity. Using the Landolt ring and a 1-day period of PD, a group of Japanese investigators (Suzuki, Ueno, & Tada, 1966) reported no significant change, although a trend toward improved visual acuity was observed. Similar results, but with no trend, were reported by Gendreau et al. (1968) after a week of PD, and by Pollard, Uhr, and Jackson (1963) after 8 hours of PD.

Perception of Brightness and Flicker. A variety of measures of brightness discrimination appear to be unaffected by either short or prolonged periods of deprivation. Doane et al. (1959) reported no changes in brightness contrast (method of Thurstone) after 3 days of PD. Similar results have also been observed for brightness discrimination tasks, involving standard and comparison stimuli, after 1 hour of PD (Batten, 1961), 3 days of SD (Weinstein et al., 1967), and 7 days of PD (Zubek, 1964c).

Measures of critical flicker frequency (CFF) have also been employed in a number of laboratories. No significant changes in CFF have been reported after 2 to 6 hours of PD (Leiderman, 1962), 3 days of PD (Doane et al., 1959), and 14 days of PD (Zubek, 1964b). Contrary results, however, have been reported by the Japanese investigator Nagatsuka (1965). A significant decrease in CFF occurred in 10 subjects after 2 days of PD. A "pre-post" decrease of 1.70 cps was shown in contrast to an increase of 0.80 cps in a group of 10 control subjects. Although these results appear to be at variance with those reported from other laboratories, they may in fact not be so. A duration of 2 days was employed, which Vernon et al. (1961) have shown produces a greater deficit than either shorter or longer durations on such measures as color perception, mirror-drawing, and rotary pursuit. In view of these results, it is possible that CFF is perhaps only affected by deprivation periods of medium duration. Further support for this hypothesis has been provided by two other Japanese studies in which changes in electrical flicker, using Motokawa's method, were appraised. Whereas "the value of electrical flicker increased remarkably" after 2 days of PD (Nagatsuka & Maruyama, 1963), no significant changes on the *same* measure occurred after 1 day of PD (Ueno & Suzuki, 1967).

From these results, and also others that have already been described, it is clear that a recognition of the possible existence of "critical periods" for certain optimal deprivation effects can resolve much of the apparently contradictory literature involving not only sensory and perceptual-motor measures but also performance measures of a cognitive nature. Fur-

ther research on the problem of critical periods is one of the most urgently
required topics for future investigation.

Color Perception. Considerable evidence is available indicating that
color perception can be disturbed by both SD and PD. Using a yellow
color-matching test, Doane et al. (1959) observed a significant impairment of color matching at the end of 3 days of PD. Vernon et al. (1961)
administered the Dvorine Color Test to three groups of subjects who
were sensory deprived for 1, 2, and 3 days. This test required the subject
to identify numbers on the plates in the usual manner of color vision testing. Although all three experimental groups performed worse than the
controls, only the deficits shown by the 2- and 3-day groups were significant. Furthermore, the deficit in color perception was worse after 2 days
than after either 1 or 3 days. An examination of the color plates missed
showed that no particular color was consistently missed and that the failures occurred primarily for the desaturated hues.

Another measure of color perception, the Farnsworth-Munsell 100-
Hue Test, was administered by Zubek et al. (1962) to a group of 29 subjects who endured a week of PD, and to a group of 10 subjects who terminated isolation prematurely (mean duration = 53 hours). Both groups
showed a significant impairment of color discrimination. Similar results
were again obtained in a subsequent study (Zubek, 1963a), in which the
subjects were required to perform physical exercises during a week of
PD. Apparently, increasing the level of kinesthetic and proprioceptive
stimulation during isolation is unable to counteract or minimize deficits in
color perception. Contrary to these Manitoba 7-day studies, Gendreau et
al. (1968c) reported that a 7-day period of PD produced no significant
change in color perception, as measured by the Handy-Rand-Ritter Pseudo-
isochromatic plates, in a group of penitentiary inmates placed in maximum security isolation cells. In accounting for these negative results, the
investigators suggested that an impairment probably occurred but may
have dissipated in the 4-hour postdeprivation period *prior* to testing.
Some evidence for the importance of time of test administration will be
presented in a later section.

Finally, a fascinating account of changes in visual perception has been
presented by Siffre (1964), who spent 2 months living in darkness and
silence in an underground cavern located 425 feet below the surface. A
comprehensive examination of various visual processes was made by an
ophthalmologist before and for several weeks after emergence from the
cavern. Siffre reported that his color perception was seriously affected,
with green being seen as blue. Other changes were a disturbance of binocular vision, increase in myopia, and a modification of the electroretino-

gram. All of these effects, it is important to note, persisted for more than a month after return to normal living conditions.

Bender-Gestalt Test. This test, which has frequently been used by clinical psychologists in the differential diagnosis of brain damage, consists in presenting a subject with a set of cards and asking him to copy each of them as accurately as possible. Various methods can then be used to appraise any changes in the form-quality of the Bender-Gestalt reproductions. This test has been employed in two Japanese studies, both employing the Pascal method of scoring. In the first (Hariu & Ueno, 1964), nine figures were presented to a group of subjects immediately after 2 days of PD. The figures were presented until all of the subjects could complete their copying. The results revealed a significant deterioration in the form-quality of the figures in relation to a group of control subjects.

In the second study (Ueno & Tada, 1965), two modifications were introduced—an 18-hour period of PD, and two different times of test administration. Although a significant change in form-quality was present when the Bender-Gestalt was administered immediately after PD, no effect was observed when the test was delayed for an hour, an excellent example of the importance of time of test administration. Using an 8-hour period, Freedman and Greenblatt (1959) also observed the presence of a poorer form-quality in both SD and PD subjects when the Bender-Gestalt was administered immediately after the termination of isolation. Contrary results were reported in two PD studies, using a 4-hour duration (Reitman & Cleveland, 1964; Cleveland, Reitman, & Bentinck, 1963). These negative findings could be due either to the briefness of the deprivation period, or to the fact that the Bender-Gestalt was administered late in the battery of numerous other tests.

Visual Illusions. A wide range of illusory phenomena have been investigated. One of these is the autokinetic phenomenon in which the subject has to watch a pinpoint source of light in a dark field. Unfortunately, the results are inconsistent. In a survey of this literature, Zubek (1969b) has concluded that "no consistent pattern of changes in the autokinetic effects seems to occur after either brief or prolonged deprivation periods with increases, decreases, or no change in latency of response being reported. The presence of these random-like results is perhaps not too surprising because it is known that a variety of psychological variables, such as expectancies, set, and attitudes, can easily influence this phenomenon" (p. 219).

In contrast to the results on the autokinetic effect, the experimental evidence clearly indicates an increase in the duration of the spiral aftereffect (Archimedes spiral). This was demonstrated by Doane et al. (1959) after 3 days of PD, and by Ormiston (1961) after 8 hours of PD. An increase in duration of the aftereffect was also reported in one of the Japanese studies (Suzuki, Fujii, & Onizawa, 1965), when the Archimedes spiral was administered immediately after 18 hours of PD but not when it was delayed for an hour. Time of test administration, therefore, has again emerged as an important variable, a finding consistent with the Doane et al. (1959) statement that "tests of perception have to be completed in a short time since the major effects seem to wear off in an hour or two" (p. 211). A lack of sufficient attention to this variable in much of the isolation literature may account for some of the contradictory results, for example in the research on the autokinetic effect. Another example is the failure of Gendreau et al. (1968) to demonstrate an impairment in color perception, a finding contrary to all of the earlier studies. In this particular experiment, the visual measure was not administered until 4 hours after the termination of PD.

The magnitude of the Muller-Lyer illusion has been studied at two laboratories. Suzuki, Fujii, and Onizawa (1965) reported a significant decrease in the magnitude of the illusion when it was presented immediately after the termination of 18 hours of PD but no change when the administration was delayed for an hour, a test administration difference which they also observed on the Archimedes spiral. Freedman and Greenblatt (1959), on the other hand, observed no significant changes in this illusion after 8 hours of either SD or PD. It is important to note, however, that a lengthy battery of tests was administered, and the Muller-Lyer was *always* presented in the middle of the series.

Another illusion that has received some attention is the perception of reversible figures (Necker cubes). The results from the McGill laboratory indicated no significant change in the frequency of reversals after a 3-day period of PD (Doane et al., 1959). Contrary findings were obtained at the Manitoba laboratory, where a significantly slower frequency of reversals per minute after a week of PD was reported (Zubek et al., 1962). In another study, employing a week of SD rather than PD, a slower reversal rate was again observed, but the results were not statistically significant (Zubek et al., 1961). The apparent discrepancy in the effects of PD observed at these two laboratories can probably be attributed to differences in time of test administration. At the Manitoba laboratory the figures were presented almost immediately after deprivation, whereas at McGill they were always presented in the eleventh position of a 2-hour battery of 13 tests.

In addition to these illusions, scattered references are made in the literature to such measures as the Two-Faces-Vase illusion, figural aftereffects, the phi-phenomenon, and "perceptual lag," a test of the apparent speed of a moving line. A survey of these studies, largely involving deprivation durations of from 30 minutes to 8 hours, has been provided by Zubek (1969b).

Reaction Time and Vigilance. The Japanese investigators Nagatsuka and Suzuki (1964) administered two types of reaction time tests to a group of subjects before and immediately after 2 days of PD: simple reaction time in which the subject released a key at the appearance of a yellow light, and choice reaction time in which he had to react to one of three colored lights presented successively in the same place. On both measures, the experimental subjects reacted more slowly in relation to a control group. The only other long-term study on visual reaction time was conducted by Vernon (1963). A simple reaction time test was administered to two groups of subjects: a group who successfully completed 4 days of SD, and a group who quit prematurely after approximately 2 days. According to Vernon, the isolation quitters showed a significantly slower reaction time whereas the successful endurers revealed essentially no change. Although these results appear to suggest that successful and unsuccessful subjects react differently to isolation, this may in fact not be the case. The critical factor may be a shorter deprivation period, 2 days, rather than "quitting," particularly in view of Vernon's earlier demonstration that a 2-day period frequently produces greater perceptual impairments than does a longer duration. This hypothesis could account not only for the negative results in Vernon's 4-day successful subjects, but also for the slower reaction time in the Japanese 2-day study, all of whose subjects, incidentally, were successful endurers.

Subjects who have been exposed to a prolonged period of isolation frequently appear dull, sluggish, and not very alert. This would suggest that objective measures of visual vigilance might reveal a poorer state of alertness, particularly because it has just been noted that isolated subjects show a slower visual reaction time. Such has been found to be the case in two studies from the Manitoba laboratory, one employing a week of SD (Zubek et al., 1961), and the other a similar duration of PD (Zubek et al., 1962). The apparatus consisted of an electric laboratory clock with a single rotating hand which was briefly stopped and then started at eight irregular time intervals during each of four successive 30-minute intervals. The subject's task, in his Mackworth-type situation, was to indicate the presence of a signal by pressing a key. The results revealed that under both types of deprivation conditions the experimental subjects consistently showed a poorer visual vigilance performance than did the controls at all four time periods.

AUDITORY MEASURES

Auditory Vigilance and Reaction Time. Undoubtedly the most careful work on this topic has been performed by Myers and his colleagues, first at the HumRRO laboratory and later at the Naval Medical Research Institute, Bethesda, Maryland. In the first study (Myers et al., 1962; Smith, Myers, & Murphy, 1967), vigilance was measured by requiring the subjects to respond to infrequently and irregularly occurring 61 db tones presented before and at the end of 3 days of SD. Furthermore, since it is known that irrelevant stimulation can facilitate vigilance, two control groups were employed, one tested in a lighted room and the other in a darkened test room. The results revealed a significant *improvement* in auditory vigilance when compared to controls tested in the dark, but no significant change relative to controls tested in the light. Observations were also made on a measure of simple auditory reaction time. Again different results were obtained: a significantly *faster* reaction time relative to the darkness controls, but no change relative to lighted-room controls. The presence of these two auditory facilitatory effects is puzzling, particularly since it has already been shown earlier that conditions of reduced sensory input produce a slower visual reaction time and poorer visual vigilance.

Further evidence for a facilitatory effect was provided in the second study, in which a 1-week period of SD was employed and auditory vigilance was appraised at intervals of 25, 75, and 145 hours (Johnson, Smith, & Myers, 1968). Relative to darkness controls, a significant improvement was again observed at all three test periods. Furthermore, since auditory thresholds were not affected it was concluded that the facilitatory effect on vigilance was not due to an increase in auditory sensitivity. In another 7-day study, a more complex task was employed (Smith & Myers, 1967). This task, which was presented at the 53rd and 125th hours of SD, simultaneously involved tracking, keeping a white noise turned off, and turning off location-coded tones. A significant improvement in performance again occurred at both test periods.

Partial support for some of these findings has been provided by the Manitoba laboratory (Zubek et al., 1961). A group of subjects tested after a week of SD showed no significant change in auditory vigilance relative to controls tested in a lighted room. Unfortunately, no control group tested under a condition of darkness was employed. In a subsequent experiment from the same laboratory, a significant *impairment* of auditory vigilance was observed, but the condition consisted of PD rather than SD (Zubek et al., 1962). This difference is not too surprising since there is some evidence to suggest that greater behavioral deficits (such as cognitive measures) and physiological deficits (such as slowing of EEG activity) seem to occur after the PD condition (see Zubek, 1964a). In commenting on this problem of the greater disruptive effects of PD, Weinstein et al. (1967) have drawn an interesting analogy from another field—it is a frequent finding in the neurological literature that partial destruction of a sensory system where some stimulation is present (as in PD) may prove to be more impairing to a patient than total destruction where stimulation is absent (as in SD).

Absolute and Difference Thresholds. Neither absolute nor difference thresholds for loudness appear to be affected by 18 hours of PD (Suzuki, Fujii, & Onizawa, 1965) or 3 days of SD (Weinstein et al., 1967). Similar results have been obtained with even longer durations. Gendreau et al. (1968), who determined the absolute threshold of hearing for seven frequencies (125 to 8,000 cps) before and after a week of PD, observed no change on any frequency. Johnson, Smith, and Myers (1968), using a 1-week period of SD, also observed no significant changes in the absolute threshold of hearing for a 1,000 cps tone presented at intervals of 25, 75, and 145 hours.

OTHER SENSORY AND PERCEPTUAL MEASURES

Tactile Perception. A considerable body of evidence indicates that not only auditory vigilance but also tactual acuity can be facilitated by isolation. The earliest demonstration of an increase in tactual acuity was made at McGill (Doane et al., 1959). Two-point threshold determinations were taken at intervals of 2 and 3 days of PD. An increased acuity of the forehead and upper arm was observed at both time intervals, an effect which was greater after 2 than after 3 days. No significant changes in acuity were seen on the finger and forearm, although the latter did show a trend toward increased sensitivity. Although no significant effects were observed on the finger and forearm, Zubek (1964c), using a more sensitive measure of tactual acuity (tactual fusion), reported a significant increase in acuity of both the index finger and forearm after a week of PD. A facilitatory effect has also been reported in two Japanese studies (Nagatsuka & Maruyama, 1963; Nagatsuka & Suzuki, 1964). In both, a significant increase in the tactual acuity (two-point threshold) of the back of the hand was observed after 2 days of PD. It is interesting to note that virtually all of the experimental subjects showed this increase, a finding also reported in the Zubek study.

In view of these clear-cut results on tactual acuity, one might expect to observe an increase in the absolute pressure sensitivity of the skin. This apparently is not the case. Using a von Frey hair technique, Weinstein et al. (1967) reported a significant *decrease* in pressure sensitivity on the palm of the nonpreferred hand after 3 days of SD. In attempting to account for these unexpected results, Weinstein has suggested that the ef-

fect may be related to the severity of their experimental condition. Since
the subjects were exposed not only to darkness and silence, but also wore
a special glove so constructed as to eliminate all tactile stimulation on the
palm, it is possible that "total" sensory deprivation (visual, auditory, and
tactual) may impair pressure sensitivity while partial deprivation, involving only one or two sense modalities, may improve it. Some support for
this hypothesis has been provided in a series of studies on partial deprivation, in which it has been shown that a prolonged period of visual deprivation alone (Phelps & Zubek, 1969) or tactual deprivation alone (Heron
& Morrison, unpublished paper; Weinstein et al., 1967) produces a significant increase in absolute pressure sensitivity as measured by the von
Frey technique. It still remains to be determined, however, whether a
deprivation of two or more sense modalities will produce the opposite effect.

Pain Perception. An increased sensitivity to pain can also occur, but
apparently only under a condition of SD. Vernon (1963) and Vernon
and McGill (1961), measuring the absolute threshold of electrical pain
of the earlobe, reported a 42 per cent increase in pain sensitivity after 4
days of SD in contrast to an increase of only 5 per cent in a group of controls. Of the nine experimental subjects, all but one showed this change.
In a second relevant study (Weinstein et al., 1967), a modified cold pressor method was employed to determine the pin sensitivity of the hand before and after 3 days of SD. Two measures were used, pain threshold
(time in seconds from immersion of the hand in ice-cold water until S reported pain) and pain tolerance (time in seconds until S reported that
the pain was intolerable). Although the results were not statistically significant, a trend toward increased sensitivity was observed on both measures and on both hands. One possible explanation for these nonsignificant
results may be the inaccuracy of the cold pressor method. Since it produces a vague rather than a clearly discriminable sensation of pricking
pain, as obtained by either the electrical or radiant heat method, the subjects may have experienced some difficulty in making accurate pain judgments, a fact suggested by the presence of unusually large intra- and in-
tersubject variability scores. Another possible explanation may be the
severity of the experimental condition—not only visual and auditory deprivation but also tactual deprivation of the hand was employed.

Contrary results were reported by Zubek et al. (1962). Using a 1-week
period of PD and a radiant heat technique for eliciting pricking pain,
they reported a significant *decrease* in pain sensitivity of the forearm.
This decrease probably can be accounted for by the use of white noise in
the PD condition. Gardner and Licklider (1959) and Carlin et al.
(1962) have both reported that white noise possesses certain analgesic

properties. Furthermore, Licklider (1961) has stated that "Mountcastle has found cells, both in the posterior group nuclei and in the cerebral cortex, which respond to nociceptive stimulation and whose responses are suppressed by acoustic stimulation" (p. 70). It would appear, therefore, that the presence or absence of white noise may be the critical factor. Furthermore, these results suggest that *qualitatively* different results may be produced by SD and PD, a finding also applicable to auditory vigilance. SD seems to facilitate auditory vigilance whereas PD tends to impair it.

Gustatory Perception. In view of the improved performance on certain auditory and cutaneous measures, it is not surprising that a facilitatory effect on taste sensitivity should have been demonstrated. The Japanese investigator Nagatsuka (1965) reported a 36 per cent increase in sensitivity to sweet and bitter after 1 day of PD, in contrast to no change in a group of controls. Measures of sensitivity to sour and salty substances were unfortunately not taken.

Kinesthetic Acuity and Spatial Orientation. Measures of kinesthetic acuity appear to be unaffected by prolonged periods of deprivation. Zubek (1964c) reported no changes in acuity after a week of PD. In this study, the subjects were required to bend their elbow to what they felt was either a 20° or a 60° angle. Hanna and Gaito (1960), in a 6-day experiment, also observed no changes on a test measuring the ability to discriminate seven small cubes differing slightly in weight. In the final study, Weinstein et al. (1967), using a similar weight-lifting task, reported no significant change in a 3-day SD study. However, a definite trend toward *improvement* was observed, particularly in the subjects who terminated the experiment prior to the 3-day prescribed period.

On the other hand, kinesthetic measures involving spatial orientation appear to be disrupted. Doane et al. (1959) appraise spatial orientation in two ways, both requiring that the subject follow directions in making a series of movements while blindfolded. The first was a paper-and-pencil test in which a route, consisting of five right-angle turns, had to be drawn, while the second required that the subject follow directions by walking in an empty room. The results revealed that the performance on the walking test was poorer after 3 days of PD than after 2, while the performance on the paper-and-pencil test of spatial orientation was much poorer after 2 days than after 3, a temporal effect seen on several other types of sensory and perceptual-motor measures. This impairment of spatial orientation is attributed by Doane et al. to a visual dysfunction resulting from an inability to visualize the external world. "This made it impossible for them to form a mental picture of the route that had to be followed in the orientation test, and thus to locate the starting point" (p. 218).

Effects of Visual Deprivation Alone

In the preceding sections it has been shown that significant increases in tactual acuity, pain sensitivity, gustatory sensitivity, and in auditory vigilance performance can occur after prolonged periods of deprivation. Recently, a series of studies at the Manitoba laboratory have indicated that similar facilitatory effects can result from visual deprivation alone. An overall reduction in sensory input from several modalities is not essential. In these studies, the subjects were placed, in groups of two, in total darkness for a period of a week. They were permitted to talk, listen to a radio, had freedom of movement, and were visited periodically by the experimenters. Various sensory and perceptual measures were then administered before and immediately after the week of darkness and subsequently at follow-up intervals of 1, 2, 5, and 7 days.

In the first study (Zubek, Flye, & Aftanas, 1964), measures of tactual acuity (two-point threshold and tactual fusion) were taken from the index finger, palm, and forearm. In addition, a dolorimeter was used to measure the heat and pain sensitivity of the forearm. Briefly, the results revealed a significant increase on all measures, on all skin areas, and by all 16 experimental subjects. Furthermore, this increased sensitivity was still present, to a statistically significant degree, several days after the subjects' return to their normal environment. In the second study (Duda & Zubek, 1965), two types of auditory measures were administered: auditory discrimination, using an auditory flutter technique (interrupted white noise at a 0.90 on-off ratio), and absolute threshold of hearing for five frequencies (100 to 9,000 cps). The results again revealed a significant increase in auditory discrimination with the aftereffects persisting for one day. All subjects but one showed this effect. The absolute thresholds were not changed, a finding that might be expected since it has been demonstrated in several studies that auditory thresholds are not affected by prolonged periods of either SD or PD (Gendreau et al., 1968; Johnson, Smith, & Myers, 1968; Suzuki, Fujii, & Onizawa, 1965; Weinstein et al., 1967).

In the third experiment (Phelps & Zubek, 1969), a variety of other types of cutaneous and auditory measures were employed. Briefly, these indicated a significant increase in absolute pressure sensitivity of the finger, forearm, neck, and leg with the aftereffects, on certain skin areas, persisting for several days. Measures of tactual and auditory localization (absolute and differential), however, were not affected by visual deprivation.

The final published study (Schutte & Zubek, 1967) was concerned with the determination of olfactory and gustatory sensitivity. A significant increase in olfactory sensitivity (recognition threshold for benzene) was observed, but with no persistence of aftereffects. The measures of taste thresholds yielded a differential pattern of results. Sensitivity to NaCl (salty) and sucrose (sweet) was increased significantly relative to a control group, with the aftereffects persisting for 1 day. Sensitivity to HCl (sour) and quinine (bitter), on the other hand, was not affected significantly, although a marked trend toward improvement for sour was evident. Eleven of the 12 experimental subjects showed an increased sensitivity to sour, a proportion identical to that observed with salt and sucrose.

Since the measurements in these Manitoba studies were confined exclusively to the pre- and postexperimental period, it is important to determine the temporal course of development of these facilitatory effects. For example, will certain of these sensory measures show an optimal effect at the 2-day period, as some of the literature seems to suggest, and then diminish with increasing duration of visual deprivation, or will some other type of functional relationship be present? Some answers to this question have recently been provided by Milstein and Zubek (1971) in several experiments conducted at the Manitoba laboratory. Measures of pain sensitivity, absolute pressure sensitivity, and tactual acuity (tactual fusion frequency) were administered to a group of experimental subjects at intervals of ½, 1, 2, 3, 5, and 7 days of visual deprivation. The results on pressure and pain revealed a noticeable increase in sensitivity, relative to controls, but only after the third day of deprivation.

A different picture emerged for tactual acuity. This measure revealed a linear improvement in acuity with increasing duration of visual deprivation. Since this effect was already present to a statistically significant degree at the first test period (12 hours), a further study was conducted in which this measure was taken at intervals of 0, 4, and 12 hours of deprivation. The results revealed a significant improvement in tactual acuity after 12 but not after 4 hours, indicating that this phenomenon first appears somewhere between 4 and 12 hours of visual deprivation.

In view of this differential temporal pattern of development characterizing tactual acuity and the two threshold measures, further research using various noncutaneous measures is required.[2]

---

2. Recently at the Manitoba laboratory, Pangman and Zubek (1972) reported a linear increase in auditory flutter fusion frequency (a task analogous to tactual fusion frequency) with increasing duration of visual deprivation. Although the facilitatory effect was clearly evident at the 12-hour test period, only the results after the third day of deprivation were statistically significant. These results, together with the earlier ones on tactual fusion frequency, appear to suggest that when sensory measures of a temporal discriminatory nature are employed, a linear improvement is performance will occur, a phenomenon similar in some respects to that observed in some of the stimulus-seeking experiments.

These results obtained at the Manitoba laboratory are significant in three respects. First, they indicate that the *minimum* duration of deprivation required to produce the various facilitatory effects is related to the type of sensory measure employed; some tasks require 3 days, others, less than 12 hours. Second, they suggest that some of the other facilitatory effects (on auditory vigilance, for example) produced by multimodality deprivation may also occur after visual deprivation alone. Third, these results are of considerable theoretical importance since they appear to provide experimental support for the sensoristatic model formulated by Schultz (1965). According to Schultz, sensoristasis is a condition in which the organism strives to maintain an optimal range of sensory variation, a range which is capable of shifting to some degree as a function of various variables. The monitor serving to maintain the sensoristatic balance is the reticular activating system that Lindsley (1961) conceives of as a "homeostat" or regulator adjusting input-output relations.

One of the predictions that Schultz derives from his model is that "when stimulus variation is restricted, central regulation of threshold sensitivities will function to *lower* sensory thresholds. Thus, the organism becomes increasingly sensitized in an attempt to restore the balance" (p. 32). The demonstration of an increase in cutaneous, auditory, olfactory, and gustatory sensitivity following visual deprivation supports this theoretical prediction. Furthermore, according to this theory the failure of one of the Manitoba studies to demonstrate an improvement in tactual and auditory localization is not surprising, since these performance measures largely involve learning rather than threshold determinations of sensitivity. Finally, one other prediction can be made from Schultz's model. Auditory deprivation alone or tactual deprivation alone should also produce facilitatory effects on nondeprived modality measures. An experimental test of this prediction will be undertaken at the Manitoba laboratory.

Physiological Effects

EEG ACTIVITY

Of the various physiological measures, changes in EEG activity have been studied the most extensively. This research has been conducted not only in North America but also in a number of laboratories in England, the Netherlands, Russia, and Japan. With only a few exceptions, all of these laboratories have reported changes in EEG activity regardless of the duration of deprivation.

Changes in electrical activity of the brain during isolation were first reported at McGill University (Heron, 1957, 1961; Heron, Doane, & Scott, 1956). Daily EEG records from six subjects who endured 4 days of PD revealed slow alpha waves of high voltage and marked delta wave activity, effects that were still present 3 hours after the termination of isolation. In order to obtain a quantitative measure of these changes, the Engel period-count technique (Engel et al., 1944) was employed to measure occipital alpha frequency. This involves counting, by means of a calibrated ruler, the number of waves occurring in each of 200 1-second samples of artifact-free occipital lobe tracings, and then obtaining the mean frequency per second. This procedure revealed a progressive slowing in mean alpha frequency with increasing duration of isolation; more slow activity was evident after 4 days than after 2 in all six subjects. This regular progression was still present even when the tracings were analyzed in 24-hour time blocks. Using the same period-count technique, a similar decrease in alpha frequency with time was also reported by Gendreau et al. (1968b) in subjects tested at intervals of 1, 4, and 7 days of PD. Unfortunately, no observations were made on the duration of the aftereffects.

Undoubtedly the most impressive evidence for EEG changes, of considerable magnitude and long-lasting nature, has been provided by the Manitoba laboratory in a 14-day PD experiment (Zubek, 1964b; Zubek, Welch, & Saunders, 1963). EEG records were taken before isolation and then during isolation at intervals of 7, 10, and 14 days. In addition, follow-up records were taken 1, 2, 7, and 10 days after the termination of PD. The results for 10 subjects, based on the period-count technique employed in all of the Manitoba studies, are summarized in Table 2.1. It can be seen that the subjects show a progressive decrease in mean alpha frequency with time in isolation. Furthermore, the mean decrease during

TABLE 2.1—*Mean occipital alpha frequencies at various intervals during and after 14 days of perceptual deprivation*

Subject No.	During Deprivation				After Deprivation			
	day 0	*day 7*	*day 10*	*day 14*	*day 1*	*day 2*	*day 7*	*day 10*
1	10.10	9.16	8.60	7.15	7.89	8.62	9.57	—
2	13.03	12.65	11.40	10.44	11.04	11.34	12.50	—
3	11.56	—	10.14	8.00	10.21	—	11.01	—
4	11.27	10.13	9.87	9.08	9.61	9.83	10.14	10.68
5	9.67	9.27	8.75	8.39	8.57	8.97	9.18	9.46
6	11.51	11.04	10.93	9.96	10.35	10.54	10.36	10.94
7	10.66	10.06	10.02	9.72	10.01	10.30	10.45	10.50
8	10.92	10.65	10.63	10.66	10.75	10.67	10.67	10.65
9	10.65	10.70	10.56	10.16	9.91	10.04	10.38	10.61
10	10.46	10.50	10.42	9.90	10.11	10.32	10.47	10.44
Mean	10.98	10.46	10.13	9.35	9.84	10.07	10.47	10.47

SOURCE: Reprinted by permission from J. P. Zubek, 1964, *Psychon. Sci.* 1:57–58.

the second week (1.11 cps) is approximately twice as great as during the first (0.52 cps).

It is interesting to note that a group of Russian investigators (Lebedinsky, Levinsky, & Nefedov, 1964), using unusually long periods of *social isolation* (not SD or PD), have also reported a similar phenomenon. The change in EEG activity was always greatest toward the end of an experimental period, whether its duration was 10, 30, 60, or 120 days. Table 2.1 also indicates a progressive return to the normal, preexperimental frequency following termination of deprivation, with indications of EEG abnormality still evident, in several subjects, 10 days after release from isolation. Although these long-lasting aftereffects may appear surprising, some supporting evidence has been reported by Lebedinsky and his colleagues (1964), who observed indications of EEG abnormalities 2 months after the termination of a 2-month period of social isolation. Collectively, these Canadian and Russian results seem to suggest that certain physiological aftereffects may persist for periods equal to the initial isolation duration. Whether the same relationship exists for durations below 2 weeks remains to be determined.

Finally, Table 2.1 shows the existence of large individual differences, with the mean decrease in frequency, after the 14-day period, ranging from 0.26 to 3.56 cps. Large individual differences, incidentally, were also present in the duration of postisolation motivational losses, indicated by inability to study or to engage in a variety of activities. These effects persisted from less than a day to 8 days (mean = 3.5 days). A correlation of +0.67 was found to exist between the magnitude of the EEG decreases and the duration of the motivational losses. These results suggest that certain individuals are much more influenced by conditions of reduced sensory input than others, a finding also observed in some prison situations in Eastern European communist countries (Hinkle, 1961).

In addition to these three long-duration studies, numerous others employing much shorter deprivation periods have indicated a slowing of EEG alpha activity: 1 hour of PD (Marjerrison & Keogh, 1967); 2 hours of SD (Van Wulfften Palthe, 1958, 1962); 6 hours of PD (Leiderman, 1962; Mendelson et al., 1961); 18 hours of PD (Ohyama, Kokubun, & Kobayashi, 1965); 1 day of PD (Sato & Kokubun, 1965; Kato et al., 1967); 2 days of PD (Nagatsuka & Kokubun, 1964); 2 days of SD (Smith, 1962); and 3 days of SD (Weinstein et al., 1967). A review of these and other studies has been provided by Zubek (1969c).

Several variables can influence the nature and pattern of the changes in EEG activity. The first is whether a longitudinal or a cross-sectional testing procedure is employed. Strong evidence has already been presented indicating a progressive decrease in alpha frequency with increasing duration of isolation. These results, it is important to note, have been obtained with a longitudinal procedure; that is, the same subjects have been tested periodically during an initially prescribed duration of isolation.

Recent evidence from the Manitoba laboratory appears to indicate that such a temporal pattern does not exist when a cross-sectional approach is employed (Zubek, Shephard, & Milstein, 1970). Three *different* groups of subjects were exposed to *either* 1, 4, or 7 days of SD. EEG records were taken before and after each duration. The results revealed no indication of a progressive decrease in mean alpha frequency over days; in each duration group the decrease was approximately 1 cps. Three control groups tested before and after the same duration showed virtually a zero change in frequency. These results are puzzling, particularly in view of the progressive decrease in frequency reported by Gendreau et al. (1968b), who employed the same temporal durations (1, 4, and 7 days) and the same period-count technique as in the present study. The main difference was their use of a longitudinal approach.

Of the various theories postulated to account for the various deprivation effects reported in the literature (Suedfeld, 1969c; Zuckerman, 1969c), the set-expectancy hypothesis of Jackson and Pollard (1962) appears to be the most relevant in interpreting the present findings. According to this hypothesis, the experimental subjects may have developed a set or "preparedness" to complete a goal-oriented task (successful endurance of isolation), this set being unrelated to the duration required for its completion. Although this does not explain specifically how set could produce the same degree of EEG slowing after the three different deprivation durations, it is interesting to note that there is some evidence indicating that "preparedness" or set for a given duration can affect the magnitude of EEG changes observed in isolation experiments (Lebedinsky, Levinsky, & Nefedov, 1964; Saunders & Zubek, 1967). Clearly more research on this phenomenon is required. Furthermore, the results of this study are of considerable importance for future research in the area of SD and PD. They suggest that a different temporal pattern of performance not only on physiological but also on various behavioral measures may occur, depending on whether the data are collected in a longitudinal or a cross-sectional manner.

A second important variable is the type of deprivation condition. The role of this variable was demonstrated in another Manitoba experiment (Zubek & Welch, 1963), in which 40 subjects were employed, 10 in each of four conditions—SD, PD, recumbent control, and ambulatory control. The duration was 1 week; EEG records were taken before and after each condition. The results indicated that all 20 subjects in the two experimental groups showed a postisolation decrease in alpha frequency. The mean decrease was significantly greater under the PD (1.21 cps) than under the SD condition (0.85 cps). On the other hand, both the recumbent and ambulatory controls showed only negligible changes over the 1-week period (−0.04 and +0.01 cps, respectively). The records of the subjects in both experimental groups were also characterized by an excess of theta wave activity, particularly in the temporal lobes, a phenomenon observed in several other long-duration studies (Kato et al,, 1967; Smith, 1962; Zubek et al., 1961). However, the incidence of these theta waves appeared to be the same for both experimental groups. The results of this experiment indicate, therefore, that conditions of both SD and PD can produce a slowing of alpha frequencies, but that the latter condition exerts a greater effect. This differential EEG effect may be related to the greater perceptual-motor and cognitive impairments that seem to occur under PD than under SD, a finding discussed in several earlier sections.

A third variable that can affect the magnitude of EEG changes is the severity of the deprivation condition. In one of the Manitoba studies (Zubek, 1963a), a comparison was made between a group of subjects who were permitted to engage in various physical exercises during a week of PD, and a group who were confined to a bed for the same duration of PD. Although both groups showed a decrease in mean alpha frequency at the end of the experimental period, the decrease in the exercising-group was approximately one-half that observed in the nonexercising group. In the second Manitoba study (Zubek et al., 1969), also involving a 1-week period, a group of subjects exposed to both PD and "whole-body" immobilization showed a greater decrease in alpha frequency than did two other groups who were either perceptually deprived or immobilized. Thus, increasing or decreasing the severity of deprivation can influence the magnitude of EEG changes.

Changes in Skin Resistance (GSR)

Only a handful of studies have investigated changes in skin resistance over a period of several days. In the earliest of these, conducted at Princeton (Vernon et al., 1961) GSR measures were obtained from 18 subjects before and after 1, 2, or 3 days of SD, and from 18 controls at the same time intervals. Because of the quiet and sleep-conductive nature of the SD environment, it was predicted that the skin resistance of the confined subjects would increase since an increase (low arousal) normally occurs in sleeping subjects. This prediction was not borne out. Regardless of duration, all confined groups showed a decrease in skin resistance (greater arousal) and, conversely, all control groups exhibited an increase over the same intervals. Follow-up measures taken a day after the termination of isolation did not differ significantly from the preisolation values. Because the skin resistance dropped progressively over time, the authors have predicted that "longer confinements would lead to greater alertness than shorter ones" (p. 55). Unfortunately, no durations longer than 3 days have as yet been employed.

Essentially similar results were reported by Weinstein et al. (1967). The skin resistance of 10 subjects was monitored *continuously* for periods of up to 3 days of SD without interruptions to apply electrodes. The progressive decline in basal skin resistance level was particularly noticeable when the results were plotted as a function of objective or calendar time rather than in terms of hours in isolation. Three other studies, using 1 to 2 days of PD, have been conducted by a group of Japanese investigators, but because of certain methodological weaknesses such as absence of control groups, no really meaningful conclusions can be drawn from them (Kato et al., 1967; Nagatsuka & Kokubun, 1964; Sato & Kokubun, 1965).

Although few investigators have employed long durations, a considerable amount of research has involved brief deprivation periods ranging from 1 to 8 hours. Since most of it is of a correlational nature, relating GSR changes to such factors as preisolation information, task demands, personality traits, etc., and since the results are somewhat complex, a description of this material will not be included (see Zubek, 1969c for details). However, reference will be made to some important research that has been conducted at Zuckerman's laboratory at the Albert Einstein Medical Center, Philadelphia.

In the first study that was concerned with the role of duration (Zuckerman, Levine, & Biase, 1964), continuous skin conductance records (reciprocal of skin resistance) were taken from 36 female subjects confined for 3 hours to "total" isolation (SD) and to two conditions of partial isolation: visual deprivation alone and auditory deprivation alone. During the first 1½ hours there was little differentiation of the three groups. However, during the second 1½-hour period the skin conductance of the total isolation group rose sharply, indicating greater arousal, while that of the partial isolation groups remained level or rose only slightly. Measures of nonspecific GSR reactions revealed a similar picture: no differentiation during the first 1½ hours, followed by a greater number of nonspecific reactions. Of the two partial isolation groups, visual deprivation produced more nonspecific GSRs during the second 1½-hour period than did auditory deprivation. An essentially similar pattern of results was obtained in a second study using male subjects (Biase & Zuckerman, 1967).

The objective of the third study was quite different. Zuckerman and Haber (1965) wished to determine whether subjects who show a greater stress reaction (high GSR reactivity) to SD possess a greater need for stimulation than do those who are not stressed by SD. The subjects, who were selected on the basis of their high or low GSR reactions to a prior isolation experiment were tested in a second 3-hour SD condition. On this second occasion, however, they were given an opportunity to make an operant response that would produce random visual or auditory stimuli, depending on their choice. The results revealed that the high GSR reactors made almost four times as many responses to the brief sensory stimuli as did the low reactors during the 3-hour period of SD. Furthermore, all of the subjects responded more for visual than for auditory reinforcement. These findings clearly indicate that high GSR reactors have a greater need for sensory stimulation (stimulus "hunger") than do low reactors.

OTHER PHYSIOLOGICAL OR PHYSICAL CHANGES

In one of the early McGill studies (Heron, 1961), several physiological measures were recorded from six subjects during 4 days of PD. Oral temperature and blood pressure were taken twice daily, and the basal metabolic rate each morning. The results indicated that there were "no consistent changes in the subject's temperature or blood pressure and their basal metabolic rates remained constant" (p. 23). Subsequent research has indicated no changes in skin temperature (thermocouple on finger) after 3 days of SD (Weinstein et al., 1967), nor in heart rate, respiration, and muscle potential activity during 1 to 2 days of PD (Nagatsuka & Kokubun, 1964; Sato & Kokubun, 1965). Certain physiological measures, however, do change providing that unusually long durations are employed. This was demonstrated by a group of Russian investigators (Agadzhanian et al., 1963) in three subjects who were socially isolated for a period of 60 days. Both respiratory rate and blood pressure began to decrease after approximately the 20th day, while heart rate showed an increase after this period. Since these results were based on a small sample, they must be regarded as purely suggestive.

Decreases in body weight almost invariably occur during prolonged isolation under both restricted and diverse diets of a plentiful nature. For example, the Japanese investigator Kitamura (1964) reported a loss in body weight of 5.7 lb after 2 days of PD, Weinstein et al. (1967) a decrease of 3.8 lb after 3 days of SD, and Myers et al. (1966) an average weight loss of 4.5 lb after 4 days of SD. Control subjects, on the other hand, showed a slight increase in average weight. Kitamura has also observed an increase in mean height of 11 mm, the first such report in the literature.

Losses in body weight in almost all subjects were also observed at the Princeton laboratory (Vernon, 1963; Vernon et al., 1961). The average weight losses at the end of 1, 2, 3, and 4 days of SD were 2.7, 1.8, 3.0 and 3.7 lb, respectively, a finding which suggests that the "length of confinement is not necessarily directly related to the loss of weight" (1963,

p. 187). Follow-up measures indicated that these losses were regained almost entirely within the first day of release from isolation. In addition to an appraisal of weight, strength of grip was measured with a hand dynamometer. The results revealed no significant differences between experimental and control subjects after either 1 or 2 days of SD. However, after 3 days the confined subjects showed an average decrease in strength of grip of 4 per cent whereas the controls gained on the average about 8 per cent. It is doubtful whether this loss of strength of grip can be attributed to the decrease in body weight. The decrease was only 3 lb, which could hardly be expected to affect the strength of an individual. Vernon (1963) suggests that the data may merely indicate that "weight and strength behave in a similar manner when subjected to sensory deprivation" (p. 189).

Biochemical Effects

OXYCORTICOID AND CATECHOLAMINE STUDIES

Three experiments have investigated the activity of the adrenocortical and sympathetic-adrenomedullary systems during prolonged PD. The earliest of these was conducted at McGill (Murphy et al., 1955). Urinary determinations of 11-oxycorticoids were taken from nine subjects before and during 1½ to 6 days of PD. Unfortunately, no controls were employed. Because no consistent increase in the excretion of corticoids occurred, it was concluded that under isolation the "adrenal cortex is not activated to a greater degree than it is by the minor exigencies of everyday life" (p. 1063).

The activity of the sympathetic-adrenomedullary system also appears to be unaffected by prolonged PD, according to one study from the Manitoba laboratory (Zubek & Schutte, 1966). In this experiment, daily urinary measures of catecholamines (adrenaline and noradrenaline) were taken from 31 male volunteers during a week of PD, as well as for 3 days before and 2 days after isolation. A further 24-hour sample was taken from some of the subjects 6 months after termination of confinement. Of the 31 experimental subjects, 18 successfully endured the week of deprivation while 13, the quitters, terminated it prematurely (mean duration = 56 hours). Since the recumbent position is known to decrease the output of catecholamines, particularly noradrenaline, a group of 18 recumbent controls were placed individually inside the chamber and asked to lie quietly for a week. Apart from the restriction on gross motor activity, their environment was kept as normal as possible—they had access to reading material, a radio, brightly colored pictures were placed on the walls, and they were frequently visited by the experimenters. Further-

more, to avoid a population bias all control subjects had initially volunteered for the experimental condition.

The results on noradrenaline, the neurohormone of the peripheral
sympathetic nervous system, indicated that both the successful endurers
and the quitters exhibited a noradrenaline pattern similar to that of the
recumbent controls. An analysis of variance revealed that all three groups
showed a significant decrease in mean urinary excretion of noradrenaline
during the experimental period relative to their pre- and postexperimental levels. None of the differences among the three groups, however, were
statistically significant.

Figure 2.2 summarizes the results on adrenaline, which is the main
constituent of catecholamines secreted by the adrenal medulla. Again,
there was no significant difference in mean excretion level between the
successful isolation endurers and the controls relative to their pre- and
postexperimental levels. Both groups showed a significant decrease in adrenaline while in the chamber. This decrease, together with that for noradrenaline already noted, probably resulted from the recumbent position
maintained most of the time by all of the subjects (Euler, Luft, & Sundin,
1955; Sundin, 1958). On the other hand, the quitters exhibited a complex pattern of changes. First, the adrenaline level during isolation was
related to their endurance. The early quitters who terminated confinement within the first 2 days showed a level similar to that of their preisolation (preday 2 and 3) or postisolation (postday 2) levels. The late
quitters, however, revealed a striking increase in adrenaline after the second day of isolation but not during the first 2 days. A possible explanation of this different effect may be that the early quitters terminated isolation at the first indication of discomfort and unpleasantness and hence
showed no increase in adrenaline, whereas the late quitters stubbornly attempted to endure the full week despite the stress of the situation.

A second characteristic of the quitters, as indicated in Figure 2.2, was
the presence of a significant increase in adrenaline on the day *prior* to
isolation and relative to the preceding 2 days. An increase in preisolation
noradrenaline level was also observed, but not to a statistically significant
degree. A similar increase in preexperimental catecholamine levels has
also been noted in other so-called stress situations—immediately before
centrifuge or drug studies, for example (Elmadjian, Hope, & Lamson,
1957; Goodall & Berman, 1960)—and is believed to be indicative of apprehension about experimental participation.

The third, and perhaps most important characteristic of the quitters,
was the presence of a preisolation level of adrenaline (preday 2 and 3)
significantly lower than that of the successful endurers. This low excretion level was also seen 2 days after termination of isolation as well as 6
months later. Because this adrenaline base-line difference seems to be a

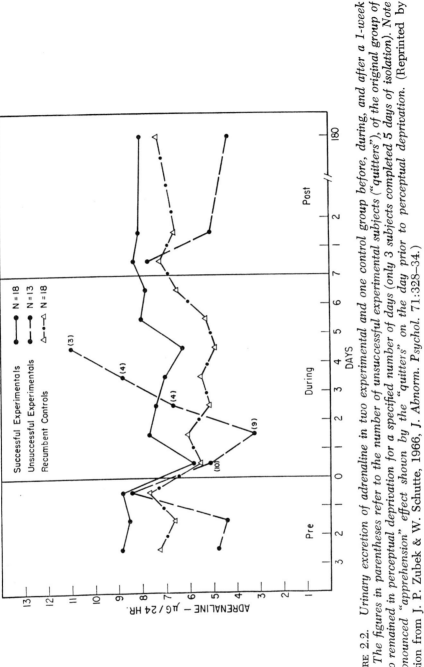

FIGURE 2.2. *Urinary excretion of adrenaline in two experimental and one control group before, during, and after a 1-week period. The figures in parentheses refer to the number of unsuccessful experimental subjects ("quitters"), of the original group of 13, who remained in perceptual deprivation for a specified number of days (only 3 subjects completed 5 days of isolation). Note the pronounced "apprehension" effect shown by the "quitters" on the day prior to perceptual deprivation. (Reprinted by permission from J. P. Zubek & W. Schutte, 1966, J. Abnorm. Psychol. 71:328–34.)*

stable characteristic, persisting over many months, it would appear that isolation quitters may be biochemically or "constitutionally" different from those who can successfully endure a prescribed period of prolonged isolation. In view of these results, further research is required to determine whether other biochemical differences may exist between these two types of subjects, a finding that may result in improved selection and screening of personnel for isolated duty assignments. This is suggested by an experiment at the Naval Medical Research Institute at Bethesda, Maryland (Haythorn, 1967). Preliminary analysis of the results of a group of subjects who were unable to endure a 1-week period of SD indicated that "they have a relatively high level of serum uric acid prior to the experiment (and before they know to which condition they will be assigned)" (p. 3).

The presence of a significant difference in base-line adrenaline level between the two types of isolation subjects suggests that they may also differ in personality. This does not appear to be the case. Administration of the Rorschach, MMPI, Edwards Personal Preference, and the Thurstone Temperament Schedule prior to isolation indicated that no single personality characteristic measured by these tests significantly differentiated the successful from the unsuccessful subject.

Finally, an analysis of the 24-hour urine volume of the successful endurers revealed a progressive decrease in excretion during the week of isolation, a decrease significantly greater than that shown by the recumbent controls. No significant difference in total fluid intake of the two groups occurred during the 1-week period. A similar progressive decline in urine volume, independent of fluid intake, has also been reported by Winters (1963) in monkeys placed in SD for 2 weeks. Since water consumption was not reduced in either experiment, this decreased urinary volume may be a primary response possibly "triggered" by a greater production of the antidiuretic hormone of the pituitary gland. This suggestion of a possible pituitary disturbance is further supported in a study from Zuckerman's laboratory in which an increased production of the pituitary thyroid stimulating hormone occurred after 8 hours of SD (Zuckerman et al., 1966).

These Manitoba catecholamine results, together with the McGill data on 11-oxycorticoids, appear to indicate that neither the sympathetic-adrenomedullary nor the adrenocortical systems are activated to any noticeable degree by prolonged periods of PD. This conclusion, however, may have to be tempered somewhat in the light of an important finding from the Soviet Union. Gorbov, Miasnikov, and Yazdovsky (1963) reported an increase in 17-ketosteroids in subjects individually confined for 15 days in an altitude chamber under a condition of *no* intercommunication. However, in experiments where some degree of two-way communication between the subject and experimenter was permitted, no changes in 17-ketosteroid output were observed. This finding is of considerable significance since in both Canadian studies some verbal contact, although infrequent, was maintained throughout the PD period. If intercommunication had been totally eliminated, it is possible that a significant increase in urinary oxycorticoids and catecholamines, relative to controls, may have occurred.

Since no significant increases in catecholamine levels were observed in the successful endurers, a second Manitoba experiment was conducted in which an attempt was made to increase the severity of PD by the introduction of kinesthetic deprivation (Zubek et al., 1969). A group of 30 subjects were not only perceptually deprived but also immobilized in a coffinlike box for a period of a week. In order to minimize physical discomfort and pain, they were unstrapped at mealtimes and during the night. Because of the severity of the condition, only 12 of the 30 subjects were able to endure the full 1-week period. The remainder (the quitters) terminated the condition after a mean duration of 33.4 hours. Briefly, the results indicated a significant increase in noradrenaline in the successful endurers relative to recumbent controls, an effect that was particularly pronounced during the second half of the experimental period. No significant differences were observed for adrenaline. A comparison of the successful endurers and the quitters again revealed that the quitters possessed a lower pre- and postexperimental baseline level of adrenaline but the difference was not statistically significant, probably because of the high quitting rate—60 per cent vs 40 per cent in the earlier PD study.

Further evidence for the importance of severity of deprivation has been provided in two short-duration experiments. In the first, Mendelson and his colleagues (1960) isolated ten subjects in a polio-type respirator, involving a severe restriction of body movements, for periods ranging from 3 to 31 hours (mean = 9.1 hr). An increased excretion level of not only noradrenaline but also adrenaline was reported. The fact that both catecholamine measures increased is somewhat surprising in view of the shortness of the deprivation periods. This finding may, however, be related to the fact that all of their immobilized subjects were quitters; none of them were able to endure the prescribed period of 36 hours. In the second study, Schaefer (1964) immersed 18 volunteers for 3½ hours in a water tank placed inside an anechoic chamber. A significant increase in both adrenaline and noradrenaline was observed.

OTHER BIOCHEMICAL STUDIES

Only limited attention has been directed at biochemical measures other than catecholamines and oxycorticoids. In one study by Zuckerman et al. (1966), a variety of urinary and plasma measures were obtained from a group of subjects during 8 hours of SD and 8 hours of a confinement control condition, in counterbalanced order. The urinary measures consisted of 17-ketogenic steroids (17-KGS), 17-ketosteroids (17-KS), and the luteinizing hormone; the plasma measures comprised the pituitary thyroid stimulating hormone (TSH), adrenocorticotropic hormone (ACTH), hydrocortisone, corticosterone, protein-bound iodine, and thyroxine. The results revealed a significant increase in 17-KGS and 17-KS during the experimental relative to the control condition. Of the five plasma measures, only the output of TSH showed an increase, with all subjects but one showing this change.

In a follow-up study, a 24-hour period of SD was employed (Persky *et al.*, 1966). Contrary to their results on the 8-hour experiment, they observed no significant difference between the isolated and confined control subjects on the output of 17-KGS, 17-KS, and TSH. However, a significant increase in output, on the first two measures, was seen in *both* groups relative to their output several months after the termination of the study. The authors interpret these later findings as indicating that social isolation and confinement are the significant sources of stress in SD and PD experiments, and that many of the effects attributed to them are really a function of the total isolation situation relative to normal life conditions. This question of the relative roles of confinement, social isolation, and sensory restriction per se is an important one that will be discussed more fully in a later section of this chapter.

Isolation Endurance

One of the intriguing isolation effects is the considerable variation in individual reactions to an impoverished sensory environment. Some volunteers can endure a duration of 2 weeks with relative ease, while others terminate isolation within a few hours. A further interesting observation has been reported by Zuckerman (1964) who, in a survey of various long duration studies, noted the presence of a surprisingly constant quitting rate: approximately one-third of the subjects failed to endure an initially prescribed period, whether the duration was 2, 4, 7, or 14 days. Subsequent research, particularly at the Manitoba laboratory, has generally confirmed this observation. One notable exception has been reported from the U.S. Naval Medical Research Institute, where approximately one-half of the volunteers were unable to endure 7 days of SD (Haythorn, 1967). This deviation is perhaps understandable since the subjects were not financially rewarded for participating in the study.

In the light of these two observations, it is not surprising that considerable attention has been directed toward determining characteristics that might differentiate successful endurers from quitters. In addition to a wide range of paper-and-pencil tests of personality, which represent the bulk of the literature, some use has been made of projective tests, questionnaires, and sensory and biochemical measures. Since it is not possible to review this extensive literature, particularly the numerous studies that have employed very brief periods of deprivation, the reader is referred to an excellent critical treatment of this topic by Myers (1969).

PREISOLATION DIFFERENTIATORS OR PREDICTORS

Paper-and-pencil Tests of Personality. One common approach in this area of investigation is to administer a battery of personality tests prior to isolation and then determine, by *t* tests, which of the numerous personality traits significantly differentiate the successful endurers from the quitters. Unfortunately, neither this omnibus approach nor the approach using a specific personality measure has been too successful.

The earliest of these omnibus studies was conducted at the Manitoba laboratory (Hull & Zubek, 1962) in which the MMPI, Edwards Personal Preference Scale (EPPS), Thurstone Temperament Schedule (TTS), and a biographical questionnaire were administered prior to either a week of SD (11 successful Ss and 5 quitters) or a week of PD (19 successful Ss and 11 quitters). The only significant finding was in the SD condition, where the quitters obtained a higher score on the Abasement scale of the EPPS. Results from pooling the two conditions revealed no significant differences on any of the 40 variables measured by the three personality tests. However, an analysis of the data derived from the biographical questionnaire indicated that the quitters were significantly more likely to be smokers and watched television more than the successful endurers. The quitters also *tended* to own fewer books and be younger. In two subsequent experiments from the same laboratory (Wright & Zubek, 1966), using a week of PD and a much larger sample, negative results were again obtained on the same three personality tests. Unfortunately, the biographical questionnaire was not employed.

Since no single personality trait was found to be effective, Wright and Zubek (1966) employed the multiple discriminant function to determine whether a combination or pattern of traits might differentiate the 1-week PD endurers from the quitters. From this multivariate analysis, 45 out of 60 successful endurers and 23 out of 30 quitters were differentiated, an overall performance of 75.6 per cent correct classification. Because these encouraging results were derived from an optimization procedure, the investigators undertook a crossvalidation study on a subsequent sample of 31 PD subjects. The previously determined multiple discriminant function weights (25 component variables) were applied to the new data with the result that all 18 successful endurers were correctly predicted to succeed. However, the isolation performance of only 4 of the 13 quitters was correctly predicted in advance. It is of interest, though, that three subjects who almost endured the week of PD were predicted to succeed. Thus, the endurance performance of 22 of 31 isolation subjects (71 per cent) was correctly predicted in advance. Although this multiple variable procedure appears to possess some merit, the predictive value of 71 per cent is not high, particularly since by chance alone one would be correct 50 per cent of the time.

Other omnibus types of studies, employing *t*-test analyses of single personality variables, have also yielded essentially negative results. Wexler et al. (1958), in a 36-hour PD condition, reported no significant differences on the MMPI and EPPS. Arnhoff and Leon (1963a) reported that only two scales, Surgency and Protension, of Cattell's 16-PF test significantly differentiated quitters from successful endurers in a 1-day PD experiment, a finding that they said "could well be due to chance factors." Similar results have been reported from a series of studies at the HumRRO laboratory (Myers, 1969; Myers et al., 1966), in which the MMPI, EPPS, and a biographical questionnaire were administered to a large sample of subjects prior to either 4 days or 6 days of SD. The questionnaire data revealed that the quitters were significantly younger and were more frequently smokers, paralleling the Manitoba findings. (Incidentally, at neither laboratory was the absence of smoking responsible for quitting, the main factors being severe boredom or anxiety.) Of no relevance to endurance were such biographical factors as birth order, educational level, and intelligence. On the personality tests, significant differences were "few and far between" (Myers, 1969). No significant differences at the .05 level or better were found in a 6-day SD study.

Some positive findings were obtained in two 4-day SD experiments, but the results formed no consistent pattern. In the first, the quitters obtained significantly lower scores on need Deference and need Affiliation and significantly higher scores on need Aggression. In the second experiment, the quitters were significantly higher on Hypochondriasis and Psychopathic Deviancy than were the successful endurers. Since no consistent pattern of results emerged, Myers (1969) next examined the *directional trends* present in all of the HumRRO and Manitoba studies, together with a field study on adjustment to work on the Arctic DEW line employing a similar battery of personality tests (Wright, Sisler, & Chylinsky, 1963). On the basis of this overview, Myers concluded that isolation quitters "tend to be youngish, television-watching, non-reading smokers who score high on Pd, Ma, and Aggression scales. Their more enduring counterparts seem to score a bit higher on some measures of mature responsibility, such as Consistency, Deference, Affiliation, Social Responsibility, and Ego Strength" (p. 305). In view of these trends, it would be interesting to determine whether a multivariate analysis, employing these specific measures, would not only differentiate between endurers and quitters but also predict their isolation endurance in advance.

In addition to these omnibus studies, numerous investigators have employed specific personality tests such as neuroticism, anxiety, introversion-extraversion, and field dependence-independence. According to Myers (1969), who has reviewed these studies, no clear picture has emerged. Myers (1969), however, has reported positive results in an unpublished study using two "life style" tests, measures of seeming proximity to the deprivation situation itself. The results revealed that subjects who were unable to endure 6 days of SD obtained significantly higher scores on scales of Thrill Seeking and Dark Quiet Cell Phobia (appraising reactions to solitude, darkness, quiet, and so forth) than did the successful endurers. Further research of this type, employing measures bearing some relationship to the actual experimental situation, may prove more rewarding than a continuation of the earlier type of research in which the personality measures have been selected on a more or less trial and error basis.

Projective Tests (Rorschach). Since the isolation situation has been conceptualized as an "unstructured behavioral projective test" (Freedman & Greenblatt, 1959), it is possible that the Rorschach test may be a better measure of PD tolerance than a variety of paper-and-pencil tests of personality because it elicits a sample of how the individual typically structures ambiguous situations according to his needs. Three 1-week PD studies, employing the Buhler-Lefever standardization of the Rorschach, have been conducted at the Manitoba laboratory. In the first experiment (Wright & Zubek, 1966), an application of the multiple discriminant function to 25 Rorschach variables yielded a prediction value of 55 per cent, a chance performance. The isolation performance of only 10 of the 18 successful endurers and 7 of 13 quitters was correctly predicted in advance. This disappointing result on the Rorschach is surprising in view of the 71 per cent correct prediction obtained on the three paper-and-pencil tests (MMPI, EPPS, and TTS), a finding discussed earlier.

Results of a more promising nature were obtained in two other Manitoba experiments, in which an examination was made of the Rorschach manifestations of an individual's defense and control mechanisms. In these two studies, the protocols were scored objectively according to the Holt-Havel method for assessing primary and secondary processes in the Rorschach and the defense and control mechanisms which these demand. The proportion of the Effectiveness of Defense score to the Defense Demand score became the Index of Control. In the first study (Wright & Abbey, 1965), a group of PD subjects were rank-ordered according to this Index of Control. The results revealed that virtually all of the successful endurers possessed a high Index of Control, while virtually all of the quitters fell in the low Index of Control group. This finding was however considered to be tentative, since the subjects were tested several months *after* completion of PD, and thus their responses may have been affected by their knowledge of success or failure in the situation. It was, therefore, decided to replicate this study but instituting a *prior* testing procedure. The results of this second study (Wright & Zubek, 1969) showed that the high Index of Control group consisted of 14 out of 15 successful endurers, while the low Index of Control group contained 12 out of the 16 quitters. A chi-square analysis of this data revealed a significant finding. From these two experiments it is evident that isolation quitters are individuals who experience difficulty in controlling the drive-dominated responses that might emerge during their attempt to successfully complete a prolonged period of isolation.[3]

Other Measures. In some exploratory research, Petrie, Collins, and Solomon (1958, 1960) reported an inverse relationship between pain tolerance and endurance of PD. Subjects showing high pain endurance remained in PD for the shortest durations, while subjects with low endurance stayed in the longest number of hours. Contrary results have been reported by Peters et al. (1963) in a PD study using a composite measure of pain tolerance (muscular contraction, electric shock, and heat). Furthermore, whatever trend was present between duration and pain tolerance took the form of a direct rather than an inverse relationship between the variables. Additional evidence for this latter finding has been provided by Zubek (1963b), who also reported a direct relationship, though not statistically significant, in a 7-day PD study. However, in the Zubek experiment absolute pain threshold was measured (dolorimeter), which may or may not give the same results as the suprathreshold tolerance measures employed in the previous two studies.

Finally, brief reference will be made to two biochemical studies that have been dealt with earlier. In the first, Zubek and Schutte (1966) reported that PD quitters possessed a significantly lower *base-line* level of adrenaline, relative to successful endurers, in the pre- and postdeprivation period, while in the second, Haythorn (1967) reported that subjects who were unable to endure a week of SD possessed a relatively high level of serum uric acid prior to the experiment. However, before these intriguing results can be used for predictive purposes it is essential that they be crossvalidated by preselecting volunteers on the basis of either high or

---

3. These results, showing the effectiveness of an Index of Control measure in differentiating between isolation quitters and successful endurers, have recently been confirmed by Dr. T. I. Myers of the U.S. Naval Medical Research Institute, Bethesda, Maryland. This unpublished experiment employed 7 days of SD and the Holtzman Inkblot Test. Despite the fact that a different projective test was used, the same pattern of results emerged.

low adrenaline and uric acid levels, and then determining whether these levels are related to subsequent performance.

EARLY-IN-ISOLATION PREDICTORS

Several studies, conducted by Myers and his colleagues, have been concerned with determining whether certain behavioral states *early in isolation* can be used to predict eventual nonendurance or quitting. These have all resulted in positive findings. In the first study (Smith, Myers, & Johnson, 1967), boring stock-market reports were available for a 1-hour period on each of days 1, 4, and 7 of a one-week SD condition. It was found that 9 of 11 subjects remaining less than 4 days in SD scored well above the median on day 1 listening, while only 7 of 21 subjects who completed the prescribed period had high listening scores.

Another excellent indicator is amount of gross motor restlessness. In one 4-day SD experiment (Smith, Murphy, & Myers, 1962), a high restlessness score during the daytime period of day 2 (but not on day 1, probably because of considerable sleeping) was strongly associated with a failure to complete the experiment. In another 4-day study (Murphy, Hampton, & Myers, 1962), estimated time passage was inversely related to endurance of SD. Subjects estimating a greater elapse of time after only 4 hours of SD (those for whom time seemed to drag) were significantly more likely to terminate the 4-day period prematurely—25 early quitters overestimated the 4-hour interval by 3.7 hours, whereas 23 endurers overestimated the period by only 1.1 hours. Finally, in several unpublished studies (referred to in Myers, 1969), Myers has reported that subjects' daily reports of affective state, such as degree of subjective stress, appear to be excellent predictors as to whether they will eventually endure either a 4- or a 7-day prescribed period of SD.

VARIABLES AFFECTING DEPRIVATION ENDURANCE

One variable that does not appear to affect isolation endurance is type of deprivation condition employed. In a series of Manitoba long-duration experiments (7 to 14 days), a relatively constant quitting rate of approximately one-third has been observed regardless of whether an SD or PD condition was used. Nor has varying the severity of the condition by eliminating test intrusions (Zubek, 1964c) or introducing physical exercises (1963a) influenced the quitting rate. Only scant attention has been paid to other possible variables. For example, Cambareri (1959) reported that more suggestible subjects remained significantly longer in a water-immersion condition than less suggestible subjects, while an Australian investigator (Francis, 1964), also using a water-immersion procedure, observed that provision of information about the passage of time was strongly conducive to successful endurance. The results on sex differences are mixed. Smith and Lewty (1959) reported that "one of the unexpected results was that the women in general seemed to last longer than the men" (p. 343). Two other experiments have failed to observe such a sex difference (Arnhoff & Leon, 1963b; Pollard, Uhr, & Jackson, 1963). All of these studies, unfortunately, have been based on a small sample. Another variable is prior isolation experience. The suggestions are that such experience does not influence endurance for brief deprivation periods, but is helpful in tolerating prolonged durations (see Myers, 1969).

Finally, there is some evidence that cultural factors may be involved. Kitamura (1965) reported that *all* 23 of his Japanese male subjects were able to endure 18 hours of PD without quitting. Essentially similar results were obtained in a series of subsequent Japanese studies involving 1 to 2 days of PD. A few quitters were present, but they were the exception. These findings are in striking contrast to those for North American males, for whom the quitting rate is approximately one-third (Zuckerman, 1964). One can only speculate as to whether certain aspects of Far Eastern culture, such as a wish to avoid "loss of face," might be the critical factor in accounting for this unusual tolerance for isolation. This Japanese finding also raises the question as to how other cultural groups would perform in isolation—certain authoritarian societies where one does what one is told to do, or certain religious groups, such as Buddhist monks, who practice inner contemplation and withdrawal from social intercourse. Another relevant question may be a rural-urban comparison within Western societies. These and other related questions await future research.

Such research might indicate that not only isolation tolerance but also other deprivation effects might be different in various cultural groups. Some evidence for this hypothesis has already been provided by Schwitzgebel (1962), who compared the reactions of a group of Africans (Zulus) and a group of English-speaking whites to 8 hours of PD. Both groups had approximately the same educational level. Although no differences in quitting rate were reported, the Zulu subjects were slower in locating embedded figures and were less accurate in estimating passage of time after PD than were the English-speaking whites. Even greater differences may have occurred had the Africans not already spent considerable time living in an urban environment.

Counteracting the Effects of SD and PD

In view of the widespread behavioral and physiological impairments reported in the literature, it is of some importance both theoretically and practically to determine whether these effects can be counteracted or minimized to any degree. Unfortunately, only limited attention has been paid to this problem.

Scattered reports in the nonexperimental literature indicate that explorers and prisoners of war have found physical exercises helpful in combating some of the effects of isolation and solitary confinement (Solomon et al., 1957). One of the most interesting of these cases concerns Major General Dean, a U.S. Army commander who was placed in solitary confinement after his capture during the Korean War. A physical fitness enthusiast, General Dean performed calisthenics even when reduced to crossing and uncrossing his fingers because of orders forbidding him to exercise. These activities, he claimed, helped him to maintain his intellectual and physical integrity.

In view of such reports, a study was conducted at the Manitoba laboratory (Zubek, 1963a) in which a group of subjects was required to perform six 5-minute exercises of a calisthenic nature each day throughout a 1-week period of PD. These exercises could be repeated as often as the subject wished. It was observed that the "exercising" subjects showed less of an impairment on a battery of cognitive and perceptual-motor tests and a significantly smaller decrease in EEG alpha frequency than did a "no-exercise" group (−0.48 cps vs −1.21 cps), also exposed to a week of PD. Surprisingly, no differences were observed in endurance rate; in both groups one-third of the subjects were unable to endure the prescribed period. It is interesting to speculate whether isometric exercises would prove to be equally effective.

Further support for these findings has been reported in some Russian social isolation studies, employing durations up to 60 days (Lebedinsky, Levinsky, & Nefedov, 1964). Although no details are given, a special set of physical exercises and certain work-cycles were said to be extremely effective in reducing both the magnitude and the persistence of various physiological and behavioral impairments (EEG and cardiovascular activity, sleep patterns, and work capacity) which in their absence could be detected to some degree 2 months after the completion of 2 months of confinement.

This beneficial effect is not too surprising, since the introduction of physical exercises during isolation may provide sufficient variability of kinesthetic and proprioceptive stimulation to counteract most of the effects of visual and auditory deprivation. This hypothesis is supported by several reports pointing to the "powerful excitatory influence of somatic sensory excitation upon the reticular activating system" (French, 1960, p. 1288), a physiological system implicated by a number of investigators in the production of deprivation phenomena (see, for example, Heron, 1961; Lindsley, 1961; Schultz, 1965; Zuckerman, 1969c).

Procedures other than physical exercises, such as the administration of certain psychopharmacological agents, may also prove beneficial in minimizing deprivation effects when introduced during isolation. Although chemical agents have not been tried on isolated human subjects, some of them have proven extremely effective in animals. Barnes (1958, 1959), for example, reported that chlorpromazine abolished virtually all of the abnormal behavioral responses developed by rats and mice placed in isolation for many days. The use of a variety of vitamin-enriched diets may also prove to be a fruitful approach, particularly in view of a claim from the Soviet Union that such diets (nature not specified, unfortunately) are particularly effective when administered during isolation (Lebedinsky, Levinsky, & Nefedov, 1964).

Another effective procedure is prior exposure to isolation. Some evidence of this was provided in an early exploratory study from the Manitoba laboratory (Zubek et al., 1962). Three of four subjects who were exposed to a week of isolation twice, a year apart, reported that the second period was far less stressful, and that they were able to get back to serious work sooner than after their first experience. Furthermore, when their performance during isolation was compared with that of four matched (on pretests) nonrepeaters, it was found that they performed better on 9 of 12 cognitive tests. Essentially similar results, based on subjective evaluations, have been observed at other laboratories. For example, Ruff, Levy, and Thaler (1961) reported that most of their eight subjects who participated in two or three consecutive experiments indicated that each period seemed easier than the last. Lilly (1956) and Lilly and Shurley (1961), using a water-immersion deprivation procedure, have also stated that repeated exposures are easier to endure and are less fear-provoking.

Further evidence of a more objective nature has been provided in three other experiments. In the first (Pollard, Uhr, & Jackson, 1963), two studies of repeated exposure found little change in likelihood of enduring either two 8-hour PD sessions or two 3-hour sessions. There were, however, significant reductions over sessions in each study in spontaneous verbalization (number of words spoken) and in certain self-report effects. In the second experiment, Suedfeld et al. (1965) reported a significant decrease in story length in a TAT-like situation after 1 day of SD. This effect, however, was not present when the same subjects underwent a second 1-day session, a week later. In the third study, a group of Russian investigators (Lebedinsky, Levinsky, & Nefedov, 1964) stated that in addition to physical exercises and enriched vitamin diets, prior experience was also effective in reducing the magnitude of various physiological and behavioral impairments occurring during prolonged social isolation periods.

Finally, one study, whose results unfortunately are only available in abstract form, has indicated that a preexperimental training program is an effective counteracting agent. Schaefer (1964) observed a significant increase in both adrenaline and noradrenaline after immersing 18 volunteers for 3½ hours in a water tank placed inside a dark anechoic chamber. These changes, according to Schaefer, could be counteracted by a program of preisolation training. In an exploratory study, six volunteers were given a month's training in "geometrical construction and projective geometry." When isolated subsequently, they revealed no significant change on either catecholamine measure. They also showed a decrease in respiration and heart rate in contrast to the no-training group, which showed an increase on both physiological measures. A replication of this important study, using a much larger sample, is warranted. Furthermore, because of its practical relevance it is essential to determine whether a shorter period of preisolation training would be equally as effective.

A possible basis for this counteracting effect of mental exercises of a geometric nature may lie in a heightened cortical stimulation of the reticular activating system (RAS). Lindsley (1961), for example, has stated that arousal and alerting of the RAS are not solely dependent upon peripheral sensory influx, but may equally well be produced by ideation and other cortical activity to past or present stimuli. Presumably, this heightened cortical activity was maintained during isolation and tended to compensate for the reduced sensory input. A similar type of explanation may apply to the beneficial effects of prior isolation experience. As a result of their first exposure, the subjects may have learned various techniques and devices to help them cope with the isolated environment on its subsequent occurrence.

Relative Effects of Confinement, Social Isolation, and Sensory Restriction

In the typical SD or PD experiment, the subject is exposed not only to a reduction in sensory stimulation but also, of necessity, to social isolation and physical confinement in a small windowless environment. Although various suggestions have been made in the literature that social isolation and confinement may be important factors, particularly in the long-duration experiments, little attention has been directed to analyzing the total isolation situation and determining the relative role of its various components. Furthermore, what research is available has only provided an incomplete picture—a comparison of the effects of sensory restriction and social isolation, for example (Persky et al., 1966; Suedfeld, Grissom, & Vernon, 1964; Zuckerman et al., 1962, 1966), or a comparison of the effects of sensory restriction and a combination of confinement plus restricted motor activity (Zubek & MacNeill, 1967; Zubek & Schutte,

1966). In none of these studies, unfortunately, was an attempt made to determine the specific role of confinement per se.

Recently, however, Zuckerman and his colleagues (1968), in an important extension of their earlier work, have analyzed the relative roles of not only sensory restriction, social isolation, and confinement, but also of experimental set and type of subjects. Using an 8-hour period of SD, measures were taken of two hormone metabolites (17-KGS and 17-KS), time estimation, affect, and responses to a variety of questionnaire items. Their main conclusion was that the "stress effects of confinement are rather massive and are found even when subjects are neither sensorily or socially isolated" (p. 194). In view of these results, it is possible that confinement alone may also be an important factor in producing some of the other effects reported in the literature, such as slowing of EEG activity and cognitive deficits.

Recently, a study was conducted at the Manitoba laboratory (Zubek, Bayer, & Shephard, 1969) in which the purpose was twofold: (1) to determine the relative effects of social isolation and confinement, of 1-week's duration, on measures of EEG activity, cognitive test performance, and various psychological and somatic symptoms elicited from a 242-item questionnaire (Myers ISQ), and (2) to compare these effects with those reported in the earlier Manitoba studies employing a week of PD. Three groups of subjects were employed: confinement (CF), socially isolated (SI), and ambulatory controls (AC).

The CF group consisted of 21 subjects who were placed one at a time in an isolation chamber for a week. All but one completed the experiment. The inside of the chamber was covered with brightly colored pictures, no restrictions were placed on motor activity (exercising, however, was not permitted), and the subjects had constant access to reading material, a radio, a television set, a mattress, and a chair with a tablet arm. The lights were put out for 9 hours at night. In order to avoid social isolation, the experimenters visited the subject at least twice each morning, afternoon, and evening. Furthermore, two visiting periods per day were scheduled for the subjects' friends and acquaintances. Finally, the two doors leading to the chamber were left open, enabling the subject to hear but not see any on-going activity in the outside control-room area.

The SI group consisted of 25 volunteers who were also placed individually in the chamber for a week. Of this group, five subjects terminated the condition prematurely (mean duration = 47 hr). The experimental environment was the same as for the CF group, with the exception of three modifications designed to achieve a condition of social isolation. First, the radio was replaced with piped-in Muzak (exclusively instrumental music). Second, a View-Master with 300 travel slides was substituted for the television set. Third, no visitors were allowed and conversation between the subject and experimenter was kept to a minimum (except at the relatively infrequent test sessions when a cognitive battery was administered). Furthermore, the two doors leading to the chamber were closed at all times.

The AC group consisted of 20 subjects who came to the laboratory at specified intervals during a 1-week control period—that is, at times corresponding to the test sessions of the experimental groups. However, they were free to leave and do what they wanted in the intervening periods. These controls, incidentally, had initially volunteered for both experimental conditions.

Using Engel's period count technique, both the SI and CF groups showed a significant posttest decrease in occipital alpha frequency (−0.62 and −0.50 cps, respectively). Furthermore, since the difference between the two experimental groups was not significant, this EEG effect appears to have resulted from confinement alone. Although a significant change was observed, its magnitude—approximately half a cycle—is considerably less than that reported by Zubek and Welch (1963) after a week of PD (−1.21 cps). These results, therefore, indicate that in the total PD situation approximately half the EEG change is produced by confinement, and half by a reduction in sensory stimulation. Social isolation, apparently, is not a contributing factor. On the other hand, an analysis of variance on the cognitive test battery revealed no significant differences on any of the 11 tests, although a general trend toward poorer performance by the SI group was observed. Since Zubek et al. (1962), using the same test battery and duration, reported that PD produced a significant impairment on various cognitive measures of a verbal, numerical, or spatial nature, it would appear that in the complex PD condition the restriction of sensory input is the critical factor in producing the various cognitive deficits; social isolation and confinement appear to exert a negligible effect.

An analysis of the results on the Myers postisolation questionnarie revealed a variety of unusual symptoms, similar to those described in an earlier section of this chapter. Of the 16 content areas that showed significant F ratios, 8 were associated solely with confinement: experiences of a hallucinatorylike nature, inefficient thought processes, subjective restlessness, restless acts, worry, reminiscence and vivid memories, and changes in body image and self-appraisal. A further two symptoms (novel idea and loss of contact with reality) also resulted to some degree from confinement, but their incidence was significantly increased by the addition of social isolation. On the remaining content areas, three (temporal disorientation, feelings of hostility, and loneliness) were associated solely with social isolation, and another three (persistent and vivid dreams, sexual thoughts, and speech difficulties) were related to a combination of social isolation and confinement.

A comparison of these results with those of an earlier 1-week PD experiment (Zubek & MacNeill, 1967), using the same questionnarie, revealed that the scores of the PD group were approximately the same as those of the SI group on most of the 22 content areas. The only symptoms in which the PD group showed substantially higher scores were experiences of a hallucinatorylike nature, temporal disorientation, speech difficulties, sexual and religious thoughts, and attitude toward the experimenters. The incidence of these phenomena appears therefore to be increased to some degree by the imposition of a reduction in sensory stimulation.

Finally, a comparison of these results with those of Zuckerman et al. (1968), who also used the Myers ISQ, shows considerable agreement. Even with their short duration of 8 hours, they observed that the effects of confinement were quite general, showing an increased incidence of most of the questionnaire-elicited symptoms. They also reported that the effects of sensory restriction "tend to be more specific, consisting of an anxiety reaction which is related to the cutting off of one's normal sensory ties with reality and the appearance of unusual perceptions and ideas" (p. 194).

In interpreting the results of this experiment, one important factor to consider is the physical dimension of the chamber. The Manitoba isolation chamber is quite small, consisting of only 45 sq ft of floor space, and in view of this it is possible that the reported results may be related, to some degree, to the use of a very restricted physical environment. In this regard, it is interesting to note that two subjects who complained about being "hemmed in" showed the largest posttest decreases in alpha frequency (-1.00 and -1.18 cps) of the CF group, indicating that the size of the physical quarters may be an important variable. Further research systematically varying the size of the confinement area (both physical and perceived space) might prove fruitful.[4] Additional research is also required on other types of performance measures as well as on durations shorter than a week. Such studies would be of considerable relevance for certain everyday situations such as working in windowless offices, or the performance of military duties in enclosed quarters.

4. In a recently completed experiment, Dr. T. I. Myers at the U.S. Naval Medical Research Institute, Bethesda, Maryland, observed that confinement for 7 days with rich audiovisual stimulation and the presence of social communication produced a slowing of the alpha rhythm, a finding confirming the Manitoba results. The magnitude of this cortical slowing appeared however to be related to the size of the chamber. Subjects confined in a small cubicle (72 sq. ft of floor area) showed a greater degree of alpha slowing than did those confined in a larger cubicle (123 sq ft).

Theoretical Formulations

In my edited book on sensory deprivation (Zubek, 1969), two chapters (Suedfeld, 1969c; Zuckerman, 1969c) are devoted to various theoretical formulations that have been proposed to account for the wide range of deprivation effects. In view of this extensive treatment, together with the fact that material of a theoretical nature has already been introduced at various points in this chapter, only a brief enumeration of the main theories will be presented.

A review of the literature reveals no dearth of theoretical accounts of how reduced environmental stimulation exerts its effects. These theories, however, can be grouped into three broad classifications. The most popular are the neurophysiological theories, which emphasize the function of the reticular activating system (RAS) because of its demonstrated importance in attention, perception, and motivation. According to them, a decrease in the level and variability of sensory input coming into the RAS via collateral fibers from the sensory systems disturbs its normal relation with the rest of the brain, thus producing both behavioral and physiological effects. The main adherents of this type of theory, in which the reticular system is conceived of as a sort of barometer or homeostat adjusting input-output relations, are Hebb (1955), Lindsley (1961), and Schultz (1965). The results that can be accounted for by this type of formulation are the slowing of EEG activity, stimulus-seeking behavior, presence of sensory facilitatory phenomena (particularly after single modality deprivation), existence of hallucinatory phenomena, and cognitive deficits. Some difficulties are encountered in dealing with cognitive improvements, changes in GSR (high autonomic arousal level concurrent with decreased cortical arousal), and large individual differences in deprivation effects. These phenomena, however, as well as most of the others, can be accounted for quite satisfactorily by Zuckerman's (1969c) Optimal Level of Stimulation theory. Furthermore, unlike the other theoretical formulations, it possesses the virtue of generating various predictions that can be tested experimentally.

A second group of theories are of a psychoanalytic nature; they postulate changes in the relationship between the functioning of the ego and id (Rappaport, 1958) or a weakening of the ego for reality testing (Goldberger & Holt, 1958). In essence, they maintain that isolation tends to cut off the ego from reality, resulting in an increase in primary process thinking (alogical, hallucinatory), a decrease in secondary process thinking involving logical processes and problem solving, and emergence of id impulses of a sexual and aggressive nature. This type of formulation, as can be seen, only attempts to account for a very limited range of deprivation phenomena.

The final group of theories are largely of a psychological nature (see Suedfeld, 1969c). These are of several varieties. First, there are the information-processing theories that attribute the deprivation effects to the organism's search for order and meaning in an unstructured sensory or perceptual environment (Freedman & Greenblatt, 1959), or postulate a disruption of the process of evaluation by which the "models" and "strategies" used in dealing with the environment are monitored and corrected (Bruner, 1961). This type of formulation has been used to explain the presence of hallucinatory phenomena and perceptual distortions and deficits on cognitive and perceptual-motor tasks.

A second theory is the expectancy-set hypothesis of Jackson and Pollard (1962), according to which many of the deprivation effects can be attributed, in whole or in part, to the subject's prior knowledge as to what is "appropriate" or expected behavior in isolation and to his motivations to report or not to report these "appropriate" behaviors. This hypothesis probably can account for the presence of various questionnaire or introspectively elicited subjective phenomena in certain experiments (with exception of the first McGill studies in which the subjects had no prior expectations or information). But it cannot account for most of the results derived from objective measures of a physiological or behavioral nature.

The third type of formulation is Haggard's (1964) three-component theory, according to which the onset of and magnitude of the various isolation effects is postulated to be related primarily to the extent and duration of the *disparity* existing between the subject's normal environment and the experimental environment that he is exposed to. Since the SD condition, involving darkness and silence, is more similar to the subject's normal living environment (at least during the sleeping hours) than is the PD condition, involving constant unpatterned light and a masking noise, this theory would predict that the latter experimental treatment would result in greater behavioral and physiological impairments, particularly if a prolonged deprivation duration were employed. Some of the experimental data appears to support this theoretical prediction. Finally, there is Suedfeld's (1969b, 1969c) arousal U-curve hypothesis, which was specifically formulated to account for the differential effects on cognitive tasks and which, with modifications, could be applied to some of the other deprivation effects.

Some years ago, both Hebb (1961) and Vernon (1963) referred to the emerging findings from deprivation experiments as "facts without a theory." This is no longer the case, since a number of explanatory models, theories, and hypotheses can be invoked, each of which explains some of the data. True, there is no single or general theory, although Zuckerman's (1969c) Optimal Level of Stimulation theory comes closest to one. But this is to be expected in view of the diversity and complexity of the phenomena and the presence of numerous variables pertaining both to the experimental condition and the subject himself.

REFERENCES

Aftanas, M., & Zubek, J. P. 1963a. Effects of prolonged isolation of the skin on cutaneous sensitivity. *Percept. mot. Skills* 16:565–71.
——. 1963b. Long term after-effects following isolation of a circumscribed area of the skin. *Percept. mot. Skills* 17:867–70.
——. 1964. Interlimb transfer of changes in tactual acuity following occlusion of a circumscribed area of the skin. *Percept. mot. Skills* 18:437–42.
Agadzhanian, N. A., Bizin, I. P., Doronin, G. P., & Kuznetsov, A. G. 1963. (Changes in higher nervous activity and in some vegetative reactions under prolonged conditions of adynamia and isolation). *Zh. vysshei nervnoi Deiatelnosti, Pavlov* 13:953–62. (In Russian.)
Arnhoff, F. N., & Leon, H. V. 1963a. Personality factors related to success and failure in sensory deprivation subjects. *Percept. mot. Skills* 16:46.
——. 1963b. Sex differences in response to short-term sensory deprivation and isolation. *Percept. mot. Skills* 17:81–82.
Arnhoff, F. N., Leon, H. V. & Brownfield, C. A. 1962. Sensory deprivation, the effects on human learning. *Science* 138:899–900.
Barnes, T. C. 1958. Effects of tranquilizers and anti-epileptic drugs on electroencephalographic flicker response and on convulsive behavior. *Anat. Rec.* 132:409.
——. 1959. Isolation stress in rats and mice as a neuropharmacological test. *Fed. Proc.* 18:365.
Batten, D. E. 1961. The effects of sensory deprivation on auditory and visual sensitivity. Ph. D. dissertation, Washington State University.
Berlyne, D. E. 1960. *Conflict, arousal, and curiosity.* New York: McGraw-Hill.
Bexton, W. H. 1953. Some effects of perceptual isolation in human subjects. Ph. D. dissertation, McGill University.
Bexton, W. H., Heron, W., & Scott, T. H. 1954. Effects of decreased variation in the sensory environment. *Canad. J. Psychol.* 8:70–76.
Biase, D. V., & Zuckerman, M. 1967. Sex differences in stress responses to total and partial sensory deprivation. *Psychosom. Med.* 29:380–90.
Bliss, E. L., & Clark, L. D. 1962. Visual hallucinations. In *Hallucinations*, ed. L. J. West, pp. 92–107. New York: Grune & Stratton.
Bombard, A. 1953. *Voyage of the Heretique.* New York: Simon & Schuster.
Brainard, D. L. 1929. *The outpost of the lost: An Arctic adventure.* Indianapolis: Bobbs-Merrill.
Brownfield, C. A. 1964. Sensory deprivation: A comprehensive survey. *Psychologia: Int. J. of Psychology in the Orient* 1:63–93.
——. 1965. *Isolation: Clinical and experimental approaches.* New York: Random House.
Bruner, J. S. 1961. The cognitive consequences of early sensory deprivation. In *Sensory deprivation*, ed. P. Solomon et al., pp. 195–207. Cambridge: Harvard University Press.

Byrd, R. E. 1938. *Alone.* New York: Putnam.

Cambareri, J. D. 1959. The effects of sensory isolation on suggestible and non-suggestible psychology graduate students. *Dissert. Abstracts* 19:1813.

Cameron, D. E., Levy, L., Ban, T., & Rubenstein, L. 1961. Sensory deprivation: Effects upon the functioning human in space systems. *Psychophysiological aspects of space flight*, ed. B. E. Flaherty, pp. 225–37. New York: Columbia University Press.

Carlin, S., Ward, W. D., Gershorn, A., & Ingraham, R. 1962. Sound stimulation and its effect on dental sensation threshold. *Science* 138:1258–59.

Cleveland, S. E., Reitman, E. E., & Bentinck, C. 1963. Therapeutic effectiveness of sensory deprivation. *Arch. Gen. Psychiat.* 8:455–60.

Cohen, B. D., Rosenbaum, G., Dobie, S. I., & Gottlieb, J. S. 1959. Sensory isolation: Hallucinogenic effects of a brief procedure. *J. nerv. ment. Dis.* 129:486–91.

Cohen, S. I., Silverman, A. J., Bressler, G., & Shmavonian, B. 1961. Problems in isolation studies. *Sensory deprivation*, ed. P. Solomon et al., pp. 114–29. Cambridge: Harvard University Press.

Cohen, S. I., Silverman, A. J., & Shmavonian, B. M. 1962. Psychophysiological studies in altered sensory environments. *J. psychosom. Res.* 6:259–81.

Davis, J., McCourt, W. F., Courtney, J., & Solomon, P. 1961. Sensory deprivation, the role of social isolation. *Arch. gen. Psychiat.* 5:84–90.

Davis, J., McCourt, W. F., & Solomon, P. 1960. The effect of visual stimulation on hallucinations and other mental experiences during sensory deprivation. *Amer. J. Psychiat.* 116:889–92.

de Ajuriaguerra, J., ed. 1965. *Désafférentation expérimentale et clinique.* Geneva: Georg et Cie.

Doane, B. K. 1955. Changes in visual function following perceptual isolation. Ph.D. dissertation, McGill University.

Doane, B. K., Mahatoo, W., Heron, W., & Scott, T. H. 1959. Changes in perceptual function after isolation. *Canad. J. Psychol.* 13:210–14.

Duda, P., & Zubek, J. P. 1965. Auditory sensitivity after prolonged visual deprivation. *Psychon. Sci.* 3:359–60.

Elmadjian, F., Hope, J. M., & Lamson, E. T. 1957. Excretion of epinephrine and norepinephrine in various emotional states. *J. clin. Endocrinol.* 17:608–20.

Engel, G. L., Romano, J., Ferris, E. B., Webb, J. P., & Stevens, C. D. 1944. A simple method of determining frequency spectrums in the electroencelphalogram. *Arch. Neurol. & Psychiat.* 51:134–46.

Euler, U. S., Luft, R., & Sundin, T. 1955. The urinary excretion of noradrenaline and adrenaline in healthy subjects during recumbency and standing. *Acta Physiol. Scand.* 34:169–74.

Fiske, D. W. 1961. Effects of monotonous and restricted stimulation. In *Functions of varied experience*, ed. D. W. Fiske & S. R. Maddi, pp. 106–44. Homewood, Ill.: Dorsey.

Francis, R. D. 1964. The effects of prior instructions and time knowledge on the toleration of sensory isolation. *J. nerv. ment. Dis.* 139:182–85.

Frankenhaeuser, M. 1968. Experimental approaches to the problem of sensory deprivation and confinement: A survey. *Sartrych ur Forsvarsmedicin* 4:163–66.

Freedman, S. J., & Greenblatt, M. 1959. Studies in human isolation. WADC Tech. Rept. 59–266. Wright-Patterson AFB, Ohio.

Freedman, S. J., & Greenblatt, M. 1960. Studies in human isolation. *USAF med. J.* 11:1479-97.

French, J. D. 1960. The reticular formation. In *Handbook of physiology, Section 1: Neurophysiology*, ed. J. Field, vol. 2, pp. 1281-1305. Washington, D.C.: American Physiological Society.

Fuerst, K., & Zubek, J. P. 1968. Effects of sensory and perceptual deprivation on a battery of open-ended cognitive tasks. *Canad. J. Psychol.* 22:122-30.

Gardner, W. J., & Licklider, J. C. R. 1959. Auditory analgesia in dental operations. *J. Amer. Dent. Assn.* 59:1144-49.

Gendreau, P. E., Freedman, N., Wilde, G. J. S., & Scott, G. D. 1968a. Stimulation seeking after seven days of perceptual deprivation. *Percept. mot. Skills* 26:547-50.

——. 1968b. The effect of 7 days perceptual deprivation on the visual evoked potential and EEG frequency. *Canad. Psychologist* 9:278. (Abstract.)

Gendreau, P. E., Horton, J. G., Hooper, D. G., Freedman, N., Wilde, G. J. S., & Scott, G. D. 1968. Perceptual deprivation and perceptual skills: Some methodological considerations. *Percept. mot. Skills* 27:57-58.

Goldberger, L., & Holt, R. R. 1958. Experimental interference with reality contact (perceptual isolation): method and group results. *J. nerv. ment. Dis.* 127:99-112.

Goldstein, K. M. 1965. Stimulus reinforcement during sensory deprivation. *Percept. mot. Skills* 20:757-62.

Goodall, M., & Berman, M. L. 1960. Urinary output of adrenaline, noradrenaline, and 3-methoxy-4-hydroxymandelic acid following centrifugation and anticipation of centrifugation. *J. clin. Investig.* 39:1533-38.

Gorbov, F. D., Miasnikov, V. I., & Yazdovsky, V. I. 1963. (Strain and fatigue under conditions of sensory deprivation). *Zh. vysshei nervnoi Deiatelnosti, Pavlov* 13:585-92. (In Russian.)

Grissom, R. J. 1963. Facilitation of memory by experiential restriction after acquisition. Ph.D. dissertation, Princeton University.

——. 1966. Facilitation of memory by experiential restriction after learning. *Amer. J. Psychol.* 79:613-17.

Grissom, R. J., Suedfeld, P., & Vernon, J. 1962. Memory for verbal material: Effects of sensory deprivation. *Science* 138:429-30.

Guiraud, P. 1937. La théorie des écrans sensorids et l'hallucinations. *Ann. Med. Psychol.* 95:618-26.

Haggard, E. A. 1964. Isolation and personality. In *Personality change*, ed. P. Worchel & D. Byrne, pp. 443-69. New York: Wiley.

Hanna, T. D., & Gaito, J. 1960. Performance and habitability aspects of extended confinement in sealed cabins. *Aerospace Med.* 31:399-406.

Hariu, T., & Ueno, H. 1964. Studies on sensory deprivation. II. Part 4. With reference to the genetic process of perception. *Tohoku Psychologica Folia* 22:72-78.

Haythorn, W. 1967. Project ARGUS: A program of isolation and confinement research. *Naval Research Reviews*, December: 1-8.

Hebb, D. O. 1955. Drives and the C.N.S. (Conceptual Nervous System). *Psychol. Rev.* 62:243-54.

——. 1958. The motivating effects of exteroceptive stimulation. *Amer. Psychologist* 13:109-13.

———. 1961. Discussion: Sensory deprivation: Facts in search of a theory. *J. nerv. ment. Dis.* 132:40–43.

Heron, W. 1957. The pathology of boredom. *Sci. American* 196:52–56.

———. 1961. Cognitive and physiological effects of perceptual isolation. In *Sensory deprivation,* ed. P. Solomon et al., pp. 6–33. Cambridge: Harvard University Press.

Heron, W., Doane, B. K., & Scott, T. H. 1956. Visual disturbances after prolonged perceptual isolation. *Canad. J. Psychol.* 10:13–16.

Heron, W., & Morrison, G. R. n. d. Effects of circumscribed somesthetic isolation on the touch threshold. Unpublished manuscript, McMaster University, Hamilton, Canada.

Hinkle, L. E. 1961. The physiological state of the interrogation subject as it affects brain function. In *The manipulation of human behavior,* ed. A. D. Biderman & H. Zimmer, pp. 19–50. New York: Wiley.

Holt, R. R., & Goldberger, L. 1961. Assessment of individual resistance to sensory alteration. In *Psychophysiological aspects of space flight,* ed. B. E. Flaherty, pp. 248–62. New York: Columbia University Press.

Hull, J., & Zubek, J. P. 1962. Personality characteristics of successful and unsuccessful sensory isolation subjects. *Percept. mot. Skills* 14:231–40.

Jackson, C. W. Jr., & Kelly, E. L. 1962. Influence of suggestion and subject's prior knowledge in research on sensory deprivation. *Science* 132:211–12.

Jackson, C. W. Jr., & Pollard, J. C. 1962. Sensory deprivation and suggestion: A theoretical approach. *Behav. Sci.* 7:332–43.

Johnson, E., Smith, S., & Myers, T. I. 1968. Vigilance throughout seven days of sensory deprivation. *Psychon. Sci.* 11:293–94.

Jones, A. 1961. Supplementary report: Information deprivation and irrelevant drive as determiners of an instrumental response. *J. exp. Psychol.* 62:310–11.

———. 1964. Drive and incentive variables associated with the statistical properties of sequences of stimuli. *J. exp. Psychol.* 67:423–31.

———. 1969. Stimulus-seeking behavior. In *Sensory deprivation: Fifteen years of research,* ed. J. P. Zubek, pp. 167–206. New York: Appleton-Century-Crofts.

Jones, A., & McGill, D. W. 1967. The homeostatic character of information drive in humans. *J. exp. res. in Pers.* 2:25–31.

Jones, A., Wilkinson, H. J., & Braden, I. 1961. Information deprivation as a motivational variable. *J. exp. Psychol.* 62:126–37.

Kato, T., Tonaka, H., Tada, H., & Hatayama, T. 1967. Studies on sensory deprivation. VI. Part 1. General methods and results of polygraphic records, behavioral observations, and interviews. *Tohoku Psychologica Folia* 26:1–10.

Kenna, J. C. 1962. Sensory deprivation phenomena: Critical review and explanatory models. *Proc. Royal Soc. Med.* 55:1005–10.

Kitamura, S. 1964. Studies on sensory deprivation. II. Part 3. On the estimation of the body image. *Tohoku Psychologica Folia* 22:69–71.

———. 1965. Studies on sensory deprivation. IV. Part 8. General discussion and concluding remarks. *Tohoku Psychologica Folia* 24:35–37.

Kokubun, O., & Ohyama, M. 1965. Studies on sensory deprivation. III. Part 7. On the results of the behavior observation and introspective reports. *Tohoku Psychologica Folia* 23:75–78.

Kubzansky, P. E. 1961. The effects of reduced environmental stimulation on human behavior: A review. In *The manipulation of human behavior,* ed. A. D. Biderman & H. Zimmer, pp. 51–95. New York: Wiley.

Lawes, T. G. G. 1963. Schizophrenia, "Sernyl", and sensory deprivation. *Brit. J. Psychiat.* 109:243–50.

Lebedinsky, A. V., Levinsky, S. V., & Nefedov, Y. G. 1964. General principles concerning the reaction of the organism to the complex environmental factors existing in spacecraft cabins. Paper read at XV Internat. Aeronaut. Congr., Warsaw, September, 1964. Translated from the Russian by NASA, TTF-273.

Leiderman, P. H. 1962. Imagery and sensory deprivation: An experimental study. Tech. Rept. MRL-TDR62–28. Wright-Patterson AFB, Ohio, May, 1962.

Levy, E. Z., Ruff, G. E., & Thaler, V. H. 1959. Studies in human isolation. *J. Amer. Med. Assn.* 169:236–39.

Licklider, J. C. R. 1961. On psychophysiological models. In *Sensory communication*, ed. W. A. Rossblith, pp. 49–73. Cambridge: MIT Press.

Lilly, J. 1956. Mental effects of reduction of ordinary levels of physical stimuli on intact healthy persons. *Psychiat. Res. Rept.* 5:1–9.

Lilly, J. C., & Shurley, J. T. 1961. Experiments in solitude, in maximum achievable physical isolation with water suspension, of intact healthy persons. In *Psychophysiological aspects of space flight*, ed. B. E. Flaherty, pp. 238–47. New York: Columbia University Press.

Lindsley, D. B. 1961. Common factors in sensory deprivation, sensory distortion, and sensory overload. In *Sensory deprivation*, ed. P. Solomon et al. pp. 174–94. Cambridge: Harvard University Press.

Marjerrison, G., & Keogh, R. P. 1967. Electroencephalographic changes during brief periods of perceptual deprivation. *Percept. mot. Skills* 24:611–15.

Mendelson, J., Kubzansky, P. E., Leiderman, P. H., Wexler, D., Dutoit, D. & Solomon, P. 1960. Catecholamine excretion and behavior during sensory deprivation. *Arch. gen. Psychiat.* 2:147–55.

Mendelson, J. H., Kubzansky, P. E., Leiderman, P. H., Wexler, D., & Solomon, P. 1961. Physiological and psychological aspects of sensory deprivation: A case analysis. In *Sensory deprivation*, ed. P. Solomon et al., pp. 91–113. Cambridge: Harvard University Press.

Milstein, S. L., & Zubek, J. P. 1971. Temporal changes in cutaneous sensitivity during prolonged visual deprivation. *Canad. J. Psychol.* 25:336–348.

Murphy, C. W., Kurlents, E., Cleghorn, R. A., & Hebb, D. O. 1955. Absence of increased corticoid excretion with the stress of perceptual deprivation. *Canad. J. Biochem. Physiol.* 33:1062–63.

Murphy, D. B., Hampton, G. L., & Myers, T. I. 1962. Time estimation error as a predictor of endurance in sustained sensory deprivation. Paper read at Amer. Psychol. Assn., St. Louis, 1962; *Amer. Psychologist* 17:389. (Abstract.)

Murphy, D. B., Myers, T. I., & Smith, S. 1963. Reported visual sensations as a function of sustained sensory deprivation and social isolation. Pioneer III Draft Research Rept., HumRRO, Monterey, California, November.

Murphy, D. B., Smith, S., & Myers, T. I. 1963. The effect of sensory deprivation and social isolation on the conditioning of connotative meaning. *Amer. Psychologist* 18:440. (Abstract.)

Myers, T. I. 1969. Tolerance for sensory and perceptual deprivation. In *Sensory deprivation: Fifteen years of research*, ed. J. P. Zubek, pp. 289–331. New York: Appleton-Century-Crofts.

Myers, T. I., Forbes, L. M., Arbit, J., & Hicks, J. 1957. A preliminary study of the effects of controlled isolation. HumRRO Tech. Rept., U.S. Army Leadership Human Research Unit, Monterey, California.

Myers, T. I., & Murphy D. B. 1962. Reported visual sensations during brief exposure to reduced sensory input. In *Hallucinations,* ed. L. J. West, pp. 118–24. New York: Grune & Stratton.

Myers, T. I., Murphy, D. B., & Smith, S. 1961. Progress report on studies of sensory deprivation. HumRRO Tech. Rept., U.S. Army Leadership Human Research Unit, Monterey, California, March.

――――. 1963. The effect of sensory deprivation and social isolation on self-exposure to propaganda and attitude change. *Amer. Psychologist* 18:440. (Abstract.)

Myers, T. I., Murphy, D. B., Smith, S., & Goffard, S. J. 1966. Experimental studies of sensory deprivation and social isolation. HumRRO Tech. Rept. 66–8, George Washington University, June.

Myers, T. I., Murphy, D. B., Smith, S., & Windle, C. 1962. Experimental assessment of a limited sensory and social environment. Summary results of the HumRRO program. Tech. Rept. U.S. Army Leadership Human Research Unit, Monterey, California, February.

Myers, T. I., Murphy, D. B., & Terry, D. F. 1962. The role of expectancy in subjects' responses to sustained sensory deprivation. Paper read at American Psychological Association, St. Louis, September, 1962.

Nagatsuka, Y. 1965. Studies on sensory deprivation. III. Part 2. Effects of sensory deprivation upon perceptual functions. *Tohoku Psychologica Folia* 23:56–59.

Nagatsuka, Y., & Kokubun, O. 1964. Studies on sensory deprivation. II. Part 1. Introductory remarks and results of polygraphic records. *Tohoku Psychologica Folia* 22:57–63.

Nagatsuka, Y., & Maruyama, K. 1963. Studies on sensory deprivation. I. Part 2. Effects of sensory deprivation upon perceptual and motor functions. *Tohoku Psychologica Folia* 22:5–13.

Nagatsuka, Y., & Suzuki, Y. 1964. Studies on sensory deprivation. II. Part 2. Effects of sensory deprivation upon perceptual and motor functions. *Tohoku Psychologica Folia* 22:64–68.

Ohyama, M., Kokubun, O., & Kobayashi, H. 1965. Studies on sensory deprivation. IV. Part 2. EEG changes before, during, and after 18 hours of sensory deprivation. *Tohoku Psychologica Folia* 24:4–9.

Okuma, T. 1962. (Sensory deprivation―Its physiological, psychological, and psychiatric aspects). *Seishin Igaku* 4:687–703. (In Japanese.)

Oleson, D. S., & Zubek, J. P. 1970. The effect of one day of sensory deprivation on a battery of relatively unstructured cognitive tests, *Percept. mot. Skills* 31:919–23.

Ormiston, D. W. 1961. A methodological study of confinement. WADD Tech. Rept. 61–258. Wright-Patterson AFB, Ohio.

Oyamada, T. 1966. Studies on sensory deprivation. V. Part 5. The effects of sensory deprivation on the performance of the projective test (3). *Tohoku Psychologica Folia* 25:19–23.

Pangman, C. H., & Zubek, J. P. 1972. Temporal changes in auditory flutter fusion frequency during prolonged visual deprivation. *Perception and Psychophysics.* 11:172–174.

Persky, H., Zuckerman, M., Basu, G. K., & Thornton, D. 1966. Psychoendocrine effects of perceptual and social isolation. *Arch. gen. Psychiat.* 15:499–505.

Peters, J., Benjamin, F. B., Helvey, W. M., & Albright, G. 1963. A study of sensory deprivation, pain, and personality relationships for space travel. *Aerospace Med.* 34:830–37.

Petrie, A., Collins, W., & Solomon, P. 1958. Pain sensitivity, sensory deprivation, and susceptibility to satiation. *Science* 128:1431–33.

———. 1960. The tolerance for pain and for sensory deprivation. *Amer. J. Psychol.* 73:80–90.

Phelps, J., & Zubek, J. P. 1969. The effects of prolonged visual deprivation on various cutaneous and auditory measures. *Psychon. Sci.* 14:194–95.

Pollard, J. C., Uhr, L., & Jackson, C. W. Jr. 1963. Studies in sensory deprivation. *Arch. gen. Psychiat.* 8:435–54.

Rapaport, D. 1958. The theory of ego-autonomy: A generalization. *Bull. Menninger Clinic* 22:13–35.

Reitman, E. E., & Cleveland, S. E. 1964. Changes in body image following sensory deprivation in schizophrenic and control groups. *J. abnorm. soc. Psychol.* 68:168–76.

Riesen, A. H. 1966. Sensory deprivation. In *Progress in physiological psychology*, Ed. E.fl Stellar & J. M. Sprague, vol. 1, pp. 117–47. New York: Academic Press.

Rosenzweig, N., & Gardner, L. M. 1966. The role of input relevance in sensory isolation. *Amer. J. Psychiat.* 122:920–27.

Rossi, A. M. 1969. General methodological considerations. In *Sensory deprivation: Fifteen years of research*, ed. J. P. Zubek, pp. 16–43. New York: Appleton-Century-Crofts.

Rossi, A. M., & Solomon, P. 1964a. Button-pressing for a time-off reward during sensory deprivation. I. Relation to activity reward. II. Relation to descriptions of experience. *Percept. mot. Skills.* 18:211–16. (a)

———. 1964b. Button-pressing for a time-off reward during sensory deprivation. III. Effects of varied time-off rewards. *Percept. mot. Skills* 18:794–96.

Ruff, G. E., & Levy, E. Z. 1959. Psychiatric research in space medicine. *Amer. J. Psychiat.* 115:793–97.

Ruff, G. E., Levy, E. Z., & Thaler, V. H. 1961. Factors influencing the reaction to reduced sensory input. In *Sensory deprivation*, ed. P. Solomon et al., pp. 72–90. Cambridge: Harvard University Press.

Sato, I., & Kokubun, O. 1965. Studies on sensory deprivation. III. Part 6. On the results of the polygraphic records. *Tohoku Psychologica Folia* 23:72–74.

Saunders, M. G., & Zubek, J. P. 1967. EEG changes in perceptual and sensory deprivation. *Electroenceph. clin. Neurophysiol.* Suppl. 25:246–57.

Schaefer, K. E. 1964. Counteracting effects of training in geometrical construction on stress produced by maximal sensory isolation in water immersion. *Aerospace Med.* 35:279. (Abstract.)

Schroder, H. M., Driver, M. J., & Streufert, S. 1967. *Human information processing*. New York: Holt, Rinehart and Winston.

Schulman, C. A., Richlin, M., & Weinstein, S. 1967. Hallucinations and disturbances of affect, cognition and physical state as a function of sensory deprivation. *Percept. mot. Skills* 25:1001–24.

Schultz, D. P. 1965. *Sensory restriction: Effects on behavior*. New York: Academic Press.

Schutte, W., & Zubek, J. P. 1967. Changes in olfactory and gustatory sensitivity after prolonged visual deprivation. *Canad. J. Psychol.* 21:337–45.

Schwitzgebel, R. 1962. A comparative study of Zulu and English reaction to sensory deprivation. *Int. J. soc. Psychiat.* 7:220–25.

Scott, T., Bexton, W. H., Heron, W., & Doane, B. K. 1959. Cognitive effects of perceptual isolation. *Canad. J. Psychol.* 13:200–209.

Shurley, J. T. 1962. Mental imagery in profound sensory isolation. In L. J. West (Ed.), *Hallucinations,* ed. L. J. West, pp. 153–57. New York: Grune & Stratton.

——. 1963. The hydro-hypodynamic environment. *Proceedings of the Third World Congress of Psychiatry,* vol. 3, Toronto: Canada. University of Toronto Press. Pp. 232–37.

——. 1968. Reduced sensory input states: Sensory and perceptual deprivation and isolation. In *Hypodynamics and hypogravics,* ed. M. McCally, pp. 237–284. New York: Academic Press.

Siffre, M. 1964. *Beyond time.* New York: McGraw-Hill.

Smith, S. 1962. Clinical aspects of perceptual isolation. *Proc. Royal Soc. Med.* 55:1003–5.

Smith, S., & Lewty, W. 1959. Perceptual isolation using a silent room. *Lancet* 2:342–45.

Smith, S., & Meyers, T. I. 1966. Stimulation seeking during sensory deprivation. *Percept. mot. Skills* 23:1151–63.

——. 1967. Time-shared perceptual-motor skills during 7 days of isolation. *Psychon. Sci.* 9:99–100.

Smith, S., Murphy, D. B., & Myers, T. I. 1962. Activity pattern and restlessness during sustained sensory deprivation. Paper read at Amer. Psychol. Assn., St. Louis, 1962. *Amer. Psychologist* 17:389. (Abstract.)

Smith, S., Myers, T. I., & Johnson, E. 1967. Stimulation seeking throughout seven days of sensory deprivation. *Percept. mot. Skills* 25:261–71.

——. 1968. Stimulation seeking as a function of duration and extent of sensory deprivation. Proceedings, 76th Annual Convention, APA, 1968, 625–26.

Smith, S., Myers, T. I., & Murphy, D. B. 1963. The effect of sensory deprivation and social isolation on conformity to a group norm. *Amer. Psychologist* 18:439–440. (Abstract.)

——. 1967. Vigilance during sensory deprivation. *Percept. mot. Skills* 24:971–76.

Solomon, P., Kubzansky, P. E., Leiderman, P. H., Mendelson, J., & Wexler, D., eds. 1961. *Sensory deprivation.* Cambridge: Harvard University Press.

Solomon, P., Leiderman, P. H., Mendelson, J., & Wexler, D. 1957. Sensory deprivation: A review. *Amer. J. Psychiat.* 114:357–63.

Suedfeld, P. 1963. Conceptual and environmental complexity as factors in attitude change. ONR Tech. Rept.

——. 1964. Attitude manipulation in restricted environments. I. Conceptual structure and response to propaganda. *J. abnorm. soc. Psychol.* 68:242–47.

——. 1968. The cognitive effects of sensory deprivation: The role of task complexity. *Canad. J. Psychol.* 22:302–7.

——. 1969a. Introduction and historical background. In *Sensory deprivation: Fifteen years of Research,* ed. J. P. Zubek, pp. 3–15. New York: Appleton-Century-Crofts.

——. 1969b. Changes in intellectual performance and in susceptibility to influence. In *Sensory deprivation: Fifteen years of Research,* ed. J. P. Zubek, pp. 126–66. New York: Appleton-Century-Crofts.

——. 1969c. Theoretical formulations: II. In *Sensory deprivation: Fifteen years of research,* ed. J. P. Zubek, pp. 433–48. New York: Appleton-Century-Crofts.

Suedfeld, P. & Landon, P. B. 1970. Motivational arousal and task complexity: Support for a model of cognitive changes in sensory deprivation. *J. exp. Psychol.* 83:329–30.

Suedfeld, P., Glucksberg, S., & Vernon, J. 1967. Sensory deprivation as a drive operation: Effects upon problem solving. *J. exp. Psychol.* 75: 166–69.

Suedfeld, P., Grissom, R. J., & Vernon, J. 1964. The effects of sensory deprivation and social isolation on the performance of an unstructured task. *Amer. J. Psychol.* 77:111–15.

Suedfeld, P., & Vernon, J. 1964. Visual hallucinations during sensory deprivation: A problem of criteria. *Science* 145:412–13.

———. 1966. Attitude manipulation in restricted environments. II. Conceptual structure and the internalization of propaganda received as a reward for compliance. *J. pers. soc. Psychol.* 3:586–89.

Suedfeld, P., Vernon, J., Stubbs, J. T., & Karlins, M. 1965. The effects of repeated confinement on cognitive performance. *Amer. J. Psychol.* 78:493–95.

Sundin, T. 1958. The effect of body posture on the urinary excretion of adrenaline and noradrenaline. *Acta. Med. Scand.* Suppl. 336:1–59.

Suzuki, Y., Fujii, K., & Onizawa, T. 1965. Studies on sensory deprivation. IV. Part 6. Effects of sensory deprivation upon perceptual function. *Tohoku Psychologica Folia* 24:24–29.

Suzuki, Y., Ueno, H., & Tada, H. 1966. Studies on sensory deprivation. V. Part 6. Effect of sensory deprivation upon perceptual function. *Tohoku Psychologica Folia* 25:24–30.

Švab, L., & Gross, J. 1966. *Bibliography of sensory deprivation and social isolation.* 2d ed. Prague: Psychiatric Research Institute.

Svorad, D. 1960. (Certain manifestations of "sensory deprivation"). *Cesk. Fysiol.* 9:267. (In Czech.)

Tiira, E. 1955. *Raft of despair.* New York: Dutton.

Ueno, H., & Suzuki, Y. 1967. Studies on sensory deprivation. VI. Part 3. Effects of sensory deprivation upon perceptual functions. *Tohoku Psychologica Folia* 26:17–20.

Ueno, H., & Tada, H. 1965. Studies on sensory deprivation. IV. Part 7. The effects of sensory deprivation upon genetic process of perception. *Tohoku Psychologica Folia* 24:30–34.

Van Wulfften Palthe, P. M. 1958. Sensory and motor deprivation as psychopathological stress. *Aeromedica Acta* (Netherlands) 6:155–68.

———. 1962. Fluctuations in level of consciousness caused by reduced sensorial stimulation and by limited motility in solitary confinement. *Psychiat. neurol. Neurochirug* (Amsterdam) 65: 377–401.

Vernon, J. 1961. Final report on the Princeton studies of sensory deprivation. Unpublished manuscript.

———. 1963. *Inside the black room.* New York: Clarkson N. Potter.

Vernon, J., & Hoffman, J. 1956. Effect of sensory deprivation on learning rate in human beings. *Science* 123:1074–75.

Vernon, J., Marton, T., & Peterson, E. 1961. Sensory deprivation and hallucinations. *Science* 133:1808–12.

Vernon, J., & McGill, T. E. 1957. The effect of sensory deprivation upon rote learning. *Amer. J. Psychol.* 70:637–39.

———. 1960. Utilization of visual stimulation during sensory deprivation. *Percept. mot. Skills* 11:214.

———. 1961. Sensory deprivation and pain thresholds. *Science* 133: 330–31.

Vernon, J., McGill, T. E., Gulick, W. L., & Candland, D. K. 1959. Effect of sensory deprivation on some perceptual and motor skills. *Percept. mot. Skills* 9:91–97.

———. 1961. The effect of human isolation upon some perceptual and motor skills. *Sensory deprivation,* ed. P. Solomon et al., pp. 41–57. Cambridge: Harvard University Press.

Walters, R. H., Callagan, J. E., & Newman, A. F. 1963. Effect of solitary confinement on prisoners. *Amer. J. Psychiat.* 119:771–73.

Weinstein, S., Fisher, L., Richlin, M., & Weinsinger, M. 1968. Bibliography of sensory and perceptual deprivation, isolation, and related areas. *Percept. mot. Skills* 26:1119–63.

Weinstein, S., Richlin, M., Weisinger, M., & Fisher, L. 1967. The effects of sensory deprivation on sensory, perceptual, motor, cognitive, and physiological functions. Tech. Rept. CR-727, National Aeronautics and Space Administration, Washington, D.C., March.

Wexler, D., Mendelson, J., Leiderman, P. H., & Solomon, P. 1958. Sensory deprivation: A technique of studying psychiatric aspects of stress. *Arch. Neurol. & Psychiat.* 79:225–33.

Winters, W. D. 1963. Various hormone changes during simulated space stresses in the monkey. *J. appl. Physiol.* 18:1167–70.

Wright, M. W., Sisler, G. C., & Chylinsky, J. 1963. Personality factors in the selection of civilians for isolated northern stations. *J. appl. Psychol.* 47:24–29.

Wright, N. A., & Abbey, D. S. 1965. Perceptual deprivation tolerance and adequacy of defenses. *Percept. mot. Skills* 20:35–38.

Wright, N. A., & Zubek, J. P. 1966. Use of the multiple discriminant function in the prediction of perceptual deprivation tolerance. *Canad. J. Psychol.* 20:105–13.

——. 1969. Relationship between perceptual deprivation tolerance and adequacy of defenses as measured by the Rorschach. *J. abnorm. Psychol.* 74:615–17.

Ziskind, E., & Augsburg, T. 1962. Hallucinations in sensory deprivation: Method or madness? *Science* 137:992.

Zubek, J. P. 1963a. Counteracting effects of physical exercises performed during prolonged perceptual deprivation. *Science* 142:504–6.

——. 1963b. Pain sensitivity as a measure of perceptual deprivation tolerance. *Percept. mot. Skills* 17:641–42.

——. 1964a. Effects of prolonged sensory and perceptual deprivation. *Brit. Med. Bull.* 20:38–42.

——. 1964b. Behavioral and EEG changes after 14 days of perceptual deprivation. *Psychon. Sci.* 1:57–58.

——. 1964c. Behavioral changes after prolonged perceptual deprivation (no intrusions). *Percept. mot. Skills* 18:413–20.

——. ed. 1969a. *Sensory deprivation: Fifteen years of research.* New York: Appleton-Century-Crofts.

——. 1969b. Sensory and perceptual-motor processes. In *Sensory deprivation: Fifteen years of research,* ed. J. P. Zubek, pp. 207–53. New York: Appleton-Century-Crofts.

——. 1969c. Physiological and biochemical effects. In *Sensory deprivation: Fifteen years of research,* ed. J. P. Zubek, pp. 254–88. New York: Appleton-Century-Crofts.

Zubek, J. P., Aftanas, M., Hasek, J., Sansom, W., Schludermann, E., Wilgosh, L., & Winocur, G. 1962. Intellectual and perceptual changes during prolonged perceptual deprivation: Low illumination and noise level. *Percept. mot. Skills.* 15:171–98.

Zubek, J. P., Bayer, L., Milstein, S., & Shephard, J. M. 1969. Behavioral and physiological changes during prolonged immobilization plus perceptual deprivation. *J. Abnorm. Psychol.* 7:230–36.

Zubek, J. P., Bayer, L., & Shephard, J. M. 1969. Relative effects of prolonged social isolation and confinement: Behavioral and physiological effects. *J. abnorm. Psychol.*, 74:625–31.

Zubek, J. P., Flye, J., & Aftanas, M. 1964. Cutaneous sensitivity after prolonged visual deprivation. *Science.* 144:1591–93.

Zubek, J. P., Flye, J., & Willows, D. 1964. Changes in cutaneous sensitivity after prolonged exposure to unpatterned light. *Psychon. Sci.* 1:283–84.

Zubek, J. P., & MacNeill, M. 1967. Perceptual deprivation phenomena: Role of the recumbent position. *J. abnorm. Psychol.* 72:147–50.

Zubek, J. P., Pushkar, D., Sansom, W., & Gowing, J. 1961. Perceptual changes after prolonged sensory isolation (darkness and silence). *Canad. J. Psychol.* 15:83–101.

Zubek, J. P., Sansom, W., & Prysiazniuk, A. 1960. Intellectual changes during prolonged isolation (darkness and silence). *Canad. J. Psychol.* 14:233–43.

Zubek, J. P., & Schutte, W. 1966. Urinary excretion of adrenaline and noradrenaline during prolonged perceptual deprivation. *J. abnorm. Psychol.* 71:328–34.

Zubek, J. P., Shephard, J. M., & Milstein, S. 1970. EEG changes after 1, 4, and 7 days of sensory deprivation: A cross sectional approach. *Psychon. Sci.* 19:67–68.

Zubek, J. P., & Welch, G. 1963. Electroencephalographic changes after prolonged sensory and perceptual deprivation. *Science.* 139:1209–10.

Zubek, J. P., Welch, G., & Saunders, M. G. 1963. EEG changes during and after 14 days of perceptual deprivation. *Science*, 139:490–92.

Zuckerman, M. 1964. Perceptual isolation as a stress situation: A review *Arch. gen. Psychiat.* 11:255–76.

———. 1969a. Variables affecting deprivation results. In *Sensory deprivation: Fifteen years of research,* ed. J. P. Zubek, pp. 47–84. New York: Appleton-Century-Crofts.

———. 1969b. Hallucinations, reported sensations, and images. In *Sensory deprivation: Fifteen years of research,* ed. J. P. Zubek, pp. 85–125. New York: Appleton-Century-Crofts.

———. 1969c. Theoretical formulations: I. In *Sensory deprivation: Fifteen years of research,* ed. J. P. Zubek, pp. 407–32. New York: Appleton-Century-Crofts.

Zuckerman, M., Albright, R. J., Marks, C. S., & Miller, G. L. 1962. Stress and hallucinatory effects of perceptual isolation and confinement. *Psychol. Monogr.* 76 (Whole no. 549).

Zuckerman, M., & Cohen, N. 1964. Sources of reports of visual and auditory sensations in perceptual isolation experiments. *Psychol. Bull.* 62:1–20.

Zuckerman, M., & Haber, M. M. 1965. Need for stimulation as a source of stress response to perceptual isolation. *J. abnorm. Psychol.* 70:371–77.

Zuckerman, M., & Hopkins, T. R. 1966. Hallucinations or dreams? A study of arousal level and reported visual sensations during sensory deprivation. *Percept. mot. Skills* 22:447–59.

Zuckerman, M., Levine, S., & Biase, D. V. 1964. Stress response in total and partial perceptual isolation. *Psychosom. Med.* 26:250–60.

Zuckerman, M., Persky, H., Hopkins, T. R., Murtaugh, T., Basu, G. K., & Schilling, M. 1966. Comparison of the stress effects of perceptual and social isolation. *Arch. gen. Psychiat.*, 14:356–65.

Zuckerman, M., Persky, H., Link, K. E., & Basu, G. K. 1968. Experimental and subject factors determining responses to sensory deprivation, social isolation, and confinement. *J. abnorm. Psychol.* 73:183–94.

Paul Fraisse *is Professor of Experimental Psychology and Chairman of the Department of Psychology at the University René Descartes in Paris. He received his Ph.D. from Louvain but all of his scientific career has taken place in Paris, first at the Center of Scientific Research and later at the Ecole Pratique des Hautes Études where he became, in 1952, Director of the Laboratory of Experimental and Comparative Psychology. He has been Secretary-General and President of the French Psychological Society and of the I.U.S.P., and is the Editor of* Année Psychologique. *His main work has been devoted to the study of rhythm, time estimation, and information processing. His most important books are* Psychology of Time *and* Les Structures Rythmiques. *In collaboration with Jean Piaget he edited* Traité de Psychologie Expérimentalé.

Fraisse *presents findings on behavioral rhythm from a series of studies, done in collaboration with M. Siffre, on the behavior of men confined to caves and living "out of time". Of particular importance is his analysis of the criteria of duration estimation. All of the criteria used by the subjects converge; the underestimation of time duration is such that time seems to pass twice as rapidly as under normal conditions. Given the fact that biological rhythms remain circadian, Fraisse concludes that underestimation is not due to the slowing down of a biological clock and explains it by the fact that the estimation of a temporal interval depends largely on the richness of psychological experiences lived through during an interval.*

3

Temporal Isolation, Activity Rhythms, and Time Estimation

PAUL FRAISSE

Spatial isolation may involve temporal isolation if one is completely deprived of the means of temporal estimation and orientation usually provided by the environment. There are many cues to temporal orientation. They originate in the natural environment, and the most important is the succession of days and nights. To this fundamental rhythm are added all the landmarks related to the social organization of life: mealtimes, school and work hours, and signals that occur on a regular schedule, such as the passing of trains and the ringing of church bells. In addition, we have specific devices for measuring time, such as radio and TV announcements of time. Spatial isolation can suppress some of these landmarks, but it can also exist when temporal cues are present.

This chapter is an attempt to study some consequences of complete temporal isolation of subjects confined to caves or bunkers in the "free-running" condition. In this condition, the subject is free to organize his life in his own way. Such freedom distinguishes this category of experiments from those that attempt to induce in the subject a rhythm differing from the usual 24-hour rhythm, or that investigate conditions in which there is a sudden break of the synchronization between environmental rhythm and the individual's biological rhythms, such as traveling by air through several time zones, or passing from daytime work to nighttime work. (For a recent review of these problems, see Conroy & Mills, 1970.) In all these studies, however, there is a common problem of consid-

The original results reported here were obtained from research conducted by Michel Siffre, Director of the French Institute of Speleology (Contract DRME 326-65 and 540-66) in collaboration with P. Traisse, G. Oleron and N. Zuili.

85

erable practical interest: to what extent do human activity rhythms depend on the temporal conditions in which they operate?

It is clear that sleep-wakefulness rhythms are synchronized with nycthemeral rhythms; biologists have shown that the rhythm of body temperature and of endocrine secretions (particularly corticosteroids), of urinary excretions and their composition, of cardiovascular changes, and so forth, follow a 24-hour cycle. These rhythms are not present in the newborn infant, and they are established progressively. Specialists agree that they are regulated by two mechanisms. Basically, one or several biological clocks regulate the periodicity of these manifestations and, in addition, there are *Zeitgebers* or synchronizers, that is, cues provided by the environment, which determine the synchronization between biological systems and external conditions. To put it in familiar words, these synchronizers set the clock right. Thus, the body temperature of many workers who pass from a diurnal activity to a nocturnal one is reversed: the maximal temperature is nocturnal instead of diurnal.

What happens to biological rhythms and to the behavior related to them when all external synchronizers are suppressed and when one is left with strictly endogenous processes? This is an interesting problem, especially when the studies cover a long period, as is the case with the expeditions conducted by Michel Siffre.

French Cave Studies

So far as I know, the first experiment in free-running conditions was performed in 1935 by McLeod and Roff, but it lasted only 4 days. Over the past 10 years a number of experiments have been conducted by Aschoff (1965), Mills (1964, 1967), Siffre (1963), and by several others (see Conroy and Mills, 1970). The longest experiment with which I have been associated was conducted in 1966. (Fraisse et al., 1968) A 24-year-old man, J. P. Mairetet, remained 174 days in a cave 70 m deep, located in southern France, 1,200 m above sea level. The cave was spacious. Mairetet had a tent, a bed, food, and electric light at his disposal. Except for a phone linking him with the surface, he was completely isolated from the external world. No temporal cues were delivered. An arrangement of wires allowed the organization of the experiments reported in this chapter. The subject was free to regulate his activity, meals, rest periods, and so forth.

When involved in a similar experiment (1963), Michel Siffre had made a considerable error in estimating the duration of his sojourn. Having stayed 58 days in a cave, he estimated that he had spent 33 days in it. As Mairetet was aware of this error, it was decided that he would make his evaluations according to his sleep-wakefulness cycles. It was stipulated that a cycle would begin when awaking, and agreed that if Mairetet wanted to sleep during the day (to take a nap, for example) he would not undress, so that sleep occurring at night could be distinguished from other sleep. These instructions were followed. Thus, what is meant by *cycle* is a duration corresponding to a subjective time unit experienced by the subject.

SLEEP-WAKEFULNESS RHYTHM

First, it is necessary to give a description of the subject's behavior during isolation. The circadian rhythm of slightly over 24 hours persisted for the first 9 days. After 3 or 4 more days, the sleep-wakefulness rhythm was 48 hours, that is, long wakefulness periods followed by long sleep periods, for about 40 days. After this, there was a return to circadian rhythm by the insertion of a nap after lunch. At that moment, the sequence was as follows: wakefulness, nap, wakefulness, night sleep. This rhythm persisted for about 60 days, or 31 cycles or subjective days in Mairetet's experience. By the end of the stay, the duration of some cycles was 72 and even 96 hours, with two naps.

In order to quantify these phenomena, we have extracted five stable periods out of the total duration of the stay. Since irregular rhythms appeared due to transition periods and to an illness, the selection of such stable periods is somewhat arbitrary. It is based on the following criteria: temporally contiguous cycles, homogeneity of cycle duration, and identical numbers of wakefulness and rest periods (sleep and nap). The results are summarized in the following table:

The first period is circadian; the second is circabidian (a cycle of approximately 48 hours). The third and the fourth are of the same nature; that is, objectively circadian with the nap shorter than night sleep during the third period and a complete return to original sleep-wakefulness periods in the fourth period. The fifth period is mentioned only for indicative purposes. During this fifth period, 72-hour cycles and 96-hour cycles were intermingled, and the mean duration of cycles is thus artificial.

When considering only wakefulness and sleep periods, two facts are worthy of attention. In period 2, which lasted for 30 days, the rhythm was circabidian and the sleep duration was reduced by 10 per cent from the mean of the usual sleep duration. Mills (1966) and Aschoff (1965) have found a similar, though never stable, circabidian rhythm. When experimenting with forced rhythms, Kleitman (1963) attempted to induce a 48-hour rhythm during one month; the two experimental subjects, while succeeding in maintaining this rhythm, experienced great difficulty in keeping themselves awake one night out of two. They were obliged to be awake for 39 to 40 hours and to sleep only 8 hours, a schedule which disrupted the sleep-wakefulness equilibrium.

In a new expedition, performed in 1968, Siffre has carried the above

TABLE 3.1 *Sleep-wakefulness cycles in five stable periods of Siffre (1963)
Experiment.*

Periods analyzed	1	2	3	4	5
Days of the experiment	1–6	12–42	59–82	105–152	153–170
Subjective cycles numbers	1–6	10–25	35–45	57–79	81–85
Mean duration of subjective cycles	25.9	46.1	49.6	49.8	84.8
Mean duration of wakefulness periods	15.2	32.2	13.8 + 16.6[a]	14.6 + 15.2	20 + 19.4 + 17.8[c]
Mean duration of sleep periods	10.7	13.9	6.8 + 12.4[b]	9.2 + 10.8	9.6 + 7.4 + 10.6[c]
Proportion of sleep periods in each cycle (in per cents)	41.4	30.2	38.7	40	32.5

a. The first number indicates the time elapsed between awaking until taking a nap; the second number the time elapsed from getting up after the nap to going to bed.
b. The first number indicates the duration of the nap, the second one the duration of the night, these distinctions being subjective.
c. In this period, there were two naps and three periods of awakefulness.

work a step further. In the same environmental conditions, it was observed that the subject spontaneously adopted a circabidian rhythm after 13 days; this rhythm has been maintained by submitting the subject alternately to light conditions during 34 hours and to darkness conditions during 14 hours. He succeeded in living according to this schedule for 66 days, or 33 cycles. The mean wakefulness was 36 hours (extreme values: 30 hr, 35 min—42 hr, 25 min), and the mean sleep duration was 12 hours (extreme values: 9 hr, 35 min—16 hr, 50 min). Thus, some persons are capable of living according to a circabidian rhythm for a period of one or two months. We shall consider later the effects of this rhythm on performance.

Second, since the experiment was run for a long period, it has been possible to verify the existence of an endogenous sleep-wakefulness rhythm that some authors considered unlikely. Moreover, the existence of this endogenous rhythm is supported by the fact that the longest cycles, in the subject's experience, were always in harmonic progression with the circadian rhythm—approximately 48, 72, or 96 hours. However, this rhythm is circadian, that is of about 24 hours (more precisely 24.6 hours), in the present experiment. In other experiments, Siffre has found values ranging from 24.5 to 25 hours with four subjects, and similar results have been obtained by Mills. These facts are well established and are not disproved by more variable results obtained in shorter experiments of only a few days or a few weeks in duration. Neither are they at variance with Lobban's (1960) experiments, which demonstrate that men are able to live without too much difficulty on 21 to 28 hour rhythms. The adaptability to forced rhythms that are not essentially different from 24-hour rhythms is one thing, and the observed rhythms in free-running experiments are a different matter.

THE BODY TEMPERATURE RHYTHM

In the present experiment, Colin et al. (1968) studied body temperature rhythm with great precision. Using a rectal probe (consisting of a thermocouple), body temperature was recorded continuously during the entire experiment, with the exception of a few instances due to instrument failures. The results showed the persistence of a circadian rhythm; in the beginning, it was 24 hours, 24 minutes, and it increased to 24 hours, 47 minutes ($\sigma = \pm 2$ hr 25 min). Siffre had observed this persistence in a previous experiment, when he found similar results in two subjects isolated 85 days and 121 days, respectively (Siffre et al., 1966; Reinberg et al., 1966).

The persistence of this circadian body temperature is noteworthy, since the sleep-wakefulness rhythm has changed considerably during period 2 (mean duration of subjective cycles being 46 hr, 1 min), where there was a single wakefulness period. Even during this period, which lasted for more than a month, the body temperature rhythm remained circadian, a fact which demonstrates that it depends on an internal synchronization and is not under the influence of the sleep-wakefulness rhythm alone. This result had previously been found in some subjects who did not present any reversal of body temperature cycle when passing from diurnal to nocturnal work.

The diachronic study by Colin reveals, however, that the body temperature rhythm might have had an influence on the changes observed in the sleep-wakefulness rhythms (passing to a circabidian rhythm and return to a sleep-wakefulness circadian rhythm by the introduction of naps). The time lags between the phases of maximal and minimal body temperature and the phases of sleep and wakefulness might have introduced these changes. However, the maximal temperature has never been observed when the subject was sleeping. It is possible that the relative stability of the body temperature corresponds to the fact that sleep-wakefulness rhythms are most often harmonics of the circadian rhythm.

THE EVOLUTION OF VIGILANCE AND PERFORMANCE

A simple visual reaction time task (RT) provided the measurement of the level of vigilance, via the measurement of performance level. (Oléron et al, 1970) Every time the subject called the team on the surface, he was asked to undergo 12 RT trials. The present analysis considers only the mean RT recorded on homologous times of calls for each cycle. The results, which are given in Figure 3.1, show a double variation in RT.

First, RT increases significantly from period 1 to period 2, that is, during 81 days. It decreases during period 4, when the circadian rhythm is perfectly stabilized. It can be concluded that the increase in RT is not attributable to the duration of the underground stay, but is due to the circadian equilibrium of the sleep-wakefulness rhythm which is synchronized with the body temperature rhythm.

Second, if subjective cycles are considered, the rhythm is circadian for period 1, the minimum appearing before noon $(p < .01)$, and circabidian for period 2, still with a minimum before noon $(p < .10)$. When the subjective cycle remains circabidian while the sleep-wakefulness rhythm becomes circadian again (periods 3 and 4), the RT cycle also becomes circadian again $(p < .05$ during period 3; $p < .01$ during period 4). Vigilance evolves parallel with the sleep-wakefulness rhythm but not with the body temperature nor with subjective duration rhythms. If there had been more series of measurements during the day, a more discriminating analysis might possibly have shown a relationship between RT and body temperature, as could be assumed on the basis of the results obtained by Kleitman (1963).

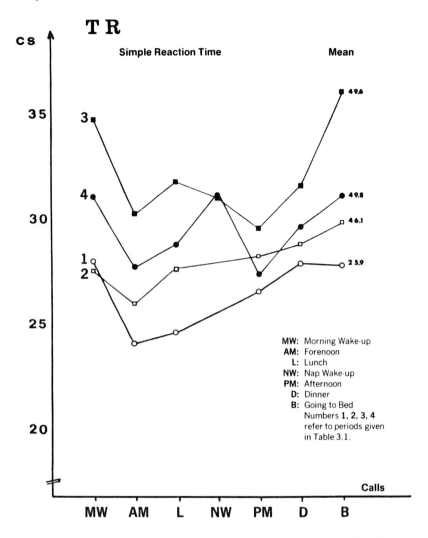

FIGURE 3.1. *Evolution of reaction times through the "day."*

The circadian RT rhythm is similar to that found by Kleitman for different sensorimotor tasks, with a minimum RT in the forenoon, and two maximums, one at the beginning and one at the end of the wakefulness period. It also corresponds to the results obtained by Klein et al. (1968), who found the same rhythm with a simple visual reaction time task. Let us add that in the present experiment, these maximums have the same duration for periods 1 and 4, but for period 2 (circabidian sleep-wakefulness rhythm), the maximum when going to bed is superior to the maximum when getting up ($p < .01$). It should also be mentioned that no differences in short-term memory for word lists were found in the course of the stay underground, and no difference was found in long-term memory between morning and night.

ESTIMATION OF DURATION

Measuring a duration from A to B consists of counting the number of time units that have elapsed between the instant A and the instant B. Estimating duration without access to means of measurement involves guessing the number of time units that might have elapsed between the two events. Estimation as well as measurement is done by referring implicitly or explicitly to a system of measurement through which two events are put in coincidence with two temporal cues, the temporal distance of which is known. When a subject is completely deprived of any temporal cue provided by the environment, he must use his memory and try to estimate duration on the basis of subjective criteria. Everyone has experienced the difficulty of such an operation when no watch or clock is available. This difficulty is certainly greater for a subject living "beyond time."

ESTIMATION OF THE LENGTH OF THE STAY UNDERGROUND

Completely isolated subjects cannot help evaluate the duration of their stay, if only to predict its end. In 1963, Siffre spent 58 days in a cave. He tried to establish a calendar by evaluating the duration of his successive activities and of his nights. When he was removed from the cave, he estimated that he had spent 33 days in it. This estimation was genuine from his point of view, as testified by the fact that, although he had entered the cave with a quantity of food calculated to last for 2 months, he had saved food in relation to the subjectively elapsed time. Thus, Siffre was more confident in his subjective estimations than in the objective criteria that he could have used by referring to the quantity of consumed food.

In the same way, he did not take into account the possible existence of a circadian rhythm of sleep-wakefulness. Had he taken this cue into consideration, he would have made an error of only 24 hours, since in 58 days he had 57 periods of sleep-wakefulness.

Mairetet was aware of these results when he undertook his experiment in 1966. It was decided that he would estimate the duration of his stay on the basis of the number of sleep-wakefulness cycles alone. As previously mentioned, he would try to distinguish between nap and night sleep by not undressing for naps. The subject followed instructions; however, he had 48-hour cycles during period 2, and during period 3 he was not conscious that naps were equivalent to nights. Therefore, he counted only 86 cycles, which he interpreted as 86 days, whereas he actually remained in the cave 174 days. Like Siffre, he underestimated his stay by about one-half.

Considering the experimental setting, these results seem paradoxical. Long sojourns in uncomfortable conditions might be thought to lead to an overestimation of the time elapsed, analogous to the overestimation observed when one is waiting or suffering. Nothing of this kind appears. The results should be compared with the observation made in the course of a mining accident at Courrieres, in 1906, when buried workers managed to get out after excavating a passage for 3 weeks. Upon emerging, they estimated that they had spent only 4 to 5 days at the bottom of the mine. After reporting other results, we shall take a closer look at this problem.

ESTIMATION OF LONG DURATIONS

What we refer to as long durations here are periods less than 24 hours, usually corresponding to several hours. The first estimation consisted in evaluating the duration between waking up and lunch. The median of the objective duration corresponding to 64 cycles (there were some omissions) was 10 hours, 26 minutes. The semiinterquartile range (SIR) was 2 hours, 4 minutes. The median of the subject's estimates, in hours and minutes, was 4 hours, 40 minutes (SIR: 28 min). The underestimation of these durations exceeds 50 per cent.

Fifty-four estimates of the duration between nap and dinner have also been analyzed. The median of the objective duration is 11 hours, 48 minutes (SIR: 3 hr, 15 min), the median of the estimates is 4 hours, 15 minutes (SIR: 55 min). The underestimation is of the same order as that which occurs during morning.

What is responsible for this underestimation? It has to be pointed out that Siffre, in establishing his calendar, made errors of the same order. It might be assumed that Mairetet's *knowledge* contributed to his more organized behavior, and that the estimates of these durations were made on the basis of time duration in his ordinary life experience. This factor might have played a role and it might explain the small variation of his estimates which, at first sight, appeared stereotyped. Note that the correlation between objective durations and estimated durations is .44 ($p <$ .001). Underestimations of the same order of magnitude are also found when shorter durations are estimated.

ESTIMATION OF SHORT DURATIONS

Short durations are defined as 1 or 2 minutes; they do not correspond to intervals between habitual actions, as in the two previous cases. Here, the subject was asked to estimate durations varying between 30 and 120 seconds (median: 75 sec; SIR: 25 sec). These stimulus values were used in the three classic methods: (1) estimation in time units—the subject received two clicks on the telephone from the team on the surface, and was asked to estimate verbally the elapsed temporal interval; (2) reproduc-

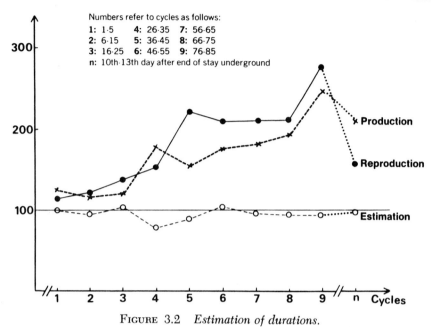

FIGURE 3.2   *Estimation of durations.*

tion—the subject had to press the key for the length of time separating the two clicks; (3) production—the subject was given a verbally defined interval and he had to press the key for the corresponding length of time. The three series of measurements were randomized and performed successively at various times during the day.

In order to standardize the results, we transformed each estimation, reproduction, and production measurement into percentages of the standard interval. We combined the values obtained for every 10 cycles, except the 5 first cycles, in order to have a standard of comparison affected as little as possible by the underground stay. Furthermore, values are given as obtained from the 10th to the 13th day after the termination of the stay in the cave.

As shown in Figure 3.2, the estimation was exact from the beginning to the end of the experiment, but this result does not appear valid. Actually, estimation and production trials were made so close to each other that the subject quickly understood that the range of stimuli was the same in production and estimation and made his responses accordingly.

Production and reproduction trials give parallel results. In the course of time, the productions and the reproductions become longer, attaining twice the length of the standard by the end of the experiment. This effect is not attributable to the mere repetition of the task, since 10 days after the termination of the underground stay the corrections are very noticeable.

These important results cannot be given a general explanation in terms of lowered vigilance or performance. On the other hand, the three temporal tasks (estimation of the duration of sleep-wakefulness cycles, estimation of the duration of the period between two activities within a cycle, and production and reproduction of brief intervals) give homogeneous results. In the light of the results obtained in the production and reproduction trials of brief intervals, the explanations that can be proposed for the results to the two first tasks must remain partial. Actually, the fact that Mairetet confused 24-hour and 48-hour cycles, the fact that he did not understand that the need to sleep that he felt after 15 hours of wakefulness was his need for night sleep and not for a nap, the fact that he could delay his lunch up to 10 hours after his breakfast, shows that there has been a systematic change in his time estimates.

Summary

The results described above are parallel to those obtained in other experiments under conditions of isolation, in spite of the difference in situation and methods. Vernon and McGill (1963) found that six subjects who stayed 96 hours in sensory deprivation conditions had a mean underestimation of 20 hours, one of the subjects making an error of 40 hours in only 4 days. Reed and Kenna (1964) also found an underestimation for short periods of sensory deprivation. Jirka and Valousek (1967) studied three speleologists who, after an expedition of 477 hours, estimated that 345 hours had elapsed; periods of rest and sleep were more underestimated than periods of activity, but even periods of activity were underestimated.

The facts being well established, how can they be interpreted? In these types of studies, the existence of a biological clock is often hypothesized, the period of which would be modified. It is difficult to give a definite content to this explanation since all studies on the physiological or biochemical effects of isolation (Zubek, 1969) have not revealed considerable changes. The circadian body temperature is maintained. In some cases, there is about a 10 per cent decline in the EEG rhythm, a result which is not important as regards the magnitude of the phenomena observed in Mairetet's reactions.

It has also been shown that estimation of duration varied with body temperature (François, 1927; Hoagland, 1933; Pfaff, 1968); however, Mairetet's temperature remained normal and stable during the entire experiment. Analyses in progress will perhaps show, besides variations of the estimation of duration in the course of the sojourn, slight circadian variations due to body temperature. But it will not be possible to explain the longitudinal results on the basis of amplitude of these variations.

This being so, the psychological explanation previously put forward (Fraisse, 1963) might throw some light on these results. The estimation of time elapsed would be proportional to the number of changes perceived in a given objective duration. If changes become very frequent, as is the case when waiting, suffering, or expending effort, each instant that elapses is paid attention to, and the duration is overestimated. If changes are few, as is the case when half-sleeping or when motor activity is reduced, duration is underestimated. Situations of perceptual deprivation with restricted activity, as was the case for Mairetet, probably fall within this category. The biological clock would not be affected to a considerable extent but, since the psychological clock registers fewer events for a given duration, there would be an underestimation of duration.

REFERENCES

Aschoff, J. 1965. Circadian rhythms in man. *Science,* 148:1427–32.

Colin, J., Timbal, J., Boutelier, C., Houdas, Y. and Siffre, M. 1968. Rhythm of the rectal temperature during a 6-month free-running experiment. *J. appl. Physiol.* 25:170–76.

Conroy, R. T. W. L., Mills, J. N. 1970. *Human circadian rhythms.* London: Churchill.

Fraisse, P. 1963. Perception et estimation du temps. In *Traité de Psychologie expérimentale,* Eds. P. Fraisse and J. Piaget. fasc. VI, chap. 19, p. 59–95, Paris: Presses Universitaires de France.

——. 1967. *Psychologie du temps.* 2d ed. Paris: Presses Universitaires de France.

Fraisse, P., Siffre, M., Oléron, G. and Zuili, N. 1968. Le rythme veille-sommeil et l'estimation du temps. In *Cycles biologiques et psychiatrie,* Symposium Bel-Air III. Paris: Masson 257–65.

François, M. 1927. Contribution à l'étude du sens du temps: la température interne comme facteur de variation dans l'appréciation subjective des durées. *Année psychol.* 28:186–204.

Hoagland, H. 1933. The physiological control of judgments of duration: Evidence for a chemical clock. *J. gen. Psychol.* 9:267–87.

Jirka, Z. & Valousek, C. 1967. Time estimation during prolonged stay under ground. *Studia Psychologica,* 9:194–97.

Klein, K. E., Wegmann, H. M. & Brüner, H. 1968. Circadian rhythm in indices of human performance, physical fitness and stress resistance. *Aerospace Med.* 39:512–18.

Kleitman, N. 1963. *Sleep and wakefulness.* Chicago: University of Chicago Press.

Lobban, M. C. 1960. The entrainment of circadian rhythms in man. *Cold Spr. Harb. Symp. quant. Biol.,* 25:325–32.

McLeod, R. B., and Roff, M. F. 1935. An experiment in temporal disorientation. *Acta Psychol.* 1:381–423.

Mills, J. N. 1964. Circadian rhythms during and after three months in solitude. *J. Physiol.* 174:217–31.

——. 1966. Sleeping habits during four months in solitude. *J. Physiol.* 189:30–31.

——. 1967. Keeping in step away from it all. *New Scientist*, 33:350–51.

Oléron, G., Fraisse, P., Siffre, M. and Zuili, N. 1970. Les variations circadiennes du temps de réaction et du tempo spontané au cours d'une expérience "hors du temps". *Année psychol.* 70:347–56.

Pfaff, D. 1968. Effects of temperature and time of day on time judgments. *J. exp. Psychol.* 76:419–22.

Reed, G. F. and Kenna, J. C. 1964. Personality and time estimation in sensory deprivation. *Percept. Mot. Skills*, 18:182.

Reinberg, A., Halberg, F., Ghatta, J. and Siffre, M. 1966. Spectre thermique (rythmes de la température rectale) d'une femme adulte avant, pendant et après son isolement souterrain. *C. R. Acad. Sci.* 262:782–85.

Siffre, M. 1963. *Hors du temps.* Paris: Julliard.

Siffre, M., Reinberg, A., Halberg, F., Ghata, J., Perdriel, G. and Slind, R. 1966. L'isolement souterrain prolongé. Etude de deux sujets adultes sains avant, pendant et après cet isolement. *La presse médicale*, 74:915–19.

Vernon, J. A. and McGill, T. E. 1963. Time estimation during sensory deprivation. *J. gen. Psychol.* 69:11–18.

Zubek, J. P. 1969. Physiological and biochemical effects. In *Sensory deprivation* ed. J. P. Zubek, pp. 207–53. New York: Appleton-Century-Croft.

Ernest A. Haggard *is Professor of Psychology in the Department of Psychiatry at the University of Illinois, where he holds a Career Research Award from the National Institute of Mental Health. He received his Ph.D. from Harvard University in 1946 and has held faculty positions at Harvard University, the University of California, Berkeley, Sarah Lawrence College, and the University of Chicago. His major interest is in learning and personality theory, although he has published in such areas as autonomic and perceptual conditioning, statistics and research methodology, the psychotherapy process, decision-making, and social influences on cognitive, intrapsychic, and interpersonal functioning.*

Haggard *presents a study of children reared either on geographically and socially isolated farms or in an urban setting in Norway. Findings are discussed in terms of two hypotheses: first, family-to-family variation should tend to be greater among isolated than among urban families, and this tendency should be manifest in the test responses of the children from the two types of families; and, second, children from isolated and urban families should differ on a variety of indices, including how they are reared, how they view and relate to their world, and on various cognitive, intrapsychic, and interpersonal characteristics. Cognitive and personality tests and measures drawn from translated standardized tests or developed as a part of this research were used to test the two hypotheses. On most of the measures the hypotheses were supported, with the findings indicating that the children from each subculture developed in ways that enabled them to function effectively in their own physical and social ecology, but not necessarily in that of children from the other group.*

4

Some Effects of Geographic and Social Isolation in Natural Settings

Previous chapters have considered how individuals responded when placed in experimental or other controlled situations involving some form of isolation in an enclosed space for relatively short periods of time—say, from a few hours to several months. Other chapters will consider how individuals and groups have adapted to a variety of situations involving enclosed or limited space for periods up to a year or more. In all such instances, however, those persons being studied had to adapt to situations

I began this research on the effects of being reared in social isolation, as compared to being reared in a small rural community or in an urban setting, in 1959–60, while visiting at the University of Oslo and the Institute for Social Research in Oslo on a Special Research Fellowship (MF-9415) from the National Institute of Mental Health. U.S. Public Health Service. At that time, a pilot study of social isolates in central Norway (Telemark) was conducted with the help of Erik Rinde, Per Tiller, and Sverre Brun-Gulbrandsen from the Institute for Social Research, and Alfred Baldwin and Harold Raush from the United States, and was supported by a Small Grant (MH-4019A) from the National Institute of Mental Health in 1960. The present study, which was conducted in eastern Norway in the area between Lake Femund and Elverum, near the Swedish border, was made possible by a U.S. Public Health Service Career Award (MH-K6-9514) from the National Institute of Mental Health and Research support from the Foundations' Fund for Research in Psychiatry (Grants 62-259, 65-321, and G69-465). Colleagues who played important roles in the data collection and other aspects of this research include: Anna von der Lippe, the director of the research activities in Norway, who made invaluable contributions, and Arvid Ås, Carl-Martin Borgen, Anne Brekke, and Claus Fasting. After the project was essentially completed, Marida Hollos collected two much-needed samples of data: the Q-sort (see Block, 1965 and Tables 4.1 and 4.5), and the Marbles Tests (see Usandivaras et al., 1967, 1970). In addition, Arvid Amundsen, R. Darrell Bock, Sissel Eide, Logan Green, Albert Kilburn, Donald Kolakowski, Sita Norum, and Astrid Simonsen aided in the preparation, coding, and analysis of the data collected between 1960 and 1970.

that were more or less novel or unfamiliar in terms of their customary experiences and life styles.

The present chapter, in contrast to the others, will be concerned with individuals who have spent most of their lives on geographically remote farms in Norway, isolated from practically everyone but the other members of their family. These farms, well away from the public roads, exist because only 3 per cent of the land in Norway can be cultivated, and over the centuries isolated farms have been developed in a remote valley, or by the sea, a fjord, or a river or lake. The isolated farms tend to be small, but are largely self-sufficient, and usually provide a livelihood above the level of bare subsistence.

The children, when old enough, tag along with, imitate, and help the same-sex parent in whatever needs to be done on the farm. Norwegian children start public school at age seven; those from the isolated farms go to state-run boarding schools, and are away from home for periods ranging from a week to a month or more, depending on how far they live from the school. At the boarding schools the children associate with a dozen or more children from other isolated farms in the same area and, except for those at school, the child's regular playmates are limited to his own brothers and sisters. When the children are not at the boarding school, as during the summer months, they usually are at home on the farm.

Traditionally, isolated farm children lived out their lives on such a farm, but increasingly they tend to leave when they finish the public elementary school. They move initially to the nearest town where they have relatives or friends, and where they can find work. If they return to the farm, as during a vacation, it is typically from a sense of nostalgia for what was once their entire world and life; they seldom return to live again as isolated farmers. Consequently, the isolated farm, with its hard and lonely life and its uncertain economic future, is less and less a characteristic part of Norway's increasingly technological society.[1] For example, in the period between 1959 and 1968, 46.4 per cent of the smallest farms in Norway (1.25 to 4.9 acres) were abandoned.[2] Such farms are being abandoned in part because of the rapidly expanding transportation and communications systems in rural Norway.

1. A somewhat more detailed account of the life on the isolated farms of the children who participated in this research is given in Haggard and von der Lippe (1970); most of this type of material will be given later in a full report of the research (in preparation). In addition, Hollos (1971), an anthropologist, who has recently studied families in the same general area in Norway (including using Elverum as the urban control sample) has given examples of her observations and descriptions of how some of the isolated families live.

2. Percentages taken from the *Statistical Yearbook* (1970) published by the Norwegian Central Bureau of Statistics, Oslo, Norway (p. 62).

What is the possible relevance of children reared on isolated farms in the Norwegian mountains to the other concerns of this book, such as the sensory or perceptual deprivation studies, or "wintering over" at the South Pole? The basic point of relevance is the assumed relation between how the child is reared and his developing emotional, mental, and interpersonal life—that is, how he learns to deal with his inner life and his outer reality. This assumption is supported by a 5-hour perceptual isolation (or deprivation) study, using samples of young adults from isolated farms and their matched controls from Oslo (Haggard, Ås, & Borgen, 1970).

As had been hypothesized (Haggard, 1964), the isolates tended to suffer significantly fewer sensory-perceptual and cognitive-affective disturbances than did their matched urban controls. Furthermore, the two groups responded to the experiment in characteristically different ways. Presumably, the isolates were able to adapt to the perceptual isolation experience with relatively greater ease than the urban controls because, from their prior style of life, they were far more accustomed than the urbanites to "periods of unstructured time and reduced bodily activity, minimal social interaction and stimulation, and reduced sensory stimulation, especially in terms of variety" (Haggard, Ås, & Borgen, 1970, p. 2).

Our Limited Knowledge of Social Isolates

Except for the anthropologists and ethnologists, perhaps the major thrust of psychology and closely related behavioral science research has been to study man's efforts, from infancy on, to develop his motor, perceptual, affective, cognitive, and interpersonal skills in order to adjust to and function effectively in a modern, highly complex social world. Relatively little attention has been paid to the development of individuals who happen to live far from the beaten path of university or other research-oriented institutions.[3] By definition, social isolates of the sort discussed here have minimal contact with society at large and they seldom have been studied by behavioral scientists. And, unfortunately, little systematic research will be done on individuals living in extreme social isolation: not only are such persons difficult to locate and to study, but also with the rapidly increasing communication and transportation networks throughout the world, isolation is rapidly vanishing as a way of life (see Asimov, 1970).

3. For example, at a time when numerous isolated families lived on the American frontier, psychologists such as James and Titchener were more interested in problems of consciousness, perception, and so forth, as studied by introspective-experimental methods, than the frontiersmen. Hall, who founded the *Pedagogical Seminary* in the field of child development 80 years ago, did not publish studies of children living in isolation on the frontier.

The knowledge we have of the social isolate (in Norway as elsewhere) is meager and comes from scattered sources. From a broad psychological point of view, perhaps our most astute insights come from the ancient teller of folk and fairy tales (for example, Christiansen, 1964), or the novelist (for example, Hamsun, 1921a, 1921b; Undset, 1928, 1929a, 1929b), or the naturalistic observer who recorded anecdotal incidents and impressions, like Eilert Sundt in Norway (see Allwood, 1957). All these sources describe how the social isolate lives and feels, how he relates to others, and how he manages to realize his destiny as best he can within his microcosm. In Norway, Tiller (1963, 1967), following an earlier pilot study with the author, reported a number of differences between isolates and urban children, based primarily on projective test data.

Other sources of insight into the individual or community isolated from society at large come from the planned study of isolated communities (for example, Aubert et al., 1970) or from unplanned events in nature, such as the volcanic eruption on the island of Tristan da Cunha (see Churchill, 1963; Munch, 1964), a shipwreck at sea, and so on (see Haggard, 1964). There are, of course, also numerous descriptions of mountain or rural farm families and the ways in which rural and urban individuals and families differ (for example, Lewis, 1946; Inkeles, 1968),[4] studies of infants isolated from their normal "societies"—that is, their families, and especially their mothers (for example, Patton and Gardner, 1963; Ribble, 1943; Spitz, 1945; Spitz & Cobliner, 1965; Whitten, Pettit, & Fischhoff, 1970; Yarrow, 1964), and an increasing number of animal studies concerned with the effects of isolation or crowding (for example, Bronfenbrenner, 1968; Fuller, 1967; Harlow & Harlow, 1962; Palmer, 1969; Welch, 1964; Zajonc, 1969), and the effects of early experience on later behavior (see Thompson & Grusec, 1970)—all of which bear di-

---

4. Inkeles (1968, p. 119) cites a study by Lanneau and Malrieu (1957) of French farm and urban families. Some of the characteristics of the two types of families are similar to those observed among the Norwegian isolated (rural) and the urban children: "the slow social awakening of the rural children, their fear and suspicion of strangers, and their lack of experience with diverse perspectives. This much may perhaps be attributed to isolation. But their sensory motor functions are highly developed, whereas their imagination, language, and intellectual functions are underdeveloped. This should be attributed not solely to isolation but also to the occupation of their parents as farmers. Presumably, the children of a professional in the same isolation would show the reverse balance of skills." There are also apparent differences between the French rural children and the Norwegian isolated children. Inkeles reports that "in the farm families children grow up in an atmosphere of warm affectivity and with a strong sense of security, which again may be cultural or may be related to an ecological factor—since in French farm families the grandparents live in the home and apparently have a tendency to overindulge their grandchildren." The differences between the French and the Norwegian children probably are a function of both the general cultural differences between the French and Norwegian societies and the psychosocial factors that accompany the extreme social isolation experienced by the Norwegian farm families in this study (see also Hess, 1970; LeVine, 1970).

rectly or indirectly on the isolated children and their urban counterparts discussed in this chapter.

Reasons for Studying Social Isolation

The present study of social isolates in Norway was undertaken for several reasons. An initial theoretical interest was whether social isolates, for whom life normally involves their learning to relate to a minimal number of persons, were possibly similar in their character and cognitive structures, interpersonal relationships, and so forth, to those individuals reared in an urban society who also relate to a minimal number of persons— namely, the withdrawn person. If fundamental similarities exist between these two groups of individuals, one might think of the isolated farm as a "natural laboratory" in which persons develop normally—but without many of the intrapsychic structures and interpersonal skills that characterize the emotionally healthy urbanite. Thus, it was reasoned that the study of individuals reared in such a natural laboratory might provide insights into the development of the mechanisms of interpersonal isolation, but unconfounded with the maladaptive patterns that characterize the withdrawn or isolated person in society.

Another reason for studying social isolation lies in the fact that the isolated farm is a social microcosm. Thus, by virtue of its small size and relative lack of complexity as a social system, the isolated farm conceivably might provide insights into relations among, for example, the parents' value systems and methods of child rearing and training, and the consequences of such factors on the development of the child's character structure and corresponding cognitive, emotional, and interpersonal adaptations. The study of life on the isolated farm offers an opportunity to trace much of the individual's development and many of his relations to his physical and social ecologies, and what they provide and require of him. It thus may permit some integrated articulation of the findings and theories generated among many of the disciplines known as the social or behavioral sciences. Or, in less technical terms, modern urban society is so complex and changing that the behavioral scientist who studies only urban individuals cannot hope to unravel the many threads of influence on the growing child which, when woven together, will make up the fabric of his mind and character.

The isolated farm is not only a social microcosm; the nuclear (or extended) family living on an isolated farm can be thought of as a society of minimal size. If one defines a society as a stable social system that must perform various functions—such as to provide for the basic physical needs of its members; to socialize its young in terms of the societal norms; to establish and maintain a variety of individual and interpersonal roles; to control and regulate the behavior of its members, as by defining and enforcing acceptable modes of affective expression and other forms of communication; and to set realizable goals for them—then the isolated farm meets most of the criteria of a viable society (see Inkeles, 1968, pp. 78–83), its very small size notwithstanding.

If the isolated farm is thought of as a society of minimal size, several assumptions can be made about its members and their interactions, as compared to individuals reared in a much larger society. Two general assumptions or hypotheses will be considered here: first, family-to-family variation should tend to be greater among isolated than among urban families, and this tendency should be manifest in the test responses of the children from the two types of families; and second, children from isolated and urban families should differ on a variety of indices, including how they are reared, how they view and relate to their world, and on various cognitive, intrapsychic, and interpersonal characteristics. Furthermore, such differences should be reasonable in terms of the differences in the physical and social ecologies in which the isolate and urban children are reared.

Hypothesis 1: Isolation and Interfamily Heterogeneity[5]

It can be assumed that any stable society, regardless of its size, imposes pressures and constraints upon its members (expectations, rewards, and sanctions, for example) which, in turn, tend to shape the members' character structure and behavior patterns (ego defenses, modes of affective expression, value systems, and linguistic habits). On the isolated farm, relatively few direct external pressures and constraints from society at large impinge upon the family-society; hence most of the socialization norms and pressures exist within the family itself—at least until the child goes off to school at age seven. In one isolated area, for example, the parents permitted the radio to be used only to listen to folk music and weather reports, not to the "cultural" programs from Oslo. In addition,

5. This general hypothesis is similar in many respects to Redfield's hypothesis that led to his comparative study of four communities in Yucatan (an Indian tribal village, a peasant village, a small town, and a city), and his observation that "the four communities are in this order less isolated and less homogeneous" (1941, p. xv). With respect to his definition of a "little community," however, Redfield (1955) thought in terms of social units larger than the single nucelar or extended family, and listed four qualities of such communities: "distinctiveness, smallness, homogeneity, and all-providing self-sufficiency" (p. 4), and asserted that a family "is sectional or segmental contrasted with the integral little community" (p. 4). But few if any social units (regardless of their size) are in fact entirely self-sufficient, and the criteria that define social units are somewhat arbitrary. Consequently, in this study various characteristics of children drawn from the two social units (the isolated family and the town) have been compared and/or contrasted.

the parents frequently said they wished the school would teach more "practical" things and less "book learning." The parents were not foolish: they wanted their children to be socialized as they themselves had been, namely, to be able to work the farm and to stay there; otherwise in their old age they would be left alone as the children were drawn to the easier and more exciting life in the city.

In a society as small and closed as an isolated farm, the children have little chance to escape from the family's socialization pressures or to learn different ways of behaving. On any particular farm, then, one would expect to find a relatively high degree of uniformity on many forms of behavior and minimal open conflict among the family members: the single family-society is just too small to tolerate, for long, many sharp and highly charged differences among its members.

In contrast to the isolated farm, individual families in a city of several thousand persons and in close contact with the larger society will be exposed to many and varied nonfamilial influences, pressures, and constraints. Normally, such influences will have a "leveling effect" (that is, not only the society at large will influence its members, but also what "the neighbors" do and say and think will matter), so that one would expect to find relatively less interfamily heterogeneity in terms of a variety of behavioral characteristics among urban families than among the socially isolated families.

If, however, the society is large enough for subsocieties to function within it, one can also expect a greater acceptance of any obvious differences among the individuals within it than within a society that is smaller and/or more isolated. These intrasociety differences often are evident in the linguistic forms used by the members of any such subgroups. For example, members of the same social set in Oslo—or any other city—will tend to "talk the same language." Apparently, as the social group becomes larger and more differentiated, there is an increase in the tolerance for intragroup differences, between as well as within families. In one very isolated area, for example, practically all the families protested (too much) that "every one here is alike"; the notion of status or other differences among the families seemed almost intolerable, although everyone knew very well that they existed and precisely what they were.

If it be true that the isolated family is relatively less influenced by the socializing pressures of the larger society than is the urban family, then the isolated family should tend to show more idiosyncratic qualities than the urban family. But if this be so, what might one expect regarding the range of interfamily differences among the isolated as compared to the urban families? It can be assumed that the characteristics of a particular isolated family-society will be determined by many factors. These factors include: what the parents are like (for example, their backgrounds, ego structures, value systems, habits, work skills); the location, size, and productivity of the farm; the number and type of individuals (grandparents, other relatives, and children), animals, and machinery on the farm; and the degree of isolation from other farms and the larger society. Because the strength and patterning of such factors will vary from farm to farm, one would expect not only a higher degree of intrafamily homogeneity, but also a higher degree of interfamily heterogeneity in a sample of isolated farm families than among otherwise comparable urban families.[6]

If isolated families tend to differ from each other in a variety of important ways more than urban families do, one would expect that (as representative samples from the two "populations") the test responses of children from isolated farms would tend to be more variable than the responses of their urban counterparts. Or, stated differently, one would expect that since urban children are exposed to the general societal norms and pressures more than are the children from the isolated farms, the responses of urban children to measures of cognitive, intrapsychic, and interpersonal functioning would show less variation than the responses of children from the isolated farms. To test this general hypothesis, the variances on each of the WISC scales (Wechsler, 1949) were compared, as well as a number of other scales which indicate the two groups' cognitive, intrapsychic, and interpersonal functioning.

Hypothesis 2: Differences Between the Isolated and Urban Samples

In accordance with the well-established finding that an individual is, in large part, the product of the kind of society or culture he is born into, it is reasonable to expect a variety of differences between persons born into the isolated and the urban societies. In most instances where comparisons are made between two or more cultural groups, differences may be expected on many of the parameters of the societies being compared, and hence on the characteristics of the individuals within those societies. For example, any systematic comparisons between samples of the Sioux or Yurok Indian children on a reservation (see Erikson, 1950) with samples of urban "American" children could be expected to show differences on practically all the cognitive, intrapsychic, and interpersonal variables generally used by behavioral scientists.

---

6. In very isolated areas, some single families have developed their own identifiable dialects. On a broader scale, families from one valley often are easily recognized by their particular dress and general manner of speaking and acting, as being different from those from another nearby valley. And, in an earlier period in the Westward development of the United States, the members of certain family groups (such as the Hatfields and the McCoys) could identify each other without a personal introduction.

The comparison between Norwegian children from isolated farms and their matched urban controls differs from most "cross-cultural" studies in several important respects: both groups have a relatively common geographic, genetic, and cultural (including linguistic) heritage; and both groups are exposed to essentially the same educational background, namely, the elementary school system which is, as far as possible, standardized throughout Norway. Consequently, insofar as the social as well as other complexities of the isolated farm and urban centers differ so enormously, it can be assumed that the intrapsychic structures and interpersonal skills in the members of the two groups also will differ in a number of significant ways. But since the children in both samples are exposed to roughly comparable academic experiences, what differences can be expected in terms of the isolates' and controls' cognitive or intellectual characteristics?

In describing any similarities and differences between the social isolates and their urban controls, comparisons will be made in terms of: how the parents in both settings say they think their children are or should be reared; and differences in the children's apparent phenomenological world and their characteristic modes of relating to it, based on a linguistic content analysis of projective test protocols. Further comparisons include: the scores of the children on the Wechsler Intelligence Scale for

TABLE 4.1   *Design and number of subjects*

Number of subjects:
Basic sample

	Isolates	(Semi-isolates)[a]	Controls	Subtotal	(Total)[a]
Boys	19	(10)	13	32	(42)
Girls	21	(9)	15	36	(45)
Total	40	(19)	28	68	(87)
Average age	10.4	(10.6)	10.3		
Number of subjects: Essay sample[b]					
Boys	16	(50)	21	37	(87)
Girls	20	(56)	19	39	(95)
Total	36	(106)	40	76	(182)
Average age	11.8	(12.0)	12.2		
Number of subjects: Q-sort sample[c]					
Boys	6	(8)	10	16	(24)
Girls	10	(10)	16	26	(36)
Total	16	(18)	26	42	(60)

a. Data for the semiisolates are not discussed in this chapter. Consequently, most of the findings are based on the subtotal of 68 Ss.

b. The Essay includes many children not in the basic sample.

c. The Q sort (Block, 1965) was administered by Dr. Marida Hollos to both parents with respect to their attitudes and child-rearing practices toward the eldest child, in case there were more than one child in the family.

Children (WISC) and other indices of cognitive functioning; various indices of intrapsychic (or ego) structures and functioning; their characteristic style of interpersonal relationships with their parents, peers, or other persons; and some general indications of how they see themselves in the future.

Methods Used to Study Social Isolates

Selection of the Samples

Norway, with its magnificently varied geography—mountains, valleys, glaciers, forests, rivers, lakes, fjords, and the approximately 150,000 islands that lie along its coast—contains many subcultural groups with rather different value orientations and life styles. As a consequence, several months were spent locating an area with relatively homogeneous genetic, cultural, and socioeconomic characteristics that also contained a sufficient number of isolated farms with children of school age and the necessary small community and urban control groups.[7] The final core or basic sample of subjects ($N = 87$), with complete data from a dozen or so tests, is given in Table 4.1, and is made up of social isolates and two control groups. The three groups are: 40 children from isolated farms (from five schools), 19 children from two loosely-knit communities of 200 to 500 persons (from two schools), and 28 children from one urban school in a town of about 7,000 persons in the same general ecological-cultural area.

The children in the two control groups were matched with the social isolates on: age (spread as evenly as possible over the 7 to 14 year span), sex, sibling position in the family, the father's education and, as nearly as possible, on the type of his occupation, to avoid confounding the degree of social isolation with socioeconomic or other factors. Thus, in all three samples the children's fathers worked primarily with things (as farmers, truck drivers, or machinists, for example), rather than with people. The sample sizes for the Essay and the parent Q-sort tests, which only partially overlap the basic sample, are also given in Table 4.1.

Although there were 87 children in the basic sample, this discussion will be based on a sample of only 68 children. The semiisolates will be

7. Because the small rural farms, especially the isolated ones, are not only difficult to work but also economically vulnerable, many are being abandoned. Nevertheless, many isolated farms are still run by the remnants of families, such as the grown brothers and sisters who never left the farm and, as adults, are unable to adapt to any other way of life. The sample of children from isolated farms is, practically speaking, all the isolated children in the parts of the ecological area where this research was carried out. The isolation sample is larger than the other two samples primarily because social isolation in Norway is a vanishing way of life; the size of the semiisolate and urban control groups could be increased without much difficulty, if that were necessary to increase the stability of the findings.

excluded for two reasons. First, this group is small in size and some types of data, such the Rorschach, are not available for all subjects. The other, and more important, reason is that to include them would complicate unduly the presentation of findings: the semiisolated children often tend to differ from the isolates and urbanites more than the latter groups differ from each other. An apparent reason for this frequent tendency is that the semiisolates seem to suffer from more intense and pervasive socialization pressures than either the isolates or the urban controls. Thus, whereas the isolated children are subjected to almost constant family pressures, they are not required to conform to many of the pressures imposed by the general society. Likewise, if the urban center is large enough the children reared in it are subjected to a variety of societal pressures, but can escape rather easily from their families, and even the neighbors, by visiting a friend or relative across town, by going to the cinema, or by playing with their nonfamily peers. The semiisolated child is subjected to both family and societal pressures and, being unable to escape either of them completely, often seems to be, or actually is, more inhibited and less independent than either the isolated or the urban child of the same age.

RESEARCH STRATEGY

There are many ways of studying the effects of being reared in social isolation. One might actually live and work on a few farms for extended periods and try to absorb the nuances of the interpersonal interactions that occur in the child-rearing, marital, and in-law relationships, or in dealing with neighbors or "outsiders." This procedure, frequently used intentionally by anthropologists and inadvertently by novelists like Hamsun or Undset, no doubt gives the most intensive, interesting, and perhaps most valid, picture of what it is like to grow up and live on an isolated farm. But then, one could study and describe only a few such isolated families, each of which would almost of necessity be atypical in one way or another. In this research, for reasons of practicability as much as preference, it was decided that a more extensive picture of the effects of social isolation could be gained by studying a large sample of children reared on isolated farms, and to learn some of the ways they were similar to and different from their counterparts growing up in a loosely-knit community or in a small city.

After the decision was made to do a normative or "statistical" study, several methodological steps were taken. First, the samples were decided upon and then repeated and extended visits were made to some of the isolated families to learn how they live and how they work their farms. Second, on the basis of the interviews with and observations of the families, decisions were made as to which cognitive, intrapsychic, and interpersonal characteristics of the children should be measured. Then, a battery of standardized tests and measures was assembled, either from the child-development literature, or developed for the purposes of this research. All the test instruments developed for this research were pretested on samples of isolated and urban control children not used in the study proper.

TESTS AND MEASURES

The tests and measures referred to in this chapter fall into three groups.[8]

1. *Translated Standardized Tests.* These included: the Wechsler Intelligence Scale for Children (WISC) (Wechsler, 1949); the Rorschach Test (R) (see Klopfer et al., 1954); the Child-Rearing Practices Q sort (Q) (Block, 1965); and the Children's Embedded Figures Test (CEF) (Karp & Konstadt, 1963).

2. *Tests Developed for This Research.* A complete description of the tests developed for this research, with some of their psychometric properties, will be presented elsewhere. Tests developed in connection with this research and referred to in this chapter include: first, the Children's Picture (Bear) Test (CP)—ten 8" × 10½" black-and-white watercolor pictures of bears in various situations (a young bear sitting alone while others play in the background, seeing the parents embrace, choosing a path to the forest or to the town, etc.). The test was administered like the Thematic Apperception Test but scored according to categories relevant to intrapsychic and intrafamily dynamics and other interpersonal relationships. Second, the Story Completion Test (SC), presented nine stories or situations to be completed by the child (reasoning as to causality in natural phenomena, belief in magic, self-reliance in solving practical problems, etc.). Third, the Essay "Myself in 15 Years" (E), was a class assignment by school teachers to children of ages 10 to 14, to focus on the nature of the children's aspirations and their projected view of themselves and their lives as young adults.

3. *Measures Developed for This Research.* Most of the measures developed for this research fall into two broad categories: global and logit

---

8. This list does not include all the tests and/or measures used in this research, but does indicate the types of information obtained (see also Haggard & von der Lippe, 1970, for some additional types of data on the isolates and the controls). The battery of tests given to the basic sample, which was administered privately in the school to each child in the study, usually ran a total of 10 to 12 hours spread over several occasions; whenever possible, each child's responses were tape recorded and later transcribed. A complete report of all the research procedures and findings is in preparation.

scales. The global scales (usually with from 5 to 7 points) were based on either a single test stimulus (such as a picture or a story-to-be-completed) or on all the stimulus situations in a test (such as all 10 cards of the Children's Picture or the Rorschach tests), and were rated by trained clinical psychologists. Whenever possible, each of the scalar points were anchored by representative responses in order to obtain uniformity of scoring as well as relatively normal distributions over the entire sample of children studied. The logit scales (ratios of two logarithms) were used to obtain a variety of quantitative measures based on samples of the children's linguistic behavior in response to several projective tests and the "objective" scores (that is, the content, location, and determinant codings) based on their responses to the Rorschach test. A more detailed description of the "linguistic" categories and scales will be given in a later section. The measures developed in connection with this research, and which will be referred to in this chapter, are: Children's Picture Test: global scales [CP(S)]; Children's Picture Test: linguistic analysis scales (logit) [CP(L)]; Rorschach Test: global scales [R(S)]; Rorschach Test: scoring category scales (logit) [R(Sc)]; Essay Test: global scales [E(S)]; and Essay Test: Linguistic analysis scales (logit) [E(L)].

SOURCES OF BIAS IN THE DATA

Despite attempts to use tests and procedures that would be of equivalent familiarity, interest, and relevance to each group of children, certain biases were found to exist in the data. These biases stemmed from both the backgrounds of the investigators, and from some of the data-collection instruments.

Investigator Biases. In this project, the persons trained in clinical psychology and/or psychoanalysis (as the members of the project were) showed themselves prone to two types of bias. One type, the clinical bias, is the sensitivity to the maladaptive and possibly pathological aspects of behavior somewhat more than to its adaptive and integrative aspects, especially in the unfamiliar context of social isolation. In other words, the meaning of the children's responses tended to be viewed unwittingly as though they were from patients in a psychological or psychiatric clinic. The second type, the urban bias, is the implicit assumption that the meaning of the children's responses can be viewed as though they were from persons reared in an urban setting, perhaps because of the investigators' unfamiliarity with the effects of being born and reared on an isolated farm.

Test Biases. Four standardized tests were selected because of their extensive use in other contexts, their relevance to particular research questions, and/or their relative freedom from the middle-class, urban biases that mark many psychological tests (see group 1).[9] Consequently, several new tests were developed to obtain data that pertain to the effects of social isolation, with minimal bias in favor of any one group of children (see group 2). Even so, it became apparent that two important sources of bias still existed in the data. For one thing, the data had a strong verbal bias: in retrospect, more observations of the children's behavior in free or structured situations should have been obtained.[10] In addition, the data had a strong intrapsychic-affective bias, due largely to the research staff's professional backgrounds and their speculations (or projections) about what the inner life of the social isolate must be like. As an attempt to correct for this type of bias, several measures were developed to give a fuller picture of the children's cognitive-adaptive characteristics (see group 3).

Certain practical considerations entered into the testing procedures along with the attempts to obtain unbiased data. For example, social isolates tend to be less talkative than urban children, especially with strangers and with respect to topics involving strong affect or ambivalence. Frequently the topics of greatest interest to the investigator may be seldom if ever discussed openly by the isolates among themselves, let alone with a stranger. Consequently, the investigator must be sensitive and careful in his probing, lest he either obtain glib and "proper" responses, or else break off the interview and even the possibility of further interviewing or testing.

Two procedures were used to cope with the shyness of the social isolate. One procedure was to use indirect methods of data collection (such as projective techniques) to obtain information on some of the isolate's attitudes and feelings about himself, his family, and his world. The other procedure was to employ (for some types of data) a psychological tester who, like the isolate, could be in no hurry at all, who could wait out the

9. Many of the psychological tests available in the child-development literature are based upon experiences and problems encountered in middle-class urban life and standardized upon such children. These tests are no more appropriate to the "culturally deprived" Norwegian social isolate than some IQ tests are as measures of the mental ability of lower-class children in a United States city slum (see Davis, 1948; Haggard, 1953).

10. An example from the Doll Play Test (not otherwise referred to in this chapter) illustrates the importance of behavioral observations: "Since impressions from overt behavior may be more vivid (and valid) than those from recorded speech or typed protocols (the source of most of our data), 'important findings' may have escaped our procedures. For example, in one test two dolls get into a fight, and the child being tested was required to strike them together and describe what they said to each other. Ratings were made of both the child's verbal response and his vigor in striking the dolls together. For this situation, the ratings based on overt behavior differentiated among the three groups much more clearly ($P = .002$) than did the ratings of the children's verbal behavior ($P = .21$)" (Haggard & von der Lippe, 1970, p. 471).

most reticent isolate, and who could silently communicate: "I can wait until you are ready to express your thoughts and feelings."[11]

DEVELOPMENT OF SCALES OR MEASURES

As noted previously, several well-known tests were adapted for use with the children being studied and, in addition, it was necessary to develop several tests and measures specifically for this research. Among the more important measures thus developed were the objective content analyses of samples of the children's linguistic behavior, and scales based on the content, location, and determinant scorings of the children's responses to the Rorschach test.

Linguistic Scales. The objective content analyses of samples of the children's linguistic behavior under relatively standardized conditions (for example, projective tests) were carried out to obtain particular sets of data or scales not otherwise available, and to minimize some types of bias which, if ignored, might seriously distort the "findings" of this research.

Since many of the psychological tests used in the research were recorded and later transcribed it was possible to computer analyze the protocols for several different tests. The children's verbal responses to these tests were thus analyzed for aspects of their manifest and latent content. The procedure used was similar to that of the *General Inquirer System* (see Gerbner et al., 1969; Holsti, Loomba, & North, 1968; Stone et al., 1966), insofar as a "dictionary" was constructed and, for any given test, every word spoken by each child was coded or tagged in accordance with the dictionary definitions. From a substantive point of view the work of Sanford (1942a, 1942b) was helpful in developing the dictionary.

The basic rationale for the procedure used is simply that everything said by an individual should reveal something of what he is like—how he sees himself in his world and how he tends to manage his inner life and his behavior in relation to his world—since it is he who said it. This rationale parallels that of the psychotherapist who assumes that a patient's reported dream should reveal meaningful things about the patient since it was, after all, the patient who dreamed (or "made") and recalled his own dream. It is likewise assumed that an individual's language somehow

---

11. The clinical psychologist who administered the Rorschach Test elicited an average of about eight responses to each of the 10 Rorschach cards for the children in both the isolate and control groups, and in no instance elicited fewer than five responses per card. Although initially two trained clinical psychologists were scheduled to administer the Rorschach test, the difference in the number of responses they obtained was so great that the data gathered by them obviously were not comparable. For the projective tests on which such differences occurred, the protocols obtained by the tester who elicited the most complete and meaningful data were used.

reflects, directly or indirectly, the matrix of perceptions, attitudes, values, interests, conflicts, memories, etc., that comprise "the mind," and that a study of the individual's linguistic behavior should indicate something of what is "in his mind." (Or, stated more simply, a correspondence is assumed to exist between the children's mental processes and their use of language.) But since one cannot examine directly "the mind" of another individual, objective scales were developed and used to "measure" the children's linguistic behavior in terms of explicitly defined scales or categories. An attempt was made to develop categories and scales that pertained to more-or-less specific research interests and questions.

The fact that each individual word was coded, independent of its context, places some burden on the coding scheme and necessarily results in a loss of important information about the manifest and/or latent content of any verbal communication.[12] However, the task of constructing a dictionary based on particular words and their context, or of more complex or subtle units such as phrases or themes, would have made the dictionary-construction phase, the coding, and/or the computer processing of these data much more complicated. For example, the isolates and the controls frequently used different dialects, idioms, and even different words, to designate the same objects or events, so that the use of specific words would have resulted in several more or less parallel dictionaries. It should also be noted in this connection that one purpose of the content analysis procedure was to try to by-pass any group differences in language usage by the use of numerical codes rather than the childrens' original words and linguistic styles, which cannot quite be ignored by clinicians making ratings based on subjective appraisals of the protocols.

The protocols for two tests, the 10-card Children's Picture Test and the Essay, "Myself in 15 Years," provide the data base for the content analyses reported in this chapter (Table 4.2). The Children's Picture Test (CP) provides data on a variety of dimensions, such as indications of the children's phenomenological world and their modes of adapting to it, including how they tend to relate to other persons. The Essay (E) data throw light on the children's characteristic time orientation, that is, the extent to which they are oriented toward the past and/or the present when asked to project themselves into the future.

---

12. In coding the individual words for manifest content the prime normative (that is, standard dictionary) definition was used. In some contexts (such as psychotherapy research), however, it may be more fruitful to assume that every word uttered by the patient contains all possible meanings simultaneously, especially when one is not so much interested in what particular words a patient is using, as in "what the patient is trying to say" but may be unable to express openly at the time (see Garduk & Haggard, 1972; Haggard, Baittle, & Isaacs, 1968; Isaacs & Haggard, 1966; Sklansky et al., 1966). A review of methods of linguistics analysis as applied to psychotherapies protocals is given in Gottschalk and Auerbach, 1966, chpts. 9-13, pp. 70-153.

TABLE 4.2   *Content analysis of two samples of children's language*

Type of Protocol	Words in Dictionary[a]	Subject Groups		Total
		isolates	controls	
Children's Picture (Bear) Test	$N = 7{,}310$	$N = 40$	$N = 28$	$N = 68$
Total "words"[b]		126,355	112,686	239,041
Total coded words[c]		119,419	107,875	227,294
Per cent "words" coded (i.e., in dictionary)		94.5	95.7	95.1
Essay Test	$N = 9{,}392$[d]	$N = 36$	$N = 40$	$N = 76$
Total"words"[b]		12,265	16,073	28,338
Total coded words[c]		10,561	13,776	24,337
Per cent "words" coded (i.e., in dictionary)		86.1	85.7	85.9

a. Identifiable words, correctly spelled, against which all the "words" in all the protocols were compared.

b. Includes all the individual verbal utterances or units; in addition to the correctly spelled words, typing errors (misspellings), nonwords (such as, . . . uhh . . .), and various noncoded categories of words (such as place names) were also included.

c. Includes all words that corresponded to those in the dictionary.

d. The dictionary for the Essay test contains 2,082 words not in the Children's Picture Test protocols (i.e., 7,310 + 2,082 = 9,392).

The linguistic dictionary of several thousand coded Norwegian words was developed by the following stages:

1. An examination of the stories of the children (in the isolation and control groups) told in response to the CP test, in order to learn whether consistent and meaningful differences might exist in the linguistic behaviors of these two groups of children;

2. The preparation of a set of preliminary categories (for example, active vs passive verbs, abstract vs concrete nouns);

3. A check on the utility of the preliminary categories by tallying the codes for all the words in the children's responses to 3 of the 10 stories from the CP test which, after being punched on cards, were listed with their frequencies for each of the children in the isolation and control groups;

4. From an examination of the data thus generated, the coding scheme or dictionary was revised by Dr. von der Lippe and the author, who also coded enough of the words to establish working definitions of the categories;[13]

5. In developing the dictionary for the CP test, each word, with its frequency for each group of children, was alphabetized and listed. As addi-

13. In its final form, the dictionary contained over 100 separate categories. This too-large number was reduced by dropping some with very small frequencies, and combining most of the remaining categories into about 50 scales, 28 of which are referred to in the tables and text of this chapter.

tional (and as yet uncoded) words occurred (as in the Essay, but which had not occurred in any of the CP protocols), they were alphabetized, listed, coded, and added to the dictionary;

6. After the dictionary was completed, a third party was trained to code each of the Norwegian words in the protocols according to the category definitions in the dictionary, with periodic checks of the codings; in cases of doubt, a three-way decision was made as to how the word should be coded. Any particular word might be coded under as many as five or six categories, and some "words," such as those not known to the coders, misspellings, or place names, were not coded; hence the difference between "Total 'words' " and "Total coded words" in Table 4.2.

All the protocols for the Children's Picture Test, the Essay, the Story Completion Test, and the Rorschach Test have thus been listed and coded, with the same codes and scales used for each type of protocol. With respect to the linguistic scales cited in this chapter, the assumption is made that the strength of any particular characteristic, tendency, interest, and so forth can be "measured" by the frequency of its occurrence, as reflected initially in the separate codings and ultimately in the transformed scales.

The scales cited in this chapter will be described or defined in the order of their occurrence in each of the tables in the text. From each type of protocol, the separate scales were generated for each individual child, then transformed and treated as a scale score for determining whether differences might exist between the children in the isolate and control groups. (The same scale scores were, of course, also obtained from the protocols of the children in the semiisolate sample.) A summary discussion of how the scales were transformed so as to be amenable to statistical analyses will follow the brief description of the scales.

Linguistic Categories and Scales for Affects. Four affect categories were coded (*anxiety, aggression, pleasure,* and *dejection*) on two levels: *explicit affect* (words that indicate the individual's actual or conscious experience of the affect in question–anxious, angry, joy, and sad, respectively; and *implicit affect* (words that only imply the presence of the affect in question by some act, object, or event–nightmare, kill, laugh, and cry, respectively).

Scales for each of the four explicit and four implicit affects were formed by the ratio: the sum of the frequency per category divided by the sum of the coded words, minus the sum of the frequency per category.

Linguistic Categories and Scales Reflecting Phenomenological World. Objects: nouns were classified as animate (a person, animal, and bird, for example) or as inanimate (a river, house, ball). Scales were formed by the ratio: (sum animate / sum inanimate) terms.

Behavior: verbs were classified as overt (walk, throw, talk) or as covert—that is, a cognitive act or affective experience (think, imagine, experience). Scales were formed by the ratio: (sum overt / sum covert) behavior terms.

Actions: verbs were classified as active (run, throw) or as passive (sit, sleep). Scales were formed by the ratio: (sum active / sum passive) terms.

Tempo: verbs were classified when possible as fast (run, hurry) or slow (dawdle, wait). Scales were formed by the ratio: (sum fast / sum slow) terms.

Communication or mode of contact with others: communication-contact verbs were classified when possible as verbal (ask, tell) or non- (or not necessarily) verbal (meet, visit). Scales were formed by the ratio: (sum verbal / sum nonverbal) terms.

Total number of coded words: the total number of words coded in one or more of the categories (excluding misspellings, stammerings, etc., which did not qualify as codable words).

Linguistic Categories and Scales for Cognitive Styles. Enumerative/Integrative: enumerative terms are the connectives that imply a mere listing or enumeration of objects or events (and, also); integrative terms are the connectives that imply an interdependence or other relationship between objects or events (therefore, because). Scales were formed by the ratio: (sum enumerative / sum integrative) terms.

Certainty/Uncertainty: certainty terms imply an absence of doubt or ambiguity (definitely, sure); uncertainty terms imply the presence of doubt or ambiguity (maybe, perhaps). Scales were formed by the ratio: (sum certainty / sum uncertainty) terms.

Concrete/Abstract: concrete terms designate tangible objects (house, boy); abstract terms designate nontangible objects or events (idea, dream). Scales were formed by the ratio: (sum concrete / sum abstract) terms.

Logic/Fantasy: logic terms imply rational, purposive cognitive processes or events (think, plan); fantasy terms imply wishfulfilling processes or events (hope, dream). Scales were formed by the ratio: (sum logic / sum fantasy) terms.

Linguistic Categories and Scales for Time References. Verbs were classified according to whether the past, the present, or the future tense was used. For these scales the data were taken from the Essay, primarily because a central aspect of the task of writing the Essay had to do with the child's ability to picture himself and his life 15 years hence. The scales were formed in terms of the proportion of verbs of each tense to the total words used (such as: sum past tense verbs / sum coded words − sum past tense verbs).

Linguistic Categories and Scales for Morals and/or the Internalization of Norms. The "morals" categories have to do with the extent to which externally imposed norms or expectations have been internalized successfully by the child. A presumed indication of *internalized morals* was inferred by terms indicating necessity or propriety (such as should, must, ought); a presumed indication of *corruptible morals* was inferred by terms that violate the customary proprieties (lie, cheat, steal). With respect to their dictionary categories, then, some of these terms in the protocols might pertain to relationships among natural phenomena (for example, "When one is tired, he should rest"), although they pertain predominantly to ethical considerations (for example, "One should not steal"). Scales for internalized/corruptible morals were formed by the ratio: (sum internalized / sum corruptible morals terms). Scales for the internalized and corruptible morals scales were formed separately on the basis of the proportion of each type of morals terms to all coded words (for example: sum internalized morals terms / sum coded words − sum internalized morals terms).

Linguistic Categories and Scales for Personal/Impersonal References. Three categories of *personal/impersonal references* to other persons were included to provide an index of one aspect of how the children in the isolation and control groups tend to relate, at least linguistically, to other individuals, and especially to those of greatest psychological importance to them. The codings were made in terms of whether the children used the personal form for designating persons in each of the three categories (mother, father, or "others" such as grandmother, brother, friend) or the impersonal form (the mother, the father, or the grandmother, the brother, the friend). Codes for each of the three categories were formed by the ratio: (sum personal / sum impersonal) terms.

Rorschach Scales. Nine scales based on the content, location, and determinant scorings of the isolate and control children's responses to the

Rorschach test (see Haggard & von der Lippe, 1970, Table 1) are cited insofar as they provide evidence of the relative dispersion of the two groups on these measures.[14]

TRANSFORMATION OF THE SCALES

Many forms of behavioral data, especially frequencies, percentages, or ratios involving small Ns, fail to meet the assumptions underlying such statistical procedures as the analysis of variance. When such procedures are used, data that deviate too much from the assumptions of normality, independence of means and variances, etc., may yield highly distorted or misleading "findings" (Haggard, 1949a, 1949b). Thus, it may be necessary to transform such data before they are analyzed statistically.

The transformation for the scales used in this chapter is: $X' = \log (X + .5)$, where X is the original frequency and X' is the transformed score for each category for each child (Bock, 1973, chap. 9). The addition of .5 to each frequency avoids the problem of taking the logarithm of a 0 frequency score for some children for some categories, should that event occur. The transformed scales were considered to be normal, continuous variates and were used in all the statistical analyses involving the linguistic and Rorschach scales—except for the computation of the isolation and control group means given in the tables.

The 28 linguistic and the nine Rorschach scales were thus transformed before F and P values were obtained. More specifically, for each scale the first step was to sum the frequency of tallies, X, in each category for each child. The scales were then developed by transforming each X, or combination of Xs, according to the following examples:

Untransformed Linguistic Scales
Actions: (sum active/sum passive)

Internalized morals

Transformed Linguistic Scales
log (sum active terms + .5) − log (sum passive terms + .5)

log (sum internalized morals terms + .5) − log (sum total coded words − sum internalized morals terms + .5)

Untransformed Rorschach Scales
Intellectual integrative capacity: (sum W/Sum $D + Dd + dd + dr$)

Transformed Rorschach Scales
log (sum W responses + .5) − log (sum $D + Dd + dd + dr$ responses + .5)

---

14. A more detailed discussion of scales based on the content, location, and determinant scorings of the Rorschach test is given in an unpublished manuscript: "On quantitative Rorschach scales" by E. A. Haggard.

General Data Analysis Procedures

Two general hypotheses were proposed regarding the social isolates and their urban controls.[15] The first hypothesis has to do with the proposition that interfamily differences should be greater among the isolated than among the urban families. With respect to this hypothesis, a simple test of the difference between the variances for the isolated and control samples (that is, the *F* ratio) was computed for a variety of measures and the tabulated *P* values doubled (see Snedecor, 1946, p. 249). The *F* ratios given in Tables 4.3 and 4.4 bear on this hypothesis insofar as they are an index of the relative dispersion of the responses of the children from the isolated and urban control groups.

The second hypothesis has to do with the proposition that differences should exist between the isolates and the urbanites on a variety of cognitive, intrapsychic, and interpersonal measures. With respect to this hypothesis, a multivariate analysis of covariance procedure (with age as the covariate) was used to test for differences on either single measures or sets of measures (Bock, 1973; Bock & Haggard, 1968). Data relevant to this hypothesis are given in Tables 4.5 to 4.10 and in the text.

Each child's age was used as a covariate and was partialled out before making any comparisons between the isolate and control groups for two reasons: first, to provide statements regarding the isolation and control groups which, presumably, represent general characteristics of the two subcultures (at least over the 7 to 14-year age span) and, second, to provide correlation coefficients (*r*s) that indicate the extent to which the traits or characteristics, as indicated by the scores on the variables, tend to become more or less pronounced as the children get older.

In addition to age, the possible effects of any sex differences, any differences among the five boarding schools from which the isolate children were drawn, and any interactions that contain the main effect of isolation were partialled out before making the comparisons between the isolate and control group means. In comparing the group means given in the tables and the text, it should be noted that the means are based on untransformed data, even though the corresponding *P* values for the differences between the means are, whenever appropriate, based on the transformed data. Consequently, the group means should be read to determine the direction and relative magnitude of the average scores for each group[16] and the *P* values, which are based on univariate *F* tests, should be read as

15. Practically all the statistical analyses were run on the MESA 98 Program (based on the article by Bock & Haggard, 1968) at the Computation Center, University of Chicago. The *P* values cited in the text and tables are based on the more conservative "two tailed" tests of significance.

16. In general, the larger group mean indicates "more of" the particular trait, characteristic, tendency, etc., in question.

indicators of the statistical significance of the difference between the two group means for each of the measures cited.

Representative Findings

The findings presented in this chapter are restricted in several ways. For example, the data on the semiisolates are not included here, and for the isolate and urban control groups the data based on several tests and measures have not been cited. But the findings that are presented with respect to these two groups of children are representative of (in the sense of being compatible or congruent with) the total body of findings. The selected findings are given to highlight some of the major similarities and differences between these two groups of children. The findings will be presented in terms of the two general hypotheses discussed in the introductory section.

Hypothesis 1: Isolation and Interfamily Heterogeneity

It was assumed that, with respect to the families living on isolated farms, the relative absence of any leveling effect due to social norms, pressures, and so forth directly imposed on the family by the larger society during the child's early years should foster the development of idiosyncratic family life styles or patterns of values, traits, and behaviors in such "family-societies." These, in turn, should result in relatively greater heterogeneity among the isolated than among the urban control families. It was thus assumed that, as representatives of such "family-societies," the children drawn from isolated farms should give test responses that are more heterogeneous than the responses of their urban counterparts. To test this hypothesis, the variances of the measures obtained from each group of children were compared and used as an index of their relative dispersion or heterogeneity.

Two considerations should be kept in mind in evaluating any differences between the isolates and controls in terms of their dispersion on the various tests or scales: first, the relative objectivity or subjectivity of the scales—sometimes called "hard" or "soft" data[17] and, second, whether any differences in the dispersion of the isolates' and controls' scores can be attributed essentially to artifacts of the scales, such as merely the correlation between scales' means and variances. Other things being equal, one can place more confidence in data based on scales that are objectively defined and standardized, and for which a negligible correlation exists between their means and variances.

17. Examples of "hard" data are the WISC and linguistic scales, and examples of "soft" data are ratings based on subjective judgments or interpretations of projective test protocols, such as the Children's Picture Test.

TABLE 4.3   *Response heterogeneity (variance) of isolates and controls on the WISC scales*

WISC Scales[a]	Group Variances isolates	controls	F[b] (σ_1^2/σ_c^2)	Difference[c] (2P)
	1	2	3	4
Picture arrangement	7.48	4.98	1.50	$<.50$
Coding	12.80	7.19	1.78	$<.20$
Comprehension	10.04	8.08	1.24	$>.50$
Vocabulary	7.41	2.89	2.56	$<.02$
Object assembly	12.91	7.79	1.66	$<.20$
Similarities	9.67	6.74	1.43	$<.50$
Picture completion	14.58	6.97	2.09	$<.05$
Information	12.83	5.76	2.23	$<.05$
Arithmetic	12.50	6.21	2.01	$<.10$
Block design	16.54	6.30	2.63	$<.01$
Digit span	13.36	3.78	3.53	$<.002$
Total verbal score	179.82	60.94	2.95	$<.01$
Total performance score	214.89	70.14	3.06	$<.01$

a. Scales listed in the order in which the control group means are larger than the isolation group means (as in Table 4.7).

b. The F ratio is used here merely to test whether the two variances (variance for isolates $= \sigma_1^2$; variance for Controls $= \sigma_c^2$) differ; hence F is defined simply as: larger σ^2/ smaller σ^2.

c. Because the ratio of the two variances (F) is used as a test of their homogeneity rather than the usual test (controlled σ^2/ error σ^2), the tabulated P value is doubled.

Although the variance of the responses of the isolates tended to be greater than that of the controls for every type of data collected in this research, perhaps this tendency can best be seen in the WISC scales, as given in Table 4.3. For this test the variances of the isolates were greater than those of the controls on each of the 11 scales (cols. 1 and 2).

The scales in Table 4.3 are ordered in terms of the average relative performance of the two groups—that is, from greater to less superior average performance of the controls with respect to the isolates. With the WISC scales thus ordered, it is clear that the isolates tend to show relatively more dispersion in their responses to those scales on which they approximate or equal the performance of the controls (rho = .69; compare Tables 4.3, col. 3, and 4.7, col. 5). Or, in other words, the dispersion of the isolates on the WISC scales is greater than that of the controls, especially on the scales on which both groups do about equally well.

The differences between the variances of the isolates and controls on the WISC scales are summarized in Table 4.4, along with the corresponding dispersion differences on measures from several other types of data. According to this summary, on all 11 (or 100 per cent) of the available WISC scales the variances were greater for the isolates than for the controls (col. 2). Furthermore, over the 11 scales the average rela-

TABLE 4.4 *Comparison of isolates and urban controls on indices of response heterogeneity*

Data Source	Total Number of Scales 1	Per Cent $\sigma_i^2 > \sigma_c^2$ 2	Average[a] F ratio 3	Per Cent $\sigma_c^2 > \sigma_i^2$ 4	Average[a] F ratio 5
WISC[b]	11	100	2.06	—	—
Linguistic scales in tables (CP Scales only)[c,d]	17	64.7	1.57	35.3	1.12
Affect Scales (not in Tables)					
Explicit affect (CP)	4	100	1.39	—	—
Implicit affect (CP)	4	100	8.26	—	—
Rorschach Scales[e]	9	77.8	1.33	22.2	1.19
Children's Picture (Bear) Test	33	69.7	1.74	30.3	1.68

a. See footnotes b and c, Table 4.3.
b. See data in Table 4.3.
c. The F ratios for the Rorschach Scales (in Table 1, Haggard & von der Lippe, 1970) and the Linguistic Scales (in Tables 4.6, 4.8, 4.9, and 4.10) are based on transformed scores.
d. Comparable data are not available for the three Essay scales in Table 4.8.

tive dispersion (as indicated by the average F ratio) was about twice as great for the isolates as for the control children (col. 3).

For the 17 linguistic scales based on the Children's Picture Test (as cited in Tables 4.6, 4.8, 4.9, and 4.10), the isolates tended to show substantially more dispersion than the controls. Two findings support this conclusion: first, on about two-thirds of the scales the variances of the isolates were larger than those of the controls (col. 2) and, second, the average F ratio was appreciably greater when the variances of the isolates were greater (cols. 3 and 5).[18] The difference in the relative dispersion of the isolates and controls is, as one might expect, much more pronounced on some types of linguistic scales—such as words having to do with affects, especially affects that are implicit rather than openly expressed. Although it is not presumed that the linguistic scales are ideal measures of an individual's overt or covert affective life, these findings are compatible with other data on these children, some of which will be discussed under Hypothesis 2.

The Rorschach scales cited in Table 4.4 were based upon the content, location, and determinant scorings of the isolate and control children's responses to this test. For these data, the variances of the isolates were greater than those of the controls on seven of the nine scales and, as in the case of the linguistic scales, the average F ratio tended to be greater for the scales on which the isolates showed greater dispersion than for the two scales on which the controls showed more dispersion.

Finally, on a set of 33 scales from the Children's Picture Test, the isolates again showed greater dispersion than the control children on about two-thirds of the scales. For these scales, the variance appears to be closely related to the scale's content. For example, on all of the 14 scales having to do with the intrapsychic control or the overt expression of various types of affect, the isolates showed relatively more dispersion than the urban children. However, on 7 of the 10 scales on which the controls showed greater dispersion, the content had to do with social or interpersonal behavior; the remaining 3 scales had to do with sundry aspects of behavior that one would expect to be of greater relevance to urban living (such as time perspective).

With respect to Hypothesis 1, then, on most of the scales the isolates showed relatively more dispersion, heterogeneity, or variance than did the urban control children, regardless of the kind of data being compared. It is true, of course, that for one or both groups the relative dispersion on a scale frequently was related to the group's average perform-

18. Since the linguistic and Rorschach scales were transformed to logarithmic scores, the differences in the means given in cols. 3 and 5 of Table 4.4 would have been numerically much larger for these two sets of data if the original scores had not been transformed.

ance on the scale. This tendency was more pronounced on scales based upon the Children's Picture Test[19] than upon the WISC, where the isolates showed relatively more dispersion on those scales on which they approximated the performance of the urban controls. Consequently, it cannot be inferred that the relatively greater dispersion among the children reared on isolated farms, in relation to the urban children, is merely an artifact of the characteristics of the scales.

HYPOTHESIS 2: DIFFERENCES BETWEEN THE ISOLATE AND THE URBAN SAMPLES [20]

Granting negligible genetic differences between groups, it is generally assumed that any clear differences in character structure, etc., will be a function of how the individuals in the groups are socialized.[21] It is furthermore assumed that the child's parents, as the prime socializing agents, play the predominant role in shaping the child's behavior patterns and the corresponding intrapsychic structures that underlie his behavior. In line with these assumptions, Block's (1965) Q sort was given to samples of parents in the isolated and urban areas, in an attempt to identify differences in their child-rearing attitudes and practices.

Parents' child-rearing attitudes. It is clear from the Q-sort data that the parents of the isolates claim to hold to the "traditional" and parent-centered child-rearing attitudes and practices more than do the parents of the urban children, who appear to be more "modern" and child-centered. Although it is probably true that the differences cited in Table 4.5 are valid, they may not be quite so great as some of the P values suggest. For example, from observations of families on isolated farms, it is clear that the parents often are quite permissive in their treatment of their children, so that the differ-

19. Since the CP scales are based on clinical psychologists' ratings of the projective test protocols, it is possible that linguistic differences between the isolates and the controls (such as vocabulary and style) may have contaminated the ratings, since, because of these linguistic differences alone, it was practically impossible to disguise by any arbitrary coding system whether the child was in the isolate or urban samples.

20. The reported differences between the isolate and control groups can be taken at face value because the sample sizes are not unduly small or dissimilar (Ns of 40 and 28), and the variances (or sigmas) of the measures as discussed in this section are not sufficiently different for the two groups to tax unduly the "robustness" of the F test.

21. Although the dominant flow of emigration is from the farm or rural areas to the urban centers, there seems to be no clear-cut pattern in terms of whether "superior" or "inferior" persons move to the towns. Emigrés typically include, for example, the gifted and ambitious who want to get ahead in the world and the infirm or otherwise handicapped who must go to the city for treatment or specialized training, as well as the run-of-the-mill individuals who just choose to live in the city or must leave the farm because it is too small to support them. In addition, children of Lappish descent were excluded from the study in order to minimize genetic as well as cultural differences between the separate samples of children in the study.

TABLE 4.5   *Parents' child-rearing values and practices*[a]

| | Group Means | | |
	isolates ($N = 16$)	controls ($N = 26$)	Difference (P value)
More characteristic of isolated parents			
I sometimes tease and make fun of my child	4.19	1.96	.0001
I think children must learn early not to cry	3.81	2.23	.004
I sometimes talk about supernatural forces and beings in explaining things to my child	3.00	2.15	.03
More characteristic of control parents			
I usually take into account my child's preference in making plans for the family	4.00	5.23	.01
I believe it is very important for a child to play outside and get plenty of fresh air	5.19	6.42	.01
I make sure my child knows that I appreciate what he tries or accomplishes	4.88	6.12	.03

a. Based on a translation of Block's (1965) 91-item Child Rearing Practices Q sort, in which 1 = the "most undescriptive" and 7 = the "most descriptive" statement, in the parent's judgment. The statement means are an average of both the fathers' and mothers' statements from the isolated and control group families. In sorting the statements, the parents arranged the items in seven piles, with 13 items in each.

ences in Table 4.5 may be due in part to the verbal habits of the parents as well as to how they actually treat their children. There is little doubt that the urban parents are familiar with the "modern" views of how children should be reared, and their greater knowledge of these views also may be accompanied by somewhat less candor than is shown by the isolates.[22]

Although a number of clear differences exist in how the two groups of parents describe their child-rearing attitudes and practices, these data by themselves do not guarantee the existence of corresponding differences in practice. Evidence to date indicates that one can hardly be reassured with respect to the assumed correspondence between what parents say they do and feel with respect to their children and their actual behavior, either with respect to their remembrance of things past (Haggard, Brekstad, & Skard, 1960) or with respect to concurrent events (Zunich, 1962). Questions regarding the data in Table 4.5 are not, however, meant to suggest the absence of real and significant differences between the child-rearing attitudes and practices of the parents of the isolated and the urban children; rather, such questions indicate that more than the parents'

22. It may well be that, because of the relative paucity of their interpersonal experiences, the isolates have not developed some of the social skills of the urbanite, such as the telling of socially convenient "little white lies," as many urban parents have learned to do. Rather, the isolates appear more apt either to keep their silence or to tell the "unvarnished truth."

verbal reports are needed to establish and delineate any such differences. Unfortunately, it was not within the scope of this research to collect sufficient data of this sort.

In Tables 4.6 to 4.10 a variety of differences between the isolate and control children will be cited. In evaluating these differences it should be noted that all the children, ages 7 to 14, were attending the public elementary school, hence were exposed to both social and intellectual influences. It is not possible to measure the socializing effects of school attendance, which no doubt vary from child to child regardless of which group he is in. In some cases the role of the school as a socializing agent appears to be minimal. For example, a young (19 years old) isolate adult in a perceptual isolation experiment (Haggard, Ås, & Borgen, 1970) was asked to describe his childhood friends. He cited the three brothers on an adjacent farm. When asked about the other children in the boarding school (whom he had known over the 7-year span), he did not consider them to be "friends," but merely "acquaintances." In most cases, however, it appears that children from isolated farms adapt to school life sometime during the first school year, to the extent that they begin to form friendships and engage in group activities with the other children in the boarding school.

Phenomenological World. According to the findings in Table 4.6, one difference between the two groups of children is the hardly-unexpected finding that, in telling stories to the 10-card Children's Picture Test, the urban children mentioned animate objects relatively more frequently than the children reared on isolated farms. The animate objects were, of course, predominantly persons or person-surrogates (such as teddy bears), as depicted in the test stimuli.

If one assumes that the phenomenological world of the isolate is made up of inanimate objects relatively more than is the world of the controls, this assumption is compatible with the language of the isolates in describing how persons (or teddy bears) tended to respond to their world. From the analysis of the linguistic behavior of the children in the two groups, the isolates appear to engage relatively more in overt actions than in subjective thoughts and feelings, and to be more active—but at a more leisurely pace. When they do communicate or have contact with others, they appear to be relatively less verbal. Finally, the isolates tend to be less verbal in general in their response to the test stimuli. In other words, from these data the isolates appear to respond motorically to the world of physical reality relatively more than to the world of interpersonal-intrapsychic reality, with its verbal buttressing, which seems better to characterize the world of the urban controls.

In addition to any overall differences between the isolate and control

TABLE 4.6   *Some views of and relations to the phenomenological world*: A
linguistic analysis of the Children's Picture (Bear) Test

Variables	Correl. (r) with age[a]	Group Means isolates	controls	Diff. (P value)
Objects (animate/inanimate)[b]	.07	1.00	1.45	.008
Behavior (overt/covert)	−.25[*]	1.85	1.49	.0001
Actions (active passive)	−.19	2.46	2.16	.0008
Tempo (fast/slow)	.18	7.26	12.10	.02
Communication (verbal/non-verbal)	.02	1.46	1.94	.08
Total number of coded words	.36[**]	2985.48	3852.68	.004

a. [**] $= P \leqslant .01$; [*] $= P \leqslant .05$ for the total sample (including the semiisolates)
b. Within the "inanimate" category, the isolates spoke relatively more frequently than the controls about natural objects, as opposed to man-made objects ($P = .002$).

groups, it should be noted that on some of the scales the children's linguistic behavior changed appreciably between ages 7 and 14. Thus, for the scales in Table 4.6 the older children tended to describe relatively more covert behavior (that is, thoughts and emotional experiences) and to use more words in telling their stories than did the younger children, as indicated by the correlation coefficients of these two variables with age.[23] It is also of interest that on several of the scales these tendencies were more pronounced for the isolates than for the controls. For these two groups separately the correlations with age are, respectively: Objects (rs = .18, −.05), Tempo (rs = .43, .12), Communication (rs = .26, −.13), and Total number of coded words (rs = .42, .34). These correlations for the separate groups suggest that between ages 7 to 14 the isolates were catching up with their urban counterparts in various ways.

Cognitive or Intellectual Abilities. The 11 WISC scales in Table 4.7 are ordered according to the relative superiority of the controls' performance over that of the isolates (col. 5). From the univariate F tests and P values it can be seen that the controls did significantly better on only four of the scales (cols. 6 and 7), regardless of the extent to which the home environments of the isolates are "culturally disadvantaged" in terms of many of the skills required for superior performance on tests of this type. From this point of view, the four scales (Picture Arrangement, Coding, Comprehension, and Vocabulary) are all heavily saturated with one or both of two factors: experiences likely to occur in a town but not on an

23. In all the rs based on the total sample for the Children's Picture Test (N = 87) or for the Essay (N = 182), which indicate the relationship between the children's age and particular variables, the within-cells correlation coefficients were computed so that any differences among the isolate and semiisolate subgroup means were removed (see Bock & Haggard, 1968).

TABLE 4.7 WISC scores of isolates and controls

WISC Scales	r with Age[a]		Group Means		Mean Diff.	Difference	
	isolate 1	controls 2	isolates 3	controls 4	5	$F_{1/56df.}$ 6	P value 7
1. Picture arrangement[b]	.05	-.10	7.53	10.33	-2.80	20.90	.0001
2. Coding[b]	.19	-.25	8.40	10.41	-2.01	8.34	.006
3. Comprehension	.15	-.23	9.00	11.00	-2.00	8.13	.006
4. Vocabulary	.04	-.12	7.43	9.07	-1.67	13.37	.0006
5. Object assembly[b]	-.12	-.06	10.95	11.93	-.98	1.57	.22
6. Similarities	.05	-.04	9.28	10.22	-.94	2.18	.15
7. Picture completion[b]	-.03	-.12	11.45	12.00	-.55	.69	.41
8. Information[c]	.31	.33	9.68	10.15	-.47	.71	.40
9. Arithmetic	.02	-.28	10.37	10.70	-.33	.02	.90
10. Block design[b]	.11	-.09	12.62	12.85	-.23	.26	.61
11. Digit span	.27	-.03	10.10	9.37	.73	1.76	.19

a. Product-moment correlations with age (over the 7 to 14 year span) after group differences among the isolated subsamples (i.e., schools attended) are removed (See Bock & Haggard, 1968).

b. For all the performance scales (nos. 1, 2, 5, 7, 10), time is an important factor in scoring, and for scales 1, 2, 5, and 10, a "time bonus," is also given.

c. The correlation with age for the total sample is significant ($P = .008$) only for the information scale (see text).

isolated farm, and emphasis—that is, bonus scores for speedy performance on the separate items comprising the scale. As impressive at the fact
that the controls did much better on four of the scales is the fact that they
did not do very much better, if as well, on seven of the WISC scales, giv-
en the great differences in the variety of nonacademic cognitive and related experiences of the children in the two groups.

It has been clear for some time that individuals from homes where verbal skills are not emphasized tend to do poorly on tests such as the
WISC, which rely heavily on verbal facility (Davis, 1948; Haggard,
1953). But it is also clear that children from "culturally deprived" home
backgrounds can rather quickly acquire mastery of the symbol systems
necessary for successful performance on IQ tests (Haggard, 1954).

The data in Table 4.7 also suggest that different cognitive skills tend
to characterize the isolate and the urban children. More specifically, the
isolates appear to do relatively better when accurate perception, memory,
and nonfantasy reasoning is called for, whereas the control children appear to do relatively better when speed, verbal skills, and tests based on
familiarity with social norms are involved. Perhaps this is just another
way of saying that the children's cognitive styles tend to correspond to
the requirements of their life styles.

In connection with Table 4.6 it was noted that children from the isolated farms appear to be catching up with their urban counterparts during
the time they are in school. The same phenomenon is seen in the correlations with age on the 11 WISC scales (cols. 1 and 2 of Table 4.7). Thus,
on 9 of the 11 scales the isolates tend to improve in their performance
the longer they stay in school, whereas the urban children tend to lose
their initial advantage on all the scales except information. But the Information scale is unique, since it is the only one that correlates significantly
with age for the total sample. This correlation probably can be accounted
for by the fact that Norwegian children begin school at age seven, not five
or six as in the United States samples on which the test was standardized;
they then acquire the types of information sampled by this scale at a
more rapid rate than the children in the standardization samples.

In addition to the WISC, a variety of other cognitive measures were
obtained in an attempt to give a broad picture of the children's intellectual functioning. On some measures the difference between the isolates
and the controls was negligible; on others it was marked, usually with the
controls getting the higher scores. A comparison of the group means in
Table 4.8 shows no significant difference between the isolates and controls on the Children's Embedded Figures Test (Karp & Konstadt,
1963), or on the children's explanations of such natural phenomena as
why clouds move across the sky or why it rains in the summer and snows

TABLE 4.8   *Some non-WISC cognitive measures*

Variables	Data Source	Correl. (r) with Age[a]	Group Means isolates	controls	Diff. (P value)
General scales					
Embedded figures test	CEF	.44**	19.08	19.36	.50
Explanation of natural phenomena	SC	.59**	1.90	1.46	.72
Perceptual organization	R(S)	.33**	3.15	4.31	.0001
"Intelligence"	R(S)	.31*	3.80	4.72	.0004
Linguistic scales					
Cognitive styles:					
Enumerative/Integrative	CP(L)	−.09	30.77	28.68	.57
Certain/Uncertain	CP(L)	−.46**	2.90	2.36	.48
Concrete/Abstract	CP(L)	−.31**	5.35	4.83	.60
Logic/Fantasy	CP(L)	−.16	11.57	8.61	.78
Time references:					
Past	E(L)	−.19**	.004	.001	.0001
Present	E(L)	−.17*	.005	.010	.0001
Future	E(L)	−.14	.003	.003	.79

a. ** $= P \leqslant .01$; * $= P \leqslant .05$ for the total sample (including the semiisolates)

in the winter. The children's answers to such questions were scored (in a Piaget-like fashion) in terms of the extent to which they gave integrated naturalistic explanations.[24] However, on two ratings based on all 10 cards of the Rorschach test—Perceptual organization and "Intelligence" —the controls tended to receive substantially higher scores than the isolates, probably because verbal facility contributes to high scores on measures of this type.[25] Finally, as the children grew older they tended to receive higher scores on the four general scales of cognitive functioning in Table 4.8, as indicated by the correlations of these scales with age.

The four linguistic scales based on the Children's Picture Test did not show any significant differences between the isolates and controls, a finding that may contradict some urbanites' preconceptions regarding the isolates' mental abilities and processes. On two of the scales, however, the total group of children showed substantial correlations with age. The children tended to describe life situations with less certainty as they got

24. Hollos (1971), who administered a series of Piaget-type tests to young children from essentially comparable groups (that is, isolates and urban controls) from the same area of Norway, reported that the isolates tend to do at least as well as or better than the urban controls on such nonsocial cognitive tasks as conservation.

25. Whether one or two measures are involved may be open to some debate. Although these two scales are conceptually different, they are far from being independent statistically, since they correlate .82.

older,[26] and they also tended increasingly to use abstract terms in their descriptions.

The three linguistic scales that pertain to the children's use of verbs in the past, present, or future tense were taken from their Essay, "Myself in 15 Years." These data were used since, given the task of projecting themselves into the future, it was of interest to compare the isolates' and the controls' tendencies to refer instead to the past and to the present.[27] These data show that, although there was no difference in terms of the relative frequency of the isolates' and controls' references to the future —the assigned task—they differed clearly in their tendencies to refer to the past and to the present. The isolates seem far more rooted in their past, the controls more rooted in their present.

In summary it can be concluded that, considering the indices of cognitive functioning used in this research, the children's performance on such measures tends to correspond to the characteristics and requirements of the kinds of social and physical ecologies in which they are reared. Whereas the controls tend to excel on tasks involving knowledge of interpersonal (and especially verbal) skills, the isolates tend to do at least as well as the controls on tasks requiring accurate perception, knowledge, and mastery of the physical world.

Intrapsychic (Ego) Structures and Functions. As urbanites, the members of the research staff assumed that individuals reared in the peace and quiet of an isolated farm would probably develop a rich fantasy life. In general this assumption is false. The findings indicate that it is the child reared in the more stimulating urban setting who tends both to develop a flourishing fantasy life and also to use it to advantage in adapting to his more complex interpersonal world.

One can speculate as to why this should be so. Is it because, in the social microcosm of the isolated farm, the socialization process is relatively uncomplicated and can be accomplished essentially by the child's identification with and imitation of his elders? Or is it due to the greater role played by language in the socialization of the urban child, such as the parents' frequent generalizations regarding what one should or should not do, that aids the development of the internalized psychic structures that regulate his behavior? Or is it due to the greater number and variety of the urban child's social relationships, with the result that his feelings to-

26. If "life is simple for the simple," then as the children got older they tended increasingly to speak of the complexity of interpersonal situations. This tendency is also reflected in other linguistic scales not cited in the tables, such as a ratio of precise/diffuse descriptive terms, which correlates .39 ($P = .0004$) with age over the seven-year span.

27. The corresponding rs from the Children's Picture Test protocols for the use of past, present, and future tense verbs are .17, .03, and .22, respectively.

TABLE 4.9 *Some characteristic intrapsychic (ego) structures and functions*

Variables	Data Source	Correl. (r) with Age[a]	Group Means isolates	Group Means controls	Diff. (P value)
Ego resources					
Richness of fantasy life	CP(S)	.29**	2.83	3.46	.05
Ability to integrate conflict in fantasy	CP(S)	.50**	2.60	3.25	.002
Reliance on external controls	CP(S)	−.62**	3.18	2.93	.08
Affect and its expression					
Total positive affect	CP(S)	.30**	4.53	5.61	.20
Total negative affect	CP(S)	−.01	4.47	5.36	.30
Socialized expression of aggression	CP(S)	.46**	2.78	3.46	.01
Internalized societal norms					
"Morals" (internalized/corruptible	CP(L)	−.26*	5.61	1.51	.01
"Morals": internalized	CP(L)	−.15	.003	.001	.001
"Morals": corruptible	CP(L)	.25*	.001	.001	.24

a. ** $= P \leqslant .01$; * $= P \leqslant .05$ for the total sample (including the semiisolates)

ward the parents do not become so highly charged as to preclude his freedom to distance himself from them enough to develop relatively autonomous ego structures? Or is it due to combinations of such factors? The
data in Table 4.9 do not answer these questions. But the findings do indicate that the urban child tends to be better able to use his fantasy life as
an ego resource, whereas the isolate, at least in fantasy, tends to rely on
external agents (such as parents or fortuitous natural events) as the primary locus of control of his impulses, thoughts, and behaviors (see Haggard, 1964).

In their responses to the situations depicted in the Children's Picture
Test, the urban children tend to express feelings and emotions somewhat
more than the isolates, regardless of whether positive or negative affects
are involved. Another difference between the groups lies in the fact that
when anger, aggression, or related affects are involved, the urban children express them (more than the isolates) in ways that are socially acceptable. The children's responses to the situations on this projective test
appear to correspond to their behavior in everyday life.

In Table 4.9 the correlations between age and the ego resources and
affective expression measures are about what one would expect. As the
children grow older, they not only develop their fantasy life but also increasingly rely on inner resources (rather than external controls) in
adapting to representative life situations; and they increasingly express
such affects as anger or aggression indirectly, that is, in socialized ways.
These findings, along with the differences in the group means between
the isolates and the controls, suggest that from a developmental point of

view the isolates lag behind their urban counterparts in terms of the ego
mechanisms and modes of affective expression appropriate to urban living. This is not to say that, for any given age group, the ego development
of the isolate is not appropriate for living on an isolated farm or that at
the same age the urban child's ego development would be optimal for or
even adaptive to living in isolation.

The scales in Table 4.9 that pertain to the development of "morals"
(or the internalization of norms) appear to bear out what many adult
isolates say about life in the city—namely, that it corrupts the isolate. In
general the isolates, as children, express internalized norms far more frequently than the urban controls. According to the descriptions of the
scales given earlier, the isolates thus tend to use more words that indicate
internalized norms (such as ought, should) in their stories than do the
urban children.

The correlations between the morals scales and age for the isolate and
control groups separately raise some interesting questions. The correlation coefficients for the three scales in Table 4.9 for the isolates and controls are, respectively, morals: internalized/corruptible (rs = $-.44$,
.17); morals: internalized (rs = $-.33$, .09); and morals: corruptible
(rs = .36, $-.13$). The P values which correspond to these rs range
from .04 to .006 for the isolates, but only from .39 to .64 for the control
children.

Do these correlation coefficients indicate that the isolates tend to become morally corrupted by their experiences in the somewhat larger social group of the boarding school as they are faced (possibly for the first
time) with opportunities to lie to or to steal from nonfamily members?
Or do the isolates' shift in the usage of "internalized" to "corruptible"
terms as they grow older suggest a waning of the role that the parents'
presence had served as part of their ego—in the sense of controlling and
regulating their behavior—and that the isolates' progressive absence from
the parents reveals the relative weakness of their autonomous internalized
ego controls? Although the data from these scales do not answer such
questions, they do suggest that the ego controls developed by the isolates
during their preschool years apparently are not sufficient to enable them
to cope with certain intrapsychic and interpersonal conflicts that emerge
during the school years—at least, not so well as those of the urban children.

Interpersonal Relations. The parents' Q-sort data in Table 4.5 strongly
suggest that the parents of the isolates take a stance that shows much less
empathy with respect to the feelings and wishes of their children than the
urban parents show. With such differences, plus the fact that affective
expression in general tends to be appreciably less in the isolated than in

the urban families, it is not surprising that isolated children should feel less close emotionally, and more rejected by, their parents than do urban children.

The difference in how the children in the two groups refer to parental figures in their stories to the Children's Picture Test is of particular interest. The isolates tend to use the personal, rather than the impersonal, form in referring to parental figures far more frequently than do the control children. This difference between the two groups does not occur when the children mention nonparental figures such as siblings, grandparents, or peers. The fact that the isolates tend to use the personal form more often than the controls in their reference to parental figures might be interpreted to suggest that children reared on an isolated farm have a much closer and more dependent (or even semisymbiotic) relationship with their parents than do the urban children. However, these differences in linguistic usage might also be interpreted in other ways, such as mere stylistic differences between the isolate and urban subcultures that do not imply any psychological differences in the child-parent relationships among the families in the two groups.

Two lines of evidence suggest the interpretation that children reared on isolated farms, who by definition lack a variety of nonfamily adults to whom they can relate, tend to be far more emotionally dependent upon

TABLE 4.10 *Some characteristic differences in interpersonal relationships*

Variables	Data Source	Correl. (r) with Age[a]	Group Means isolates	controls	Diff. (P value)
Parental relationships					
Emotional closeness to parents	CP(S)	.64**	2.55	3.21	.005
Feels rejected by parents	CP(S)	−.22*	.70	.46	.02
Personal/Impersonal references:					
The mother figure	CP(L)	−.32**	6.25	1.64	.0001
The father figure	CP(L)	−.31**	7.05	1.36	.0001
All other "persons"[b]	CP(L)	.02	.55	.48	.71
General social relationships					
Humans in interaction	R(S)	.31*	1.50	1.69	.004
Contact with larger society	CP(S)	.20	4.60	5.43	.05
Social contact function	CP(S)	.66**	2.73	3.54	.005
Social contact function	R(S)	.36**	3.28	3.93	.002
Number of peers introduced into stories	CP(S)	.36**	4.20	6.36	.01
Amount of social play	CP(S)	.26*	4.43	5.89	.001
Amount of solitary play	CP(S)	−.04	5.20	4.82	.12

a. ** $= P \leqslant .01$; * $= P \leqslant .05$ for the total sample (including the semiisolates)

b. Since the 10 stimulus cards of the Children's Picture Test used teddy bears (not humans) as subjects in various situations, humans and teddy bears are coded as being "persons."

their parents than the urban children. One line of evidence stems from the fact that the discrepancy in the use of personal/impersonal terms applies only to parental figures, not to other persons or person-surrogates referred to by the children in their stories. The other line of evidence stems from the fact that the tendency to use a relatively large proportion of personal terms in referring to parental figures decreases with age, which indicates that the use of such terms is not a general characteristic of that subculture.

Do the negative correlations in Table 4.10 correspond to the tendency among many children of ages 7 to 14 to seek autonomy or emotional independence from their parents? If this interpretation of the negative *rs* be correct, it is interesting to compare these correlation coefficients for the two groups separately: the correlations for the isolates and the controls are, respectively, $-.29$ and $-.42$ for mother figures, and $-.18$ and $-.55$ for father figures. The P values that correspond to these *rs* range from .07 to .28 for the isolates and from .02 to .003 for the controls, suggesting that as the children in the two groups grow older the urban children tend to achieve emotional independence from their parents more than do the children in the isolated families. This interpretation of the *r*'s corresponds to the behavior of individuals in isolated families, insofar as the emotional dependence of isolates upon their parents tends to remain an important factor in the dynamics of the family as long as the parents live on or near the farm.

The measures in Table 4.10, which indicate the nature of the general social relationships of the isolate and control children, are in line with what one would expect to find. For example, on the Rorschach test the urban children perceived more "humans in interaction" and, on the Children's Picture Test they showed more "contact with the larger society" than the children from isolated farms. Furthermore, on each of these tests a scale called "social contact function" was rated on the basis of each test as a whole. This latter scale was defined in terms of the child's presumed ability to establish and maintain meaningful relationships with other persons. As expected, the urban children showed a higher level of social contact function than the isolates, although all the children showed an increase in this characteristic as they grew older. And in their stories to the Children's Picture Test, the urban children also introduced more peers and spoke more of social play, and less of solitary play, than did the social isolates. Again, the children's verbal responses to the tests correspond generally to their customary behavior which is, in turn, compatible with the kinds of lives they lead.

The Future. Finally, some note should be taken of how the children in the two groups appear to view their future lives, according to what they

said in writing the Essay, "Myself in 15 Years." In their essays the isolates frequently brought parents into their future, which is essentially a
continuation of the past and present. In contrast, the urban controls appear to assume that they will be mobile both geographically and socio-
economically, and already frequently have fixed upon glamorous and sophisticated occupations, which often are far beyond their current position
in life.[28] These differences between the two groups of children suggest
that the isolates are not prepared for any drastic changes in their life
styles, whereas the urban children not only are better prepared to adapt
to such changes but also seem eager to bring them about.

Concluding Remarks

Although the two subcultures upon which these samples are based have
much in common, such as a relatively common genetic and cultural heritage, they also differ in a number of important ways. Among the most
important differences are the extent to which the families, and the children in them, interact with other individuals, and the extent to which their
lives are thereby influenced directly by the matrix of forces in the society
at large. The most general conclusion to be drawn from the findings of
this research is that each subculture appears to foster the development of
various adaptation patterns in its members which are appropriate to, and
congruent with, the physical-cultural ecologies in which the members of
each subculture live and function.[29]

Two general hypotheses underlying the research were used to organize
the findings reported in this chapter. The first hypothesis has to do with
the proposition that children reared on isolated farms will tend to show
greater interfamily heterogeneity on various measures of how they view
their world and learn to function in it than will children from urban families. The findings reported in Tables 4.3 and 4.4 support this proposition.

A corollary of this proposition—namely, that members of isolated
families will show greater intrafamily homogeneity than members of urban families—was not tested. To test this notion would require the sys-

28. These findings are taken from an unpublished manuscript: "Degree of social
isolation and projections of the future self" by Anna L. von der Lippe & E. A. Haggard.
29. One may ask whether a town of approximately 7,000 persons is really "urban."
A town (or small city) of this size certainly is not urban in the sense that London,
New York, or Rome is. But from a behavioral and interpersonal point of view one
may assume that the town used in this research is "urban enough." That is, it may be
assumed that, in terms of some hypothetical threshold that has to do with the variety
and complexity of available interpersonal relationships and relative freedom from the
constraints of family pressures, the children reared in the town are "urban." The
many significant differences between the two samples support this assumption.

tematic study of a substantial number of both isolated and urban families, each with several siblings per family, a task that was beyond the scope of this research. However, from the observation of isolated families it often seemed that the members of each family tended to possess common ego-defense mechanisms and modes of affective and verbal communication with others. It is not difficult to rationalize such an impression: the single isolated family may not be able to tolerate the frictions that might develop were wide differences in character structure, defense mechanisms and modes of affective expression to exist among its members. The apparent phenomenon of the "common group ego" which seems to exist in such natural groups as the isolated family suggests that the members of small purposely-formed groups that are required to function for long periods under stress and/or in isolation from others should possess similar (or at least compatible) character structures.[30]

The second hypothesis has to do with the proposition that children reared on isolated farms will tend to differ in a variety of ways from children reared in urban families. The findings reported in Tables 4.5 to 4.10 and in the text support this proposition. Briefly, the reported differences have to do with how the children in the two families presumably are reared; how they tend to view their particular worlds and how they function in them; their cognitive structures and styles; their character structures (including various ego controls, mechanisms, and resources); how they relate to themselves, to their parents, to others such as peers, and to society at large; and with how they tend to view their future lives. In addition to the many reported differences between the isolates and the controls in terms of how they have learned to adapt to their separate worlds and ways of life, there are also differences in their ability to adapt to new and different situations, styles of life, and ways of behaving. By and large, the urban children, who have a broader experience base, appear to be better able to adapt to changes in their environmental context.[31]

The fundamental importance of the degree of congruence between the characteristics of the individual and of the environmental context in which he is required to function, as illustrated by the findings of the pres-

30. Wilkins (1967) made essentially the same point regarding the composition of small groups when he observed: "We should mention that dissimilarities in background can provide a breeding ground not only for misunderstanding but also for hostility, which is a very contagious emotion, especially in isolated settings" (p. 281).

31. For example, on a measure of the degree of ego control of impulse, "the urban children tended to be scored in the middle range (i.e., flexible, appropriate control), whereas the isolates more often were scored as showing under- or overcontrol ($P = .05$). This difference was not so clear in the younger group, ages 7 to 10 ($P = .25$), but was marked in the older group, ages 11 to 14 ($P = .005$)" (Haggard & von der Lippe, 1970, p. 483).

ent study and by the reactions of the isolates and controls to the perceptual isolation experiment, bears directly upon the basic concern of this book, namely, how men can best adapt to and function effectively in situations involving isolation and confinement. The adaptation of the individual, both in terms of his inner life and the effectiveness of his performance, cannot be considered apart from the parameters of his environmental context. Any review of instances in which urban individuals are placed in environmental settings involving short-term or extended isolation can be expected to show that the individual's adaptation patterns will be stressed or even break down if the isolation situation in question is sufficiently long, especially if it is very different from those to which that individual is accustomed (see Haggard, 1964; Zubek, 1969).

In a study of the characteristics of individuals who were able to function effectively under high stress in an enclosed space, data were collected on a group of enlisted men who had adapted successfully to life aboard a submarine under wartime conditions. From their responses to a modified Thematic Apperception Test, the men possessed a set of character traits that included "a superficial need for independence, with a deeper dependence on outside support; frequent unresolved conflict, ambivalence, or fluctuation of aggressive and sexual drives; and a reliance on external stimulation to determine their thoughts, which tend to be specific and concrete rather than elaborate and abstract" (Haggard, 1949c, p. 455). Although not all of these traits may be of crucial importance to the men aboard a submarine, and even though the men may disclaim some of the traits, it is not difficult to see how they at least do not interfere with successful adaptation to life aboard a submarine during wartime. In fact, to turn the person-situation paradigm around, one could state a priori from a thorough analysis of the objective and emotional demand characteristics of life aboard a submarine that the submariner should possess the sorts of traits revealed by the men's responses to the projective test.

One can take hope in the fact that man has shown himself able to adapt successfully to the most unlikely environmental situations, many of which no doubt have been more taxing to his resourcefulness than those discussed in this book. To achieve a reasonable degree of congruence between the characteristics of the individual and the potentially stressful or dangerous situations in which he must function will require selection of the individual in terms of more than just his technical skills or his apparent interests and abilities. It will require selection also in terms of his basic character structure, including his latent or unconscious needs, fantasies, and ego defenses. Because the range of situations involving isolation differ in so many ways, there is no one character structure or mode of adaption that is ideally suited for all situations. Rather, the individual's inner adjustment and his behavioral effectiveness rest on the congruence of his character structure and the parameters of his environmental context, and the flexibility of his adaptive mechanisms to accommodate to changes in it.

REFERENCES

Allwood, M. S. 1957. *Pioneer in sociology and social anthropology.* Oslo, Norway: Nordli.

Asimov, I. 1970. Toward the global village: The fourth revolution. *Saturday Review* October 24:17–20.

Aubert, V., Bratrein, H. D., Irgens-Jensen, O., Kjellberg, F., & Mathiesen, P. 1970. Isolation and integration: A community study in Northern Norway. Oslo: Institute for Social Research. (Mimeo.)

Block, J. 1965. The child-rearing practices report. Institute of Human Development, University of California, Berkeley. (Mimeo.)

Bock, R. D. 1973. *Multivariate statistical methods in behavioral research.* New York: McGraw-Hill. (In press.)

Bock, R. D., & Haggard, E. A. 1968. The use of multivariate analysis of variance in behavioral research. In *Handbook of measurement and assessment in behavioral sciences,* ed. D. K. Whitla, pp. 100–142. Reading, Mass.: Addison-Wesley.

Bronfenbrenner, U. 1968. Early deprivation in mammals: A cross-species analysis. In *Early experience and behavior,* ed. G. Newton and S. Levine, pp. 627–764. Springfield, Ill.: Charles C. Thomas.

Christiansen, R. T., ed. 1964. *Folktales of Norway.* Trans. P. S. Iverson. Chicago: University of Chicago Press.

Churchill, R. 1963. Out of this world! *Daily Mail* (London), May 20–24, 1963.

Davis, A. 1948. *Social class influence upon learning.* (The Inglis Lecture.) Cambridge, Mass.: Harvard University Press.

Erikson, E. H. 1950. *Childhood and society.* New York: Norton.

Fuller, J. J. 1967. Experiential deprivation and later behavior. *Science* 158:1645–52.

Garduk, E. L., & Haggard, E. A. 1972. Immediate effects on patients of psychoanalytic interpretations. *Psychological Issues* 7, monogr. 28.

Gerbner, G., Holsti, O. R., Krippendorff, K., Paisley, W. J., & Stone, P. J. 1969. *The analysis of communication content: Developments in scientific theories and computer techniques.* New York: Wiley.

Gottschalk, L.A., & Auerbach, A.H. 1966. *Methods of Research in Psychotherapy.* New York: Appleton-Century-Crofts.

Haggard, E. A. 1949a. On the application of analysis of variance to GSR data: I. The selection of an appropriate measure. *J. exp. Psychol.* 39:378–92.

——. 1949b. On the application of analysis of variance to GSR data: II. Some effects of the use of inappropriate measures. *J. exp. Psychol.* 39:861–67.

——. 1949c. Psychological causes and results of stress. In *Human factors in undersea warfare,* pp. 441–61. Washington, D. C.: National Research Council.

——. 1953. Techniques for the development of unbiased tests. Proceedings: 1952 Invitational Conference on Testing Problems, pp. 93–120, 125–28. Princeton, N. J.: Educational Testing Service.

———. 1954. Social-status and intelligence: An experimental study of certain cultural determinants of measured intelligence. *Gene. Psych. Mono.* 49:141–86.

———. 1964. Isolation and personality. In *Personality change,* ed. P. Worchel & D. Byrne, pp. 433–69. New York: Wiley.

Haggard, E. A., Ås, A., & Borgen, C. M. 1970. Social isolates and urbanites in perceptual isolation. *J. abnorm. Psychol.* 76:1–9.

Haggard, E. A. with Baittle, M. R., & Isaacs, K. S. 1968. The diagnostic interview as a data collection instrument. In *Studies in psychotherapy and behavioral change,* ed. M. J. Feldman, vol. 1, pp. 1–34. Research in individual psychotherapy. Buffalo, N.Y.: The State University of New York at Buffalo, University Publications.

Haggard, E. A., Brekstad, A., & Skard, A. G. 1960. On the reliability of the anamnestic interview. *J. abnorm. soc. Psychol.* 61:311–18.

Haggard, E. A., & von der Lippe, A. 1970. Isolated families in the mountains of Norway. In *The child in his family, vol. 1, International Yearbook of Child Psychiatry,* ed. E. J. Anthony and C. Koupernik, pp. 465–88. New York: Wiley.

Hamsun, K. 1921a. *Growth of the soil.* Trans. W. W. Worster. New York: Knopf.

———. 1921b. *Pan.* Trans. W. W. Worster. New York: Knopf.

Harlow, H. F., & Harlow, M. K. 1962. Social deprivation in monkeys. *Science Amer.* 207:136–44.

Hess, R. D. 1970. Social class and ethnic influences on socialization. In *Carmichael's manual of child psychology,* ed. P. H. Mussen, vol. 2, pp. 457–557. 3rd ed. New York: Wiley.

Hollos, M. C. 1971. *Community, family, and cognitive development in rural Norway.* Ph.D. dissertation, University of California, Berkeley. Ann Arbor, Mich.: University Microfilms, no. 71–15, 788.

Holsti, O. R., with Loomba, J. K., & North, R. C. 1968. Content analysis. In *The handbook of social psychology,* ed G. Lindzey and E. Aronson, vol. 2, pp. 596–692. Reading, Mass.: Addison-Wesley.

Inkeles, A. 1968. Society, social structure, and child socialization. In *Socialization and society,* ed. J. A. Clausen, pp. 73–129. Boston: Little, Brown.

Isaacs, K. S., & Haggard, E. A. 1966. Some methods used in the study of affect in psychotherapy. In *Methods of research in psychotherapy,* ed. L. A. Gottschalk and A. H. Auerbach, pp. 226–39. New York: Appleton-Century-Crofts.

Karp, S. A., & Konstadt, N. L. 1963. *Manual for the Children's Embedded Figures Test.* Brooklyn, N. Y.: Cognitive Tests.

Klopfer, B., Ainsworth, M. D., Klopfer, W. G., & Holt, R. R. 1954. *Developments in the Rorschach technique, Vol. 1: Technique and theory.* Yonkers-on-Hudson, N.Y.: World.

Lanneau, G., & Malrieu, P. 1957. Enquête sur l'éducation en milieu rural et en milieu urbain. *Enfance* 4:465–85.

LeVine, R. A. 1970. Cross-cultural study in child psychology. In *Carmichael's manual of child psychology,* ed. P. H. Mussen, vol. 2, pp. 559–612. 3rd ed. New York: Wiley.

Lewis, C. 1946. *Children of the Cumberland.* New York: Columbia University Press.

Munch, P. A. 1964. Culture and super-culture in a displaced community: Tristan da Cunha. *Ethnology* 3:369–76.

Palmer, F. H. 1969. Inferences to the socialization of the child from animal studies: A view from the bridge. In *Handbook of socialization theory and research*, ed. D. A. Goslin, pp. 25–55. Chicago: Rand McNally.

Patton, R. G., & Gardner, L. L. 1963. *Growth failure in maternal deprivation.* Springfield, Ill.: Charles C. Thomas.

Redfield, R. 1941. *The folk culture of Yucatan.* Chicago: University of Chicago Press.

———. 1955. *The little community.* Chicago: University of Chicago Press.

Ribble, M. 1943. *The rights of infants.* New York: Columbia University Press.

Sanford, F. H. 1942a. Speech and personality. *Psychol. Bull.* 39:811–45.

———. 1942b. Speech and personality: A comparative case study. *Charac. and Person.* 10:169–98.

Sklansky, M. A., Isaacs, K. S., Levitov, E. S., & Haggard, E. A. 1966. Verbal interaction and levels of meaning in psychotherapy. *Arch. gen. Psych.* 14:158–70.

Snedecor, G. W. 1946. *Statistical methods* 4th ed. Ames, Iowa: Iowa State College Press.

Spitz, R. A. 1945. Hospitalism: An inquiry into the genesis of psychiatric conditions in early childhood. In *The psychoanalytic study of the child,* ed. A. Freud, H. Hartmann, & E. Kris, vol. 1, pp. 53–74. New York: International Universities Press.

Spitz, R. A., & Cobliner, W. G. 1965. *The first year of life.* New York: International Universities Press.

Stone, P. J., Dunphy, D. C., Smith, M. S., & Ogilvie, D. M. 1966. *The general inquirer: A computer approach to content analysis in the behavioral sciences.* Cambridge: MIT Press.

Thompson, W. R., & Grusec, J. E. 1970. Studies of early experience. In *Carmichael's manual of child psychology,* ed. P. H. Mussen, vol. 1, pp. 565–654. 3rd ed. New York: Wiley.

Tiller, P. O. 1963. Isolation: Center and periphery. *The Scandinavian J. of Psych.* 4:90–96.

———. 1967. Growing up in rural periphery. Oslo, Norway: Institute for Social Research. (Mimeo.)

Undset, S. 1928. *The master of Hestviken: The axe.* Trans. A. G. Chater. New York: Knopf.

———. 1929a. *The master of Hestviken: The snake pit.* Trans. A. G. Chater. Knopf.

———. 1929b. *The master of Hestviken: In the wilderness.* Trans. A. G. Chater. Knopf.

Usandivaras, R. J., Grimson, W. R., Hammond, H., Issaharoff, E., & Romanos, D. 1967. The marbles test: A test for small groups. *Arch. gen. Psych.* 17:111–18.

Usandivaras, R. J., Romanos, D., Hammond, H., & Issaharoff, E. 1970. *Test de las bolitas: Grupo e imagen (manual).* Buenos Aires: Editorial Paidos.

Wechsler, D. 1949. *WISC Manual: Wechsler intelligence scale for children.* New York: The Psychological Corporation.

Welch, B. L. 1964. Psychophysiological response to the mean level of environmental stimulation: A theory of environmental integration. In *Symposium on medical aspects of stress in the military climate,* pp. 39–96. Washington, D.C.: Walter Reed Army Institute of Research, Walter Reed Army Medical Center.

Whitten, C. F., Pettit, M. G., & Fischhoff, J. 1970. Evidence that growth failure from maternal deprivation is secondary to undereating. In *Annual progress in child psychiatry and child development*, ed. S. Chess & A. Thomas, pp. 261–78. New York: Brunner-Mazel.

Wilkins, W. W. 1967. Group behavior in long-term isolation. In *Psychological stress*, ed. M. H. Appley & R. Trumbull, pp. 278–88. New York: Appleton-Century-Crofts.

Yarrow, L. J. 1964. Separation from parents during early childhood. In *Review of child development research*, ed. M. L. Hoffman & L. W. Hoffman, vol. 1, pp. 89–136. New York: Russell Sage Foundation.

Zajonc, R. B. 1969. *Animal social psychology: A reader of experimental studies*. New York: Wiley.

Zubek, J. P. ed. 1969. *Sensory deprivation: Fifteen years of research*. New York: Appleton-Century-Crofts.

Zunich, M. 1962. Relationship between maternal behavior and attitudes toward children. *J. genetic Psychol.* 100:155–65.

E. K. Eric Gunderson *is Head of the Epidemiology and Operational Psychiatry Division, Navy Medical Neuropsychiatric Research Unit, San Diego, and Adjunct Professor of Psychiatry at the University of California, San Diego. He received his Ph.D. in psychology from the University of California, Los Angeles, in 1953 after completing a Veterans Administration clinical internship. His research interests have included experimental treatment programs for Navy delinquents, basic and applied research concerned with human behavior in stressful environments, and the epidemiology and etiology of mental illness. He has served on consultant panels for the National Research Council concerned with long-duration space flight and human biology and medicine in polar regions. He edited* Physiological and Pyschological Research in Antarctica *and* Life Stress and Illness.

Gunderson *reviews psychological studies conducted in polar regions from 1956 through 1968. The development of individual performance criteria at U.S. Antarctic stations is presented in detail, and the predictive validities of a wide array of screening methods is evaluated. Typical adjustment problems and emotional reactions of individuals to the isolation of the long Antarctic night are described, and the many social tensions engendered by confined group living are noted. Gunderson also notes the complexity of the prediction problem and the high degree of specificity in predictor-criterion relationships, but demonstrates that important insights into group and individual behavior can be gained from research in this unusual and stressful environment.*

5

Individual Behavior in Confined or Isolated Groups

E. K. ERIC GUNDERSON

For the typical urban dweller from temperate zones living above the Arctic circle or on the Antarctic continent, the harsh climate and continuous darkness of the winter period impose severe restrictions on work and recreational activities. While certainly not all members of isolated groups find close, confined living monotonous, routine, and unrewarding, a large proportion of participants describe the environment in such terms. Prolonged isolation from the outside world, together with the inevitable confinement experienced during the winter months, may adversely affect emotional equilibrium, motivation, and effectiveness.

Little research has been done on psychological problems of living in the far north. Willis (1960) described psychological problems of Hudson Bay Company employees and government officials living in the Canadian Arctic. Sells (1965), by means of trained observers and interviewers, studied factors affecting morale at remote Air Force stations in Alaska and emphasized the great importance of leadership and organizational factors in maintaining morale and effective performance. In the present volume Sells has proposed a taxonomy of isolated microsocieties based upon similarities in group and environmental dimensions. From research conducted in another type of isolated group setting, Radloff and Helmreich (1968) reported many types of behavioral observations from the Sealab II experiment, which provided an excellent model for quasi-exper-

Report Number 71-12, supported by the Bureau of Medicine and Surgery, Department of the Navy, under Research Work Unit MF12.524.001-9003D. Opinions expressed are those of the author and are not to be construed as necessarily reflecting the official view or endorsement of the Department of the Navy.

imental field studies in the undersea environment. Research at Antarctic stations has provided a body of data relevant to many questions concerning the effects of confined living and individual and group behavior.

Psychological studies, sponsored by the Navy Bureau of Medicine and Surgery, were conducted at United States Antarctic stations during the International Geophysical Year (1957–58). Mullin and Connery (1959) interviewed and tested members of two winter parties in 1957–58, and Rohrer (1961) gathered interview observations concerning individual and group adjustment problems during 1958–59. Smith (1961) and Smith and Jones (1962) investigated selection methods for scientist participants in the International Geophysical Year (IGY), and Smith (1966) studied group structure and social relations during a dangerous Antarctic traverse. McGuire and Tolchin (1961) evaluated individual and group adjustment at South Pole Station in 1959, based upon psychological tests, diary observations, and medical records. Nardini, Herrmann, and Rasmussen (1962) evaluated the psychiatric screening program during and immediately after the IGY and concluded that psychiatric evaluations had been relatively successful in predicting Antarctic performance as indicated by leaders' ratings.

Law (1960) provided a summary of extensive experience with psychological problems in the Australian Antarctic program, and Palmai (1963a, 1963b) gathered extensive test and observation data at one Australian station. Palmai, in the difficult role of participant observer, noted a decline in morale and increases in group conflict and dispensary visits in the third quarter of the year.

Eilbert and Glaser (1959) studied the differences between U.S. Air Force enlisted personnel rated well-adjusted or poorly adjusted by immediate supervisors while serving at isolated Arctic bases. Well-adjusted subjects tended to describe themselves as conscientious and responsible individuals who accepted authority. The poorly adjusted group described themselves in other and less consistent terms. Poorly adjusted subjects were found to be more complaining and more fearful of the Arctic, to go to sick call more often, to have greater interpersonal problems, and to be no more than marginally concerned about their work, as compared with well-adjusted subjects.

Wright, Sisler, and Chylinski (1963) investigated personality characteristics associated with favorable adjustment to northern isolated living. The sample consisted of 197 civilian electronic technicians employed by the Bell Telephone Company to staff the Mid-Canada Defense Line. Many of these technicians manned outlying Doppler sites in groups of from two to eight men. Supervisor ratings defined high and low adjustment groups after one year of duty. A battery of personality tests, including the Minnesota Multiphasic Personality Inventory and Edwards Personal Preference Schedule, were given to the men prior to beginning their northern duty. The findings indicated that variables associated with antisocial behavior and psychotic tendencies were related to less efficient functioning in conditions of isolation.

In a second and more extensive study, using a larger, more heterogeneous, and unscreened sample, Wright et al. (1967) investigated personality characteristics associated with favorable work and social adaptation in isolated, semiisolated, and urban settings. Subjects completed the Minnesota Multiphasic Personality Inventory, Edwards Personal Preference Schedule, and Brainard Occupational Preference Inventory. Work performance and social adjustment were appraised by means of station supervisor ratings concurrently with the testing for the initial samples, and after one year of duty for the second isolated station group. Results were considered supportive of the findings of Eilbert, Glaser, and Hanes (1957), who had reported that most of the factors that were found to differentiate between the well-adjusted and poorly adjusted groups seemed to be relatively independent of the Arctic. The authors concluded that the particular combination of three psychological tests employed in the study would, however, be of limited value in the selection of candidates for northern service.

Owens (1966, 1967a, 1967b, 1968) has reported a series of psychological studies at Australian National Antarctic Research Expedition (ANARE) stations. These reports described the development of performance criteria and the relationships of personality and biographical variables to these criteria in wintering-over parties. The results of a factor analysis of station leaders' performance ratings closely resembled those obtained at U.S. stations by Gunderson and Nelson (1966). Relationships of personality attributes, as measured by the Leary Interpersonal Check List (ICL), and the performance criteria were analyzed; the *love* score on the ICL was related to an interpersonal criterion factor, while the ICL *dominance* score correlated with task and intrapersonal criterion dimensions. Based on their relationships with criterion measures, the following desirable personality attributes (ICL dimensions) for Antarctic service were identified: agreeableness, leadership, self-reliance, group cooperation, and openness. Undesirable qualities were: rigid defensiveness and dependence upon others for task direction.

In another study, Owens investigated a number of biographical variables as indicators of Antarctic adjustment. Age was not related to overall performance, but marital status was, suggesting that prolonged separation from family affected emotional adjustment. Occupational specialty, education, family stability, and birth order were unrelated to overall performance. Previous Antarctic experience was related to performance for radio operators and meteorological technicians, but not for scientists or maintenance personnel. Owens agreed with U.S. investigators that task or occupation moderated relationships between biographical characteristics and performance criteria.

Taylor (1969) reported on psychological data collected at New Zealand's Scott Base. By means of interview responses, members of two successive wintering parties indicated demographic and employment backgrounds, motives for volunteering, plans and accomplishments for the year, time perception, sleep disturbances and other adjustment problems, group relations, and suggestions for improved selection.

Three wintering parties were given the Cattell 16 Personality Factor Test and were compared with U.S. norms. These Antarctic groups appeared more reserved, shy, intelligent, trusting, self-sufficient, and controlled than the population at large.

Taylor (personal communication, 1970) compared a Scott Base group and a South Pole group tested by Shurley and his associates on the 16 Personality Factor scores before and after winter isolation. The South Pole men indicated a high degree of self-sufficiency, which the author attributed to the extreme degree of isolation and confinement experienced at South Pole. Taylor's studies are continuing at Scott Base and at the new five-man year-round station established at Lake Vanda in 1958.

A new research program on Antarctic groups was initiated at the Navy Medical Neuropsychiatric Research Unit, San Diego, in 1961 and 1962. Primary objectives were to evaluate the nature and degree of stress experienced in this environment, to develop viable performance measures, and to construct prediction equations from screening examination data to aid in future selection. Antarctic personnel are volunteers and generally spend a year at one of several stations. Groups in our studies varied in size from 8 to 36 men. Groups were composed of diverse occupational specialists needed to maintain the stations and to collect data in various scientific disciplines. Group membership was generally 60 per cent Navy personnel and 40 per cent civilian scientists and technicians. The most important sources of data were clinical examinations, military records, questionnaires, rating scales, sociometric instruments, station leaders' logs and diaries, debriefing interviews, and on-site visits. The remainder of this chapter will be concerned with the development of individual criterion measures for the Antarctic setting, and with the evaluation of various types of predictor information.

The Development of Individual Performance Criteria

The underlying assumptions and concepts that guided the construction of criterion measures for the Antarctic setting were largely derived from an examination of organizational goals and analysis of preliminary data available from the period of the International Geophysical Year (1957–58). Since 1959 the National Science Foundation has administered the Antarctic science program, and the Navy has provided logistic support, including construction and maintenance of stations, transportation of men, equipment, and supplies, support of field parties, and provision of communication, meteorological, and medical services. The objective of the U.S. Antarctic Research Program is to conduct basic research in a number of scientific disciplines, principally in the atmospheric and earth sciences and recently in biology as well. This program entails placing investigators and their instruments in the field to collect data and, at several sites, maintaining these field parties through the austral winter. The permanent interior stations are located in the most hostile environments inhabited by man. It seemed apparent from the outset that hard work, at times under extremely adverse conditions, would be required of participants in order to accomplish organizational objectives and perhaps to survive. Task performance then appeared unequivocally relevant to program goals. Preliminary data gathered during the IGY confirmed the importance of job performance in judgments of overall effectiveness.

It was soon recognized that measurement of task performance in this setting would be difficult. Each of the many occupational specialties represented at the small stations had quite different tasks to accomplish. Furthermore, it was impossible to know in advance how much work would be required in a given area or what disruptions might occur due to factors beyond the individual's control. One thing appeared certain; the only available source of information about an individual's work behavior was the station membership itself. It was decided that measurement of work performance could be best achieved in this type of intimate, closed community by seeking a concensus of leaders and group members.

A second area of behavior evaluation which assumed major importance in our early thinking was that of emotional health. The importance attributed to possible emotional problems arose largely from concern with the deleterious effects of long-term isolation and confinement and from the knowledge that the specialized skills of each group member were largely irreplaceable. During the IGY, the Navy Bureau of Medicine and Surgery was assigned responsibility for physical and psychiatric screening of all Antarctic personnel. Psychiatric evaluations were intended only to identify and disqualify potentially psychotic or seriously disturbed individuals. Within a population of healthy volunteers it was considered difficult, if not impossible, for examiners to differentiate individuals in terms of probable future adjustment in the Antarctic without having much more relevant information about environmental and social conditions.

Fortunately, cases of psychosis or severe neurosis have been extremely rare at Antarctic stations, so that severe psychopathology has not provided a meaningful criterion for differentiating individuals on emotional behavior. Minor emotional disturbances are quite prevalent, however, as indicated by self-report questionnaires and symptom check lists filled out by medical officers (Gunderson, 1963). In early studies, station members seemed capable of observing and reporting emotional distress in their associates, and, indeed, there was no practical way for an observer outside the station to monitor an individual's emotional behavior.

Many minor annoyances and frustrations are to be expected in the Antarctic environment. Because of the extreme cold and required heavy clothing, outdoor work is slow and difficult. Equipment breakdowns are frequent, and spare parts may not be available. Water is carefully rationed and, generally, only one shower each week or 10 days is permitted. Clothing is washed infrequently. Water pipes and drains often freeze. Crowded living and working spaces make privacy difficult. Ham radio contacts with families and loved ones may be disrupted by communications blackouts for days or even weeks at a time. In short, the direct and indirect restrictions imposed by the harsh environment tend to make even simple daily tasks and activities slow, uncertain, and generally difficult.

As indicated previously, minor emotional problems are not uncommon during the winter months. Stress and tension may arise from or be expressed in incidents of interpersonal friction, some of which seem to be triggered by trivial events, as illustrated by the following excerpts from station leaders' logs:

One civilian's coffee cup had become so dirty that I threw it in the garbage can. We had soup for evening meal and he used his cup. After finishing his soup he hung his cup in the rack without cleaning it. About an hour later he found the cup and he wanted to know why I had put it where I had. I told him why whereupon he lost his temper and started acting like a child.

Morale not very good. C——who has generally been in good spirits was antagonized by the scientific leader over an inconsequential matter. Later C—— after drinking, finally departed for the summer camp because "he couldn't stand anybody any longer."

Some degree of emotional regression is suggested by occasional temperamental displays:

Cook's at it again. He's moody, definitely emotionally immature. Threw a lemon pie and cookies all over the galley the other day, then went to his room for a couple of days and wouldn't come out.

General lethargy and malaise tend to appear after several months of winter confinement:

One thing to mention about the duty here and that has been trouble in sleeping. Personnel can work hard all day and then when they go to bed cannot sleep. This has been happening a lot within the past month. I also catch myself and all others sitting down and staring at the bulkhead and not thinking about anything. I guess this must have something to do with being inside the trailer so long and seeing the same people day in and day out and also the darkness outside.

Everyone seems "grouchy"—no clear reason. Probably antarcticitis catching up.

There just isn't enough work to keep everyone busy now. It's becoming ironic that the less work there is to do, the harder it is to get it done.

The above excerpts are intended to illustrate the emotional and motivational problems that may arise during prolonged confinement; the examples given tend to be extreme rather than typical. Such reactions when they occur are readily observable by other station members.

The importance of the third major area of behavior, social compatibility or likability, was not clearly recognized in the beginning phases of the Antarctic research program. Incomplete sociometric data gathered from the IGY period indicated that popularity or likability was substantially correlated with overall performance evaluations. Later studies replicated and confirmed this relationship and psychiatric debriefings as well as observer reports tended to emphasize the importance of social relationships in overall adjustment.

The wide range of skill requirements in Antarctic groups results in heterogeneity in social and educational backgrounds, interests, and values. The individual's adjustment problems are complicated by these differences, and interpersonal conflicts are more likely where viewpoints and attitudes are so varied. The Navy men tend to have common traditions and expectations, which are generally not shared by the civilian personnel. Tensions and overt conflicts may arise around issues of housekeeping chores, cleanliness, group standards, rules of conduct, and so forth.

A general concept of effective individual performance evolved from these earlier studies which included three essential components: task performance, emotional stability, and social compatibility. Factor analysis of behavior trait ratings by supervisors and peer nominations for "best friend" or "easy to get along with" resulted in a rotated factor structure, so that three pairs of items emerged as salient dimensions: (1) emotional control and acceptance of authority, (2) industriousness and achievement motivation, and (3) likability (from supervisor ratings) and friendship-compatibility (from peer nominations). These factors matched closely the three behavior components or concepts that had been postulated to account for overall effective performance at small Antarctic stations.

Scores representing the three clusters were obtained by averaging rankings (converted to T scores) on the two items in each cluster. The relationships between the three factors and a composite criterion representing the most meaningful general index of performance (rankings of "select to serve with again in the Antarctic") were determined by means of multiple regression. The multiple correlation between the three behavior clusters and the general criterion was .89. The importance of the social compatibility cluster was apparent when multiple correlations were obtained between various combinations of clusters and the criterion. By removing the social compatibility cluster, the value of R was reduced to .75. The three factors tended to have the same multiple correlation relationship with the overall criterion for various subgroups of personnel.

Overall performance variance then could be accounted for by three behavior trait clusters. The addition of other characteristics to these clusters did not improve the multiple correlation. Our initial efforts, then, to measure separate aspects or components of desired performance appeared to be successful in identifying a parsimonious and general set of factors. The next phase of the research involved collecting new criterion data over several years by means of rating and sociometric instruments. Two station leaders, the Officer in Charge and the Scientific Leader, independently filled out 10 behavior trait ratings on 8-point scales. Performance evaluations were made twice during the winter period, in March and September. A sociometric form was administered to all station members in September. Three of these items were utilized in deriving the three behavior factor scores. The supervisor trait items and sociometric items that contributed to each of the behavior factor scores are shown in Table 5.1.

Group members at each station were ranked and assigned T scores in terms of average supervisor ratings and number of peer nominations in each of the behavior areas. T scores are utilized in order to control for station size and differences in supervisors' rating distributions.

Measures of the three trait areas by the two methods (supervisor ratings and peer nominations) were intercorrelated in several samples. Results are summarized in Table 5.2. All intercorrelations of trait areas within and between methods are shown. These data can be meaningfully

TABLE 5.1 *Supervisor tract items and sociometric items contributing to behavior factor scores*

Behavior Factor	Supervisor Items	Peer Items
Emotion	Emotional control; acceptance of authority	Calm and even tempered
Task	Industriousness; Motivation; proficiency	Industrious and hard working
Social	Likability; cheerfulness; considerate of others	Friendly and popular

TABLE 5.2   *Intercorrelations for different methods of measuring performance*

	E_s	T_s	S_s	E_p	T_p	S_p
I. Supervisor ($N = 128$)						
Emotion$_s$						
Task$_s$	.43					
Social$_s$	.65	.41				
Peer ($N = 139$)						
Emotion$_p$	.54	.32	.41			
Task$_p$	.37	.54	.31	.58		
Social$_p$	.38	.37	.49	.61	.56	
II. Supervisor ($N = 110$)						
Emotion$_s$						
Task$_s$	.40					
Social$_s$	.63	.41				
Peer ($N = 105$)						
Emotion$_p$	.62	.36	.51			
Task$_p$	.41	.55	.28	.48		
Social$_p$	.48	.25	.54	.53	.56	
III. Supervisor ($N = 100$)						
Emotion$_s$						
Task$_s$	.46					
Social$_s$	.50	.45				
Peer ($N = 109$)						
Emotion$_p$	.65	.34	.37			
Task$_p$	.38	.67	.35	.49		
Social$_p$	.35	.20	.47	.63	.42	

interpreted in terms of the Campbell and Fiske (1959) model for the evaluation of convergent and discriminant validities. This method of analysis is appropriate where more than one trait area is measured by more than one method. Convergent validity is demonstrated when different methods of measuring the same trait areas significantly agree. Discriminant validity requires that correlations between measures of the same trait areas by different methods should exceed correlations between different trait areas (1) across different methods, and (2) within the same method. The latter requirement is a rigorous condition that has seldom been met in studies of behavior traits.

Convergent validities are underlined in the diagonals of the crossmethods correlations in Table 5.2. All coefficients are highly significant ($p < .001$) and provide substantial evidence for the presence of convergent validity.

Discriminant validity was determined by averaging all correlations of each trait area with other trait areas both across different methods and within the same method. A comparison of average validities for each trait area over all samples and average correlations with other trait areas are

TABLE 5.3   *Discriminant validities of criterion components*

	Mean Validities[a]	Mean Correlations with Other Areas[b]
Emotion	60	47
Task	59	46
Social	50	46

a. Values are averaged over all samples.

b. Correlations with other trait areas are averaged both across methods and within methods.

shown in Table 5.3. Discriminant validities were indicated by the fact that average validities in each case exceeded average correlations with other trait areas. Further details concerning these relationships are available in Gunderson and Nelson (1966) and Gunderson and Ryman (1970).

The overall results were most striking because of the stability or consistency in relationships from one sample to another. The development of these criteria represented a major step toward developing useful predictions of performance in future Antarctic groups.

A problem common to many studies in the trait domain was reflected in the relatively high correlation between the emotion and social behavior areas. The fact that emotional and social behavior tend to be closely associated makes it difficult to achieve sharper delineations in measurement of these concepts.

The behavior factors derived in this study and those reported by Borgatta (1964) labeled emotionality, sociability, and task-interest or responsibility, appear to be equivalent concepts.

In a recent study an attempt was made to estimate the relative importance of the three behavior factors in overall performance as perceived by two groups of Navy enlisted men (Construction or Seabee personnel and Technical-Administrative personnel) and the civilian scientists (Doll & Gunderson, 1970). Peer nominations on the emotion, task, and social items were correlated with peer nominations for a general criterion item, "If you were given the task of selecting men to winter over at a small station, which men from this station would you choose first?" A control variable, peer nominations on friendship, was included in the analysis. The rank order of importance of these behavior traits as indicated by the magnitude of their correlations with the overall criterion was: (1) emotional stability, (2) task performance, (3) social compatibility, and (4) friendship for both the Navy Seabee group and the Navy Technical-Administrative group. For the civilian group the rank ordering was (1) social compatibility, (2) emotional stability, (3) task performance, and

(4) friendship. Social compatibility was judged to be most important for civilians' adjustment. Generally, there was agreement among all groups in stressing a personality-oriented trait rather than task-oriented behavior.

Prediction of Individual Performance

With the development of a stable system of performance evaluations, predictive studies, using a variety of personnel assessment methods, became possible. Prediction of personnel performance in an industrial or military setting tends to be difficult even within stable and well-defined organizational structures. Whether actuarial or clinical methods are employed, predictive validities tend to be low and crossvalidities often are insignificant. The need for valid personnel selection devices remains, however, and the development of useful selection models is an urgent concern in the Antarctic setting as well as in other, less extreme environments. In any personnel assessment program the need to consider and integrate many kinds of information about an individual is apparent, as is the need to define as clearly as possible the specific criterion behaviors to be predicted.

Many studies have demonstrated that the validities of predictors tend to vary over types of criteria and groups to be predicted. In an attempt to obtain an overview of the Antarctic selection problem, a study was conducted of 240 winter-over personnel to evaluate the relative predictability of three Antarctic occupational groups (Navy Seabees, Technical-Administrative, and Scientists) on five performance measures (Emotion, Task, Social, Leader, and Overall), utilizing a variety of predictor sources (Doll, Gunderson, & Ryman, 1969). Specificity of predictors for the various groups and criteria was demonstrated, and it was seen that this type of analysis could aid in the early identification of areas of information which could contribute to meaningful prediction of performance in the Antarctic setting.

A more thorough analysis of a similar type was undertaken with larger samples of the same three occupational groups. A large number of screening information items were grouped into five predictor sources. The *Personal History and Hobbies* category included 21 variables derived from factual information pertaining to family background, religious interests, marital status, education, delinquency history, and military status and experience. In addition, this category contained attitudes toward a list of 19 hobbies and recreational activities. *Opinion Survey* items included 76 attitude and personality self-description statements rated on 6-point scales ("strongly agree" to "strongly disagree"). The *FIRO-B Inventory* (Schutz, 1958) contained 54 items referring to basic social needs. The *Friend Description* items were 50 personality trait adjectives

TABLE 5.4 *Numbers of significant predictor source, occupational group, and criterion*

Group and Criterion	Personal History and Hobbies	Opinion Survey Items	FIRO-B Items	Friend Description Items	Psychiatric Ratings	Row Total
Seabee						
Emotion	8	6	1			15
Task		6		2	4	12
Social	2	11	1	1		15
Leadership	8	12		3	10	33
Technical						
Emotion	4	3	3	3		13
Task	4		2	2	3	11
Social	4	4	2	3	1	14
Leadership	2		3		3	8
Scientists						
Emotion	7	2	11	4	3	27
Task	10	2	10	2		24
Social	9	4	14	6	2	35
Leadership	6	4	8	2	1	21

that were rated on 8-point scales in terms of degree of preference for these traits in close friends. The *Psychiatric Evaluations* were combined ratings by psychologists and psychiatrists on 16 personality traits and adjustment predictions.

The results of the analysis are summarized in Table 5.4. The numbers in the table represent the numbers of items that were significantly correlated ($p < .05$) with each criterion for each group. Certain screening sources contributed many more significant items than did others for predicting performance in specific occupational groups. For example, *Opinion Survey* items were far more relevant for predicting adjustment among Navy Seabee (construction) personnel than among the civilian scientists, while for the *FIRO-B* test items the opposite was true. Psychiatric evaluations were highly relevant for only one criterion and for one group, that is, leadership ability in the Seabee group. The *Friend Description* items, which were designed to predict dyadic friendship choices rather than individual performance, nevertheless made minor contributions, particularly in the scientist group. Personal history data and hobby interests provided the greatest overall contribution to the prediction of adjustment. Clinical evaluations appeared to make the least overall contribution and made an important one only in the prediction of leadership for the Seabee group.

The row totals in the table indicated the relative predictability of the various group-criterion combinations. Social adjustment among the scientists and leadership ability among the Seabee personnel were most predictable, while task motivation was least predictable in both of the Navy groups. The analysis provided an example of the complexity of performance prediction in natural isolated groups and demonstrated a high degree of specificity in the relevance of various types of personnel information for different criteria and for different job roles. Ghiselli (1963) and others have demonstrated similar specificity in different types of groups and situations. This method appears useful for providing an overview of the prediction problem and for identifying the types of predictor variables that are most relevant to the performance criteria. The percentage of predictors that proved to be significant for the various screening sources tended to be low, suggesting that the prediction task in this setting is not an easy one.

In this section some of the specific findings with respect to significant predictors of Antarctic adjustment will be considered. This survey of performance indicators will necessarily be highly selective because of space limitations, but can perhaps serve to illustrate major trends.

The predictive value of past military performance records of Navy enlisted men was examined in order to test the proposition that past performance was a significant predictor of future performance in a new and different setting. In an earlier study, it was estabished that Navy volunteers for Antarctic service had better performance records than did other Navy men of comparable experience (Gunderson, 1964). Performance marks are semiannual ratings by superiors on scales ranging from 1.0 to 4.0 in five trait areas: professional performance, military behavior, leadership and supervisory ability, military appearance, and adaptability. For purposes of this analysis, the averages of the six most recent sets of performance marks were utilized. Initially it appeared that past performance marks were significantly correlated with Antarctic performance criteria, but when pay grade (rank) was controlled by correlating performance marks with Antarctic adjustment criteria separately for several pay grade levels, past performance records did not significantly predict Antarctic performance. Further analyses are continuing to determine if certain subgroups of Navy personnel are more predictable from past performance records than the Navy group as a whole.

Previous Antarctic experience might be expected to be a favorable indicator for wintering-over at small stations. Seabees who had previous summer season or wintering-over experience at the large McMurdo base tended to score lower on the Emotion and Social criteria than did others. Past Antarctic experience generally had little predictive value for future expeditions.

Life history data generally are viewed as an important source of information from which to predict future behavior. Biographical questionnaires have been part of the psychiatric screening program for Antarctic personnel since its inception. An earlier report (Gunderson & Nelson, 1965) described the relationships between the personal history variables and performance criteria for a 5-year sample of small station Navy personnel. Subsequent data have been gathered on personal history-criterion relationships for three occupational groups over a 4-year period. Some of these results are summarized below.

Pay grade or rank clearly discriminated Antarctic performance for the Navy Seabee and Technical groups. Nonrated Seabees (those not yet petty officers) performed relatively poorly as a group, while second class and first class petty officers performed well. Comparable results were evident on the closely related variable, years of occupational experience. Navy men with more than 7 years of experience generally performed well. Relatively inexperienced Seabees and civilians (2 or 3 years or less of occupational experience) did not perform as effectively.

Religious preferences were related to performance in that Seabees who were Lutherans or Baptists did exceptionally well, as did civilians who were Lutherans. Civilians who professed no religious preference tended to do poorly on Task, Social, and Overall criteria. Frequency of worship was a discriminating variable in that civilians who reported attending worship once or twice a month performed well, while Navy Technical personnel who reported not attending worship at all tended to do relatively poorly.

Size of family was a significant variable; Technical personnel from small families (only child or one sibling) performed below average, while civilians with two siblings tended to do less well than others. Navy Technical personnel who were middle children (neither oldest nor youngest) tended to do exceptionally well on all criteria. Urban-rural residence had different implications for the two Navy groups; Seabees who had lived on farms tended to do well on the Task criterion, while Navy Technical personnel from large cities did exceptionally well.

The relationship of father's education to performance was quite striking, in that civilians who had fathers with little education performed well in the Antarctic. Navy men whose fathers had completed high school did not perform well, and civilians whose fathers were college graduates did poorly on the Overall and Social criteria. Seabees whose mothers had relatively little education did well, while civilians whose mothers were college graduates did less well than other civilians. Navy men whose fathers were in skilled occupations performed well, while civilians whose fathers were in professional occupations were less effective. Navy men from southern states tended to perform relatively poorly in the Antarctic environment.

Civilians and Navy men who professed interests in many hobbies tended to do poorly at small Antarctic stations. This finding has been a consistent one over the years and leaves little doubt that persons with needs for high activity levels have difficulty in adjusting to Antarctic confinement. In an earlier study (Gunderson, Nelson, & Orvick, 1963), high activity needs were positively related to performance at a large Antarctic base (McMurdo) where opportunities for activity were far less restricted.

The FIRO-B scales were included in the test battery primarily for studies of mutual attraction. The relationship of these measures of social needs to popularity or likability in Antarctic groups was of some interest, however, and it seemed plausible that these scales might contribute to prediction of social adjustment. The six FIRO-B scales—Expressed and Wanted Inclusion, Expressed and Wanted Control, Expressed and Wanted Affection—were correlated with the Emotion, Task, Social, Leader, and Overall criteria. Results for the civilian personnel are shown in Table 5.5. The correlations for Navy personnel generally were not significant.

It is first notable that virtually all of the correlations were negative; several were significant ($p < .05$). Generally, it appeared that high scores on any of the FIRO-B dimensions had unfavorable implications for Antarctic adjustment among civilians. High Expressed Affection scores were negatively related to all three behavior criteria. The contents of the Expressed Inclusion and Expressed Affection scales strongly sug-

TABLE 5.5   *Correlations between FIRO-B scales and performance criteria for scientists*

FIRO-B Scales	Criteria			
	emotion	task	social	overall
Expressed inclusion	−12	−25[a]	−18	−20[a]
Wanted inclusion	−11	−10	−17	−11
Expressed control	−12	−01	−11	−05
Wanted control	−25[a]	−16	−16	−20[a]
Expressed affection	−20[a]	−20[a]	−20[a]	−17
Wanted affection	−10	−10	00	−05

a. $p < .05$

gested an underlying dimension of extroversion; evidence from psychiatric debriefings as well as clinical examiners' ratings suggested that persistent extrovertive behavior in members of Antarctic groups was atypical and unpopular. The FIRO-B Wanted Control scale appears to be closely linked to strong dependency needs, which would explain the unpopularity of individuals high on this trait. The FIRO-B relationships tended to verify participant observers' impressions concerning positively valued attributes in Antarctic scientists: mild introversion and self-sufficiency.

Examination of specific Opinion Survey items that correlated significantly with performance criteria yielded further impressions of valued Antarctic behavior traits. The item, "I like to keep my car clean and polished all the time," had high negative correlations with all criteria for the civilian group, suggesting a strong dislike of excessive neatness or compulsive cleanliness in successful civilians. The issue of neatness and cleanliness is often a source of controversy between Navy men and civilians at Antarctic stations. The other significant Opinion Survey items for civilians tended to be heterogeneous, but suggested introversion as well as lack of orderliness. The "absent-minded professor" is not an acceptable image to the successful Antarctic scientist.

The successful Technical-Administrative Navy men described themselves as both fearful and critical of authority, intolerant of change and of persons with different beliefs, and suspicious.

Successful Seabees saw themselves as firm in basic beliefs but tolerant of different viewpoints, persevering but not compulsive, trusting but not sympathetic or helpful, and conforming.

These varied and perhaps surprising partial personality composites of the "ideal Antarctic man" should dispel any notions that prediction of adjustment in this setting is a simple exercise. The differences between the Navy Seabee and Technical-Administrative groups appeared consistent with their respective roles at Antarctic stations. Seabees tended to be interdependent in their jobs and gregarious socially, while radio operators and electronics technicians more often were isolates within the station group.

Finally, the contribution of clinical evaluations to the prediction of Antarctic performance has been of continuing interest over the years. As indicated previously, clinical ratings, based upon semistructured interviews by psychologists and psychiatrists, were an excellent source of information for predicting leadership ability in Navy men. Averaged independent ratings by psychologists and psychiatrists on Emotional Control $(r = .30)$, Flexible $(.24)$, Acts Out $(-.21)$, Persevering $(.21)$, Acceptance by Peers $(.26)$, Acceptance by Supervisors $(.26)$, Overall Adjustment $(.30)$, and Alert $(.19)$ were significantly related to leadership scores among Seabees. Similar trait items were significantly correlated with the leadership criterion in the Technical-Administrative group, and the combination of the variables Pay Grade $(r = .44)$, Conforming $(.34)$, and Emotional Control $(.26)$ yielded a multiple correlation of .60 with the Leader criterion for this group. Clinical ratings generally have not been important predictors of other criteria, but specific traits have contributed uniquely to prediction equations for several criterion-group combinations.

Multiple regression equations have been developed for each occupational group and each criterion, utilizing those screening items from various sources which contributed uniquely to prediction. The validities of these equations are continuously being evaluated and improved.

Future Research

The Antarctic provides a useful setting for the study of behavior under conditions of long-term confinement. A large data file of varied personnel assessments has been assembled, and continued data acquisition is planned. The problems, limitations, and advantages of behavior measurement in this setting have been well-delineated during several years of research in Antarctica. A major objective has been to establish a viable system for evaluating individual performance, encompassing a wide array of behavioral indices from multiple sources and emphasizing replication and generalization of findings. Another objective, only partially realized at this time, is to conceptually integrate and understand the many interrelated factors that account for behavior variance in this setting.

Problem areas in human biology and psychology that could be investigated in polar regions in the future with great benefit to medical and behavioral science have been outlined recently in "Polar Research: A Survey," published by the Committee on Polar Research of the National Academy of Sciences (Gould, 1970). Shurley and his associates (1970) initiated a new era in Antarctic biomedical research by establishing a sophisticated sleep laboratory at the South Pole. This comprehensive psychophysiological research program established a valuable framework for future quantitative studies of sleep and activity schedules and physiological functions at high altitude, which can be related to behavioral and environmental data and provide the basis for systematic ecological and psychobiological studies. Other aspects of current research on adaptation of individuals and groups in the Antarctic, including group composition and effectiveness (Gunderson, 1968a), leisure activities (Doll & Gunderson, 1969), job motivation and satisfaction (Ryman & Gunderson, 1970), and physical and mental health (Gunderson, 1968b), have been detailed elsewhere. These studies, which relate directly and indirectly to individual performance in many ways, should contribute to better understanding of man's adaptation to isolation and confinement.

REFERENCES

Borgatta, E. F. 1964. The structure of personality characteristics. *Behav. Sci.* 9:8–17.
Campbell, D. T., & Fiske, D. W. 1959. Convergent and discriminant validation by the multitrait-multimethod matrix. *Psychol. Bull.* 56:81–105.
Doll, R. E., & Gunderson, E. K. E. 1969. Hobby interest and leisure activity behavior among station members in Antarctica. Unit rept. 69–31, September, Navy Medical Neuropsychiatric Research Unit, San Diego, Calif.
———. 1970. The relative importance of selected behavioral characteristics of group members in an extreme environment. *J. Psychol.* 75:231–37.
Doll, R. E., Gunderson, E. K. E., & Ryman, D. H. 1969. Relative predictability of occupational groups and performance criteria in an extreme environment. *J. clin. Psychol.* 25:399–402.
Eilbert, L. R. & Glaser, R. 1959. Differences between well and poorly adjusted groups in an isolated environment. *J. appl. Psychol.* 43:271–74.
Eilbert, L. R., Glaser, R., & Hanes, R. M. 1957. Research on the feasibility of selection of personnel for duty at isolated stations. AFPRTR 57-4, ASTIA Document No. 134241, NSAF Personnel Training and Research Center, Lackland AFB Tex.
Ghiselli, E. E. 1963. Moderating effects and differential reliability and validity. *J. appl. Psychol.* 47:81–86.
Gould, L. M. (Chairman, Committee on Polar Research). 1970. *Polar research: A survey.* Washington, D.C., National Academy of Sciences.
Gunderson, E. K. E. 1963. Emotional symptoms in extremely isolated groups. *Arch. gen. Psychiat.* 9:362–68.
———. 1964. Performance evaluations of Antarctic volunteers. Unit rept. 64-19, August, Navy Medical Neuropsychiatric Research Unit, San Diego, Calif.
———. 1968a. Group compatibility in restricted environments. In *APA Symposium on Factors Affecting Team Performance in Isolated Environments,* ed. S. B. Sells, pp. 11–25. Institute of Behavioral Research, Texas Christian University, Fort Worth, Tex.

———. 1968b. Mental health problems in Antarctica. *Arch. environ. Health* 17:558–64.
Gunderson, E. K. E., & Nelson, P. D. 1965. Biographical predictors of performance in an extreme environment. *J. Psychol.* 61:59–67.
———. 1966. Criterion measures for extremely isolated groups. *Personnel Psychol.* 19:67–80.
Gunderson, E. K. E., Nelson, P. D., & Orvick, J. M. 1963. Personal history correlates of military performance at a large Antarctic station. Unit rept. 64-22, August, Navy Medical Neuropsychiatric Research Unit, San Diego, Calif.
Gunderson, E. K. E., & Ryman, D. H. 1970. Convergent and discriminant validities of performance evaluations in extremely isolated groups. Unit rept. 70-8, January, Navy Medical Neuropsychiatric Research Unit, San Diego, Calif.
Law, P. 1960. Personality problems in Antarctica. *Med. J. Australia*, Feb. 47:273–81.
McGuire, F., & Tolchin, S. 1961. Group adjustment at the South Pole. *J. Ment. Sci.* 107:954–60.
Mullin, C. S., & Connery, H. J. 1959. Psychological studies at an Antarctic IGY station. *U.S. Armed Forces Med. J.* 10:290–92.
Nardini, J. E., Herrmann, R. S., & Rasmussen, J. E. 1962. Navy psychiatric assessment in the Antarctic. *Amer. J. Psychiat.* 119:97–105.
Owens, A. G. 1966. The assessment of individual performance in small Antarctic groups. Part I. OIC's Rating Scales. Research rept., Psychological Research Unit, Australian Military Forces, Melbourne, Australia, August.
———. 1967a. The assessment of individual performance in small Antarctic groups. Part II. Ratings on the Leary Interpersonal Checklist. Research rept., Psychological Research Unit, Australian Military Forces, Melbourne, Australia, August.
———. 1967b. The assessment of performance in small Antarctic groups. Part III. Factor analysis of Leary Interpersonal Checklist items. Research rept. Psychological Research Unit, Australian Military Forces, Melbourne, Australia, October.
———. 1968. Some biographical correlates of assessed performance in small Antarctic groups. Research rept., Psychological Research Unit, Australian Military Forces, Melbourne, Australia, October.
Palmai, G. 1963a. Psychological aspects of transient populations in Antarctica. *Medicine and Public Health in the Arctic and Antarctic*, Geneva, World Health Organization, (Public Health Papers, No. 18), pp. 146–58.
———. 1963b. Psychological observations on an isolated group in Antarctica. *Brit. J. Psychiat.* 109:364–70.
Radloff, R., & Helmreich, R. 1968. *Group under stress: Psychological research in SEALAB II.* New York: Appleton-Century-Crofts.
Rohrer, J. H. 1961. Interpersonal relationships in isolated small groups. In *Psychophysiological aspects of space flight*, ed. B. E. Flaherty, pp. 263–71. New York: Columbia University Press.
Ryman, D. H., & Gunderson, E. K. E. 1970. Factors affecting the stability of job attitudes in long-term isolated groups. Unit rept. 70-13, March, Navy Medical Neuropsychiatric Research Unit, San Diego, Calif.
Schutz, W. C. 1958. *FIRO: A three-dimensional theory of interpersonal behavior.* New York: Rinehart.

Sells, S. B. 1965. Research report on leadership and organizational factors in effective A. C. & W. sites. Contract No. AF41(657)-323. Arctic Aeromedical Laboratory. Institute of Behavioral Research. Fort Worth, Tex.

Shurley, J. T. 1970. Man on the south polar plateau. *Arch. Internal Med.* 125:625–29.

Smith, W. M. 1961. Scientific personnel in Antarctica: Their recruitment, selection, and performance. *Psychological Rept.* 9:163–82.

———. 1966. Observations over the lifetime of a small isolated group: Structure, danger, boredom, and vision. *Psychological Rept.* 19:475–514.

Smith, W. M., & Jones, M. B. 1962. Astronauts, Antarctic scientists and personal autonomy. *J. Aerospace Med.* 33:162–66.

Taylor, A. J. W. 1969. Ability, stability and social adjustment among Scott Base personnel, Antarctica. *Occupational Psychol.* 43:81–93.

Willis, J. S. 1960. Mental health in the north. *Med. Services J. Canad.* 16:689–720.

Wright, M. W., Sisler, G. C., & Chylinski, 1963. Personality factors in the selection of civilians for isolated northern stations. *J. appl. Psychol.* 47:24–29.

Wright, M. W., Chylinski, J., Sisler, G. C., & Quarrington, B. 1967. Personality factors in the selection of civilians for isolated northern stations: A follow-up study. *Canad. Psychologist* 8a:23–31.

Paul D. Nelson, *Commander, Medical Service Corps, U.S. Navy, is Head of the Human Effectiveness Branch, Research Division, Bureau of Medicine and Surgery, Department of the Navy, and coordinates psychiatric and psychological research among Navy Medical Department laboratories. His Ph.D. in social psychology was conferred by the University of Chicago in 1961. He served as a staff psychologist for the Chief of Naval Air Training and as a research psychologist at the Navy Medical Neuropsychiatric Research Unit, San Diego prior to assuming his present position in 1966. Among his research projects (together with E. K. Eric Gunderson) was the development of psychiatric screening criteria for Antarctic wintering-over volunteers, a project related to his chapter here. His research interests include leadership, management, small group and organizational effectiveness; the formation and change of attitudes and values; and the relationship of life stresses, life styles, and personality to mental and physical health.*

Nelson *addresses the problem of studying isolated and confined groups through use of indirect observational methods. He argues that the choice of observational methods selected for use in the study of such groups must be in part a function of the conditions under which groups are formed (e.g., was their isolation or confinement planned or accidental?), the environmental conditions in which the group functions (e.g., isolation and/or confinement), and the characteristics of groups to be measured (e.g., goal patterns, group structure, group culture, and group effectiveness criteria). Nelson discusses the utility of the interview, questionnaire, personal diary and log, organizational records, and site-visit methods for observation and measurement of various group characteristics under different conditions of group formation and environmental constraint.*

6

The Indirect Observation of
Groups Under Confinement
and Isolation

PAUL D. NELSON

Relatively rare among the documented accounts of human feats accomplished under conditions of confinement and isolation are those described by Byrd (1938), when he camped alone in his Antarctic base in order to avoid the ever-possible complications inherent in group experience. Numerous occasions of individual heroism have, of course, been observed in time of war or in man's conquest of the unknown, occasions in which lone men have faced confinement or isolation voluntarily or involuntarily. Seemingly more common, however, have been those accounts in which groups of men, by intent or accident, have faced the problems of confinement and possibly isolation in the course of pursuing a personal or societal goal.

Among such accounts are those of exploration parties: Shackleton's crew in quest of the Antarctic (Lansing, 1959), Scott's fatal expedition across the Antarctic continent (Huxley, 1957), the first colony of men to "winter-over" at the South Pole (Siple, 1959), crossing an ocean by raft (Heyerdahl, 1950), the climbing of Mount Everest (Lester, 1964), and exploration of the underwater world by aquanauts (Radloff & Helmreich, 1968). Still other accounts come from wartime experiences of combat units under fire (Little, 1964; Marshall, 1947), of air crews downed at sea (Rickenbacker, 1943), and of groups under duress as prisoners of war (Bettelheim, 1943; Leighton, 1964; Meyers & Bider-

The author is presently Head, Human Effectiveness Branch, Research Division, Bureau of Medicine and Surgery, Department of the Navy. Opinions asserted herein are those of the author and are not to be construed as necessarily reflecting the official views or endorsement of the Department of the Navy.

man, 1968; Nardini, 1952; Schein, Schneier, & Barker, 1961). And, there are those accounts of military and scientific groups which, under somewhat more routine conditions, work for relatively long periods of time under the isolation and confining conditions imposed by submarine duty (Campbell, 1953; Weybrew, 1963) and by the manning of Arctic and Antarctic scientific stations (Boag, 1952; Braun & Sells, 1962; Eilbert & Glaser, 1959; Gunderson & Nelson, 1965).

The examples cited are of real-life groups. Neither the groups nor the situations they faced were contrived for the purposes of studying human behavior. In some instances it was possible for the behavior of those groups to be directly observed by participant observation or by monitoring techniques from outside the group's environment. For the most part, however, the accounts of human experience cited were derived from official records, personal diaries, interviews following confinement or isolation, or from questionnaires designed to be completed by group members during the course of their experience. It is to such groups and methods of data collection that this chapter is addressed.

Somewhat in contrast to the chapters by Haggard and Gunderson, in which focus is predominantly upon the individual, the orientation here is upon the group as a unit of analysis. In still further contrast to the chapters by Radloff and Haythorn, in which predominant focus is upon direct observation of groups in field or laboratory environments, the intent here is to discuss indirect methods of observing the behavior of confined and isolated groups.

The nature of behavior observed in previous studies of confined and isolated groups will not be discussed in this chapter. Several notable reviews (Biderman, 1967; Sells, 1961; Smith, 1967; Wilkins, 1967) already provide such discussions. Rather, an effort will be made to discuss general characteristics of isolated and confined groups that warrant observation, the conditions of group formation and group environment that circumscribe the experience of confinement and/or isolation, and the efficacy of various indirect observational methods for collecting data, given those considerations. Such matters should of course be interrelated. A discussion of observational methods in any discipline or field of study should reflect some theoretical and conceptual basis, the nature of constructs and variables to be inferred and observed, and the conditions under which observations can and should be made.

Altman (1966), in reviewing the literature on small group analysis and related contributions on group dimensionality by Borgatta (1956), Cattel, Saunders, and Stice (1953), Golembiewski (1962), Hemphill and Westie (1950), Thelen (1959), Thibaut and Kelley (1959), and others, specifically addresses the question: "What behavior (in groups) should be studied?" The answer to that question should at least in part dictate the method of observation to be used. Within still another chapter of this text Sells emphasizes the need for a taxonomy of environmental and group characteristics such that greater standardization might be achieved in observational methods and greater generality of interpretation achieved in summary of data obtained.

Reflecting agreement with the points of view advanced by Altman and Sells, the remainder of this chapter will be addressed to concepts of group formation, group environment, and group behavior, and their significance for appropriate choice of methods for indirect observation of groups under conditions of confinement and/or isolation.

Concepts of Group Formation

The circumstances under which individuals become isolated and/or confined as a physical group are important both for understanding behaviors which occur under those conditions and for ascertaining the possibilities available for observing group behavior under such conditions. Two important categories of group formation concepts are:

1. *Planned vs accidental confinement and/or isolation*—to what extent was group formation under conditions of confinement or isolation planned, anticipated, or accidental; to what extent were group members aware of the circumstances they would face as a group prior to their confinement or isolation; to what extent were group goals identified relative to confinement or isolation, by the group itself or by others prior to such experience; and to what extent were group members purposely selected and assembled for conditions of confinement or isolation?

2. *Group structure prior to confinement and/or isolation*—to what extent did group members, prior to confinement or isolation, have established patterns of interaction, established positions of authority and responsibility within the group, and shared expectations concerning the behavior of other group members as a function of their being members of the group or some common parent organization (norms) or as a function of the specific positions held in the group (roles); and to what extent were such structural, normative characteristics a function of previous experience by the isolated or confined group as a group, or a function of group members' affiliation with a common parent organization, or prescribed solely for the purposes of the confinement and/or isolation experience?

The extent to which a group's confinement and/or isolation was by plan or by accident and the extent to which such a group, prior to its confinement or isolation, was structured in regard to task and interpersonal roles and norms, either as a function of prior group history or specifically for the purposes of the confinement or isolation experience, may not necessarily be related to group effectiveness in confinement or isolation. It is presumed, however, that such conditions of group formation have an impact upon the group behavior that does occur under conditions of confinement and/or isolation. Essentially, they refer to preparedness of the group, in terms of the expectations the group has of its future environment, and in terms of its internal structure as a group. To cite examples, the astronaut crews represent an extreme of preparedness, both in terms of awareness of their future environment and in terms of their role structure to cope with an environment. A shipwrecked party might represent the other extreme of unpreparedness. The former had been assembled and trained together as a group specifically for the confinement and isolation experience; the latter of course had not.

Concepts of Group Environment

It is within the scope of this book, of course, to attend to confining and/or isolating characteristics of environment. Within the context of this chapter those concepts should be defined in terms of their constraining character for groups. Their nature is important both in regard to group behavior and assessment methods possible.

Confinement is the extent to which group members are physically restricted to a fixed space or geographical area by virtue of man-made or natural barriers, territorial boundaries, or hostile surrounds of environment; within a confining environment, personal space, as a function of group size and of the physically or socially prescribed boundaries limiting movement, can be a most important dimension.

Isolation is the extent to which group members are restricted, either by physically or socially prescribed limits, from communicating with others outside the immediate group or from receiving information, directly or indirectly, from others outside the immediate group; it is important to differentiate those groups that can send but not receive from those that can receive but not send, and to differentiate those groups from others that can do neither or both.

The very restricted space per man in an astronaut habitat surrounded by a formidable physical environment, and the somewhat greater mobility potential per man in an Antarctic station or a prisoner-of-war compound, with a hostile physical environment enveloping the former and a hostile social environment enveloping the latter, represent differences in condition of confinement. And yet astronaut crews in continuous communication with earthbound monitors, both sending and receiving, differ in condition of isolation from prisoners-of-war who can receive letters but not send them or vice versa; from military units that can monitor radio messages but not initiate them; or from groups such as those of Antarctic stations whose communications or lack thereof with the outside are determined by weather conditions or equipment failures.

To this point attention has been given to the circumstances under which a group enters an environment of confinement and/or isolation and to the nature of confinement and isolation as environmental constraints for a group. Their significance will now be further developed through discussion of concepts of group behavior to be observed and of the possible methods for indirect assessment of such group behaviors.

Concepts of Group Behavior

It is all too easy, and somewhat common, to refer to groups but, in fact, to analyze individuals. Smith (1967), for example, reviews the literature of small-groups research appropriate to the problems of confinement, but discusses in great part the reactions or behaviors of individuals quite apart from an interactive point of view appropriate in discussions of groups. Behaviors of individuals are, of course, important and necessary components of group behavior; in fact some might argue that there is no behavior other than that enacted by individuals. But, there are indeed characteristics of groups which are unique to groups as units of analysis, characteristics which require that individual behaviors in some way be integrated into an interpersonal matrix. As Altman (1966, p. 128) puts it, in summarizing his literature review and development of a scheme for evaluating small group criteria:

> The general criterion question regarding small group behavior, namely, "How is the group doing?" was expanded to include questions concerning the total behavior of group members as they worked on a task, i.e., their interpersonal behavior, their goal-contributory behavior as well as those behaviors directly related to task performance. Thus, the criterion question was defined to include a very broad range of behaviors which conceptually and sequentially link to each other and which eventually interact and combine to affect final group output.

Group behaviors, then, are generally of two broad categories. One has to do directly with goal attainment and the other has to do with maintenance of the group itself, or, in Slater's (1955) framework regarding small group role differentiation, task-oriented and social/emotional-oriented behaviors. The attention to groups under confinement and/or isolation should, as with any group, be focused upon both types of behaviors and their resultants, the latter to include goals, values, attitudes, and as Altman calls it, "group output." Within either or both the task and interpersonal domains of group behavior one can conceptualize four major domains of inquiry: group goal patterns, group structure, group culture, and group effectiveness criteria.

GROUP GOAL PATTERNS

The goal patterns within an isolated or confined group represent the aggregate of those objectives held by individual group members during the the group's experience. Such individual goals become group goals to the extent that they are shared by group members and, furthermore, to the extent that such group members are collectively aware of such shared orientations. Sheer survival is a goal at least implicitly shared by most groups experiencing conditions of confinement or isolation, though it may be given second-order priority in groups for which the attainment of another objective comes first at any cost. The importance of group goals, pertaining to both survival and interpersonal responsibilities is discussed in accounts of prisoners-of-war who become apathetic or lose a sense of social responsibility for or identity with their fellow prisoners (Biderman, 1967; Nardini, 1952).

Not all individual goals can necessarily be expected to be shared as group goals. And, at times, individual goals can be strongly at variance with group goals, a matter that should not be neglected in accounting for variability of behavior among group members. The total absence of even one shared goal, of course, renders the group little more than an aggregate of individuals sharing a common environment, a physical group only in contrast to a psychological group.

Even when the group's confinement or isolation is highly planned, and goals set in advance of such experience, the complexity of goals may afford occasion for conflict over the course of time. In astronaut activities, for example, there are the publicly discussed differences of opinion regarding scientific data collection and engineering feats as sometimes competing goals. In Antarctic station groups, discussed in the previous chapter by Gunderson, different occupational subgroups, as extensions of different parent organizations, often have different and sometimes competitive goals related to task functions. Gunderson, with Doll (1969), points out how group member goals, varying somewhat by occupational subgroup in the Antarctic, may also serve as an important moderator variable in the relationship over time between feelings of accomplishment or morale and measures of task accomplishment.

Important, too, in the study of group goal patterns is their continuity over time. Are initial goals abandoned or placed in lower priority by group members over time? Even if initial goals are maintained, to what extent are they shared by group members over time? If the goals for a planned group experience of confinement and/or isolation are prescribed by a parent organization rather than set by the group members themselves, are they sacrificed over time, or modified by the group, particularly under conditions of extreme isolation wherein communications with the parent organization are virtually severed?

One might hypothesize, for example, that as the fate control by a parent organization over a confined or isolated group decreases as a function of time and severity of confinement and particularly of isolation, goal patterns pursued by the confined or isolated group become increasingly those set by the group itself. Hardly a more poignant account of group goals as a driving force, a source of deep frustration, an image of a group's morale and its physical condition, and as a changing pattern in the face of new circumstances and alternatives for human survival could be rendered than that derived from the day-to-day diary of Scott, as he heroically led his men on that ill-fated journey across the Antarctic continent to the South Pole and back to the base they never reached (Huxley, 1957).

GROUP STRUCTURE

By group structure I refer broadly to the way in which members of a group are organized, the predominant relatively regular patterns of interaction that occur, formally and informally, and the distribution, both expected and actual, of authority and responsibility among group members in regard to both the attainment of task-related goals and group maintenance.

To the extent that some degree of stability in role structure and interaction patterns is necessary for the maintenance of social order and continuous pursuit of group goals, group structure is especially important to assess over time in confined or isolated groups. Without some such stability, as with the sharing of common goals, a group can be reduced in time to little more than an aggregate of individuals, each concerned solely with his own survival or livelihood. That group structure can be degraded, particularly in the face of extreme hardship, is indicated in POW accounts (Biderman, 1967; Schein, Schneier, & Barker, 1961), Arctic traverse parties (Seaton, 1964), and military groups under stress of escape and survival training (Torrance, 1957b). As Scott wrote in his diary toward the end, with his men suffering from ill-health, fatigue, cold, hunger, and frustration, "we cannot help each other; each has enough to do to take care of himself" (Huxley, 1957, p. 404).

Under such conditions of duress, one might hypothesize from the accounts given that over time there is a tendency for formal authority to become less tolerated, for group structure in general to become less complex, and for interpersonal concern and responsibility among group members for one another to diminish, in fact if not in spirit. The extent to which such change in group structure is primarily a function of the most severe physical hardship, or whether it is more a function of interpersonal conflict and an erosion of social order, is not clear. In the case of Scott's expedition, it was probably the former, since Scott, even in death, was found with his arm draped across his closest friend (Huxley, 1957, p. 410).

The extent to which an experience of confinement or isolation was well planned and the extent to which the group began its experience with a well-differentiated role structure, as discussed earlier under conditions of group formation, may be a contributing factor to the stability of group structure during confinement or isolation. The importance of the group goals, for which group structure has meaning, may also account for differences among groups in structural stability. In the perhaps less physically punishing, though no less threatening, environment of Antarctic scientific stations, wherein task-related roles are reasonably well specified in advance and group members carefully selected, there is some indication that while group structure may become less complex over time there is general stability of structure over the 6-month "wintering-over" period, especially in task-related, in contrast to informal friendship, dimensions of structure (Nelson, 1964). Even there, however, some differences in trend were noted between different station groups.

A particularly critical element of group structure in confined or isolated groups, or perhaps any group under stress, is that of leadership, both in regard to task and social-emotional problems of the group. Formal and informal leadership patterns would appear to be most important in regard to total group unity, over and above subgroup structures related to pursuit of different tasks or subgoals, as in the Antarctic stations. Leadership, addressed as an interaction process involving reciprocal roles or expectations as well as individual behaviors of assertiveness, has been a major focus in the writings of Boag (1952), Braun & Sells (1962), Campbell (1953), Marshall (1947), and Torrance (1957a), covering groups in the Arctic, submarine crews, combat field units, and survival training groups, respectively. Leadership continuity, especially under emergency or crisis, is regarded by most writers as essential.

Perhaps a more perplexing problem in regard to leadership in small confined or isolated groups is that related to the matter of "interpersonal distance" between leaders and other group members. To what extent can formal group leaders, with prescribed roles of authority, rely on institutionalized status alone, particularly as length of confinement and isolation increases and "status-leveling" forces of environment are operative? Also, how "autocratic" or "democratic," as the case may be, can a designated leader afford to be under such conditions of group life?

Day (1968), with an historical perspective, renders an appropriate account of such concepts in regard to authority structure of sailing ships of the past century. Fiedler (1957), summarizing experimental and field studies, addresses the matter in terms of differing relationships between "leaders," "key men," and other group members, offering an intriguing notion that perhaps there is a meaningful difference between "how close the leader becomes to his men" and "how close the men feel to their leader."

In accounts of living-working groups at Antarctic stations (Nelson, 1962), leadership status and esteem are regarded in terms of the types of decisions required and expected of designated leaders by their men. On matters of a technical, task-specific nature, leader decisions are expected to be based upon consultations with appropriate task specialists. Decisions regarding general, routine, station policy matters, affecting all men alike (such as station housekeeping or recreational schedules), are expected to be rendered by the formal leader after consultation with the entire group ("democratic" style). Decisions on emergency matters, differing from other decisions on time allowed for decision-making, are expected to be made by the leader as quickly and "autocratically" as required by circumstance. In any instance, the formal leader's role is not to be abdicated; his sense of timing and appropriate relationship to his men may, however, be different from one situation to another.

Thus, to adequately assess leadership, as group structures in general, it is essential to assess patterns of interactions, as well as expectations or roles, over time, observing such patterns in the context of conditions facing the group at that time as well as in context of previous patterns. As Biderman (1967) puts it, in regard to the initial adjustment of prisoners of war, "a fundamental problem facing the captive is that of working out definitions of his new social and physical environment" (p. 346). Such adjustments, of course, can be expected to be faced by confined or isolated groups on a continuing basis.

GROUP CULTURE

A frequently overlooked, though important, aspect of group behavior under conditions of confinement or isolation is that of group culture—those values, attitudes, norms, activities, symbols, signs, sources and types of humor, and general life-style characteristics that tend to be more or less shared by group members as a function of their being confined or isolated as a group, and that tend to have unique meaning or significance to the particular group within which they exist.

Derived from a common awareness and acceptance of the fate of confinement or isolation, from a mutual feeling held by group members of being in a sense "removed" from the outside course of life, and from sharing an experience private to the collective membership of that particular group, the characteristics of group culture can be hypothesized as in part determining the nature of group goals and group structure over time. Reciprocally, group culture can also be viewed as resulting from those same patterns of orientation and interaction and might be hypothesized as determining in part the general effectiveness of the group. For group culture represents a form of group identity, in much the same sense that we refer to the "personality" of the individual in its broadest context. Depending upon its nature, aspects of group culture can be functional or dysfunctional in regard to the achievement of any given set of goals, including survival itself. Biderman (1967), for example, discusses the importance of group norms and cultural value systems in POW settings, as does Nardini (1952) in regard to risks of individual escape plans vis-à-vis group sanctions.

Group members initially bring into the circumstance of confinement or isolation their personal life-styles, including those values, attitudes, norms, and symbol systems referent to their common and unique domains of cultural heritage, much the same as, and even related to, their private goals. The manner in which those cultural, and even personality, idiosyncrasies are integrated into a cultural form common to the confined or isolated group members is worthy of study; It serves as another source of information concerning the extent and manner by which the group achieves a sense of unity, pride, and even accomplishment. Scott, for example, in describing the character of his expeditionary team, cites "the Soldier" (nickname) who never tires of "girding at Australia, its people and institutions," and the Australians who "retaliate by attacking the hide-bound prejudices of the British Army." Yet "never a temper [was] lost in these discussions" (Huxley, 1957, p. 299).

In more contemporary fashion, the cryptic language system, symbols of humor, and even the nicknames assumed by astronaut crew members and those given their spaceships reflect a sense of culture shared variably by the crew members, by the parent space organization, and even by the public as it gradually becomes acculturated to the business of space flight. While such cultural elements are not always unique to the confined and isolated crew itself, they are nevertheless important in welding a cohesive link between the crew, the parent organization, and the nation. By contrast, the "inside" pranks (such as the ham sandwich taken aboard by a space flight crew to the surprise of its colleagues in the parent organization) exemplify not only the sense of humor of the individuals involved but also a sense of their confidence, esprit de corps, and uniqueness as a crew.

Humor, in fact, while being an asset to men confined or isolated, might be hypothesized as a significant form of culture for any group faced with arduous conditions. In describing POW survival, Nardini (1952) states it in the following way: "Cleverness, adroitness of thinking and dealing with people, and general cunning were often great contributing factors to survival whereas pure intelligence unrelated to interpersonal dealing and long-range prediction was of less advantage. The more sense of humor an individual was able to retain the greater were his chances for survival" (p. 245). One of the difficulties with humor as an effective coping mechanism for truly isolated groups is that its potency is in great part a function of surprise, the unexpected context, the novelty of use, and the necessity of a "target audience." Astronaut pranks, for example, might have much less meaning to the crew members were they unable through audiovisual communications to surprise their colleagues in the earthbound parent organization. Other groups, for whom isolation is greater, have a less readily available target audience upon which to reinforce the private or in-group quality of humor.

In visiting Antarctic station groups, one can observe many cultural features that over the years have differentiated groups. Some are surmised to have been of short-term value to the groups; others perhaps "carried them through" the long winters. Examples are the "home town" street names assigned to snow paths in a camp; the Burma Shave limerick signs alongside a snow trail leading to "town," a reference to the station camp; a winter "Olympics" held at another station; an institutionalized pet cat at one station and the adopted indigenous penguins at another; and a station "flick" created by group members who spliced segments of many different commercial movies, all of which had been viewed individually to the point of boredom.[1]

The types of leisure activities pursued by group members provide further insight to group culture. Doll and Gunderson (1969) reveal differences in hobby interests and in activity levels for various subgroups of Antarctic station personnel over two time periods of the year. One rather intriguing observation was that, despite expressed hobby interest in competitive games by most group members, there was relatively little participation by small station members in such activities, perhaps as the authors suggest due to a concern for potentially disruptive effects upon group harmony.

Another type of cultural reference is that of time orientation, noted by Wilkins (1967) as a most important element for men in confinement or isolation. Reports that Antarctic wintering-over personnel seem unable to persevere in personal pursuits of reading or completing privately scheduled training courses, and the abrupt cessation of checking days off on calendars,[2] suggest a number of questions about the perspective of time and the consequent orientation to events of the past, present, and future among men isolated together under conditions of confinement. Certainly,

1. From personal observation during site visit.
2. From personal observation during site visit.

it would be of value to assess over time the extent to which group orientation and activity is focused upon the past, present, or future.

The extent to which the group knows the length of its confinement or isolation and the extent to which it has normal cues about the passage of time, as in lightness and darkness cycles, are probably important aspects of the time orientation problem. For such is the dimension on which activities are planned; it is a common element underlying many cultural patterns in all societies, on an hourly, daily, weekly, monthly, or yearly basis. It can be a source of hope and a grounds for despair. In his last diary entry Scott records: "I do not think we can hope for any better things now. We shall stick it out to the end, but we are getting weaker, of course, and the end cannot be far" (Huxley, 1957, p. 410).

GROUP EFFECTIVENESS CRITERIA

Despite the intrinsically interesting aspects of studying group goal patterns, group structure, and group culture over time under environmental constraints of confinement or isolation, our interest in such phenomena is essentially prompted by an interest in predicting the relative effectiveness of groups of specified characteristics under equally specified environmental conditions of confinement and/or isolation. Man's search for a better understanding of the universe, be it through exploration of the oceans or remote regions of the earth, or through extended flights into outer space, provides a contemporary and prospective context for such an interest.

One must, if interested in predicting effectiveness, specify some criteria on which to evaluate groups. Effectiveness, of course, as with the very concepts of confinement and isolation, is a relative concept. Knowledge about how any given group was formed, the reason for which it was formed, and the circumstances by which it was confined or isolated is necessary prior to the establishment of any concrete and meaningful criterion or set of criteria by which to evaluate its effectiveness. There are, nevertheless, at least three general criterion concepts applicable to confined or isolated group effectiveness, within which a range of more or less specific criterion measures could be established depending upon the nature of the group and the circumstances of its confinement or isolation. Those three broad group effectiveness criteria include survival, task achievement, and group cohesion.

Survival is a self-explanatory criterion. In addition to sheer survival, health of group members could be a more specific criterion, including aspects of both physical and mental health. For example, Gunderson (1968) analyzes the prevalence of emotional symptoms among different Antarctic station groups, and different occupational subgroups within stations, at different times of the year. For groups confined or isolated by accident, as among shipwrecked parties or prisoners of war, survival is generally the foremost criterion of effectiveness just as it is the group goal. Escape from conditions of confinement or isolation can, in those instances, constitute another criterion as well as goal related to that of survival. Both Biderman (1967) and Nardini (1952), however, allude to some of the complications in analyzing prisoner-of-war survival and escape records as indices of group, in contrast to individual, effectiveness. The individual who ignores the safety of his fellow men in order to "save his neck," may survive or even escape, but at the expense of his group. Consequently, despite acknowledgment of the apparent relationship between ineffective POW organization and the high death rate among American prisoners in the Korean conflict, Biderman (1967) concludes: "The survival of an individual, or survival rates among a group, provide no neat bases for valid evaluations of the virtuousness of their behavior in terms of any social standards" (p. 264). This is not to rule out such criteria as meaningful indices of group effectiveness, but merely to cast a cautionary note in regard to their use for such purposes.

In groups confined or isolated by plan, on the other hand, there are generally goals in addition to survival toward which the group is at least initially oriented. Survival still remains a goal, perhaps only implicitly, but the purpose for which the group is confined or isolated is more likely to be one of a task-achievement nature. To assess task-achievement effectiveness one must obviously know the intended tasks or mission of the group, and perhaps even to some extent the initial estimate by group members or their parent organization of the likelihood that such tasks will be achieved. Those who establish goals, be they the members of an organization responsible for forming the confined or isolated group or members of that group themselves, must have some concept of the likelihood of task achievement if they are to be able to assess the relative success or failure of the group achievement.

One of the problems encountered in assessing task achievement among many confined or isolated groups, particularly those with complex structure and goal patterns such as Antarctic stations, is that specific task goals are often not formulated in advance of the group's confinement and isolation experience, nor is an estimate of the likelihood of those tasks being achieved always specified in any detail. Rather, broad goals are set, the details of which are to be established by the group once in its novel environment. On new construction tasks in the Antarctic, for example, likelihood of task achievement would have to be in part a function of materials available. In scientific data collection, likelihood of task achievement could be based in part upon predicting to what extent weather conditions will inhibit or facilitate the collection of certain new data. Gunderson and Nelson (1965) discuss this in a study of group effectiveness criteria among Antarctic groups.

Another aspect of task-achievement criterion assessment has to do with the multiplicity and complexity of goal patterns. If the group is totally oriented to the achievement of one goal, or a series of goals in a particular sequence as is somewhat characteristic of space flight missions, the measurement of group task-effectiveness is somewhat different from that of a situation in which various occupational subgroups have different goals, as in the case cited for Antarctic station groups.

A third consideration in assessing task effectiveness of relatively confined or isolated groups is the extent to which group members are self-reliant in achieving goals. When a group is totally isolated, it must be self-reliant. If it is only moderately isolated, there is the possibility that outside support could be sought. The astronauts and even Antarctic station group members are not totally isolated except under conditions of communications blackouts.

Antarctic groups vary in the extent to which they seek outside advice or assistance in problem solution.[3] In some instances such assistance is necessary. Under emergencies requiring facilities that are simply not available, of course, one could not necessarily conclude that the seeking of outside assistance was indicative of ineffectiveness. But when the resources for problem solution do in fact exist within the group's immediate environment, seeking outside support can very well be an index of relative ineffectiveness.

Finally, quite related to the ability of a group to survive and to achieve its goals is the criterion of group cohesion. A group divided or disorganized under confinement or isolation has little chance for task effectiveness, and even perhaps survival. While a summary of the literature on small group research offers equivocal evidence of a relationship between group cohesion and task achievement (Lott & Lott, 1965), at least moderate cohesion seems necessary, though it may be insufficient, for task achievement. Cohesiveness can also in some instances deter a group from achieving a goal, as when a group establishes its own goal (for example, survival at any cost), the achievement of which is incompatible with the achievement of another goal established for the group by an outside organization (such as completion of a mission at any cost). Such instances, on occasion, have been observed in military air crews in regard to aborting missions.[4]

The relative absence of conflict within the group, a high degree of esprit de corps, and a strong sense of teamwork and "sharing the load" are indicators of group cohesion, all of which are related to independent measures of confined or isolated group effectiveness (Gunderson & Nel-

3. Personal communication with station leaders and Antarctic support staff.
4. From personal communication with Dr. W. W. Haythorn.

son, 1965). Sociometrically, a high degree of mutual interpersonal esteem and a relatively low percentage of social isolates is also indicative of cohesion. Attitudinally, a high mean level of positive attitude regarding teamwork or harmony within the group, with concomitant low variance, might similarly be indicative of cohesion. Without assessing group cohesion, it would be difficult to fully appreciate the implications of stability or change in goal patterns, group structure, or group culture.

Certainly, neither the measurement nor the prediction of group effectiveness is simple. But, with some specification of group formation and environmental restriction characteristics—the conditions under which and the reasons for which a group becomes confined or isolated—some valid measures of group effectiveness criteria can be specified. In turn, the membership composition of groups, their goal patterns, structural characteristics, and culture can be viewed over the course of time as variable categories from which group effectiveness criteria might be predicted.

A few ideas bearing upon indirect observational methods that might be used in assessing group characteristics and behavior under conditions allowing the investigator neither control over nor direct observation of groups during their confinement or isolation experience are outlined below.

Methods for Indirect Assessment of Groups

This chapter began with a discussion of concepts related to the ways in which groups become confined and/or isolated, as well as to the nature of confinement and/or isolation faced by a group. Such conditions rather strongly dictate the possible alternatives for assessing group behavior under confinement or isolation. Next, a few major concepts regarding group behavior under conditions of confinement and/or isolation were summarized, using the pretext that knowledge about "what one wants to study" in some ways also affects the selection of appropriate methodological tools. Therefore, methods of assessment will be discussed in the present section in terms of their relevance to preceding concepts.

For a general review of methods appropriate in the present instance, one might refer to the text on social research methods by Selltiz et al. (1963), and also to the insightfully written work on "unobtrusive" methods by Webb and colleagues (1966). This discussion, however, will focus on five principal methods for collecting data indirectly: interview, questionnaire, diary or log, organizational record, and site visit. The investigator should use as many methods in combination as the situation permits to increase breadth of understanding as well as reliability of observation. As Webb and his colleagues (1966) have it: "So long as we maintain, as social scientists, an approach to comparisons that considers compensating error and converging corroboration from individually contaminated outcroppings, there is no cause for concern. It is only when we naively place faith in a single measure that the massive problems of social research vitiate the validity of our comparisons" (p. 34).

THE INTERVIEW

Of the five methods for data collection, the interview is the only method that necessarily entails "face-to-face" communication (or some approximation thereof, as in telephone interviews) between investigator and group participants or others knowledgeable about the group and its experience. If the group's confinement or isolation is planned, the interview can be a useful tool for preconfinement or preisolation assessment of group members' anticipations about the experience, and their goals and motivation together with their perceptions of the goals of other group members. It also helps assess their perceptions of the roles to be assumed by other group members and by themselves or the extent to which such roles even exist prior to the group's confinement or isolation. If there is a past group history, the interview also allows for assessment of group members' perceptions of significant features about the group's past structure, formal and informal, its culture, and its effectiveness both in attainment of earlier goals and cohesiveness in that process. If the group's confinement or isolation evolves by accident, of course, there is no possibility for preconfinement interviewing unless such was conducted under some pretense that accidental confinement or isolation was possible, given the nature of mission upon which a group was about to embark.

The interview can also be conducted with persons other than immediate members of a group to be confined or isolated, as with responsible individuals from a parent organization of the group or its members. When the confinement or isolation experience is planned, this source of information can be especially fruitful for exploring concepts of goals that the organization holds for group attainment during confinement or isolation. These data can then be used for comparison with group members' perceptions of goals. In the same way, information can be obtained about role structure elements in the group, as prescribed or perceived by persons other than group members themselves.

In documented studies of confined or isolated groups, the preconfinement interview has probably been used more for the assessment of individuals' emotional strengths and weaknesses, their personal motivations, and to some extent their role perceptions, as in the screening of volunteers for Antarctic duty (Gunderson, 1966). Less frequently reported is the use of preconfinement interviewing for the explicit purpose of gathering data about group phenomena. Even the assessment of goals held for the group by a parent organization, in a planned confinement or isolation experience, is frequently difficult except in a general sense, since as Gunderson and Nelson (1965) point out the unusual circumstances of carrying out an assigned task often preclude statement of specific goals beforehand.

When conditions allow interviews by phone during the course of confinement, some information on "how the group is doing" can be obtained. But the use of interview in such instances is rare, except in those situations as in the astronaut flights where direct monitoring is conducted. And it will probably be limited to communication with one or two persons, such as group leaders or radio operators, in which case perceptions of group phenomena would be limited to the perspectives of a few nonrandomly selected group members.

Most frequent use of the interview for assessing qualities of the group and its confinement or isolation experience has been the postconfinement interview with group members or survivors. In instances such as prisoner-of-war experiences from which only part of a group survives there is always the uncertainty explained by Biderman (1967) that the perceptions of survivors represent those who didn't survive. Has the process of surviving, in other words, affected survivors' recall and interpretation of past events in various ways?

Postconfinement interviews can, however, yield information about general group effectiveness and major trends of group behavior during confinement or isolation. When all group members, or a proper sample, can be interviewed, consensus among reports can be measured if the interview is structured so that all persons are questioned in the same manner and about the same things. Gunderson and Nelson (1965) have reported on the utility of postconfinement interview assessments of group effectiveness for comparison with other data, related to the same criteria but gathered by other means during the course of confinement.

In general, the interview when conducted expertly is a flexible tool, allowing information probes to clarify or broaden one's understanding of behavior and the surrounding circumstances. Perhaps its greatest utility is for the development of insights which, under another circumstance and perhaps with different methods of observation, can be more rigorously pursued or validated.

THE QUESTIONNAIRE

The questionnaire, if considered to be a structured, "self-administered" interview, can be used in much the same ways as the interview. It can be somewhat open-ended or highly structured in format. While it generally accomplishes the standardization of inquiry quite well (except for the ever-possible difference of interpretation of questions), it lacks some of the flexibility for probe inherent in an interview.

On the other hand, it lends itself somewhat better than the interview to quantification of judgment, as might be obtained for example in ratings of frequency and quality of interaction among group members in assessing group structural elements. It can also be used by group members during the course of confinement or isolation if prepared beforehand and group members properly instructed on its use. In the latter instances, adequate care must be given to instruct group members or leaders of the conditions under which questionnaires should be administered. Instructions pertaining to the matter of protecting the confidentiality of information must be clearly understood, particularly if any information might be considered "sensitive" or "threatening to the group" by members of the group. The key to the latter problem lies as much in the way questions are constructed as in the administrative management of the questionnaire. Also important is arranging, whenever possible, for questionnaires to be completed by group members as a natural part of the normal duties or tasks they perform. Certainly, in several years of research conducted with groups manning Antarctic stations, there have been some instances of complete failure by the groups to fill out questionnaires. But far more often full sets of questionnaire data have been obtained, with and without personal identity of the respondent revealed. The validity of such data is often open to question, but here again the use of multiple observational methods can be an effective means of verification.

Taking the Antarctic groups as an example, the questionnaire has been used at different times during the confinement experience to assess group member interactions (sociometric questionnaire) related to work tasks, formal and informal communication networks, roles, leisure activities, and friendships (Nelson, 1964). When all group members respond to such relatively nonthreatening questions, the customary completeness of data allows ample opportunity to assess important aspects of group structure, even its complexity as revealed through "who-to-whom" matrix analysis of interaction reciprocity and indirect linkages of interaction. Examples of these questions are: "With what group members have you most frequently worked during the past month," "With whom do you most frequently spend off-duty time," and "To whom do you generally go for information related to your job or to other matters such as station policies."

Similarly, questionnaires containing items of attitude about one's work as well as of the teamwork or esprit de corps that seems to exist in one's group have been useful in assessing the perceived quality of group effectiveness. Important, too, is the variance of response in different attitudinal domains, indicative of the degree of group member consensus or lack thereof, in regard to "how well the group is doing." As Gunderson and Nelson (1965) imply, in discussing criterion measures for confined or isolated groups, the group members themselves are often as good a source as any for assessing the effectiveness of their group, particularly as pertains to cohesiveness and spirit of accomplishment, if not actual productivity relative to a clearly specified goal. Group members serve in a sense as a collective participant observer.

Another possible use of questionnaires during the course of confinement, particularly in regard to the environmental constraint of confinement per se, might be the assessment of territorial behavior of group members, an important quality of behavior in confined space addressed by Altman and Haythorn (1967). In settings such as the Antarctic stations where the physical layout of each station is known in advance, one could have the group members indicate on a station blueprint where they spent their time for various types of activities and the proportion (on an average daily basis) of time spent there. By virtue of occupation and personal disposition, men in Antarctic stations appear to use geographical space quite differently over the course of a year.[5] Such behavior, of course, has implications for interactions within the group, and possibly reflects consequences of group life.

Finally, for those situations in which it may be neither possible nor politic to obtain information by questionnaire during the course of a group's confinement or isolation, postexperience questionnaires, as interviews, can be used. In the most difficult of circumstances, where group members disperse upon release from their confinement or isolation, and there is thus no possibility of group questionnaire administration, the mail-questionnaire can be useful.

In full awareness of the potential methodological pitfalls of such a method, the mail-questionnaire was used one year with Antarctic station group members on whom data had also been collected during the course of the year of confinement (Nelson, 1963). Some of the group members, from four different station groups, received the questionnaire 6 months following Antarctic experience. The remainder received the same questionnaire 12 months after leaving the Antarctic. An overall return rate of 64 per cent was realized, slightly higher for the 12-month followup sample than the 6-month sample. Such a return rate, though appreciably lower than the 93 per cent return rate reported in the National Research Council and Veterans Administration follow-up study of World War II prisoners (Cohen & Cooper, 1954), is not greatly out of line with what might be expected of mail-questionnaires in general, and better than many such instances.

The important findings of that study, however, were the significantly positive relationships between judgments (mostly about other group members' behavior and performance) rendered after the fact, even 12

---

5. From personal observation during site visit and interviews with station members.

months later, and judgments made earlier (through questionnaire assessment) at three different times during the course of confinement in the Antarctic. There was furthermore no significant difference in earlier performance (as revealed by peer and supervisor ratings in the Antarctic) between those who returned the questionnaires and those who did not.

In addition to the apparent validity of postconfinement judgments (in relation to judgments rendered during the confinement period), the mail-questionnaire, through use of open-end questions, provided a rich source of data to be used in subsequent studies of adjustment to Antarctic life, including information, freely offered and consensually validated by different respondents, which led to the development of individual adjustment criteria discussed in another chapter by Gunderson. Those criteria are now routinely obtained in the Antarctic and were used by Lester (1964) and by Radloff and Helmreich (1968) in different environmental settings with relatively isolated and confined groups, respectively.

In general, the questionnaire, properly constructed and administered, is probably the most valuable of the methods discussed in this chapter in assessing elements of group structure and their change or stability over time. It can be used to assess such elements of group behavior, and member perceptions thereof, both prior and subsequent to confinement or isolation as well as during the experience. The latter is dependent upon knowledge beforehand of what the confinement will entail as well as, of course, adequate briefing of the individual or individuals who administer the questionnaire.

THE DIARY OR LOG

In contrast to interviews and questionnaires, initiated and designed by persons other than those whose behavior is subject to study, the personal diary or log, informal or formal, is primarily designed and completed on the initiative of the individual recorder. In some instances, of course, as aboard ship or in military or scientific bases, official logs are customarily required by a parent organization. Such logs generally are descriptive of time-date events, general group activities, or perhaps critical incidents, sometimes involving specific members of the group. Since they are self-initiated or at least institutionalized, as are official logs, they offer a somewhat less obtrusive source of information about groups than either the interview or questionnaire. And in many instances they offer the only source of information about behavior of men during confinement and isolation. Scott's daily recordings are a case in point (Huxley, 1957).

The diary or log, if maintained by only one or two group members, can of course fail to reveal much of significance in regard to group behaviors, particularly estimates of group goals, structure, or culture. In other words, if the diary consists of little more than personal reflections of feeling states, aspirations, or a chronology of events in the physical environment (such as weather), the information has little or no use for assessing groups. Diaries and even logs can contain, on the other hand, information about interactions between the recorder and other group members, as well as perceptions the recorder has of other group members or of the group as a whole. Use of subjunctive language, for example, might reveal perceptions of roles; use of active tense language reveals behavior as enacted, or at least as perceived or interpreted by the recorder.

The maintenance of diaries by many group members affords, to the extent that recording style is at all similar from one person to another, a somewhat richer source of information. This may include information on group goals (if only through independent agreement among recorders' personal expression of goals or aspirations), and on group structure (both formal and informal, task and interpersonally oriented, and on roles as well as interactions). Data on culture (as revealed through personal anecdotes, special language, or reference to nicknames or symbols of unique value to the group), and on group effectiveness (through similarity of personal observations about group achievement or spirit) also may be obtained.

Work logs, maintained as an integral part of conducting one's daily task-related activities, can provide data concerning time spent on tasks, difficulties encountered, achievements realized, and interactions with others in a work-related way. In that sense they can serve as sources of information about task-related group structure, territorial behavior in terms of where one spends time during the day's work, and task-achievement criteria. Likewise, official logs such as those of ships, which served as an historical source of information for Day (1968), can be analyzed for insights into institutional norms, group activities, and critical incidents pertaining to achievement or cohesiveness of the group.

Often overlooked are medical logs, as surveyed by Doll, Rubin, and Gunderson (1969) in recent shipboard studies of health in relation to demographic and work environment characteristics, and as maintained by Nardini (1952), whose personal observations of men and their survival under extremes of confinement were made in his role as a medical officer in prisoner-of-war camps. The use of sick-call data by Stouffer and his colleagues (1949), in their studies of World War II combat units, is still another example. Such sources of data are of course specific to group criteria of survival. But they are also suggestive of general health trends that might be as indicative of interpersonal and work-related stresses as of physical hardships alone.

Diaries, and even logs, are not always easy to analyze, particularly for inferences about group behaviors. Content analysis is tedious and as much an art as a science, though if properly conducted a rather revealing procedure. The utility of content analysis for study of mass media communications, as discussed by Berelson (1952), is well known. Were the same technique of analysis applied to such documents as Scott's diary (Huxley, 1957), one might note changes over time in number of words per daily entry; the proportionate use of the pronoun "we" in contrast to "I," "he," or "they;" the affect reflected similarly in language; and the attention given to interpersonal, introspective, and physical environment phenomena. Even estimates of time perspective both in regard to perceived attainability of goals and in a more general sense of focus upon the past, present, or future may be obtained.

THE ORGANIZATIONAL RECORD

When the confined or isolated group has at least one parent organization to which its members have some type of formal relationship, records maintained by that organization relative to the group and its members can be useful. Such records could be analyzed for information about the group prior to its confinement or isolation or for information on the group's effectiveness. Organizational records would less likely be a major source of information about dynamics of group behavior during confinement or isolation, unless they were of critical incident form in relation to success or failure in achieving organizational goals.

The extent to which the confinement or isolation experience was planned, the purposes for which the group was formed, the extent and rationale of special selection of group members for the experience, the assignment of specific roles as in group leadership and task functions, and the extent to which specific goals were delineated are possible types of information to be gleaned from organizational records. Even for groups whose confinement or isolation was a matter of accident, it is possible if group members are from a common organization, that organizational records might contain information on the circumstances leading to the group's confinement or isolation. Military records, for example, are sometimes useful for describing the conditions of battle or defense under which groups of men were captured as prisoners of war.

Organizational rules and regulations can be a source of information for assessing the extent to which group norms, operative during confinement or isolation, were consistent with or departures from institutionalized forms of behavior. Day's (1968) analysis of the authority structure in sailing ships of the English Royal Navy contains frequent references to personal letters or logs maintained by ships' captains, on the one hand, and official institutionalized documents related to maritime law and customs, on the other.

Another type of information that might be obtained from organizational records is that of communications with the confined group whose isolation is not sufficiently severe as to prohibit such communications. The frequency and content of communications received by the parent organization from a confined group can provide information about the group's effectiveness, its problems, and the relative ability or inability of the group to resolve such problems without assistance from the outside. Communications sent by the organization to the confined group, on the other hand, can also be assessed for information about goals held by the organization, their possible alteration during the course of a group's confinement, and for evaluative information portraying organizational perceptions of the group's effectiveness at various points in time.

Finally, records maintained by the parent organization of a confined or isolated group, for which a task objective or set of objectives had been established prior to the group's experience, may be among the only sources of information at the conclusion of such group experience for assessing task accomplishments of the group, if only of a general evaluative nature. Less likely, of course, would be information about the more informal and interpersonal aspects of the group's experience. But comparisons of organizational evaluations of the group's task effectiveness with other types of data gleaned from interviews, questionnaires, personal diaries, and logs could yield a breadth of information spanning formal and informal, task and interpersonal effectiveness indices of the group's behavior.

THE SITE VISIT

When a group's confinement or isolation is restricted to a fixed geographical location, or when in the absence of confinement an isolated group's path of movement is known, visits to such locations after the group's experience can be a further source of information about what the group did and what the physical conditions of its existence might have been. Archeologists, of course, have long been expert in drawing inferences about human culture from ancient ruins or physical traces of group life in locations of former habitation.

In the Antarctic scientific stations, where groups turn over occupancy each year, site visits can reveal changes made in the station environment from one group to the next. The extent to which a group "adds to its physical environment" may be one index of its effectiveness in coping with confinement or isolation. The physical layout of functional spaces can provide information useful for interpreting data from other sources on group interactions or even culture. One needn't be a mariner, for example, to infer characteristics of group structure aboard fighting ships of the past or present from the physical arrangement of working and living quarters.

So too, the observation several years ago of living quarters at one of the Antarctic stations can be as revealing of interpersonal strains within the group as a set of attitudinal responses yielded by questionnaire.[6] The living quarters were built by a subgroup of men during their confinement to allow them both privacy and as much distance as possible from others in the group. The signs of culture, mentioned earlier, symbolic of "bringing a little of home into the Antarctic," the surveillance of calendars on the walls of work and living spaces, the existence of certain recreational equipment in frequented areas of the station in contrast to that equipment stashed away in the storage areas, and the pictures and other symbols of significance to group members displayed in various parts of a station provide further bits of information about confined groups in the Antarctic.

The site visit may be no more revealing of how groups behave under confinement or isolation than any other method. If done alone, without other sources of information, it may even be less revealing. But if made in addition to the benefit of other collected forms of data, site visits can add a depth of perspective which otherwise might be lacking. As one follows Scott and his men across the Antarctic ice cap through the personal diary notes, there is a sense of tragedy in the account of a highly cohesive group of men reduced, by necessity of circumstances, to individual survivors, each responsible for himself. How significant it was that Scott was found, some months after the end, in an attitude of camaraderie with his closest friend, even in death. Had the "site visit" in that instance not been made, or the men not found, that subtle observation would never have been made, nor, in fact, would the diary have been available to posterity.

One is not customarily able to directly observe what goes on with groups confined or isolated by intent or accident in the course of pursuing a meaningful objective. Under these circumstances, the student of group behavior must make the most of what he has in theory as in method, if for no other reason than to further develop hypotheses that might, under more scientifically favorable conditions, be subjected to test. When concerned with groups, he must bear in mind those concepts applicable to groups; and he must use as many methods of data collection pertinent to those concepts as are applicable in any instance.

The conclusion applied by Webb and his colleagues (1966) to their writing about unobtrusive measures in social research was an excerpt from a review of statistical theory by Binder (1964). The same conclusion is also fitting for this chapter: "We must use all available weapons of attack, face our problems realistically and not retreat to the land of fashionable sterility, learn to sweat over our data with an admixture of judgment and intuitive rumination, and accept the usefulness of particular data even when the level of analysis available for them is markedly below that available for other data in the empirical area" (p. 294).

---

6. From personal observation during site visit and through interview with station members.

REFERENCES

Altman, I. 1966. Aspects of the criterion problem in small groups research. *Acta Psychologica* 25:101–31.

Altman, I., & Haythorn, W. W. 1967. The ecology of isolated groups. *Behav. Sci.* 12:169–82.

Berelson, B. 1952. *Content analysis in communication research.* New York: Free Press.

Biderman, A. D. 1967. Life and death in extreme captivity situations. In *Psychological stress: Issues in research,* ed. H. Appley & R. Trumbull, pp. 242–64. New York: Appleton-Century-Crofts.

Bettelheim, B. 1943. Individual and mass behavior in extreme situations. *J. abnorm. soc. Psychol.* 38:417–52.

Binder, A. 1964. Statistical theory. *Ann. rev. Psychol.* 15:277–310.

Boag, T. J. 1952. The white man in the Arctic. *Amer. J. Psychiat.* 109:444–49.

Borgatta, E. F. 1956. On the dimensions of group behavior. *Sociometry* 19:223–40.

Braun, J. R., & Sells, S. B. 1962. Military group performance under isolation and stress: A critical review. Ft. Wainwright, Alaska: Arctic Aeromedical Laboratory Technical rept., AAL-TDR-62-33, June.

Byrd, R. E. 1938. *Alone.* New York: Putnam.

Campbell, D. T. 1953. A study of leadership among submarine officers. Columbus, Ohio: Ohio State University, ONR rept. N6 ori-17, III, NR 171 123.

Cattell, R. B., Saunders, D. R., & Stice, G. F. 1953. The dimensions of syntality in small groups. *Human Relations* 6:331–56.

Cohen, B. M., & Cooper, M. Z. 1954. *A Follow-up study of World War II prisoners-of-war.* Washington, D.C.: U.S. Government Printing Office, September.

Day, R. M. 1968. Authority in the sailing ship. Ft. Worth, Texas: Institute of Behavioral Research, Texas Christian University, NASA Grant NGR 44-009-008, Rept. no. 8, December.

Doll, R. E., & Gunderson, E. K. E. 1969a. Occupational group as a moderator of the job satisfaction–job performance relationship. *J. appl. Psychol* 53 (5):359–61.

———. 1969b. Hobby interest and leisure activity behavior among station members in Antarctica. San Diego, Calif.: Navy Medical Neuropsychiatric Research Unit rept. 69-34.

Doll, R. E., Rubin, R. T., & Gunderson, E. K. E. 1969. Demographic variables and illness onset in an attack carrier's crew. *Arch. environ. Health* 19:748–52.

Eilbert, L. R., & Glaser, R. 1959. Differences between well and poorly adjusted groups in an isolated environment. *J. appl. Psychol.* 43:271–74.

Fiedler, F. E. 1957. Non-fraternization between leaders and followers and its effects on group productivity and psychological adjustment. In *Proceedings of the WRAIR and NRC Symposium on Preventive and Social Psychiatry.* Washington, D.C.: Walter Reed Army Institute of Research, Walter Reed Army Medical Center.

Golembiewski, R. 1962. *The small group: An analysis of research concepts and operations.* Chicago: University of Chicago Press.

Gunderson, E. K. E. 1966. Selection for Antarctic service. San Diego, Calif.: Navy Neuropsychiatric Research Unit Rept. 66-15, March.

——. 1968. Mental health problems in Antarctic. *Arch. environ. Health* 17:558–64.

Gunderson, E. K. E., & Nelson, P. D. 1965. Measurement of group effectiveness in natural isolated groups. *J. soc. Psychol.* 66:241–49.

Hemphill, J. K., & Westie, C. M. 1950. The measurement of group dimensions. *J. Psychol.* 29:325–42.

Heyerdahl, T. 1950. *Kon Tiki.* Chicago: Rand McNally.

Huxley, L., ed. 1957. *Scott's last expedition: The journals of Captain R. F. Scott.* Boston: Beacon Press.

Lansing, A. 1959. *Endurance: Shackleton's incredible voyage.* New York: McGraw-Hill.

Leighton, A. H. 1964. *The governing of men.* New York: Octagon Books.

Lester, J. T. Jr. 1964. Men to match Mount Everest. *Naval Research Review* 17 (12):7–14.

Little, R. W. 1964. Buddy relations and combat performance. In *The new military,* ed. M. Janowitz, pp. 195–224. New York: Russell Sage Foundation.

Lott, A. J., & Lott, B. E. 1965. Group cohesiveness as interpersonal attraction: A review of relationships with antecedent and consequent variables. *Psychol. Bull.* 64:259–309.

Marshall, S. L. A. 1947. *Men against fire.* New York: Morrow.

Meyers, S. M., & Biderman, A. D., eds. 1968. *Mass behavior in battle and captivity.* Chicago: University of Chicago Press.

Nardini, J. E. 1952. Survival factors in American prisoners-of-war of the Japanese. *Amer. J. Psychiat.* 109:241–48.

Nelson, P. D. 1962. Leadership in small isolated groups. San Diego, Calif.: Navy Medical Neuropsychiatric Research Unit Technical Rept. no. 62-13.

——. 1963. A study of the validity of mail questionnaire data. San Diego, Calif.: Navy Medical Neuropsychiatric Research Unit Technical Rept. no. 63-7.

——. 1964. Structural change in small isolated groups. San Diego, Calif.: Naval Medical Neuropsychiatric Research Unit Technical Rept. no. 64-24.

Radloff, R., & Helmreich, R. 1968. *Groups under stress: Psychological research in Sealab II.* New York: Appleton-Century-Crofts.

Rickenbacker, E. 1943. *Seven came through.* New York: Doubleday.

Schein, E. H., Schneier, I., & Barker, C. H. 1961. *Coercive persuasion.* New York: Norton.

Seaton, R. W. 1964. Deterioration of military work groups under deprivation stress. In *The New Military,* ed. M. Janowitz, pp. 225–49. New York: Russell Sage Foundation.

——. 1961. *Military small group performance under isolation and stress: An annotated bibliography.* Fort Worth, Tex.: Texas Christian University, U.S. Air Force Contract 41(657)-323, October.

Selltiz, C., Jahoda, M., Deutsch, M., & Cook, S. W. 1963. *Research methods in social relations.* New York: Holt, Rinehart and Winston.

Siple, P. 1959. *90° south.* New York: Van Reese Press.

Slater, P. E. 1955. Role differentiation in small groups. *Amer. Sociol. Rev.* 20:300–310.

Smith, S. 1967. Studies of small groups in confinement. In *Sensory deprivation: Fifteen years of research,* ed. J. P. Zubeck, pp. 374–403. New York: Appleton-Century-Crofts.

Stouffer, S. A., et al. 1949. *The American soldier: Combat and its aftermath,* vol. 2. Princeton: Princeton University Press.

Thelen, H. A. 1959. Work-emotionality theory of the group as organism. In *Psychology: A study of science,* ed. S. Koch, vol. 3, pp. 545–608. New York: McGraw-Hill.

Thibaut, J., & Kelley, H. H. 1959. *The social psychology of groups.* New York: Wiley.

Torrance, E. P. 1957a. Leadership in the survival of small isolated groups. In Proceedings of the WRAIR and NRC Symposium on preventive and social psychiatry. Washington, D.C.: Walter Reed Army Institute of Research, Walter Reed Army Medical Center.

———. 1957b. What happens to the sociometric structure of small groups in emergencies and extreme conditions? *Group Psychotherapy* 10:212–20.

Webb, E. J., Campbell, D. T., Schwartz, R. D., & Sechrest, L. 1966. *Unobtrusive measures. Nonreactive research in the social sciences.* Chicago: Rand McNally.

Weybrew, B. B. 1963. Psychological problems of prolonged marine submergence. In *Unusual environments and human behavior,* ed. N. Burns, R. Chambers, & E. Hendler, pp. 87–125. New York: Macmillan.

Wilkins, W. L. 1967. Group behavior in long-term isolation. In *Psychological stress: Issues in research,* ed. M. Appley & R. Trumbull, pp. 278–90. New York: Appleton-Century-Crofts.

Roland Radloff *is Program Director for Social Psychology at the National Science Foundation. He received his Ph.D. from the University of Minnesota in 1959 and after a one-year academic career at Yale University became a research psychologist for the federal government. This includes two and one-half years at H.E.W., Public Health Service, and eight years at the Naval Medical Research Institute. He has worked both as an experimental and field researcher. At N.M.R.I. his attention focused on the study of group reactions to stress. His most extensive publication on the topic is the book* Groups Under Stress: Psychological Research in Sealab II, *co-authored with Robert Helmreich.*

Radloff *advocates an increase in the use of naturalistic observation, unobtrusive measures, and multivariate, multimethod approaches to research. The proposed methods are presented as essential to the growth and development of social psychology in general. While the concepts and methods proposed are based on research on saturation diving, their potential for broad application is stressed.*

7

Naturalistic Observations of Isolated Experimental Groups in Field Settings

ROLAND W. RADLOFF

Introduction

This chapter will present methods and concepts designed to describe, explain, and predict the behavior of individuals and groups in isolated, exotic environments. The background for the following material is 6 years of research on saturation diving groups. The general goals of the research have been to develop and refine multivariable, multimethod, objective criteria and predictors of adjustment and performance, and to develop and refine a conceptual framework. The approach emphasizes naturalistic, unobtrusive observations of behavior.

While concepts and methods discussed here are based on research on saturation diving, they have broad application. Their application to other exotic environments such as space and remote sites on earth is especially appropriate. With modifications, they can be used in the study of groups in more normal environments. Such groups can range from the prosaic to the sublime—from athletic teams through school classes and industrial work groups to departments of psychology. Wide use of these concepts and methods can serve the interests of both applied and basic research. Some applied goals are the improvement of selection, group composition, adjustment, and productivity. Basic research goals are the definition and development of concepts and theories.

From Bureau of Medicine and Surgery, Navy Department, Research Subtask MF022.01.03-1004. The opinions and statements contained herein are the private ones of the writer and are not to be construed as official or reflecting the views of the Navy Department or the naval service at large.

METHODOLOGICAL ORIENTATION

Although this discussion may appear quite prosaic, it arises from an intense dissatisfaction with the present state of psychological knowledge and psychological research. In attempting to predict the behavior of men and groups in real-life settings, a large number of two types of research studies have been and continue to be done. First, we have esoteric, rigorously controlled laboratory studies, limited in their ability to generalize to real-world problems (for example, Zubek, 1969.) Second, we have applied man-machine, human engineering studies, designed to answer highly specific questions (for example, Fraser, 1966.) There has also been a limited number of a third type of study, which is closer to the experimental groups discussed here. Examples are fallout shelter studies (Rasmussen & Wagner, 1962; Rasmussen, Wagner, & Morris, 1966; and Georgia, University of, 1962–63). However, such groups are in an "as if" environment. The main research goal is usually to shed light on how equipment would function and persons would behave *if* they were involved in an emergency.

Mention of these types of studies does not imply any criticism of the research conducted or of the investigators doing the work. The criticism rather is of the relative paucity of studies of behavior in the field, broad and general enough to yield information on the totality of individual and group reactions to the environment. This viewpoint has been well stated by Dr. Saul Sells in *Psychological Stress* (Appley & Trumbull, 1967). In discussing the lack of research in the real world, Dr. Sells talks about the possibility of working out arrangements for studying life where it occurs: "I think that psychologists need to come out of the ivory tower and go into the world where life actually takes place and not simply reject it on the grounds that it is too difficult, or too expensive, or that there have been people who have tried it and it hasn't worked out. The problem is rather one of looking on this as a challenge for which we need to mobilize our efforts. There is no lack of ingenuity. More than anything else it appears to me to be a matter of apathy" (p. 277).

The reluctance to study behavior in the field is not limited to the study of man in exotic environments. This problem pervades the entire field of psychology, a point that will receive elaboration later in this paper.

SATURATION DIVING

In recent years a number of experimental and commercial undersea projects have employed the technique of saturation diving. Teams of divers have lived in, and worked in the water from, small habitats on the ocean floor. The habitats have been pressurized with exotic gas mixtures, with pressures up to 300 psi and helium contents up to 96 per cent. Noteworthy examples are the U.S. Navy's Sealab Program and French explorer Jacques Cousteau's Conshelf studies. Employment and development of saturation diving capabilities may be expected to increase markedly in the next decade, and thus the topic should be of more than passing interest. Indeed, in the foreseeable future, far more man-days are likely to be spent in sea floor habitats under pressure than in the more publicized space vehicles and stations.

Small groups in saturation diving projects are subject to naturally existing conditions of interest to psychologists who desire to study humans under stress. Saturation divers are under severe stress; furthermore, those stresses have not been imposed or contrived by psychologists. Saturation divers are in exotic environments. While their spacial separation from a normal environment may seem slight, they are separated by many hours or even days—6 days if saturated at 600 feet—from a return to the normal world, because of decompression requirements. Saturated divers live in constant danger from equipment failure or human error which could result in fatal or disabling accidents. They breathe exotic gas mixtures under pressure and are often subject to severe thermal stresses. They live in close confinement and are highly dependent on each other and on surface support personnel. In brief, saturation divers are pioneers on a novel, often hostile, always demanding and exciting frontier.

PSYCHOLOGICAL RESEARCH ON SATURATION DIVING

Research on saturation divers presents some unusual opportunities not present in other exotic environments such as the Antarctic. Since safety and medical monitoring require television and audio access, psychologists can observe behavior with a minimum likelihood of affecting reactions to observations, a Hawthorne effect (see Roethligsberger & Dickson, 1939; Rosenthal & Rosnow, 1969). Divers realize that the watchful eye of "big brother" is there for their safety. The psychologist is well advised to take full advantage of this situation, eliminating, in so far as possible, any reminders that he is present. Thus, he is provided with unusually free and unobtrusive access to ongoing behavior which can be observed with minimal bias and interference.

The approach to research on saturation diving described here has evolved during the course of observation and research on five saturation diving projects: Sealabs I, II, and III, and Projects Tektite I and II. In addition, extensive reading of studies on other natural groups supplemented and influenced the approach.

No psychological research was conducted on Sealab I. I spent 2 days observing the project on site, from the medical monitoring van. This brief study proved to be extremely fruitful. During observations on Sealab I, many concepts and methods germinated that did not mature until 5 years later. The basic approach of collecting unobtrusive measures of behavior by observation derived from the Sealab I experience. During Sealab II, Dr. Robert Helmreich of the University of Texas and I conducted an extensive program of research. This research is reported in *Groups Under Stress* (Radloff & Helmreich, 1968). In planning for research on Sealab III, extensive effort went into developing predictive measures to supplement criterion variables carried over from Sealab II. Unfortunately, due to a fatal accident early in 1969, Sealab III operations have been suspended indefinitely.

In research on Project Tektite, excellent observation and data collection facilities permitted a detailed analysis of behavior. Project Tektite I employed one group of men for a period of 60 continuous days living in and working from an underwater capsule. In Project Tektite II, nine different groups of men and one group of women worked for periods ranging from 14 to 30 days.

(Project Tektite II was under the auspices of NASA and the Dept. of Interior and my participation was limited to the role of consultant. Dr. Robert Helmreich was in charge of psychological research. To date, only brief reports of the research have appeared.)

Lack of field research in recent years has resulted in a dearth of methods and concepts directly applicable to field studies designed to assess overall individual and group effectiveness. Because of this absence of methodological and conceptual guide lines, a relatively new approach has been developed in the studies of saturation diving. It has developed slowly, and is incomplete.

The central feature of the approach has been the observation, by closed circuit television, of the day-to-day behavior of saturation diving crews. The data have been objective, emphasizing the identification of man, time, place, and activity. Records have been made of where the men were physically—in what section of the capsule or the water; and what they were doing—diving, working in the capsule, talking to each other, preparing or eating meals, relaxing, getting up, going to bed, maintaining the habitat, and so on. We recorded whether the men were working alone or in groups of two, three, or more, and in some cases, the order in which things were done. These records have been taken systematically and regularly for up to 24 hours per day and for missions ranging in length up to 60 days. Data were precoded and recorded numerically. In recent studies, the recording has been directly onto punched cards for computer analysis.

The approach outlined here may not appear to be very psychological. It is unsophisticated; it is only common sense. The methodological and conceptual rationale is simple and straightforward. This approach is both forthright and relatively novel; its underlying assertion is that psychology has been studiously ignoring the obvious.

General Characteristics of Criteria and Predictors

In observing behavior in natural settings, the psychologist must divest himself of the laboratory orientation to manipulate and control. Naturally existing influences (independent variables) are so powerful that they are virtually certain to override or obscure variables a researcher might insert into the environment. This is especially true under either or both of the following conditions: (1) if participants are aware that interventions have been made in order to study their reactions; (2) if the manipulation interferes with vital work or life support activities. Whenever possible, measurement of behavior in natural groups must derive from and not be imposed upon naturally occurring behavior.

The research on saturation diving began with a specification of the criteria of performance and adjustment to be predicted. While this may seem to be a logical approach, in another sense it may appear to be putting last things first, since dependent variables are specified before independent variables. In an attempt to measure criteria relevant to important aspects of adjustment and performance, variables with the following characteristics were chosen. Criterion variables have been: (1) based on relatively broad concepts that derived from an analysis of the environment; (2) based on measures of real performance and adjustment; (3) multiple measures rather than single indices; (4) dependent on a variety of methods of measurement and have come from a variety of data sources; (5) quantitative and, whenever possible, based on multiple data points; (6) objective; and (7) measured unobtrusively. Finally, (8) criteria have *not* been based on subjective self-report nor on artificially contrived tests.

Predictors should be derived from the criterion variables. It is desirable to have predictors that are as similar to the criteria as possible. Actual performance at a prior time in exactly the same situation is the best and most precise predictor of performance in the target situation. However, this level of correspondence between criteria and predictors is seldom possible for exotic environments. Divers cannot be put in saturation diving conditions in the open sea in order to select them for such work. Similarly, astronauts cannot be put in orbit in outer space to select them for that mission. Therefore, in broad terms the predictors should have the same characteristics as the criteria specified above, with the exception of reliance on real performance in the target environment.

It may be necessary to rely on performance in a similar, rather than the same, situation. Returning to the previous illustration, performance of a diver working in nonsaturated conditions could be used to predict his performance in a saturated setting. Jet test-pilot performance was used to predict performance in a spacecraft. With increasing automation of spacecraft it is questionable that the same predictor will work in the future. Training in geology appears to have been as important as experience in jet aircraft for our men on the moon. Following the principle of maximum similarity between predictors and criteria it should be possible to specify the kinds of tests that make the best predictors of the criterion.

CRITERION COMPONENTS—CONCEPTS

Criterion components employed in research on saturation diving have been identified and used by Drs. Eric Gunderson and Paul Nelson (1966) in their research on Antarctic wintering-over groups. These concepts defined three rather broad facets of adjustment of men to unusual environments. The ready transfer of these concepts from their use in the Antarctic to use in saturation diving indicates their broad applicability. They should be useful in assessing the performance and adaptation of individuals and groups in any environment separated by time or distance from a normal environment. The criterion components are: task performance, social interaction, and emotional adjustment.

While these facets of adjustment are quite likely to be highly intercorrelated—that is, a successful adjustment in one area will be accompanied by successful adjustment in the other two areas—they nevertheless are conceptually distinct and there are advantages to using them as distinct concepts. The principal advantages of separate consideration are in directing attention toward several aspects of adjustment and in indicating the types of measures that can be used to assess those aspects. In addition, all three of these factors would seem to be of special importance in groups isolated from the normal environment.

For example, in discussions of adaptation to the Antarctic, Rohrer (1961), Wilkins (1967), and others have identified the importance of work in the exotic environment. Because men in environments separated from normal society are deprived of many of their normal roles and functions, the work role assumes added importance as a consumer of time, as the basis for a man's status, and as an index of successful adjustment.

Similarly, social interaction within a small group in an isolated environment is of crucial importance. Janis (1963) has summarized many of the reasons for the characteristic increase in group solidarity among men facing danger or the stresses of the unknown. In his analysis, depending both on Freudian and social psychology, Janis makes the point that such men depend on each other for support, self-evaluation, self-validation, and the satisfaction of a variety of needs that are either of lesser importance or are satisfied by a number of groups or persons in normal society.

Of special significance is the variety of emotions, including fear, anxiety, depression, exhilaration, pride, and excitement, which are normally experienced in isolated and confined environments. The success of individuals and groups in coping with the emotions that appear in unusual environments is a significant factor in overall adjustment and adaptation.

While the appropriate or characteristic emotional reactions will vary from one environment to another, depending upon the levels and kinds of physical and psychological stress, exotic environments have the potential of producing exotic emotional reactions. These emotional reactions will be important, not only in their own right, but also in the feedback loop by which they are linked to social interaction and performance.

Work by Schachter and his colleagues (1964) has produced fresh insights on the role of social and environmental factors in determining the development and labeling of emotional reactions. Schachter's work has demonstrated clearly the inadequacy of purely physiological approaches to the measurement and definition of emotions, emphasizing the complex interplay of social and other situational determinants.

Deciding on Criteria

TASK CRITERIA

How do we decide on criterion variables in a given situation? First, let us consider task performance. The appropriateness of task-criterion variables can be decided by an analysis of the specific situation. In work on saturation diving, the principal task criterion has been diving time. It has been fortunate, and perhaps somewhat unusual, that this one measure has applied quite well to all persons in Sealab and Tektite.

The principal reason for choosing diving time as the major indicator of task performance is that maximizing diving time has been the publicly stated and universally accepted goal of saturated diving projects. While there have been some differences in role requirements—that is, some men have had more work to do inside the undersea habitat than have others —all participants in saturation diving programs have been divers. Another reason for using diving time was that the collection of these data required no intrusion into the situation. A record of diving time is kept as an official record in diving programs and is thus minimally subject to error and distortion.

A common denominator of performance may not usually be available. For example, widely different measures of performance are necessary to assess the work efficiency of scientific and support personnel teams in the Antarctic. A further complication in the Antarctic research is that it is not possible to observe the groups under study. Through diligent and well-directed efforts Gunderson, as described in this volume, has solved these problems by using ratings of leaders and peers. Questions such as "Who is the best man in performing his work at this station?" allow the respondent to judge the person in comparison with all others regardless of differences in jobs. The criterion has been the consensus of the leaders and peers. In this situation, the group is the standard of comparison. A man's performance in relation to other persons in his group determines the adequacy of performance.

The group as a standard has also been used in the research on diving. However, in Tektite II, the most recent saturation diving studies, overall group performance has been extracted as a covariant. This refinement would be more difficult to implement in the Antarctic, but even in this setting it should be possible to obtain at least rough measures of overall group performance by some outside judge. Group estimates could then be used in order to get more precise estimates of individual performance across groups.

Thus, the problem of specifying measures of task performance is not insurmountable, and similar principles will apply in any natural setting. That is, criteria should be based upon actual work rather than reactions to some contrived or artificial test. The best measure of work for each man will depend on analysis of the situation.

The recommendation to use multiple measures of each criterion component suggests the use of measures other than a single indicator of performance, no matter how exemplary the best measure may be. Less direct measures of task performance such as leader ratings have been used in the work on saturation diving. In addition, precise measures of performance on some subtasks may be available. In this case, a behavioral scientist would be well advised to enlist the assistance of subject matter specialists who are qualified to make judgments of the particular performance. In summary, the important point about task measures is that they should measure actual performance on real tasks. If possible, at least one measure should be quantified on an ordinal scale and be objective.

TASK PREDICTORS

Predictors of task performance criteria should be as similar as possible to the performance criterion variables. For example, if diving time is a major criterion variable, each candidate's amount of prior diving, preferably a relative amount, would be the best predictor. The classic summary statement of this point is that the best predictor of future performance is past performance.

The recent establishment of computerized data banks promises great advances in this area in the near future. For example, a complete record of the logs of all Navy dives is now being collected and stored on computer tape. This data bank is a research tool of enormous potential. It can be used in evaluating the effectiveness of training programs in personnel selection on initial entry and in personnel management for all decisions in a man's diving career. For example, if men are needed for a particularly challenging assignment, the detailed record of past performance can be used to select the pool of best qualified men. Volunteers could be recruited from this group of qualified men. While the military can be expected to take the lead in this area, advances in computer technology suggest that such facilities will assume increasing importance for personnel selection and management.

If, however, detailed predictive information is not readily available, specially designed rating forms asking for previous leader or supervisor evaluations may provide excellent predictive information. Other possible predictors of diving performance would be such things as variety of diving experiences, marks in diving school, and lifelong interest in swimming. On a more general level, an indication of motivation to perform useful constructive work could be gleaned from a life history. Similar specific and general predictors of task effectiveness may be defined for the general case of performance criteria by an analysis relying on past behavior as the best predictor of future behavior.

SOCIAL INTERACTION—CRITERIA AND PREDICTORS

For both criteria and predictors of social interaction, the measurement technique of choice is some variant of sociometric instruments. From a conceptual standpoint, it stands to reason that the best assessment of successful social adjustment is the judgment of a man's peers as to how desirable a companion he is. Lindzey and Byrne (1968) observed that sociometric instruments "are designed specifically to provide a sensitive and objective picture of the interpersonal relations existing within a group. . . . Consequently, they are of singular importance to the empirically oriented social psychologist" (p. 452). Viewed as to their record of performance, Hollander (1954) maintains that: "Peer nominations present a more superior consistent predictor of performance criteria across situations than any single variable. The evidence, mainly for military studies, is quite clear on this point."

A major reason for the effectiveness of peer nominations is that they are based on multiple data sources. The value of this property of data is becoming increasingly recognized (see Campbell & Fiske, 1959.) In a group of 30, each person is evaluated by 29 different and knowledgeable judges. While each man may err in evaluating his peers, the errors are likely to cancel each other and to fix the individual with much greater accuracy than will any single measure. There is of course the possibility of negative and positive halo effects. Even if such effects are significant, however, they will doubtless have a bearing on adjustment. A man who is universally accepted or rejected by his peers, especially in an isolated environment, will adjust better or worse by reason of those evaluations.

One problem with sociometric techniques as both criteria and predictors is the reluctance of members of small or highly cohesive groups to make sociometric choices. They are especially reluctant to make negative choices. One technique is to use only positive sociometric choices. However, the relation of positive only to both positive and negative choices has not been well investigated. As noted by Lindzey and Byrne (1968), lack of methodological work is a general problem with sociometric techniques. The importance of peer choice certainly justifies far more methodological attention than it has received.

Another good measure of social interaction is contact with the outside world. For isolated groups, outside contacts are a particularly appropriate index. In most remote settings, some form of communications with the outside is provided. These communications can be monitored as to frequency and length of communication by individual. Some examples of outside contacts are telephone calls, radio communications, and letters. In Sealab II, the number of telephone calls proved to be an excellent measure of social compatibility. The number of phone calls had a strong negative correlation with sociometric choice and other measures of social interaction, as well as task measures.

In summary, there is little doubt of the extreme importance of sociometric techniques specifically, and of measuring social interaction in general as both a criterion and predictor. It does appear, however, that methodological work is needed in this area. Because of the robustness and importance of the variables, the methodological efforts can be expected to have excellent payoff.

EMOTIONAL CRITERIA

Emotional reactions are difficult to assess both as criteria and predictors. In the Antarctic, Gunderson and Nelson (1966) have used leader and peer ratings of emotional adjustment with some success. In a variety of situations, including research on saturation diving, a mood adjective check list has proved to be valuable. However, there is a requirement to develop techniques of assessment that do not depend upon subjective self-report.

Meal behavior is a potentially fruitful source of information. As an indicator, it is universally applicable, sensitive, and revealing. If observational facilities are available, the simplest type of data is of course whether or not a meal is eaten and, over the course of time, how many meals are missed. This measure was used on Sealab II. More difficult, but still possible, is an assessment of the quantity of food eaten. However, this technique depends upon knowing whether a man is eating more or less than normal. Other aspects of meal behavior related to adjustment are whether meals are eaten alone or in groups, moods during meals, and frequency and regularity of eating.

Related to meal behavior as an assessment of emotional adjustment is the measurement of how much weight a man gains or loses during his exposure to a stressful environment. For example, Rohrer (1958) and others have observed that in the Antarctic most men gain a good deal of weight. It would seem that individual deviations from the proportional gain in weight by the group would indicate favorable or unfavorable individual emotional adjustment. Similarly, records of sick calls may provide a measure of emotional adjustment. Even where attainable, however, such indicators provide only gross estimates.

The physiological measurement of emotional adjustment holds out the promise of precise evaluation. With the development of sophisticated telemetering devices, it should be possible to develop more refined physiological measures. However, a major problem with physiological measures has been identified by Schachter (1964), who has shown that similar states of arousal may be differentially labeled according to influences such as prior experiences, social contacts, and information available—in short, affected by a variety of personal and situational predisposing and "postdisposing" influences. It is sufficient to observe that the measurement of emotions is an especially tricky and difficult enterprise.

EMOTIONAL PREDICTORS

Predictors of emotional reactions are also difficult to assess. There are, of course, a host of paper-and-pencil tests available. However, such instruments suffer from at least three problems. First, despite their sophistication, it is still possible to "fake" responses to such instruments. Second, it is quite possible that an individual is unaware of his typical emotional reactions. Finally, this problem is intensified by the fact that exotic environments are not typical. Base-line measures, however accurate, may not predict well in extreme environments.

Measures that yield behavioral and/or physiological indices of emotions present a good deal of promise. Specifically, Lazarus (1966) has used films to produce emotional reactions. Relatively precise physiological reactions to realistic arousal can be assessed using this method. A similar measure, providing behavioral as well as physiological responses, is the stress threat test developed by Wherry and Curran (1965). A personality type test that yields behavioral measures is the rod and frame test developed by Witkin et al. (1962). This test measuring field dependency would seem to have high face validity for subjects such as divers for whom orientation is an important requirement. An additional important indicator of emotional reactions is the life crisis scale developed by Holmes and Rahe (1967). Scores derived from answers to objective questions about critical occurrences in an individual's life during the past year have proved to be highly effective in predicting susceptibility to disease. Such a measure would be especially useful for relatively short crucial missions.

DEVIATION SCORES

In research on saturation diving, the group has been the standard of comparison. Deviations from group means rather than deviations from a larger population of divers have been used as scores. For a variety of purposes, it is desirable to evaluate specialized groups in relation to the larger population groups from which they are drawn. If the types of measurements described here are widely employed, explanatory and predictive power will be increased by the ability to make comparisons across groups and to compare deviations from larger populations norms.

WHY HETEROGENEOUS MEASURES?

Human behavior is extremely complex. Both criterion and predictive measures lack conceptual and methodological precision. Given this state of the art, it is highly probable that any predictors will provide biased estimates of the true score of a given individual. Thus, increasing the reliability of a measure by adding more items to a test, or using additional measures highly similar and highly correlated with measures already used will only increase such biases. The solution rather is to use a variety of measures from a number of sources. Careful selection of measures will maximize the probability that the biases inherent in each measure will cancel out.

Consider the following example. Assume that there are two men whose theoretical qualifications are equal. That is, they are equally qualified as candidates for participation in a saturation diving program in the sense that they will be equal on "true" criterion scores. Suppose that one man is "person oriented" and the other is "task oriented." The first man might rate high on predictors such as sociometric choice and leader ratings, while the second would rate high on objective task-performance predictors and tests of capacity. If only one type of measure were used, one man would be favored over the other. If, however, heterogeneous measures are used, the biases in assessment will balance and neither will be favored. The position here advocated is that the greater the heterogeneity of measures employed in both predictors and criteria, the greater will be the validity of the estimate of "true" scores.

At a more general level, Webb et al. (1966) have provided compelling arguments for the use of multiple measures. Their discussion applies to all scientific concepts, but most directly to the social sciences. They state that "once a proposition has been confirmed by two or more independent measurement processes, the uncertainty of its interpretation is greatly reduced. The most persuasive evidence comes through a triangulation of measurement processes" (p. 3).

Several types of measures have been recommended and discussed in this paper. Table 7.1 presents an outline of the different types of measures proposed. This list is not exhaustive. Other methods of classification could have been used. The outline is presented to summarize and illustrate the main points of the discussion.

The use of heterogeneous measures poses considerable problems in reducing and analyzing data. The use of heterogeneous measures forces the investigator to combine apples and oranges. Not only a large number of measures but a large number of data points per measure will be accumulated if the present recommendations are followed. Fortunately, recent advances in electronic data processing have kept pace with the growth in amount of data. Similarly, the increasing sophistication and power of multiple regression techniques (see Cohen, 1968) allows the investigator to extract the maximum information from his data.

EXTENSIONS AND APPLICATIONS OF THE PROPOSED APPROACH

The preceding discussion is concerned mainly with predicting individual responses to exotic environments. The purpose of this detailed discussion is to illustrate some of the salient features of the method proposed and its utility. This has, I hope, been accomplished. However, in doing this a false impression may have been left. The reader may feel that the prediction of individual performance and adaptation is the sole application of

TABLE 7.1   *Summary of types of measures*

type of measure	criterion examples	predictor
Subjective self-report	Qualitative reports: interviews, questionnaires adjective check lists	Tests of character, such as personality tests
Objective self-report	Self-maintained quantitative logs, such as amount of sleep or work	Tests of capacity, such as IQ tests Biographic inventories
Other report	Leader or supervisor ratings Sociometric choice Employee ratings of leaders	Leader or supervisor ratings Sociometric choice Employee ratings of leaders
Observation	Objective records of work, social interaction, and emotional adjustment Clinical evaluations Audiotape, videotape, and other electronic records, such as EEG and biochemical	Objective records of work, social interaction, and emotional adjustment in training or previous jobs Clinical evaluations Physical examination Anthropometric data "Emotional" tests
Archival data	Dive, flight, ship, and communication logs Medical records	School records Performance ratings Medical records

the approach proposed here. Far from being the sole use, the prediction of individual performance and adaptation may not even be the most valuable contribution the present behavioral oriented approach can make. In this section, some extensions and applications of the proposed approach will be examined briefly.

One interesting and productive way of using data based on naturalistic observations of real-life groups is to examine variations in productivity and adaptation over time. For example, Weybrew (1963) in work in submarines and Gunderson (1963) in Antarctic groups, among others, have noted midperiod slumps in moods. Other studies have identified end spurts in performance and adjustment. Channel fever describes, in the vernacular, responses determined by time. Collection of detailed records of behavior, or in some cases existing official records, can reveal such temporally related phenomena and identify their regularity.

A special case of variations in performance over time is illustrated by the question: Are improvements, deteriorations, or steady states the norm for isolated groups? Subjective self-reports may be quite misleading in providing data on this point. For example, Smith (1966) found that members of the groups he observed in the Antarctic had the impression of no change or even deterioration in their performance, whereas objective measures indicated marked improvements in work efficiency.

Are there predictable interactions between various components of the conceptual criterion? Multiple component criterion data enables the investigator to determine if changes in productivity, for example, are accompanied by changes in social interaction and emotion, or if changes in one variable are preceded or followed by others with predictable regularity.

Are there stable temporal variations of productivity and adjustment between groups in the same environments? In different environments? For example, are periods of settling in, midslumps, or end spurts proportional to the length of stay? Detailed information from several groups will be useful in detecting normal and abnormal reactions during the history of a group.

Do successive groups exposed to exotic environments exhibit predictable changes in their ability to work and live in those environments? For example, certain problems may appear in pioneering groups but be absent in later groups exposed to the same environment. Or the opposite may occur, with new problems emerging as the novelty wears off. Restricting the identification of problems of adjustment and adaptation to measurement by subjective self-report may obscure such changes. It is quite possible that later occupants of exotic environments may report symptoms of maladjustment that have become part of the folklore of reactions, even if the causes of those symptoms have been greatly or partially eliminated. This would be particularly unfortunate if expensive or time-consuming organizational or environmental alterations had been instituted to alleviate the appearance of such symptoms. Objective records could provide a check on self-report in this instance.

Only limited data on these points are available from previous research; moreover, the presently available data are not definitive. Present information frequently cannot suggest specific courses of action. Rather, current knowledge serves to define problem areas and underscore the need for more precise, detailed, and objective information on a wider variety of groups.

In order to develop and establish the concepts and methods proposed here, the approach must be extended and applied to more as well as different natural groups. To know how individual men and groups spend their days, weeks, and months together, and to know it in detail, is a necessary first step toward a general understanding of adjustment to the environment in which their time is spent. The methods suggested here, if widely used, are capable of providing increasingly precise descriptions and lawful explanations of individual and group behavior. While it is important to collect information on other diving groups using these techniques, it is even more important to extend the methods employed here to the measurement of behavior in other groups.

An ideal opportunity for extension is the space program's proposed orbital workshop crews. While opportunities and facilities exactly similar to those used in studying undersea groups are not available for studying space crews, the basic techniques can be easily adapted to that situation. Highly comparable data can be gathered on future undersea and outer space missions. Some advantages of this joint opportunity are the similarities of the men and crews, duration of missions, and the psychological characteristics of the environments. A common conceptual and methodological approach to data collection in the two environments will greatly accelerate the understanding of, adjustment to, and performance in both environments.

To date, the National Aeronautics and Space Administration has looked to laboratory and simulation groups in order to understand and predict the behavior of men in space flight. Such information is useful. An excellent analysis and annotated bibliography of laboratory and simulation studies has been compiled for NASA by Fraser (1966). Furthermore, the Tektite projects were designed, in part, to provide data relevant to the behavior of man in long-term missions in outer space. It is perplexing and surprising that NASA has not considered space crews themselves as the most appropriate groups to study in order to predict performance and adjustment to spaceflight. However, there have been no reports of detailed systematic studies of psychologically relevant aspects of adjustment to spaceflight. Such studies are entirely within the realm of present capabilities.

Consider for one example, possible studies in the area of communications alone. Questions of interest to behavioral scientists such as the following could be asked and answered. What is the frequency and length of communications between ground control and outer space capsules over the course of a flight? What proportion of these communications is task relevant versus socially motivated? Does the frequency and length of communications vary according to the stage of the mission? Are there lawful variations according to the length of the mission and the number of crew members? Are communications related in any way to task performance within missions and across missions?

Supposedly complete records of communications have been taken and such information may still be available for analysis, but only one such mission appears to have been so studied (Matarazzo et al., 1964). Since there have been approximately 35 manned spaceflights in the U.S. program, and if communication records are available on all these flights, a wealth of material may still exist that could shed light on many questions of psychological interest, some of which have been outlined above. With the talent, money, and technical facilities invested in the space program, it seems wasteful that systematic behavioral records have not been designed as a part of those studies. Perhaps such work has not been done because the required concepts and methods have not been available.

Automated Data Collection Methods

Since field research has been relatively neglected in recent years, behavioral scientists in general and social psychologists in particular have not benefited fully from the electronic revolution. TV, tape recorders, telemetering devices, and high speed computers enable researchers to collect and process large varieties of measures hitherto unavailable. There are a number of "state of the art" methods of increasing the automation and decreasing the intrusiveness of behavioral data collection (see Sidowski & Ross, 1969). Only insight, imagination, and money are required to implement such methods.

The possibilities in automating data collection can be appreciated by considering the sophistication achieved in sensing and transmitting psychophysiological information. Surely, if it is possible to sense and transmit minute signals emanating from neurological or fine muscular responses, it should be a relatively simple matter to sense and transmit signals produced by gross muscular or whole body responses. Thus, for example, it should be feasible to obtain records of location and activity through the use of automated sensors. In undersea research, simple records of location and relative amount of activity have proved to be a rich source of information regarding the structure and behavior of groups.

A basic problem in pursuing the goals outlined here is that, in going into the field, many scientists of all stripes, and behavioral scientists especially, feel that somehow their ability to conduct sound scientific research is compromised. Many investigators seem to feel that field research is inferior to laboratory research. While it is true that field research is different, it is not thereby inferior. Could it be that naive attempts to transfer laboratory methods into the field have resulted in the self-fulfilling prophecy that the real world is a barren, sterile, and impossibly difficult environment in which to conduct psychological research?

A few years ago, a bright but discouraged young researcher delivered an interesting paper at a human factors conference. He presented an impeccably neat factorial design with which he proposed to measure the performance of a new sensing device in guiding high speed aircraft to their targets. Before giving the results, he presented a fairly long and pathetic apologia detailing a variety of predictable real-life interferences that had hopelessly confused the neat cells of his experimental design. The error term in his analysis of variance was enormous. He concluded with an observation somewhat as follows: "An investigator going into the field can rely on only one thing, the utter and complete dissolution of his experimental design."

This example represents a common complaint of researchers who attempt to transfer a laboratory orientation into a field setting. The proper response to this state of affairs is not to abandon field research. Rather, it must be recognized that the appropriate experimental design in field studies exists in naturally occurring variables that are imposed with greater force and fidelity than a researcher can possibly produce in a laboratory setting. In order to be successful, the investigator must design studies so that the naturally existing requirements of the situation work for rather than against him.

IMPLICATIONS FOR PSYCHOLOGY IN GENERAL

Twenty years ago, E. G. Boring assessed the status of psychology in his classic work, *A History of Experimental Psychology* (1950). Boring exuded confidence. He observed that, "The academics now know that psychology is not a mean and narrow subject which they themselves dreamed up in order to be able to criticize one another. It is something that the world can use and is using. Psychology has escaped from the neurosis of adolescence by getting itself wanted, for, by becoming married to reality, it has gained its maturity. The dire warning of its doubtful parent [philosophy], that it would come to no good, now seems very long ago" (p. 743).

Are psychologists as confident today as Boring was 20 years ago? In 1950, psychology had a fresh record of significant contributions to the prosecution of World War II. It was being accepted in the government, in industry, in schools, and in society at large. However, something seems to have gone wrong on the way to the future. The marriage of psychology to reality, proclaimed by Boring, is on the rocks. Separation, if not divorce, has befallen the union since 1950.

In recent years the pages of the *American Psychologist* and other journals have been filled with articles and letters admonishing psychology to become "relevant." Various paths toward the goal of relevance have been suggested, many having concluded that psychology as a profession should be directed toward social action. Toward this end, there was a recent proposal to change the tax exempt status of the American Psychological Association (Sanford, 1970) so that it might engage in political lobbying. This awkward attempt to move the entire profession from the ivory tower directly into the real world would surely fail to accomplish its goals. Even if psychologists were to become directly involved in political action as a unified group—an unlikely prospect—they would be seen as only one more small lobbying group with no more political muscle than their numbers, financial resources, and unity deserved.

If psychology is less relevant today than it was 20 years ago, how did it get that way? A large part of the problem appears to be the severely constrained methodological corner into which we have painted ourselves. Webb et al. (1966) have discussed the problem of methodological constraint in detail. They point out that the vast bulk of psychological research depends on a single method, questionnaires. Sociologists Brown and Gilmartin (1969) present highly revealing data on this point. In an analysis of reports in the two leading sociological journals, they found that "not a single study [of 242] was based on systematic observation, the recording or tallying of specific types of behavior according to a predetermined schedule." They conclude that "in actual practice, the sociologist today limits himself rather generally to the construction and conduct of questionnaries and interviews. . . . Non-verbal behavior is likely to pass unexamined, along with the crucial issue of correspondence between what is said and what is done."

Ring (1966) has criticized the excessive reliance on laboratory studies, and specifically deception studies, in social psychology. However, Ring's suggestion that "role-playing" experiments be substituted for deception experiments cannot be endorsed here. The substitution of role-playing experiments would move experimental social psychology even farther from reality than it already is. Ring's criticism was based primarily on ethical considerations. The internal validity of laboratory research has also been questioned by Rosenthal (Rosenthal & Rosnow, 1969) and others who have examined critically the problem of experimenter bias. Furthermore, using laboratory research in a concerted attack has not produced the significant theoretical advances that were promised. For example, regarding theories of cognitive consistency, Brehm (1970) points out that a flood of laboratory studies focused in this area has not produced a unified theory. The opposite has been the case, with a bewildering number of small unrelated hypotheses emerging from the work, obscuring the general propositions with which the investigations began.

Psychology may be less relevant today because we have forgotten our heritage. In the same chapter from which the above-quoted assessment of psychology was taken, Boring (1950) identified the great men in psychology. The results of Boring's analysis might surprise many psychologists. He lists four men as having had the greatest impact on the discipline. They are Darwin, Helmholtz, Freud, and James. The appearance of Charles Darwin's name on this list may seem curious to many psychologists. Darwin not only appears on Boring's list of the four most important men in the history of psychology, but he is identified as the most important of the four.

The fact that current problems of psychology may have developed partly because of the methodological influence of Charles Darwin is scarcely apparent today. To be sure, his theories concerning the nature of man are so integral a part of our thinking that they are seldom questioned by psychologists. However, Darwin's methods, primarily the observation of phenomena in the natural world, have been neglected almost completely. The bulk of psychological investigations are laboratory studies, following the model of Helmholtz, or questionnaire studies attempting to assess psychodynamic concepts derived from Freud. Psychology even has more of the philosophical, speculative endeavor exemplified by James than it does the naturalistic observations of Darwin.

The concepts and methods proposed here call for a return to field research by a significant number of psychological researchers. While this is a minority position within psychology today, it has a respectable history. In addition to Darwin, such men as Galton, Hall, J. M. Cattell, Guthrie, and Lewin exemplify the approach. Perhaps the outstanding contribution of psychological research, the intelligence test, was developed almost completely by field research. The intelligence test was an attempt to solve a problem in the real world, using information derived from real life. Furthermore, its criteria in the early stages were practical and applied.

Conclusion

New tools and methods are available for rapid advances in field research. Recent developments in the use of the camera, tape recorder, television, and more sophisticated electronic data collection and recording equipment have only scratched the surface of the potential of this equipment. Previously neglected sources of data such as archives and official records can be tapped to supplement data obtained from observations. Computer advances will assure increasingly ready access to large amounts of archival data. Various standard techniques such as sociometric measures and leader ratings can be added. Thus, it is more feasible than before, although still difficult, to employ multimethod, multivariable assessments of criteria and predictors.

Recent advances in the development of multiple regression as a data analysis tool parallel the growth of equipment (Cohen, 1968). Finally, the new approach recommended here will result in huge masses of data. Fortunately, electronic data processing is expanding to meet these needs.

These converging developments make possible totally new approaches in field research and in psychology in general. This paper has focused largely on the investigation of small groups in undersea habitats. It has attempted to outline the halting steps that have been taken in that area toward more thorough and productive field research. If these methods are generally applied and further developed, psychology's impact on government policy and human affairs can be expected to increase greatly, surpassing the high water mark of involvement and influence reached during World War II. Psychology will be able to follow the advice of a recent president of the *American Psychological Association* who recommended that we "give psychology away" (Miller, 1969). Research in the real world would not only contribute directly to the impact of psychology on mundane problems, but its theoretical propositions would at the same time, in Harlow's (1953) words, "catch up with, and eventually even surpass, common sense."

REFERENCES

Appley, M., & Trumbull, R. 1967. *Psychological stress: Issues in research.* New York: Appleton-Century-Crofts.

Boring, E. G. 1950. *A history of experimental psychology.* New York: Appleton-Century-Crofts.

Brehm, J. 1970. Review of R. P. Abelson, E. Aronson, W. J. McGuire, T. M. Newcomb, M. J. Rosenberg, and P. H. Tannenbaum, eds. *Theories of cognitive consistency, a sourcebook. Contemp. Psychol.* 15:167–69.

Brown, J., & Gilmartin, B. 1969. Sociology today: lacuna, emphasis and surfeits. *Amer. Sociologist* 4:283–91.

Campbell, D. T., & Fiske, D. W. 1959. Convergent and discriminant validation by the multitrait-multimethod matrix. *Psychol. Bull.* 56:81–105.

Cohen, J. 1968. Multiple regression as a general data analytic system. *Psychol. Bull.* 70:426–43.

Fraser, T. M. 1966. The effects of confinement as factor in manned space flight. NASA Contractor Report #511, Washington, D.C., July.

Georgia, University of. 1962–63. Shelter occupancy study—University of Georgia. Office of Civil Defense, GEOU-226-FR.

Gunderson, E. K. E. 1963. Emotional symptoms in extremely isolated groups. *Arch. gen. Psychiat.* 9:362–68.

Gunderson, E. K. E., & Nelson, P. D. 1966. Criterion measures for extremely isolated groups. *Personnel Psychol.* 19:67–80.

Harlow, H. F. 1953. Mice, monkeys, men, and motives. *Psycholog. Review* 60:23–32.

Hollander, E. P. 1954. *Leaders, groups and influence.* New York: Oxford University Press.

Holmes, T., & Rahe, R. 1967. The social readjustment rating scale. *J. psychosom. Research* 11:213–18.

Janis, I. L. 1963. Group identification under conditions of external danger. *Brit. J. Med. Psychol.* 36:227–38.

Lazarus, R. 1966. *Psychological stress and the coping process.* New York: McGraw-Hill.

Lindzey, G., & Byrne, D. 1968. Measurement of social choice and interpersonal attractiveness. In *The handbook of social psychology: Research methods,* ed. G. Lindzey & E. Aronson, vol. 2, pp. 452–525. Reading, Mass.: Addison-Wesley.

Matarazzo, J. D., Wiens, A., Saslow, G., Dunham, R. M., & Voas, R. B. 1964. Speech durations of astronauts and ground communicator. *Science* 183:148–50.

Miller, G. A. 1969. Psychology as a means of promoting human welfare. *Amer. Psychologist* 24:1063–75.

Radloff, R., & Helmreich, R. 1968. *Groups under stress: Psychological research in Sealab II.* New York: Appleton-Century-Crofts.

Rasmussen, J., & Wagner, C. 1962. Psychological studies. In *Studies of the Bureau of Yards and Docks Protective Shelter: I Winter Trials.* NRL Rept. 5882.

Rasmussen, J., Wagner, C., & Morris, C. 1966. Psychological studies. In *Studies of the Naval Facilities Engineering Command Protective Shelter: II Winter Trials.*

Ring, K. 1967. Experimental social psychology: Some sober questions about some frivolous values. *J. exp. soc. Psychol.* 3:113–23.

Roethligsberger, F. J., & Dickson, W. J. 1939. *Management and the worker.* Cambridge: Harvard University Press.

Rohrer, J. H. 1958. Some impressions of psychic adjustment to polar isolation. Georgetown University Medical School, Washington, D. C., March. (Mimeo.)

———. 1961. Interpersonal relationships in isolated small groups. In *Psychophysiological aspects of space flight,* ed. D. E. Flaherty, New York: Columbia University Press.

Rosenthal, R., & Rosnow, R. L., eds. 1969. *Artifact in behavioral research.* New York: Academic Press.

Sanford, N., ed. 1970. APA and public policy: Should we change our tax-exempt status? *Amer. Psychologist* 25:i–xvi.

Schachter, S. 1964. The interaction of cognitive and psychological determinants of emotional state. In *Advances in experimental social psychology,* ed. L. Berkowitz, vol. 1, pp. 49–80. New York: Academic Press.

Sidowski, J., & Ross, S., eds. 1969. Instrumentation in psychology. *Amer. Psychologist* 24:186–384.

Smith, W. M. 1966. Observations over the lifetime of a small isolated group, danger, boredom and vision. *Psychol. Rept.* 19:475–514.

Webb, E. J., Campbell, D. T., Schwartz, R. D., & Sechrest, L. 1966. *Unobtrusive measures: Non-reactive research in the social sciences.* Chicago: Rand McNally.

Weybrew, B. B. 1963. Psychological problems of prolonged periods of marine submergence. In *Unusual environments & human behavior,* ed. N. Burns, R. Chambers, & E. Hendler, pp. 85–125. New York: Crowell Collier and McMillan, Inc.

Wherry, R. J., & Curran, B. M. 1965. A study of some determiners of psychological stress. U. S. Naval School of Aviation Medicine, Rept. #2, July.

Wilkins, W. L. 1967. Group behavior in long-term isolation. In *Psychological stress: Issues in Research,* ed. M. Appley & R. Trumbull, pp. 278–88. New York: Appleton-Century-Crofts.

Witkin, H. A., Dyk, R. B., Paterson, H. F., Goodenough, D. R., & Karp, S. A. 1962. *Psychological differentiation.* New York: Wiley.

Zubek, J. P., ed. 1969. *Sensory deprivation: Fifteen years of research.* New York: Appleton-Century-Crofts.

William Wesley Haythorn *has been Professor of Psychology and Urban and Regional Planning at Florida State University since 1969. He received his Ph.D. from Rochester University in 1952 and after work as a social psychologist for the U.S. Air Force (1952–55) he was manager of the logistics system laboratory for the RAND Corporation from 1955 through 1962. He has since taught at a number of colleges and universities, consulted for many private and public research agencies, and from 1964 through 1969 was Director of the Behavioral Sciences Department of the Naval Medical Research Institute.*

Haythorn *identifies social isolation as an important research subject, in light of its incidence in technological innovations such as space capsules and submarines, and in consideration of social psychology as a newly-recognized major field, apart from biological and physiological psychology. Citing the results of heretofore scanty and primarily anecdotal studies in the field, he supplements previous findings with newer ones based on sound experimental laboratory methodology, particularly his and Altman's data on isolated dyads, both hypothetically compatible and hypothetically incompatible. He then demonstrates a curvilinear relationship between stress and performance: Performance is apparently enhanced under social isolation conditions up to the point of moderate stress, and only then begins to deteriorate. Haythorn concludes with a matrix analysis of needs by sources of satisfaction, drawing on Maslow's taxonomy of human needs and hypothesizing that closed systems, to date, have not provided for certain higher-level human needs. The thrust of his argument is that subsequent systems design will ideally engineer a complete human existence, an ecologically balanced "mini-world," with the potential of keeping groups socially and emotionally viable in social isolation for indefinite periods of time.*

8

The Miniworld of Isolation: Laboratory Studies

Background

It is generally recognized that man is a social animal whose behavior is significantly determined by his need for other people and his reactions to other people. This social aspect of man's existence is nowhere more evident than when he is isolated from his fellow man. The importance of social contact has long been recognized, as seen in the use of solitary confinement for purposes of punishment and voluntary isolation for religious meditation. However, social isolation per se has only become of major interest to psychologists within the last two decades.

The reasons for this belated interest are not hard to find. Historically, psychology began by adopting a biological or physiological model of man and avoided the emphasis given to social considerations, by sociologists and social philosophers, as either not concerned with the individual or not sufficiently rigorous scientifically. Social psychology as a major field of study really didn't get going, except for the work of a few individual scientists, until the late 1930s, and has developed as a separate specialty within psychology primarily within the last 30 years.

The interest of social psychologists in social isolation has been stimulated by modern technology, which increasingly permits men to enter en-

From Bureau of Medicine and Surgery, Navy Department, Research Subtask MR006.08.0001. The opinions and statements contained herein are the private ones of the writer and are not to be construed as official or reflecting the views of the Navy Department or the naval service at large. The author was formerly Director, Behavioral Sciences Department, Naval Medical Research Institute, Bethesda, Maryland 20014.

vironments such as outer space and the ocean depths in which he is phys-ically removed from the larger society and largely deprived of normal social contacts. Observations of small groups of men in Arctic and Antarc-tic weather stations, submarines, and high-altitude aircraft led to initial conclusions that such conditions were conducive to low morale, psychoso-matic complaints, and occasionally severe and bizarre stress reactions. These field observations by psychiatrists, clinical psychologists, and oper-ational personnel provided strong impetus to an interest in understanding the effects of isolation and confinement on small groups of men. Labora-tory studies designed to contribute to such understanding have thus ap-peared only within the last 10 to 15 years.

Previous Reviews

The available literature on isolation and confinement has been extensive-ly reviewed a number of times (see Fraser, 1966; Schultz, 1965; Smith, 1969). These reviews are unanimous in noting that most of the literature is anecdotal in nature and that very little of it is based on sound experi-mental laboratory methodology. The logistics involved in staffing and running a long-term isolation and confinement study are complex and ex-pensive, and the number of variables of interest is large, so that few labo-ratories have had the resources and administrative support to conduct such research. Nonetheless, the results reported in the literature are suffi-ciently important to both social psychology and systems designers to war-rant yet another review introducing additional material and providing a somewhat different conceptualization from those of previous reviews.

Stresses of Isolation

The anecdotal literature and much of the field and laboratory research indicate that isolation and confinement are stressful to many individuals, and that the stress is sometimes severe enough to result in serious decre-ments in adaptation and performance. It appears, on close examination, that there are a number of different sources of stress involved, and that individual differences in tolerance for these stresses greatly complicate the task of predicting who will be able to tolerate any specific isolation and confinement situation. In order to help clarify the picture, we can be-gin by identifying the various sources of stress and the reactions associat-ed with each.

STIMULUS REDUCTION

Most isolation and confinement situations involve a degree of stimulus re-duction that many individuals find disturbing. Even in relatively stimulus-rich settings such as modern submarines, prolonged missions are likely to become boring and monotonous to many crew members (Mullin, 1960; Weybrew, 1963). Studies of extreme degrees of stimulus reduction, usually called stimulus or perceptual deprivation studies, have recently been covered in depth by Zubek (1969; ch. 2, this volume). Individuals in relatively monotonous group settings, such as an Antarctic weather station or a Distant Early Warning radar station in the Arctic, experience some of the same subjective responses as do individuals in the more extreme conditions of individual sensory deprivation (Myers, 1969; Schultz, 1965; Smith, 1969).

Stimulus deprivation has been studied in the laboratory in a variety of ways, ranging from total immersion in water set at skin temperature to the less extreme condition of restful confinement to dark, soundproof chambers. Subjects in these studies typically report considerable subjective stress and emotional symptomatology, including hallucinatorylike visual sensations, fears of losing their sanity, vexation at the boredom and monotony, unusual and alarming thoughts about themselves, and others (Myers et al., 1962). Factor analyses of an Isolation Symptomatology Questionnaire developed by Myers and his colleagues have yielded three clusters of items that have been labeled *tedium stress,* reflecting concern with the boredom and monotony of isolation; *unreality stress,* concerned with novel and frightening reactions to stimulus reduction; and *positive contemplation,* reflecting the positive reactions of some individuals to the opportunity isolation provides for thinking about one's life and the meaning of things. The first two of these are negatively related to isolation tolerance. The latter, *positive contemplation,* is characteristic of individuals showing a high degree of isolation tolerance (Myers, 1969).

A test of whether these same reactions occur in isolated small groups was provided by a study of dyads confined to a small (12' x 12') room for 10 days during which they had no contact with the outside world except for announcements of time to awake, receive food, commence or terminate tasks, and go to sleep. In comparison with control groups that were similarly selected and given identical tasks to perform in the same rooms by the same schedule, but who were free to leave the rooms between tasks and whose members slept in the regular Navy barracks and ate in the regular Navy dining hall, the isolated groups reported more subjective stress and emotional symptomatology (Haythorn, Altman, & Myers, 1966). This difference was especially pronounced for hypothetically incompatible isolated dyads, in comparison with either incompatible control or compatible isolated groups. We shall return to this study below. At this point, the relevant find is that small, isolated groups—in this case, dyads—reported symptomatology and stress similar to, but less extreme than, individuals confined for up to 7 days in complete darkness and silence. The symptomatology results would seem to confirm the hypothesis that at least part of the stress reported by these isolated laboratory groups was attributable to stimulus reduction relative to more normal environments.

Although not a laboratory study in the usual sense, Rasmussen (1962; 1968) reports on a study of 100-man groups confined to a fallout shelter for 2 weeks. One such group was run during winter months and another during the summer. Since environmental control facilities in the shelter were minimal, the two runs differed considerably in the temperature and humidity maintained inside the shelter. The volunteer subjects were subjected to rigid medical and psychiatric screening, which eliminated about one-half of the summer group and about one-third of the winter group. Subjects were not told how long they were to be confined, and were offered no incentive for participation other than the intrinsic reward of making a useful contribution. To study psychological discomfort, subjects ranked 21 sources of discomfort. "Boredom" ranked sixth in acuteness of discomfort in the winter test and ninth in the summer test, indicating again the importance of stimulus reduction as a source of stress in isolated group settings.

CONFINEMENT

A second major source of stress, and one that is of particular importance to designers of undersea or space vehicles, is that of confinement. There is a considerable premium on available volume in such vehicles. Extra volume means extra expense, which may be prohibitive. It is therefore desirable from an engineering and cost point of view to minimize the volume per man provided for living and working quarters. Since both space and underwater vehicles operate in environments hostile to the unprotected man, crew members are required to spend most if not all of their time inside the vehicle. This obviously restricts mobility, brings crew members into contact with each other more intimately and continually, and limits opportunities for crew members to get away from each other. The normal option of voluntary withdrawal from a group is largely, if not completely, denied to crew members of such vehicles.

In an excellent review of the literature on confinement per se, Fraser (1966) identifies a number of multiman aircraft or space cabin simulator and multiman chamber confinement studies. Most of these studies ran only one crew one time, and are better described as feasibility tests than as laboratory studies. Nonetheless, by looking across studies Fraser is able to identify reasonably consistent findings regarding the deleterious effects of tight confinement. His general conclusion is that "confinement, when defined as a physical and temporal limitation on the activities and translational motions of an individual or group, is a stress-inducing entity which can be discriminated from, although it is sometimes accompanied by, perceptual and social isolation" (p. 102). Fraser notes, furthermore, that various types of perceptual aberrations such as those reported in stimulus deprivation studies are also reported by individually confined subjects, but with two subjects the incidence of such reports is markedly reduced, and with more than two its occurrence has not been reported.

Emotional reactions, according to Fraser, are not uncommon in confinees. With a multiple crew, the resentment is commonly directed against other crew members, although if motivation and discipline are high these reactions will frequently be latent rather than overt. Interpersonal relationships in carefully selected, well-motivated simulator crews, however, do not seem to give rise to problems, at least during the first 30 days of confinement.

Physical discomfort is reportedly severe in simulator studies wherein the restrictive element of confinement is great. Fraser finds an interdependency between available space per man and length of mission in determining the degree of discomfort. By locating each of 59 confinement runs, varying from one-man simulator studies to actual submarine cruises, on a volume by duration chart, and noting the degree of discomfort, stress, or difficulty reported, he generates curves of recommended minimum volumes per man for groups of different sizes, indicating increases in recommended volume per man with increases in mission duration and/or group size. The minimum volume per man recommended ranges from 50 cubic feet for 1 man on a 1-day mission, to about 240 cubic feet per man for a 10-man crew on a 400-day mission (Fraser, 1966, p. 101).

Intellectual or complex psychomotor performance in these simulator studies is relatively unaffected by confinement per se, although it is significantly impaired by sensory or perceptual isolation. Other performance changes in these studies are either minimal or are attributed by Fraser to environmental conditions other than confinement (p. 104).

In a series of laboratory studies at the Naval Medical Research Institute in Bethesda, Maryland, it has been noted that individuals confined in pairs behave as though territorial preferences were important to them. Altman and Haythorn (1967a) assigned pairs of men to isolation or control conditions, composing groups such as to complete a Greco-Latin square design in which a third of the pairs was homogeneously high, another third homogeneously low, and the remaining third heterogeneous with regard to each of four personality measures. These measures were: dogmatism as measured by the Rokeach Dogma Scale; and needs for affiliation, dominance, and achievement as measured by the Edwards Personal Preference Schedule. Analysis revealed a marked tendency for isolated dyads—and particularly those that were hypothetically incompatible—to establish mutually exclusive use of room objects and locations as the period of confinement progressed. (Results from this study regarding territoriality are summarized in more detail in the chapter by Altman.)

In a second major study at the Naval Medical Research Institute addressed to an aspect of confinement per se, Taylor, Wheeler, and Altman (1968) provided half of their isolated pairs of men an opportunity for privacy by assigning them to two adjoining rooms. Each man slept in his own room, but was free to enter the other room whenever he wished. Group tasks were scheduled in one or the other of the rooms, so that a degree of interaction was required daily. Subjective reactions were measured by the Subjective Stress Scale developed by Kerle and Bialek (1958) and the Spielberger measures of trait and state anxiety (Spielberger, 1966). Other independent variables manipulated in this study, in a 2 × 2 × 2 experimental design, were expectations regarding mission duration provided by initial instructions (4 days vs 20 days), and daily outside stimulation provided by verbal instructions, 5-minute broadcasts of rock-and-roll music, a 1964 Huntley-Brinkley documentary record, and a series of questions and answers from the "*Playboy* Adviser" column dealing with sports, law, etiquette, hobbies, food, and so forth (these audio stimuli were presented periodically to the "stimulated" pairs, but not to the nonstimulated pairs).

It had been expected that the possibility of privacy would serve to ameliorate some of the stress. The "privacy" manipulation by itself, however, contrary to expectations, produced significantly elevated levels of state anxiety and subjective stress under conditions permitting privacy. This was primarily true for dyads expecting to be confined for 20 days. It appeared that the greater degree of forced interaction in the no-privacy condition had stress-ameliorative effects, or conversely, the greater degree of social isolation in the privacy condition heightened the subjective stress response, particularly when subjects were given expectations of remaining isolated for a relatively long time.

Another aspect of confinement per se that has been noted in the anecdotal literature is that men become overexposed to each other. That is, they reportedly reveal personal information about themselves, tell their favorite stories, and display their personal idiosyncracies to the point of boring and irritating each other (Byrd, 1938, pp. 16–17; Smith, 1969). To examine this phenomenon in the laboratory, Altman and Haythorn (1965), in the dyad study previously described, included a self-disclosure questionnaire developed by Jourard (1964) that asked subjects both before and after the 10 days of isolation to indicate what items of personal information they had disclosed to their dyad partner, their best friend, and their average acquaintance in recruit training (which they had finished just prior to their participation in the experiment).

Analyses revealed that members of isolated dyads revealed both more and more intimate items of information to each other than did members of control dyads. Even in as short a time as 10 days, the isolated dyad members reportedly had revealed personal information at an intimacy level approximating what they had revealed to their best friends. This, it was felt, substantiates the field observation that co-confinement under conditions of social isolation accelerates the acquaintance process, perhaps more rapidly than the group members are able to develop common norms or otherwise accommodate to each other.

SOCIAL ISOLATION

A third hypothetically important source of stress in isolated, confined situations is social isolation per se. Small groups of men confined to small vehicles or habitats for prolonged periods of time, with minimal or no contact with the larger society, would appear to have more difficulty in satisfying social needs than would groups of men equally confined but not deprived of outside social contact. Many personality and social psychological theories would suggest that men need others for social need satisfactions, social comparisons, social reality testing, and so forth. Reduced opportunity for social contact and communication would seemingly impair these social processes. Unfortunately, however, the evidence relating to this hypothesis is largely indirect. There have been no direct laboratory tests, to my knowledge, that successfully separate effects of social isolation per se from those of confinement and stimulus reduction. The indirect evidence, however, supports the hypothesis that social isolation is by itself a significantly stressful condition for at least a substantial number of people, and that the reactions to it are distinguishable from those to confinement and stimulus reduction.

The study that best makes this distinction for small, isolated, laboratory groups is the study by Taylor, Wheeler, and Altman (1968), described above. One of the manipulations included in the study was to provide outside contact to half of the isolated dyads, but not to the other half. This condition, labeled *stimulation*, did not by itself produce a difference in anxiety or subjective stress reports, but it was involved in a couple of significant interaction effects. In describing these interactions, the authors state that "the 20-day privacy groups with lack of stimulation showed a significantly sharp increase of A [anxiety] state by Day 5, when all groups in this condition aborted. On the other hand, groups in short missions (4 days) with outside stimulation and privacy were least stressed" (p. 373). It appears, then, that outside contact had some stress-ameliorating effect when taken in context with other variables.

The most socially isolated condition in this experiment, involving no outside stimulation, privacy, and expectations of a long mission produced subjective reports of rather severe stress and a 100 per cent abort rate, while the least socially isolated condition involving no privacy, outside stimulation, and expectations of a short mission produced very low levels of reported stress.

It has been argued that, especially in lieu of objective measures, men use social comparison processes to determine the validity of their opinions, the adequacy of their performance, and the appropriateness of their emotional responses (Festinger, 1954). Members of small, isolated groups obviously have fewer opportunities for making such comparisons than have members of larger or nonisolated groups.

In an experiment designed to test the hypothesis that men make more accurate and more stable self-evaluations when they have a larger number of comparison others, Radloff (1966) provided subjects with a pursuit rotor task and gave them feedback indicating their performance in relation to that of other subjects. Under various conditions his subjects were given feedback indicating that they were similar to or deviant from (either considerably better or worse than) the average of other subjects. They were then asked to estimate what their scores would be on subsequent performances of the task. Comparisons of their expected and actual subsequent performances indicated that subjects who received feedback placing them relatively near a large number of other subjects, either because they were approximately average or similar in their deviance to a large number of others, were both more accurate and more stable in predicting their own future performances.

The importance of social needs in isolated pairs of men was directly examined in the study by Haythorn and Altman (1967). Subjects were assembled in pairs in such a way as to complete a Greco-Latin square, in which some pairs had congruent or complementary needs for affiliation, dominance, and achievement, while for other pairs these needs were incongruent, noncomplementary, or competitive. It was predicted that pairs in which social needs were congruent or complementary would report less stress and emotional symptomatology than would pairs with competitive, noncomplementary, or incongruent needs. It was further predicted that the former, hypothetically compatible, pairs would show less tendency to establish territoriality and to withdraw from each other socially than would the latter, hypothetically incompatible pairs. Both of these sets of predictions were largely confirmed (Altman & Haythorn, 1967a; Haythorn, Altman, & Myers, 1966). It seems clear from this study that dyads composed to facilitate social need satisfactions adapted to the conditions of isolation better than did dyads composed to frustrate such satisfactions.

INTERPERSONAL STRESS

Interpersonal adaptation can be a problem in any group setting. It seems, however, to be especially troublesome in isolated groups. Elsewhere I have argued that interpersonal stress constitutes one of the principal sources of trouble in isolation and confinement situations (Haythorn, 1970). The hypothetically incompatible pairs of men in the Haythorn and Altman study reported more subjective stress and emotional symptomatology, established more clear-cut territorial behavior, and withdrew from each other socially. The stress and territoriality results were most evident for pairs of men with competitive high dominance needs, while the stress and withdrawal responses were significant for pairs with incongruent (heterogeneous) achievement needs. Two of the homogeneously high dominance pairs were unable to complete the 10 days of isolation, and two of the heterogeneous need achievement pairs in isolation showed remarkably high interpersonal hostility characterized by physical and verbal abuse directed toward each other. None of the isolated pairs with complementary dominance needs showed such interpersonal hostility.

At this point, we can only conjecture about why interpersonal stress is worse in isolation and confinement than in other situations. One obvious difference, alluded to above, is that it is more difficult to escape each other in isolation. Another is that the common ego defense mechanism of displacing aggression is less available, since there is no one outside the group to whom it can be displaced. Direct expression of aggression tends to be suppressed, presumably because group members recognize a high degree of mutual interdependence (Smith, 1969). This suppression of aggression has been cited by Mullin (1960) as a probable source of increased psychosomatic complaints in Antarctic weather stations.

Performance in Isolated Groups

Many of the studies of military crews assigned to isolation and confinement situations have been primarily concerned with performance effects of such conditions. Frequently, the interest has been in determining whether or not a particular kind of vehicle, habitat, or mission was feasible from the point of view of the crew's ability to survive and continue to perform adequately. Fraser (1966) concludes from his review of the literature that "intellectual or complex psychomotor performance, even under conditions approaching the intolerable, is relatively little affected by confinement *per se* although it is reduced under conditions of perceptual isolation. Where confinement is severe enough to produce physiological incapacitation, a significant decrement can be measured . . . but otherwise the minor decrements observed are probably due to fatigue arising from demanding work schedules, or from boredom associated with performance of repetitive and apparently useless tasks" (p. 103).

Altman and I (1967b) attempted to assess performance effects of isolation in small groups by providing our subjects with monitoring, decoding, and simulated combat information center tasks administered once or twice daily throughout the 10-day period. Significant performance differences were found between isolation and control subjects on the two group tasks (decoding and CIC), but in an unexpected direction. That is, the isolated pairs performed these tasks better than the control pairs. Hypothetically incompatible pairs also tended to perform better than hypothetically compatible pairs, again contrary to expectations. In attempting to understand these unexpected results, an analysis of the relationship between stress and performance was undertaken.

The best explanation, admittedly arrived at by indirect inference, is that a curvilinear relationship between stress and performance exists such that increasing stress up to a point has an arousal effect that improves performance. Beyond this point of moderate stress, evidence of impairment was found. The stress generated in this study was predominantly in the mild-to-moderate range, where the relationship to performance is positive. This explanation fits the data rather well and is consistent with laboratory group studies by Lanzetta (1955) and by Berkun et al. (1962).

Evidences of individual performance decrement in group confinement situations have been reported in some studies Adams & Chiles, 1961; Agadzhanian et al., 1963; Altman & Haythorn, 1967b; Hartman et al., 1964; Hicks 1962; Page, et al., 1964; Rodgin & Hartment, 1966).

Smith (1969) concludes, based on his review of the groups-in-isolation literature, that neither intellectual effectiveness nor perceptual-motor ability shows any consistent change of note during short-term confinement. For longer durations, however, the picture is less clear. Impairment of memory, difficulty in concentrating, low energy for intellectual pursuits, and less team performance effectiveness are often reported, but test data substantiating these reports are frequently lacking. Motivation and morale, however, which often relate to performance, generally deteriorate under long periods of isolation. Smith (1969) notes, for example, that there are no studies of long-term confinement reporting improved motivation and morale, though many studies report a deterioration. The degree of isolation, length of mission, the nature of the task, interpersonal compatibility, and undoubtedly many other variables interact to determine the performance of isolated groups. Considerably more research and model-building is needed to understand and predict task performance in isolation adequately.

Need Satisfaction in Isolated Groups

In the course of several years of research on isolated groups, I have come to believe that human needs constitute an especially valuable target of investigation for social psychology. No other situation brings the dynamics of individual and group adaptation so sharply into focus. No other complex social situation permits such complete experimental control of relevant variables, since all other situations allow subjects to interact with a larger world that is not under experimental control. This observation is what led to the concept of the miniworld of isolation. In a very real sense, the manned space capsule on an interplanetary voyage is a tiny world entirely self-contained except for temporal considerations of having a starting point and an expected terminal point. It seems instructive to examine the capacity of such a miniworld to satisfy human needs. By viewing the isolated group as a self-contained, complete ecological system, many important aspects of system design from both an engineering and behavioral science point of view come into bold relief.

A complete ecological system obviously has to be designed to meet the needs of organisms comprising the system. Since we are concerned here primarily with man, it seems reasonable to start by examining the needs of man that must be met. The needs one can identify are legion, so it will be necessary to classify in order to limit our discussion to a manageable number. No completely satisfactory taxonomy of human needs exists, but the widely-known one proposed by Maslow (1943) will serve our present purposes.

Maslow suggests that needs are hierarchically related so that lower-level needs must be at least minimally satisfied before higher-level needs become salient. The various needs may be simultaneously operative, but frustration of lower-level needs allegedly tends to reduce the importance or salience of higher-level needs. At the lowest level, Maslow places physiological needs such as hunger, thirst, and oxygen requirements, the prolonged frustration of which will result in death to the organism. With physiological needs at least minimally satisfied, safety and security needs become paramount. These refer to needs to avoid or escape threat, fear, danger, and uncertainty. Next in order are needs for affection and belonging. This level includes needs for love, approval, acceptance, and so on. Esteem needs assume salience when the three preceding levels are adequately satisfied. This level includes needs for recognition, status, dominance, individuality, and the like.

The fifth step in Maslow's hierarchy are the self-actualization or self-realization needs. These refer to the complex set of requirements men develop to realize their full potential. This seems to mean finding a way of life that allows the individual to exercise his unique constellation of abilities and interests in meaningful ways—that is, in ways that have relevance to the social and physical context in which he is situated. The needs to achieve worthwhile goals, and to contribute usefully to society, in ways that are compatible with the individual's total configuration of capabilities, interests, and roles are included at this level. In Maslow's view,

TABLE 8.1 *Relationship of satisfaction or frustration sources to human needs*

Human Needs

Sources of Satisfaction or Frustration	A. Physiological	B. Safety & Security	C. Affection	D. Esteem	E. Self-actualization	F. Cognitive	G. Aesthetic
1. Self	Stimulus needs Activity preferences Territorial needs Life support needs Sleep patterns	Trait-anxiety Isolation tolerance Effectiveness of coping with primary process Base-line excretion of adrenalin	need Affection	need Esteem need Dominance	need Achievement Self-concept Total personality	need Cognition	Aesthetic needs
2. Other group members	Life support interdependency Stimulus value thereof Interaction preferences	Aggressiveness of partners Overexposure Leadership	Congruence of affective needs	Complementarity of dominance and esteem needs	Congruence of achievement needs and values Overall complementarity of personalities Role complementarity Compatibility of roles with personalities	Cognitive stimulation Complementarity of knowledge Congruence of cognitive interests	Congruence of interests Aesthetic stimulation

	Outside contact	Rescue possibilities	Supportive communication	Recognition afforded	Role assignment	Provision of sources of information	Provision of aesthetic opportunities
3. Embedding organization (larger social system)	Expectations provided	Intervention possibilities Provision of safeguards Expressed concern for safety Emergency procedures training	Availability as scapegoat	Group structure established	Crew composition process Role definition and reinforcement Feedback regarding value of role Cultural context of mission	Responsiveness to informational inquiries	
4. Physical environment	Life support system Recreational facilities Stimulus variety Mission duration Space available	Physical danger Built-in safety Privacy opportunities	Group size	Status symbols in living-working space	Variety of activities permitted Physico-cosmic context of mission	Sources of information	Richness, beauty of environment

relatively few people reach complete satisfaction at this level of need. As some minimum level of satisfaction of self-actualization needs is attained, however, cognitive needs become salient. These include needs to know and understand, and instigate information seeking for the sake of knowledge per se. People concerned with the most basic scientific and philosophical questions would seem to be motivated largely by cognitive needs. Finally, at the top of his hierarchy, Maslow places *aesthetic* needs, which refer essentially to needs to experience beauty.

The *sources* of satisfaction of these various levels of needs are rather limited in the closed ecology of isolated and confined groups. An analysis of sources of satisfaction or frustration of the seven levels of needs was undertaken in order to identify problematic aspects of isolated groups that had not been particularly emphasized in earlier research. The results of that analysis are presented in matrix form in Table 8.1. The matrix shows the seven levels of needs in Maslow's hierarchy as columns, and four sources of satisfaction or frustration as rows. Each cell, then, includes situational considerations, individual characteristics, or group characteristics relevant to the satisfaction or frustration of that particular need by that particular source.

The characteristics of individuals that seem relevant to need satisfaction in isolation are listed in the first row, labeled *Self,* in the column that appears most relevant. The second row identifies *Other group members* as sources of need satisfaction or frustration. The *Embedding organization,* or larger social system, is identified in the third row as a major source of potential satisfaction or frustration. Finally, the fourth row lists the *Physical environment* as a potential satisfier or frustrator.

In the design of submarines, underwater habitats, space vehicles, and the like, the necessity of satisfying the most obvious of the physiological needs has been recognized in the extensive programs of life support systems development. Men clearly must have an adequate atmosphere, water supply, food supply, and waste management system if they are to survive.

Research on isolation and confinement suggests, however, that other physiological needs exist that have not been as well recognized in the design of closed systems, such as needs for stimulation and physical activity. Myers (1969), for example, reports that activity preferences as measured by Thrill Seeking and Sociability scales were significantly correlated with Worry and Phobia measures in a stimulus deprivation study. Zubek (1963) found that physical exercise mitigated the effects of 7 days of perceptual deprivation. Fraser's review (1966) indicates the importance of the available space per man as well as mission duration in a confinement situation. The stimulus value of other group members has been commented on in the anecdotal literature (see Smith, 1969, for example), and the increased rate of self-disclosure in isolated groups has been measured by Altman and Haythorn (1965).

The existence of important territorial needs has been noted by Hall (1959), among others, and territorial behavior in isolation has been confirmed by Altman and Haythorn (1967a). The degree of contact or communication with the outside world and the expectations regarding mission duration provided by the embedding social system were found by Taylor, Wheeler, and Altman (1968) to be significant factors in determining the degree of subjective stress and state anxiety reported by isolated dyads. In a study designed to separate the effects of stimulus reduction from those of confinement per se, Smith, Myers, and Johnson (1967) found that a stimulus enriched confinement situation produced far fewer requests for release (aborts) and stimulus seeking behavior than did a stimulus reduced confinement situation (see also Smith & Myers, 1966). The stimulus enriched condition in this study provided considerable recreational opportunities for subjects.

It has also been generally recognized in systems design that safety needs must be minimally satisfied if men are to be asked to function as crew members. This recognition takes the form of built-in safety features, emergency procedures training, and the development of rescue capabilities when possible. The U. S. Navy, for example, has been publicly and explicitly concerned with developing deep submergence rescue capabilities. The National Aeronautics and Space Administration has been explicitly and publicly much concerned with safety precautions during manned space launchings and recoveries. This overt display of concern on the part of embedding organizations for the safety of crew members is, I believe, ample testimony to the fact that such needs are recognized as highly important.

The ability of individuals to tolerate the unavoidable risks and dangers inherent in many such assignments is generally considered in selection and screening procedures. The voluntary nature of participation in most such programs provides reasonably good assurance of motivated individuals who are not likely to be easily alarmed or frightened by the inherent dangers. Prior experience in similarly dangerous settings adds to this assurance. Psychological and psychiatric screening, additionally, usually seeks to eliminate anxious or emotionally unstable individuals.

Commenting specifically on individual characteristics predictive of isolation tolerance, where physical danger is not present, Myers (1969) highlights the importance of four factors, three of which seem relevant to the individual's needs for safety and security, or his proneness to anxiety and worry. The four factors emphasized by Myers are: (1) effectiveness of coping with primary process material, (2) rapid perceptual satiation, (3) lower base-line excretion of adrenalin, and (4) relatively high Pd and Ma scores on the MMPI, high thrill-seeking scores, and high need Aggression scores on the Edwards Personal Preference Schedule.

All but the second of these seem to relate to safety and security needs. The aggressiveness of other group members seemingly constitutes a source of threat to safety needs, and it has been argued (Altman & Haythorn, 1965) that overexposure to each other is somewhat threatening. Smith (1969) cites several studies emphasizing the role of leadership in group maintenance activities, including peace-keeping and guaranteeing the rights of individuals. According to the aforementioned study by Taylor, Wheeler, and Altman (1968), one of the results of providing opportunities for privacy in relatively high-stressed groups was to deny group members some of the emotional support they derived from each other in no-privacy conditions.

Needs for affection and belonging have been largely neglected by systems designers, but the available data argue for their importance. Individual differences in need for affection would seem to be related to adaptation to isolation, since there would be fewer other people from whom affection could be sought. This variable has not, however, proved predictive of isolation tolerance. On the other hand, congruence of affective needs in isolated pairs was found by Altman and Haythorn (1967a) to be related to territoriality and social interaction patterns of behavior, with isolated pairs with incongruent needs for affection, as measured by the EPPS, showing greater territorial behavior and greater social withdrawal than either their control counterparts or other isolated pairs. It can be hypothesized that affectively supportive communications from the larger society, when possible, will help mitigate the stress of isolation, but the only data supporting this hypothesis are anecdotal in nature. The physical environment per se would seem to have little relevance to satisfying or frustrating the need for affection, except for the variable of group size. Presumably, larger groups would offer more opportunity for need satisfaction, at least up to a point.

Equally ignored by systems designers have been the needs for esteem. It has long been noted that one of the principal motives for group participation is the need for control, dominance, power, or prestige. The only direct evidence available regarding the importance of these needs in isolation, however, is the data indicating that complementary needs for dominance as measured by the EPPS is strongly related to dyad tolerance for isolation and confinement (Haythorn, Altman, & Myers, 1966). These data also indicate that the individual's need for dominance by itself is not predictive of either tolerance or lack of tolerance. The individual's dominance needs have relevance only in the context of the other man's dominance needs. Homogeneity of dominance needs, whether high or low, was associated with elevated reports of stress and emotional symptomatology. When dominance needs were homogeneously high, subjects established marked territoriality, interacted vigorously, reported high levels of subjective stress, and aborted. Homogeneously low dominance pairs also reported high levels of subjective stress, but showed a pattern of social withdrawal, a declining degree of territoriality with regard to beds, and did not abort. Heterogeneous dominance pairs—those said to have complementary needs—reported lower levels of subjective stress, showed relatively no pattern of territoriality, interacted at a rate between the other two compositions, and also showed no signs of aborting.

These results highlight the importance of viewing the isolated group as a single, closed system, with individuals existing in a complex social context. The data are not available for evaluating the effect of esteem-supporting communications from the larger society, but in view of the apparent relevance of such needs, it seems reasonable to assume that such communications would be valuable. The telephone conversation, televised around the world, between President Nixon and the astronauts on the moon possibly testifies to the recognition by NASA officials of this important need. (Other interpretations of this event are, of course, also possible.)

The opportunities for satisfying self-actualization needs in isolated groups would seem to be severely limited, except in those rare situations that combine isolation and pioneering research or exploration. Routine duty assignments to isolated outposts, underwater vehicles, and long-term manned space flights when they become more common may provide crew members a sense of accomplishment. But during the mission there will, in many such settings at least, simply not be enough to do to exercise the full potential of most crew members. Evidence bearing on this point is extremely weak, since there are no recognized measures of self-actualization needs, nor of their satisfaction or frustration. Need achievement, however, seems to be related, does have recognized measures, and has been administered to laboratory isolated groups as well as to groups in real-life isolation.

The Altman and Haythorn study yields evidence that dyad composition with regard to need achievement was significantly associated with stress, activity patterns, and task performance, but not with territoriality. As with need dominance, however, the significant differences were primarily between the heterogeneously and homogeneously composed dyads, rather than between the homogeneously high and homogeneously low. It appeared that incongruent—that is, heterogeneous—achievement needs produced elevated reports of subjective stress and emotional symptomatology (Haythorn, Altman, & Myers, 1966), a greater frequency of solitary versus joint activity (Altman & Haythorn, 1967a), and better performance on cooperative tasks (Altman & Haythorn, 1967b). The

only significant differences between the homogeneously high and homogeneously low isolated dyads were engendered by the greater tendency
for low-ach dyads to report less symptomatology and subjective stress
than other compositions, but this was only slightly more true for isolated
dyads than for controls.

Other aspects of the matrix analysis remain as yet untested, but are
certainly consistent with our more intuitive and global observations. If
the concept of self-actualization needs is valid, then the individual's total
personality—and especially his self-concept—is relevant to how well he
can achieve self-actualization in an isolated group setting. The overall
complementarity of personalities, the complementarity of the roles they
assume, and the compatibility of those roles with the personalities of crew
members would be crucial in facilitating or inhibiting individual crew
members in their search for more or less total adaptation to the situation,
finding satisfactory applications for their abilities and outlets for their interests. Likewise, the manner in which the larger social system has designed the structure of the crew, assigned roles, composed crews, defined
and reinforced roles both within the crew and between the crew and the
supporting organization, and provided feedback both before and, if possible, during the mission will contribute to the ease with which individual
crew members can fit themselves comfortably and satisfactorily into their
particular niche.

The cognitive and aesthetic needs are completely unresearched in isolated small group settings. It seems clear that individuals do have interests in cognitive and aesthetic activities, and these seem difficult to pursue
in isolation. Anecdotal reports from Antarctic weather stations indicate
that men frequently go to Antarctic duty with plans to complete correspondence courses or do a lot of nonfiction reading as part of their self-
education. These plans, more often than not, fail to materialize. The low
level of activity, monotonous stimulus conditions, and/or relative lack of
social reinforcement are apparently not conducive to sustained cognitive
activity.

This is perhaps also the reason for the difficulty in concentrating or
thinking clearly that is often reported in isolation or stimulus reduction
studies. The stimulus value of other group members, mentioned earlier,
can be at least partly addressed to cognitive needs, to the degree that men
learn from each other. This thought suggests the concept of informational
complementarity, or the condition wherein one member of a pair has information that the other lacks and vice versa. This would seem to be conducive to effective mutual satisfaction of cognitive needs, to the extent
that cognitive interests were congruent, or to the degree that the knowledge each man had was interesting to the other. Examples of this kind of
relationship can be drawn from the NMRI studies, but no systematic investigation has yet been undertaken. The value of providing sources of

information, and the actual availability of sources of information, has also been mentioned in the anecdotal literature (see, Byrd, 1930, p. 210), but no systematic data are available.

Much the same observations can be made regarding aesthetic needs, except that there is even less reliable research data. Admiral Byrd (1938) eloquently describes the aesthetic experience of witnessing the aurora australis, and the recent Apollo astronauts have commented on the beauty of the earth from outer space, but these are experiences not available in most routine isolated duty stations. We have seen nothing of the aesthetic interests in our laboratory studies except for an occasional subject who is also an artist. If aesthetic needs are important to men, however, as Maslow suggests, then some provision for their satisfaction in long-term missions might be worthwhile.

There does not appear to be any good evidence that frustrations of the highest level needs—cognitive and aesthetic—have any profound effect on performance. This may be, however, because even the longest periods of isolation for which good data exist are relatively short when compared with an interplanetary trip or some longer mission. It may also be because frustrations of lower-level needs, as Maslow argues, inhibit the salience of higher-level needs. If this be true, then it might reasonably follow that satisfaction of the lower-level needs would make the higher-level needs more salient, and their adequate satisfaction might then become more important to successful adaptation and performance.

The primary points of the matrix analysis of needs by sources of satisfaction are that man has more needs than the physiological and security needs currently recognized in systems design, and that research into these higher-level needs has already yielded useful results. It seems to me that we are ready to move beyond the problems of keeping men alive and functioning in closed ecological systems for limited periods of time, to keeping them indefinitely viable as a socially and emotionally effective group. This calls for engineering a complete human existence—a miniworld—with a capability of satisfying all the human needs. Viewing laboratory research on isolated groups in this way highlights a number of problems that have not yet been attacked in any systematic way, but past research holds the promise that progress is attainable. This view also seems to me to focus on many of the shortcomings of previous research, and particularly sensitizes us to extraneous variables affecting group behavior in particular isolated situations, but which may not be generally operative.

REFERENCES

Adams, O. S. & Chiles, W. D. 1961. Human performance as a function of the work-rest ratio during prolonged confinement. ASD Technical Rep. 61–720.

(Contract No. AF33 (616)–6050, Aeronautical Systems Division, Aerospace Medical Laboratory, Wright-Patterson AFB, Ohio.) Lockheed-Georgia Co., November.

Agadzhanian, N. A., Bizin, I. P., Doronin, G. P., & Kuznetrov, A. G. 1963. (Change in higher nervous activity and some vegetative reactions under prolonged conditions of adynamia and isolation). *Zhurnal vysshi nernoi Deiatelnosti*, Pavlov, 13:953–62. Cited by Smith, 1969.

Altman, I., & Haythorn, W. W. 1965. Interpersonal exchange in isolation. *Sociometry*, 28:411–26.

Altman, I. & Haythorn, W. W. 1967a. The ecology of isolated groups. *Behavioral Science*, 12:169–82.

Altman, I. & Haythorn, W. W. 1967b. The effects of social isolation and group composition on performance. *Human Relations*, 4:313–40.

Berkun, M. M., Bialek, H. M., Kern, R. P. & Yagi, K. 1962. Experimental studies of psychological stress in man. *Psycholog. Monogr.*, 76, no. 15, (Whole no. 534.)

Byrd, R. E. 1930. *Little America*. New York: Putnam.

———. 1938. *Alone*. New York: Putnam.

Farrell, R. J. & Smith, S. 1964. Behavior of five men confined for 30 days: Psychological assessment during Project MESA. Contract no. NASW–658, The Boeing Co., Seattle, Wash., no. D2–90586.

Faucett, R. E. & Newman, P. P. 1953. Operation Hideout: Preliminary report. Medical Research Laboratory, U.S. Naval Submarine Base New London, Conn., Report no. 228, July.

Festinger, L. 1954. A theory of social comparison processes. *Human Relations* 7:114–40.

Fraser, T. M. 1966. The effects of confinement as a factor in manned space flight. NASA Contractor Report NASA CR–511, Washington, D.C., July.

Hall, E. T. 1959. *The silent language*. New York: Doubleday.

Hartman, B. O., Flinn, D. E., Edmunds, A. B., Brown, F. C., & Schubert, J. E. 1964. Human factors aspects of a 30-day extended survivability test of the Minuteman Missile. USAF School of Aerospace Medicine, Aerospace Medical Division (AFSC) Brooks AFB, Tex., Technical Documentary Rep. no. 64–62, October.

Haythorn, W. W. 1970. Interpersonal stress in isolated groups. In *Social and psychological factors in stress*, Ed. J. E. McGrath, pp. 159–76. New York: Holt, Rinehart and Winston.

Haythorn, W. W. & Altman, I. 1967. Together in isolation. *Transaction*.

Haythorn, W. W., Altman, I., & Myers, T. I. 1966. Emotional symptomatology and stress in isolated pairs of men. *J. exp. research Person.* 4:290–306.

Hicks, S. A. 1962. The effects of twenty-four hours of confinement in mobile armored personnel carriers on selected combat relevant skills: A follow-up. Technical Memorandum 7–62, Human Engineering Laboratories, Aberdeen Proving Ground, M. June.

Jourard, S. M. 1964. *The transparent self-openness, effectiveness, and health.* Princeton, N.J.: Van Nostrand.

Kerle, R. H. and Bialek, H. M. 1958. The construction, validation, and application of a Subjective Stress Scale. United States Army Leadership Human Research Unit Research Report. Monterey, Calif.: Presidio of Monterey, (Fighter IV).

Lanzetta, J. T. 1955. Group behavior under stress. *Human Relations.* 8:29–53.

Maslow, A. H. 1943. A theory of human motivation. *Psycholog. Review.* 50:370–98.

Mullin, C. S. 1960. Some psychological aspects of isolated Antarctic living. *Amer. J. Psychiat.* 117:323–25.

Myers, T. I. 1969. Tolerance for sensory and perceptual isolation. In *Sensory deprivation: Fifteen years of research*, Ed. J. P. Zubeck, New York: Appleton-Century-Crofts.

Myers, T. I., Murphy, D. E., Smith, S., & Windle, C., 1962. Experimental assessment of a limited sensory and social environment: Summary results of the HumRRO Program. Presidio of Monterey, Calif.: U.S. Army Leadership Human Research Unit research memorandum, February.

Page, R. N., Dagley, C., & Smith, S. 1964. Manned environmental system assessment (MESA) program: Final report. Contract No. NASW–658, The Boeing Co., Seattle, Wash., no. D2–00487–5, June.

Radloff, R. 1966. Social comparison and ability evaluation. *J. exper. soc. Psychol.*, *Suppl.* 1:6–26.

Rasmussen, J. E. 1962. Psychological studies. Chapter 8 in *Studies of the Bureau of Yards and Docks Protective Shelter. I. Winter Trials.* NRL Rept. 5882.

Rasmussen, J. E. 1968. Psychological studies. Chapter 8 in *Studies of the Naval Facilities Engineering Command Protective Shelter: II Summer Trials.* NRL Rept. 6656.

Rodgin, D. W., & Hartment, B. O. 1966. Study of man during a 56-day exposure to an oxygen-helium atmosphere at 258 mm hq. Total pressure: XIII. Behavioral factors. *Aerospace Med.* 37:1130–35.

Schultz, D. P. 1965. *Sensory restriction: Effects on behavior.* New York: Academic Press.

Smith, S. 1969. Studies of small groups in confinement. In *Sensory deprivation: Fifteen years of research*, ed. J. P. Zubek. New York: Appleton-Century-Crofts.

Smith, S., & Myers, T. I. 1966. Stimulation seeking during sensory deprivation. *Percep. mot. Skills* 23:1151–63.

Smith, S., Myers, T. I., & Johnson, E. 1967. Stimulation seeking throughout seven days of sensory deprivation. *Percep. Mot. Skills* 25:261–71.

Spielberger, C. D. 1966. Theory and research on anxiety. In *Anxiety and behavior*, ed. C. D. Spielberger. New York: Academic Press.

Taylor, D. A., Wheeler, L., & Altman, I. 1968. Stress relations in socially isolated groups. *J. person. soc. Psychol.* 9:369–76.

Weybrew, B. B. 1963. Autonomic resiliency, subjective symptomatology, and submarine stress. New London, Conn.: Naval Medical Research Laboratory, *Memorandum Rept. no.* 63–13, November 12.

Zubek, J. P. 1963. Counteracting effects of physical exercises performed during prolonged perceptual deprivation. *Science* 142:504–6.

———. Ed. 1969. *Sensory deprivation: Fifteen years of research.* New York: Appleton-Century-Crofts.

Irwin Altman *is Professor and Chairman of the Department of Psychology at the University of Utah. He received his Ph.D. from the University of Maryland in social psychology, and has taught at the American University and the University of Maryland. His general area of interest is in interpersonal relations, with an emphasis on the role of the physical environment as a determinant and result of interpersonal exchange. He has also co-authored a book outlining a theory of the development and deterioration of interpersonal relationships,* Small Group Research. *The work reported in this chapter grew out of several years of research he conducted at the Naval Medical Research Institute, Bethesda, Maryland, on the impact of social isolation on the interpersonal functioning of small groups.*

Altman *presents an "ecological" approach to the process of interpersonal exchange that is based on a series of studies of socially isolated groups and on studies of the development of interpersonal relationships. From these data he offers a model of interpersonal functioning based on the theme that interpersonal events function as a system, with synchronized behaviors occurring at verbal, nonverbal, and environmental levels. Particular emphasis is placed on the latter, in the form of territorial behavior and general use of space.*

An Ecological Approach to the Functioning of Socially Isolated Groups

IRWIN ALTMAN

Introduction

This chapter outlines an approach to the functioning of small isolated groups in relation to adaptation and coping processes, management of conflict, and facilitation of positive interpersonal exchange. Broadly speaking, the chapter adopts an ecological orientation to interpersonal behavior, and approaches group functioning as a complex system operating through time within relatively fixed environments.

The theoretical orientation presented later is based on two lines of research I have been engaged in for several years. The first concerns social penetration processes that occur in the development, management, and deterioration of interpersonal relationships—that is, the ongoing behavioral events that occur as interpersonal relationships proceed from strangership to friendship and beyond. Early work on social penetration emphasized verbal exchange and subjective expectancy processes at various stages of relationships (Altman & Haythorn, 1965; Altman & Taylor, 1968; Colson, 1968; Frankfurt, 1965; Page, 1968; Taylor, 1968; Taylor, Altman, & Sorrentino, 1969; Taylor & Oberlander, 1969; Tuckman, 1966). More recently, a broader orientation has been taken, which goes beyond verbal behavior to a simultaneous analysis of use of space and the physical environment (Altman, Taylor, and Sorrentino, 1968; Lett, Clark, & Altman, 1969) and nonverbal behaviors such as gestures, eye

Much of the research reported in this paper was undertaken at the Naval Medical Research Institute, Bethesda, Maryland. The statements and opinions are those of the author and do not reflect the views of the Department of the Navy or the naval service at large.

contact, posture, and head nodding. This work contributed to the ecological orientation described below by making salient the fact that interpersonal exchange is not restricted to one behavior modality alone. Rather, to understand how interpersonal relationships grow and deteriorate requires simultaneous analysis of many levels of functioning beyond the verbal one.

The second line of research that contributed to the themes of this chapter involved investigations of socially isolated groups in laboratory settings, conducted at the Naval Medical Research Institute, Bethesda, Maryland. The first large scale study investigated the relationship between group member compatibility and interpersonal and performance behaviors (Altman & Haythorn, 1965, 1967a, 1967b; Cole et al., 1967; Haythorn & Altman, 1967; Haythorn, Altman, & Myers, 1966). A second study investigated group behavior as a function of degree of privacy, outside stimulation, and expectations about length of the isolation experience (Altman, Taylor, & Wheeler, 1971; Taylor, Wheeler, & Altman, 1968). A third experiment by Smith and Haythorn investigated the effects of compatibility, crowding, and group size on the functioning of isolated groups.

The first studies on the social penetration process provided the conceptual basis for the proposed ecological approach to group functioning; the isolation studies formed the pragmatic basis for viewing groups as intact, complex, multilevel "real" units. These two lines of research have gradually led to the position that an ecological orientation is required for the understanding of group functioning in general, and socially isolated groups in particular. The basic themes of this ecological orientation will be outlined below, followed by an overview of relevant research. A general theoretical framework of group functioning will then be presented; as this goes beyond available data, it falls somewhat short of a comprehensive theory.

An Ecological Orientation to Interpersonal Behavior

An ecological orientation involves several overlapping themes that form a general strategy of research at theoretical and empirical levels:

1. *Social process occurs at several levels of functioning.* Interpersonal exchange is multichannel, with communication occurring at several levels of behavior. People not only use verbal channels, but also interact via "self-marker" and "environmental prop" behaviors (Altman & Lett, 1970). Self-markers include nonverbal bodily behaviors such as smiling, eye contact, head nodding, postures, and gestures. Environmental prop behaviors encompass use of objects, areas, and aspects of the physical environment, including physical distance from others. These levels of functioning are accompanied by various internal cognitive/motivational proc-

esses and physiological events. An ecological orientation to the study of interpersonal relationships calls, ideally, for an analysis of as many of these levels of functioning as possible within a single program of study.

2. *Social behavior functions as a system.* An ecological orientation also presumes that the various levels of behavior operate as a holistic, integrated entity through time and at any point in time. Verbal behavior does not operate independently of nonverbal or environmental prop behavior. They fit together as a system of interrelated events, with properties of substitutability, compensatory functioning, equivalency, and others often attributed to man-machine and hardware systems. Thus, a smile may substitute for a head nod; a verbal statement of agreement may be equivalent to a certain body position; nervous fidgeting may represent psychological discomfort. The ideal is to study all levels of functioning *simultaneously* at a given point in time and through time, rather than to focus on only a single behavioral "slice." By working with multiple behaviors within or across channels, *behavior patterns* can be identified, and a more holistic understanding can be achieved of the functioning of "people" and "groups" as complex entities.

3. *Social process involves a man-environment relationship.* Interpersonal relations do not occur in a situational or environmental vacuum. They vary as a function of the properties of the physical environment and simultaneously involve active use of the environment. In work on socially isolated groups described later, it was demonstrated how conditions of the environment such as privacy, length of group isolation, and degree of stimulation affected interpersonal functioning. That is, the environment "acted upon" groups in an independent variable sense. But this research also demonstrates how conflict management and interpersonal adaptation and coping involve groups acting upon the environment. As a function of their relationship, members established territories for areas and objects in the environment, used beds in certain ways, and had architectural design preferences. Thus, an ecological orientation assumes social interaction to involve an *interperson-environment unit,* with the environment viewed from both behavioral determinant and behavioral response perspectives.

4. *Social process is ideally cast within a broad conceptual and methodological framework.* The breadth of an ecological strategy seems to require an organizing conceptual framework within which to cast specific facets of research. A theoretical study of groups may lead to much useful descriptive knowledge, but if research is to be generalized, especially to a realistic situation such as that of isolated groups, a conceptual framework is necessary. While the ideal is a deductive theoretical system, other levels of conceptual frameworks can be useful, including general integrative classification systems and syntheses of knowledge in specific areas. An ecological orientation assumes some effort to develop general conceptual

frameworks within which information about specific entities, such as isolated groups, can be cast.

There is also the need for a broad methodological orientation, which employs converging research methods addressed to the same empirical questions, in accord with the multitrait, multimethod approach to research. This calls for a diversity of research methods, including experimental techniques, field observations, interviews, and questionnaires. To the extent that the same research questions are approached by only a limited number of methods, the opportunities for knowledge and generalization are severely limited.

5. *Interpersonal functioning occurs through time and in a time-bound fashion.* Another working assumption of an ecological orientation is that group processes should be studied in a dynamic sense, with an understanding of how they occur through time, in sequentially interdependent chains. This means that interpersonal events should be viewed as part of a changing system, with events at Time 1 affecting and restricting the possible outcomes at Time 2, and so on. Understanding isolated or other groups is not only a matter of understanding resultant outcomes, but should also involve consideration of how events at one time are different from and derived from events at an earlier time.

These components of an ecological orientation comprise a strategy of research for understanding interpersonal relations. While easy to talk about and perhaps easy to agree with, implementation is another matter. But even if it cannot be wholly satisfied, the strategy has been a useful guide. A review of specific research conducted within this orientation is presented below. This is followed by presentation of a substantive ecological orientation to the functioning of social groups, with particular attention to isolated groups.

Research Background

The approach proposed in this chapter draws on research in several areas —the acquaintance process, nonverbal behavior, and man-environment relationships. The goal is to weave these areas into a coherent fabric addressed to development, management, and deterioration of interpersonal relationships.

I have been studying the social penetration process for several years. This term is used to encompass the events that take place as people develop and dissolve social bonds. Such questions as the following have been addressed. What is the behavioral history of development of an interpersonal relationship? Do the processes of self-disclosure, psychological accessibility, and openness by people to one another follow a systematic behavioral history? How do factors such as personality, interpersonal compatibility, and environmental presses slow down or accelerate the process?

Our framework hypothesizes that the growth of an interpersonal bond follows a systematic behavioral flow from strangership to acquaintance-ship to friendship to deep-seated emotional bonds. Loosely speaking, this development involves gradually increasing and systematic penetration toward the core of personality by social actors. As a social relation-ship develops, there appears to be an orderly process by which people come to know one another. They gradually learn more about one another by mutual exposure of themselves. What they learn is at first superficial and at the periphery of their personalities, but later they interact in more intimate areas and at greater levels of "depth." Several classes of factors drive this process, including mutual interpersonal rewards and costs expe-rienced in a dyadic relationship, personality factors, and the environment within which the relationship is embedded.

The social penetration process is seen as a complex of several levels of behavioral functioning, from subjective covert modes of response to a va-riety of overt behaviors. In early studies, emphasis was placed on verbal facets of interpersonal exchange as affected by personality, situational, and interpersonal reward/cost factors. For example, in the personality area, investigators in our laboratories established relationships between openness to others and integrative complexity (Tuckman, 1966). They also studied interpersonal exchange with a roommate (Taylor, 1968); personality measures on the MMPI and the Guilford-Zimmerman inven-tory (Taylor, Altman, & Frankfurt, 1966). Elsewhere, Polansky (1965) and Jourard (1964) have conducted a great deal of research on verbal openness and personality.

Earlier work also emphasized the generic nature of developmental processes in interpersonal exchange and the role of interpersonal reward/cost factors on the growth of social bonds. Several studies dem-onstrated the systematic growth of interaction from outer, superficial lay-ers of personality at the beginning of a social relationship to more deeply rooted, central aspects at later stages of the social penetration process (Altman & Haythorn, 1965; Colson, 1968; Frankfurt, 1965; Page, 1968; Taylor, 1968; Taylor, Altman, & Sorrentino, 1969). Several of these studies have also shown that interpersonal rewards and costs (that is, compatibility) accelerate the process, especially in intimate areas of ex-change, as reflected in verbal output. The role of environmental and situ-ational factors has also been studied in social isolation studies by Altman and Haythorn (1965) and in a laboratory study by Altman, Taylor, and Sorrentino (1968).

A second stream of research concerns the functioning of socially isolat-ed groups. This work highlighted the idea that understanding the social penetration process demanded a broader perspective than originally held, including analysis of how people use their bodies and the physical environment, along with verbal behavior, as communication vehicles. And, most important, it was desirable to see how these different levels of functioning operated as a coherent system. A preliminary conceptual framework that integrates these different levels of functioning is described in Altman and Lett (1970). Briefly, they hypothesize that antecedent variable classes including *personality factors* (personality, demographic characteristics, physiological and physical characteristics); *interpersonal factors* (compatibility, interpersonal history); and *situation-environment* factors lead to a *subjective situation definition*. This subjective analysis of situational requirements is translated into behavioral responses at several levels of functioning—*physiological, verbal, self-marker* (nonverbal behavior), and *environmental prop* (use of the physical environment)—which, in turn, are fused into *complex behavior patterns* involving complementary, systematic sets of individual behaviors. *Subsequent subjective evaluation processes* then feed back to earlier facets of the framework to yield a dynamic temporally changing behavioral system.

The social penetration and ecological frameworks provided the initial conceptual base for understanding the management of interpersonal relationships from the vantage of a multilevel, temporally longitudinal approach. It now becomes appropriate to undertake a further development of the framework with a specification of interrelationships between levels of interpersonal behavior, and a hypothesized set of dimensions which cut across levels, and which may be indicators of effective group functioning. First, however, it would be well briefly to review representative research on the environment, nonverbal behavior, and complex behavior patterns as related to interpersonal behavior.

The Environment and Interpersonal Relationships

The physical environment can be viewed from two perspectives—as a determinant of behavior, and as an aspect of behavior (Altman, 1971). Not only does interpersonal exchange occur within an environmental milieu that affects its course and character; social interaction also involves active use of the environment. In a word, there is a truly mutual relationship between man and his environment. However, with the exception of Roger Barker's work (Barker, 1963, 1968; Barker & Gump, 1964; Barker & Wright, 1955), little environmentally oriented research was conducted relevant to the matter of interpersonal relationships until the late 1950s. But research is expected to expand during the 1970s (see reviews by Altman & Lett, 1970; Argyle & Kendon, 1967; Lett, Clark, & Altman, 1969; Patterson, 1968; Sommer, 1967, 1969).

Past research emphasized the environment as an independent variable, as a determinant or cause of behavior, and then largely in terms of the effects of lighting, color, temperature, and other "pure" physical factors on feelings, perceptions, performance, and so forth. The social impact of variations in the environment has been studied in the context of proximity and interaction (Caplow, 1950; Deutsch & Collins, 1951; Festinger, Schachter, & Back, 1950; and many others reviewed in Lett, Clark, & Altman, 1969); microspace design and friendship (Blake et al., 1956); classroom seating arrangements and friendship (Byrne, 1961; Byrne & Buehler, 1955); social isolation and self-disclosure, territorial behavior and social activity (Altman & Haythorn, 1965, 1967a; Altman, Taylor, & Wheeler, 1971; Haythorn & Altman, 1967); and classroom seating arrangements and participation (see Sommer, 1967, 1969, for a review of much of this literature). Thus, environmental design arrangements, especially proximity, seem to be consistently associated with interaction, friendship, and mutual openness. Unfortunately, there is not yet much theory of environmental impact on social functioning, perhaps because we lack a systematic body of knowledge, and perhaps because there is no relevant taxonomy of environments, situations, and tasks.

A series of studies conducted on socially isolated groups illustrate how the environment serves both as a determinant and as a vehicle of interpersonal behavior. In one study, a variety of data were obtained from pairs of men socially isolated for 10 days (Altman & Haythorn, 1965, 1967a, 1967b; Haythorn & Altman, 1967; Haythorn, Altman, & Myers, 1966). Matched isolation and control groups were formed so as to be compatible and incompatible on need dominance, need achievement, need affiliation, and dogmatism. Isolates in general, and incompatible isolates in particular (especially those incompatible on need dominance and need achievement), showed more subjective stress reactions, emotional symptomatology, and interpersonal conflict, as well as some tapering off in performance effectiveness on team tasks. Mutual self-disclosure, a verbal aspect of the social penetration process, did not vary with compatibility, although isolates were more open to one another than controls, especially in intimate topical areas. Thus, the environment as an independent variable accelerated the social penetration process.

It is also interesting to see how members coped with one another insofar as active use of the physical environment was concerned. A measure of "territorial behavior" was developed to reflect degree of exclusive use of environmental objects and areas (chairs, areas, and beds), along with measures of social activity. The results indicated that different forms of incompatibility were associated with different modes of using the environment. Pairs incompatible on dominance (both high on desire to control and dominate) were quite territorial and socially active. They gradually divided up the room and had their own territories, as reflected in exclusive use of chairs, beds, and sides of the table, but still dealt with one another in a very active, perhaps competitive way. In many respects they never accommodated to one another and never achieved a working group consensus.

A different pattern was shown by those incompatible on need affiliation, where one man was desirous of social relationships and the other man was not. These groups also were territorial, but they withdrew from one another socially. This was a "quiet" incompatibility, with men staying in their own places and having little to do with one another. These groups also showed little stress, suggesting that they had achieved some ability to cope with one another and with the environment. Thus, this study demonstrates how interpersonal adaptation and adjustment occurs at several levels of behavioral functioning, and how interpersonal relationships are not only affected by an environmental milieu such as social isolation, but also how the physical environment is actively used to cope with interpersonal compatibility and incompatibility.

In the next study, three aspects of the environment were varied in a 2 × 2 × 2 factorial design: availability of privacy, expected length of social isolation, and degree of stimulation from the outside world (Altman, Taylor, & Wheeler, 1971; Taylor, Wheeler, & Altman, 1968; Taylor et al., 1969). In a "no privacy" condition, pairs of men lived and worked in the same room for 8 days; "privacy" groups had a two-compartment chamber with each man living in separate but connected areas. Outside stimuli were also varied, with differences in communication and interaction links with the outside world. The third variable involved expectations about length of the isolation period, with some groups expecting to be isolated for 4 days and others expecting a 20-day stay. The actual period of the experiment was 8 days, with uncertainty created in the 4-day groups when they were not released after 4 days.

Over half of the groups did not complete the isolation period and aborted, somewhat more so in 20-day conditions in the first few days and in the 4-day conditions after the fourth day, and more so in the privacy vs no privacy situations. Abort rates were higher for 20-day privacy groups and 20-day no stimulation groups than for the others, attesting to the impact of these conditions on adaptation to isolation. As in the prior isolation study and in accord with the ecological orientation of this chapter, a variety of behavioral measures from several different levels of functioning were obtained over the 8 days of isolation. Because of the large number of groups who aborted, it was possible to search for behavior patterns that distinguished successful and unsuccessful groups.

In several facets of behavior prior to, during, and following isolation, members of abort groups showed a characteristically different syndrome of behavior than completers. This behavior pattern cuts across several levels of functioning from subjective reports to use of space and objects, to task performance, to physiological functioning. Taken together, these data yielded a behavioral profile which suggested that aborters misread the demands of the situation and did not undertake effective group formation processes necessary to cope with the situation. A profile of their behavior, which forms a temporal narrative of how aborters and completers progressed through isolation, was sketched. The pattern described next is not universal, but interacts with the properties of the environment, especially privacy features and expected length of isolation.

During 2 days of orientation before isolation, Holtzman inkblot data, MMPI and other personality data, subjective stress and anxiety reactions, and a physiological indicator of stress (protein bound iodine level in the blood) were obtained. The data suggest that eventual aborters generally seemed to misread and underestimate the demands of the situation they were about to enter. For example, the pretest PBI and, to a lesser extent, the state anxiety and subjective stress data (Taylor, Wheeler, & Altman, 1968) indicated lower levels of physiological stress and anxiety behavior by abort group members, who seemed to be less concerned about the impending situation than those who eventually completed isolation. While the Holtzman data showed no preisolation differences, MMPI pretest scores of certain aborters indicated that they were higher on repression-sensitization, control, and heterosexual aggression and were lower on responsibility. From other sensory deprivation research there is an indication that aborters are high on "thrill seeking." All these results point to aborters as having underestimated the difficulty of the situation and perhaps as perceiving the situation to be no problem for a "he-man" adventurous type.

This extrapolation from personality, physiological, and subjective report measures fits in nicely with the type of behavior manifested by aborters in the early days of isolation. The general interpretation of their behavior during this period was that they did not adapt to or cope with the situation in a way that would lead to success. Members of abort groups did not go about the job of effective group formation and acculturation to one another. This was particularly evident in the way in which they dealt with one another in terms of social activities and use of their physical environment during the first day or two of isolation. For example, the data show that, compared with completers, members of abort groups spent less time together talking or doing things as a pair during the early days. One would think it interpersonally adaptive to begin developing a modus vivendi with another person, a stranger, if one were going to be in close and intimate contact for several days. One might expect an attempt to learn about the other person, to determine his living and work habits, and to begin working out a pattern of life that would be

interpersonally viable, if not positive. This inattention to early group formation is also reflected in the aborters' use of the environment in terms of
territorial behavior and bed-oriented behavior.

On all three measures of territorial behavior—beds, chairs, and sides of a
table—members of abort groups were lower than completers early in isolation. Thus, they not only failed to interact socially, but also did not establish interpersonal identities in terms of use of the environment. Territorial behavior can be considered to be adaptive and facilitative of group
functioning, as reflected in a host of animal studies and in our earlier
study of isolated groups (Altman & Haythorn, 1967a). One major function of territorial behavior is to set boundaries among group members, to
facilitate and establish bases of interaction, and to smooth out functioning
in a way analogous to social norms and conventions. In reviewing earlier
data on relationships between dyadic incompatibility on need dominance,
affiliation, achievement, and dogmatism, we noted that incompatible
groups also showed very low territorial behavior early in isolation compared with compatible groups, which is analogous to the pattern reported
in this second study. Eventually unsuccessful groups omitted going about
the business of group formation and group organization during the early
days of their experience, which may have derived partly from their early
misreading of situational demands or because they denied the situation
and its difficulty.

This pattern is also reflected in the way in which aborters and completers used their beds, not just initially but throughout the experience.
While much of the data was not statistically reliable, there was an indication that aborters were more bed-oriented than completers. They tended
to be either more withdrawn (spending a great deal of time in bed),
and/or were quite restless (in and out of bed often). Furthermore,
throughout the isolation period, aborter bed data suggests a lack of interpersonal synchrony or pacing, which is congruent with the social activity
and territorial behavior reported above. Members of completer groups
showed high intradyad correlations between time spent in bed and restlessness, whereas aborter groups showed negative or zero correlations.
Therefore, restlessness or withdrawal of one man was not similar to that
of the other man in aborter groups, compared with the completers. Thus,
there was an overall profile of successful completer groups being organized and forming a group, with members attuning themselves to one another in a variety of ways. The territoriality and social activity data and,
to some extent, the bed behavior results suggest this difference to have
evidenced itself early; the PBI and stress data indicate its precursors in
the preisolation situation.

As days progressed, however, there were some dramatic behavioral
changes, which add to the picture of early maladaptation by aborters.

The difference between aborter and completer behavior profiles continued to develop beyond the initial days. Aborters began to show heightened stress, anxiety, nervousness, and hyperactivity as days progressed, perhaps as an overreaction to their initial lack of concern. Their feelings of anxiety and stress mounted rapidly, surpassing that of the completers, as reflected in self-report questionnaires (Taylor, Wheeler, & Altman, 1968). This was indirectly confirmed at physiological levels by posttest PBI scores.

Coupled with this heightened stress and anxiety, some aborters, especially in 4-day conditions, showed a high degree of arousal and energy discharge—that is, restlessness. Others, especially in 20-day conditions, showed increased amounts of withdrawal or time spent in bed. The data also indicate that aborters then began establishing territories at higher levels than completers in the later days of isolation. These data suggest either a belated attempt at group formation processes and/or a panic reaction which resulted in high energy expenditure and heightened social activity (which may either have been to plan the abort or to seek solace and support). The completers, on the other hand, seemed to settle down to a lower level of activity and a paced and ordered existence. Their levels of stress and anxiety rose but then stabilized; their restlessness and withdrawal dropped or remained stable; their social activity declined. Territorial behavior was less evident, and they gave all appearances of "settling in" to a quiet existence. They seemed to have surmounted interpersonal organization problems and made an adequate personal adjustment to isolation.

These patterns were generally consistent for completers in most experimental conditions; they varied somewhat for aborters as a function of mission expectation length and privacy conditions. As suggested above, 4-day abort groups tended to be hyperactive and acting out; 20-day groups seemed to be more withdrawn, quiet, and passive. The patterns described above were also more evident in privacy aborters.

These data suggest some of the elements of a behavioral syndrome involving use of the environment which reflects the adaptive/nonadaptive nature of group formation and functioning. Furthermore, they illustrate how different levels of organismic functioning can be pieced together to yield an "ecological" viewpoint. Finally, these data demonstrate how the man-environment complex can and should be viewed from a dual perspective—how the environment affects man and how man simultaneously acts upon the environment in the management of social relationships.

In addition, the results of these studies suggest an approach to interpersonal functioning centering around a concept of "time-linked synchrony." This means that the ability of a group to cope with a situation,

including interpersonal adaptation, is a time bound process, perhaps analogous to the notion of imprinting, and involves interpersonal synchronization in many areas of living. Our data suggest that eventual success or
failure in the situation had its precursors in early day behavior. Successful groups exhibited what might be termed a high degree of synchrony,
where group members attuned themselves to one another in terms of social activity, established physical boundaries involving use of the environment, and meshed their activity levels with one another. This may be an
essential ingredient of effective coping in group situations and only became evident when data on interpersonal functioning were considered at
several levels of behavior.

INTERPERSONAL DISTANCE: THE BRIDGE BETWEEN THE ENVIRONMENT AND
SELF-MARKERS

Edward Hall (1966), an anthropologist, proposed a system of "proxemics" concerned with physical distance and interpersonal relationships. He
described four distance zones reflecting variations in intimacy and closeness. *Intimate distance* ranges from actual body contact to about 18 inch-
es and is the distance of lovemaking and wrestling, comforting and
protecting, and highlights the possibility of physical contact. *Personal distance* ranges from 1½ to 4 feet and also permits close involvement and
transmission of detailed visual, olfactory, and auditory cues. *Social distance* spans 4 to 12 feet and is characteristic of interaction in impersonal
or casual social relationships. *Public distance*, 12 feet or more, typically
is beyond the realm of interpersonal relationships. In a review of research
on interpersonal distance we induced 31 propositional statements
grouped around a few central themes. Examples are: social bonds are associated with close physical distances; psychological abnormality is associated with distorted distances from others; and close physical proximity
leads to social ties (Lett, Clark, & Altman, 1969).

This work is significant because it provides a conceptual bridge between use of the environment in the conduct of interpersonal relationships and use of the body, in the form of nonverbal behavior. As discussed later, interpersonal distance is the linkage between the self and the
social environment. Implicit in the notion of interpersonal distance is that
it is an environmental *medium* within which social communication can
occur. Different distances allow for differential exchange of visual, olfactory, kinesthetic, and other, cues involving the body. Unfortunately,
much research views interpersonal distance as an end in and of itself.
With few exceptions (Argyle & Dean, 1965; Goldberg, Kiesler, & Collins,
1969), research has not bridged between self-markers, interpersonal distance, and the environment. Weaving together these different levels of
exchange should be a goal of future research.

Use of the Body and Self-Markers in Interpersonal Exchange

The physical self—the face and head, trunk, arms, and legs—complement the use of words and the physical environment in social communication. Hall (1966) associated different behaviors with the four interpersonal distance zones just described. These include kinesthetic, visual, thermal, and olfactory cues. At intimate distances the head, pelvis, hands, and trunk can be brought into contact. There is exchange of heat and body odors, and ability to see shifts in eye movements and in the fine musculature of the face. At greater distances such cue patterns change considerably.

At a more analytic level, Ekman and Friesen (1967c) developed a classification of nonverbal self-markers in terms of five generic categories: emblems, illustrators, affect displays, regulators, and adapter behaviors. Emblems are gestural acts having a direct verbal translation that substitutes for words. Shaking the fist as a hostile communication is an example. Illustrators are similar to emblems, but complement verbal statements as simultaneous adjuncts, not as substitutes. Affect displays convey emotional states—anger, sadness, joy, love. Regulators and adapters contribute to the management of interaction and to interpersonal synchrony. They include such things as head nods, patterns of eye contact, and postural shifts, which help pace an interaction.

Argyle and Kendon's approach (1967) is similar to that of Hall in its focus on parts of the body, whereas Ekman and Friesen (1967c) emphasize function and meaning of self-marker behavior. Argyle and Kendon classify nonverbal behaviors in terms of standing and dynamic features of social performance. Standing features, such as physical distance, bodily orientation, and posture, change infrequently, and set the structure within which dynamic changes occur, including movements of the body, changes in facial expression, eye contact, and gaze properties. There has been considerable research, which is too lengthy to review here, on many specific nonverbal cues. An example of one area concerns eye contact and gaze patterns. In a theoretical analysis, Argyle and Dean (1965) point to a number of interpersonal functions of eye contact such as information seeking, signaling that channels are open, that communications are being received, and so forth. They posit an equilibrium level of eye contact which results from a balancing of approach and avoidance forces. Visual interaction is a very heavily researched area, with studies considering such factors as variations in eye contact as a function of need affiliation, trust, embarrassment, and lying (see, for example, Exline, 1963; Exline & Eldridge, 1967; Exline, Gray, & Schuette, 1965; Exline & Winters, 1965; Kendon, 1967).

Bodily movements and facial expressions have also been of great interest to those concerned with nonverbal communication (see Davitz, 1964, and recent work by Ekman and Friesen, 1967a, 1967b, 1967c, on the contribution of static and dynamic characteristics of the face and body to communication of the quality and intensity of emotion, and by Mehrabian, 1969, on the relationship between interpersonal attitudes and posture and orientation). While there is a great body of research on nonverbal behavior, relatively little has viewed self-marker and environmental prop behavior as joint facets of a complex behavior pattern contributing to the overall social penetration process.

Complex Behavior Patterns

Self-marker, environmental prop, and verbal behaviors do not occur in an unrelated or disjointed fashion. They blend together to form complex patterns of behavior that have all the properties of "systems" described earlier—namely, interrelatedness, compensatory action, equivalence of functioning, and substitutability. Goffman (1959, 1961), a sociologist, and Scheflen (1964, 1965, 1968), a psychiatrist, adopt strategic approaches that view all levels of functioning in broad, global frameworks. According to Scheflen, complex behavior patterns are hierarchically organized and range from discrete molecular levels to holistic integrated behavior sets. Scheflen (1964) distinguishes between points, positions, and presentations. Points are specific behaviors such as shifting head positions, flexions or extensions of the neck, and so forth. A sequence of points involving gross postural orientations comprises a position, analogous to a general point of view. Presentations encompass the totality of positions and can endure for minutes or hours, terminated by a change of location.

Goffman (1959, 1961), emphasizes use of environmental props—a concept of "front" represents stable and transitory features of the environment and self arranged in accord with an intended situation definition. Certain aspects of front, such as furniture and decor, refer to the physical environment, while others, such as clothing and rank, are personal and attached to the performer. Use of the physical environment also involves the notion of "regions." Front regions are analogous to being onstage in a theatre and refer to the geographical locale of social performances where illusions, impressions, and role relationships are exhibited using the full range of self-markers and environmental prop behaviors. Back regions or backstage are areas where behavioral effects are created, where ceremonial and other equipment is kept, where characters can step out of social performance roles.

Another analytic approach to complex behavior patterns is that of Argyle and Kendon (1967), described earlier. Like Goffman, they describe complex behavior patterns as highly organized social performances, analogous in many ways to motor performances. Of particular interest is their emphasis on the "mix" of behavior modalities, interpersonal synchrony, and the nature of complex behavior patterns. They see body contact, physical proximity, gestures, posture, etc., combining in various mixes to yield patterns of behavior. However, relatively little empirical research has been done on complex behavior patterns, especially as related to group adaptation processes.

Rosenfeld (1965, 1966a, 1966b) is one of the few who provides an empirical base for complex behavior patterns associated with interpersonal compatibility. Subjects instructed to seek the approval of another person were more socially active than those in an avoidance situation. They approached the other person closer, were more talkative, smiled, and made more positive gestural responses, including head nods and postural shifts.

Mehrabian (1968a, 1968b, 1969) uses multidimensional analyses of nonverbal behavior in different types of social relationships involving friends and mixed sex pairs to identify directly complex behavior patterns. Reviewing literature on nonverbal correlates of interpersonal attitudes, with an emphasis on position and posture (Mehrabian, 1969), he reports several studies directly concerned with multilevel response patterns involving, for example, correlations between directness of body orientation and eye contact, and between eye contact and head, shoulder, and leg orientations. In considering his own and others' studies on body accessibility (open or closed arm and leg positions) and body relaxation (forward-backward and sideways leaning), the results are not always clear but depend upon such factors as seating vs standing position and sex composition of a dyad.

Clearly, work on complex behavior patterns has just begun and is relatively primitive in terms of both empirical and conceptual progress to date. Thus far, most research efforts have been directed toward intensive analyses of individual facets of nonverbal behavior, rather than toward study of complex behavior patterns.

Some of the research reviewed here emphasized verbal aspects of interpersonal processes; another line of study focused on physical environment issues; still another area involved nonverbal communication. These streams of research have typically proceeded in a parallel fashion, with only occasional bridging across areas. The goal of this chapter is to begin the integration process with the hope of pointing toward a theoretical framework of interpersonal behavior that approaches the ecological orientation described earlier.

SOME DIMENSIONS OF AN ECOLOGICAL APPROACH TO INTERPERSONAL FUNCTIONING

This part of the chapter goes beyond the empirical data of our own and others' studies and steps toward a conceptual framework for understand-

AN ECOLOGICAL MODEL OF PERSONALITY AND INTERPERSONAL BEHAVIOR

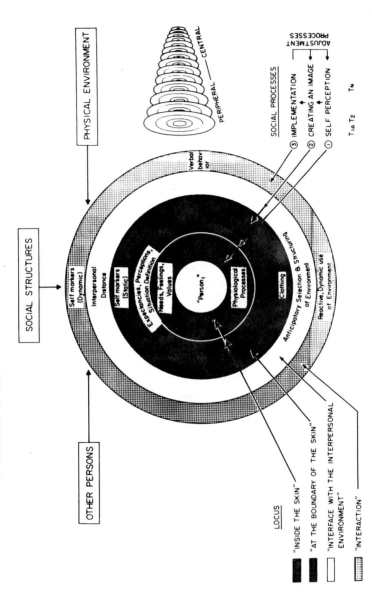

FIGURE 9.1. *An ecological model of personality and interpersonal behavior. Source: From Social Penetration by I. Altman and D. A. Taylor. Copyright © 1973 by Holt, Rinehart and Winston, Inc. Reprinted by permission of Holt, Rinehart and Winston, Inc.*

ing interpersonal functioning within an ecological orientation. The first task is to set forth a behavioral criterion domain, that is, a specification of relevant interpersonal behaviors. Subsequent steps require stating the relationships between behavioral domains and, eventually, proposal of a set of "ideal" levels of behavior or combinations of behavior that will result in effective interpersonal functioning. Figure 9.1 initiates the first part of the task—a specification of the behavioral criterion domain. This diagram has several features. It indicates what are considered important facets of behavior essential to interpersonal functioning; it links these together into a crude "model" of personality and indicates relationships between levels of behavior; and it attempts to fit the different behavioral levels into an interpersonal interaction schema with temporally dynamic features.

The main part of the figure depicts several levels of behavior involved in interpersonal relationships that function as an integrated set, and are differentially remote from the physical-social environment or, to use Lewinian terminology, the *psychological environment*. The diagram is also in accord with Lewin's distinction between inner-outer and central-peripheral regions of the person and conveys primarily the inner-outer distinction in terms of remoteness or directness of contact with the psycho-social environment. The idea of central-peripheral regions (that is, control, importance, or depth) is reflected in the insert diagram on the right side of the figure, and represents another dimension. Thus, the whole figure can be viewed as a solid cone with inner-outer distance from the psychological environment represented by the cross-section, and a central-peripheral depth dimension represented by the long axis of the cone.

The innermost layers of the person, in terms of remoteness of contact with the social environment, include *needs, values and feelings,* and *physiological processes,* all of which contribute to a core self-perception. For heuristic purposes, one might say that this is an initial process analogous to what may have occurred in the preisolation situation of the study reported earlier. This is a self-defining process that sets the framework for a host of temporally and sequentially linked behaviors and responses to the environment.

As indicated in the lower right-hand insert to the figure, the overall behavioral domain is a servo-system with continuous feedback loops and no real beginning or end. The internal complex of needs/values/feelings and physiological events is also hypothesized to be affected by other persons, environmental factors, and various aspects of the social structure, as are all levels of functioning. This complex of events results, it is hypothesized, in a general *definition of the situation,* the next layer of the diagram. This situation definition is a subjective analysis of what a situation calls for and its demands, and an internalized plan of behavior (not necessarily of an aware nature). These "inside the skin" processes are key precursors of eventual behavior and, as our isolation study indicated, are important facets of behavior to study. Thus, the data collected prior to isolation about anxiety, stress, personality, and physiological states turned out to be good predictors of subsequent behavioral events.

The figure then depicts a series of behavioral events at "the boundary of the skin," which contribute to the creation of an interpersonal image. This is a process of initial contact with the social environment. The person creates an interpersonal image through *static self-markers* and *clothing*. Static self-markers are essentially what Argyle and Kendon (1967) termed standing features of performance. They include relatively unchanging orientations, body positions, and postures. Clothing also often serves, explicitly or implicitly, to set the stage for interaction. These levels of behavior begin the process of translation of internal events into a social-psychological image. Unfortunately, little of our own research dealt with these boundary processes; it would be useful to deal with them in the future. As discussed previously, there is a considerable body of research on self-markers as an independent facet of behavior, but relatively little research within an integrated framework. There is also a lack of research in the behavioral sciences on clothing as part of an interpersonal behavioral system.

The next layer represents greater extension of the person into the environment and toward interaction with other people and includes *interpersonal distance*, and *anticipatory selection and structuring of the physical environment*. These basic "interfaces with the interpersonal environment" contribute to the overall image that was initiated by clothing and static self-markers. *Interpersonal distance* refers to the pure physical separation between people, which Hall's (1966) proxemics approach and the review of the literature by Lett, Clark, and Altman (1969) considered. Interpersonal distance is a medium within which various forms of communicaion can occur. The nature of distance relationships is a preliminary structuring device for the management of interpersonal relationships. *Anticipatory selection and structuring of environment* also establishes a framework within which social interaction can occur (see Altman, 1971, for a discussion of this aspect of use of the environment). The arrangement of furniture in a room or office, adjustment of lighting, choice of a meeting room, arrangement of seats in a class, and a host of other actions represent anticipatory processes that are designed to prestructure an impending interaction in advance of, or at the initiation of an interpersonal exchange.

An example of this type of behavior was evidenced in a laboratory study on preferences for various room designs after a favorable or unfavorable period of interaction with another person (Altman, Taylor, & Sorrentino, 1968). The result showed preferences for separate living areas in an incompatible situation and for close, combined living under the expectation of a good interpersonal relationship. Page (1968) found comparable results with different size groups. Thus, subjects had translated their feelings about the other person into an anticipatory structuring of the mutual environment.

The levels of functioning discussed thus far are all somewhat preliminary to social exchange, although they set boundaries within which interaction occurs. Actual two-way interaction is "closest" to the interpersonal environment and involves dynamic, temporally continuous *verbal behavior, dynamic self-marker behavior,* and *dynamic/reactive use of the environment.*

Verbal behavior is, of course, a major medium of interpersonal communication, and has been the subject of considerable research. Dynamic self-marker behavior includes the array of bodily events which shift and change as interaction proceeds, such as eye gaze patterns, smiling, facial expressions, and expressive hand and body movements. Again, research on social penetration has not yet included analysis of dynamic self-marker processes, and there has been relatively little research explicitly directed toward such problems (Mehrabian, 1969). Reactive, ongoing use of the environment is the third aspect of dynamic interaction and refers to shifting extensions of the self into the physical environment throughout the course of interpersonal exchange. Establishment of territories, use of beds by isolation groups in the studies reported earlier, and their changing patterns over days are examples of this facet of interpersonal exchange.

The cone-shaped insert to Figure 9.1 is intended to suggest that all the behavioral events described thus far occur at several levels of depth or intimacy of exchange. This has been an important distinction in our work on verbal aspects of the social penetration process, where verbal content was scaled for level of intimacy and where it was demonstrated that relationships gradually move toward more intimate areas of exchange as a function of experienced rewards and costs.

There are several reasons for describing classes of behavior that precede, structure, and occur directly in the course of social interaction, which tie in with the ecological orientation described earlier. First, the idea of different levels of behavior intrinsic to interpersonal exchange needs to be highlighted. Second, these behaviors function as a coherent system in both a time bound and psychologically dependent sense and as a continually adjusting servo-system. The typical approach has been for different investigators to study separate behaviors with only rare attempts at establishing linkages or interdependencies. Of course, such an extreme analytic orientation is necessary, but some attention must also be given to the synthesis of separate levels of behavior and to the empirical portrayal of "whole people."

Unfortunately, this is neither easily nor often undertaken. It is a difficult task, for integrating different levels of behavior requires an understanding of several areas of research and the conduct of a variety of studies. This can result in a watering down of intensive analysis generally necessary for researching a specific phenomenon. Nevertheless, it does appear feasible, on a limited basis, to adopt or integrate research strategy. Furthermore, it is essential if one is to understand a specific person, group, or situation. This is what the practicing clinician does, although sometimes in a qualitative, nonspecifiable, and nonreplicable way. Our dilemma as researchers is to achieve the same understanding of total entities, but in strict accord with our heritage of empiricism, rigor, and quantification.

The third function served by the discussion and figure is both a listing of relevant variables and a limited statement of conceptual and dynamic linkages between variable classes. The diagram proposes a sequential flow of events and mediating processes, with each affecting subsequent events in a complex feedback system. It does not yet specify *how* these sequential events operate, but only that such dependencies exist. The question of how and under what conditions one behavior leads to another is a specific research matter.

In essence, the figure proposes a behavior framework, not just a catalog of behaviors, relevant to social penetration and group adaptation processes. These behaviors occur as a group develops and forms, as it exhibits internal conflict processes, and as it strives for viability. The ability to tap into as many of these processes as possible, in a systematic and empirical fashion, will yield a better understanding of groups than will understanding any single class of behavior separately. Given this multitude of behaviors, how does one describe the "ideal" levels of functioning in all these behavioral domains? The following discussion continues pushing beyond the data and proposes a series of generic dimensions along which the preceding behaviors can, theoretically, vary. In many respects these will be hypotheses about some essential components of an effective interpersonal relationship, in social penetration terms, which apply to all the preceding behaviors. The set of hypothesized dimensions appears below:

1. richness-guardedness of interaction
2. uniqueness of interaction
3. efficiency of exchange
4. synchrony and pacing

5. behavior substitutability and equivalence
6. permeability and openness
7. voluntariness and spontaneity
8. evaluation

As the table indicates, it is hypothesized that an effective interpersonal relationship involves "appropriate" levels of behavior on eight dimensions that function in a time-linked fashion. That is, a particular level of richness-guardedness of exchange in verbal, nonverbal, or environmental prop areas is appropriate at one stage of a relationship and inappropriate at another stage. This temporally bound property is applicable to all dimensions. Furthermore, there are situational determinants of appropriateness on the dimensions—for example, richness of communication may be important for adaptation in one situation but be detrimental to effective functioning in another situation. Therefore, what follows is only a "naming" and description of relevant dimensions of an effective interpersonal relationship, without specification of what the ideal values on each dimension are or should be. Also, these dimensions are applicable to all the overt interpersonal behaviors described earlier. A final caveat is that the dimensions of Table 9.1 are not wholly orthogonal, but overlap somewhat. This is not a serious problem at present, since the goal now is only to crudely identify major parameters of effective interpersonal relationships.

RICHNESS-GUARDEDNESS OF INTERACTION

The growth of an interpersonal relationship is characterized by a greater amount and variety of exchange within and across behavior modalities. As a relationship proceeds from strangership to friendship, new areas of personality become mutually accessible, and at more intimate levels of interaction. The parties build more complex interpersonal cognitive models of one another and come to understand better the nuances of their respective personalities. This occurs at all levels of exchange—verbal, environmental prop, and self-marker. In a well-developed relationship, feelings, transient and permanent mood states, affective states, and so on, are communicated and received through more behavior modalities. If one examined interaction between close associates, one would observe a greater variety of behavior employed to convey a particular state. For example, disapproval behavior would involve more use of frowning, more verbal disagreement, more negative hand motions and gestures, greater body tenseness, and more willingness to employ environmental props, such as slamming the table or door or pushing objects angrily. This probably would also occur in a greater variety of behavior patterns in the more well-developed relationship. In less well-developed relationships, people tend to rely more on a limited number of culturally stereotyped modes of response. One consequence of limited behavior repertoires is the increased probability of confusion and misunderstanding about the intent of communication.

This does not mean that *all* relationships should strive toward richer communication. As indicated above, these dimensions are time and situation bound in terms of appropriate levels of behavior. If a situation required extremely close interpersonal exchange and a group did not exhibit much richness of communication after a reasonable period, then it might be concluded that they had not achieved a satisfactory level of functioning on this dimension. On the other hand, if the situation was one that called for very little interpersonal contact, and group members had achieved a tremendous richness of exchange very quickly, one might conclude that this state of affairs was also inappropriate. These dimensions are descriptive; they can be used to describe the "state" of interaction exchange achieved. One must then analyze situational and time bound requirements of the group milieu to determine the extent to which the exchange fell short or was in excess of appropriate levels of functioning. One might argue that a social isolation situation requires a moderate level of richness of exchange, enough for the men to be able to live as an integrated group for extensive periods of time, but with richness of exchange controlled to allow independence and privacy of group members. An isolated group in which the members either know very little about one another or in which men are overly accessible to one another are both likely to be ineffective.

UNIQUENESS OF INTERACTION

Members of well-developed groups often have unique and idiosyncratic communications systems. Various voice intonations, facial expressions, body movements, and handling of objects come to have unique meanings understood only by group members. A good deal of the research reported earlier on self-marker and environmental prop behavior applies primarily to early stages of relationships, and therefore reflects culturally acceptable and stereotyped ways of dealing with others. A smile, a positive head nod, or leaning forward all reflect positive behavioral indicators common to many people and appropriate to casual relationships. However, more idiosyncratic behavior complexes are also associated with reactions to intimates. Furthermore, such group uniqueness probably extends between and within group behavior. That is, a group might exhibit several unique patterns to reflect a single feeling state, and also have a different behavior repertoire regarding that state than another group. Therefore, the extent to which group members develop unique modes of communication reflects the stage of their general relationship. Again, levels on this dimension only describe the state a group has achieved; they do not specify what is "good" for a particular situation.

EFFICIENCY OF EXCHANGE

This dimension involves accuracy, speed and sensitivity of transmission, and receipt of communication. In well-developed relationships, intended meanings are transmitted between group members rapidly, accurately, and with great sensitivity and fineness of tuning. Another component of increased efficiency is reduced energy expenditure in communication in more well-developed relationships. Perhaps this is the case because members of advanced relationships use a broader range of communication modalities, while those at earlier stages of development probably employ fewer channels, especially the verbal one. This may require considerable redundancy to achieve an accurate communication since verbal behavior, or any mode of behavior alone, may not convey all aspects of what is intended.

The three characteristics of richness, uniqueness, and efficiency of communication certainly overlap. Taken together, however, they reflect the idea that advanced stages of group development involve interaction at multiple levels of functioning, with more rich, varied, and complex exchange and more efficient and sensitive transmission and receipt of communication among members.

SYNCHRONY AND PACING

This dimension refers to coordination and meshing of interpersonal actions. Goffman (1959) describes a working consensus where social actors know their mutual roles and play them in a complementary way. There is also a considerable body of research indicating that, over time, people become attuned to one another and develop synchronous patterns of interaction at all levels of functioning.

Interpersonal synchrony and pacing is analogous to the behavior of a well-functioning athletic team, where the members smoothly predict and react to one another's actions. Minimal cues are exchanged, but they are accurately responded to and interpreted. Similarly, in a well-developed interpersonal relationship, synchronous and meshed communication occurs, whether the exchange be of a routine nature or of a personal and intimate character. The differences between aborter and completer groups in the social isolation studies illustrate this synchrony concept. Aborter group members did not attune themselves to one another early in isolation, as reflected in social activity, and territorial and bed behavior. As with the other dimensions, one might hypothesize that an effective group would have to achieve a level of synchrony appropriate to the behavioral demands of the situation and that inability to do so, over time, would contribute to ineffective functioning.

BEHAVIOR SUBSTITUTABILITY AND EQUIVALENCE

With increased experience in a relationship, more ways become available to convey the same feeling state in a substitutable and equivalent fashion. The greater richness of behavior repertoires, uniqueness of dyadic interaction, and efficiency of communication make it possible to employ a broad mix of behaviors from different levels of functioning to express an intended state. In casual relationships, culturally stereotyped modes of response are probably relied on heavily; in more highly developed relationships, it is predicted that a given psychological state is conveyed by a wider range of equivalent and substitutable behaviors. This dimension is closely related to the *richness* of *communication* dimension, but emphasizes the idea that well-developed relationships have a greater behavioral repertoire to communicate a given state, as well as the ability to convey a larger number of states.

PERMEABILITY AND OPENNESS

Much of the social penetration framework revolves around the idea that, at verbal, self-marker, and environmental prop levels of behavior, increased mutual openness and accessibility characterizes growing interpersonal relationships. The notion should be added that there is also more fluidity and mobility of exchange in well-developed relationships. Members can move in and out of discussion areas in a facile way, can quickly and easily exhibit intimate touching gestures and body positions, and can just as quickly move out of such exchange patterns; they can easily move into one another's personal space, and so on. In short, group members become quite permeable and accessible to a range of interaction with one another; they can easily shift from one area to another and from trivial to intimate exchanges. The barriers between them are quite permeable at all levels of functioning. But the process is not endless. People maintain their integrity, independence, and ultimate separateness from one another at all levels of functioning. Some things are never revealed to others; certain rooms, places, or objects may be inviolate to entry or use, certain self-marker or bodily behaviors are rarely exhibited. Thus, permeability and openness are conceived of as dynamic processes, characterized by a shift and fluidity of exchange, not by unequivocal openness.

VOLUNTARINESS AND SPONTANEITY

An implicit theme in much of the preceding discussion is that increased voluntariness and spontaneity of exchange occurs in all areas of functioning in more advanced relationships. There is far more informality in interaction, a greater ease and opening of the self to others, and a parallel comfortableness in entering the personality and life of other group members. Movement across topical areas is facile and fluid and is initiated spontaneously without excessive probing. The parties enter into exchange with freedom and without hesitation.

The preceding dimensions—synchrony and pacing, substitutability and equivalence, permeability and openness, voluntariness and spontaneity —attach to the flow of interaction over time. They provide a portrayal of well-developed relationships as free flowing and interlaced, with a blend of complementary, changing, but organized interaction.

Evaluation

Concomitant with changes on the preceding dimensions, and certainly overlapping with many of them, is the increased ability of group members in well-developed relationships to evaluate or convey positive and negative judgments and affect about one another. At advanced stages of a relationship, people become more willing and able to criticize and to praise one another, to demonstrate positive and negative feelings, and to be generally less constricted in evaluation. Again, the ability to convey evaluations is not necessarily good or bad, but is differentially appropriate to the stage of a relationship and to the general requirements of the situation within which the group is embedded.

Use of these dimensions to assess the effectiveness of a group requires a process of several steps. The first involves "locating" a group on each of the dimensions—that is, determining how much richness, efficiency, synchrony, permeability and openness, etc., the group members convey to one another. Simultaneously, one must determine the "ideal" levels of behavior that the situation calls for with respect to each of the dimensions. Thus, the situation and the group must be independently "scored" on the various dimensions with respect to the various levels of behaviors discussed earlier. Matching the descriptive state of the group with the ideal requirements of the situation in the same behavioral terms will permit an assessment of how well the group is functioning relative to the situation.

The preceding discussion is not restricted to the viability of isolated groups, whether they be undersea, in space, or in geographically remote areas. While such situations have unique properties, our approach has been to seek principles and strategies applicable to the functioning of *any* small social group.

Implications for Isolated Groups

The salience of some of the issues discussed in this chapter becomes heightened in situations such as social isolation, especially when it is accompanied by physical confinement, as is often the case. The time scale, as well as the physical scale, of group life becomes telescoped, events proceed rapidly, and there is less error tolerance of an interpersonal nature. As our own research demonstrates, the early periods are critical, for these are the times of group organization, and what happens then can have an important impact on subsequent events. Therefore, it becomes essential for group members (and group managers) to be able to diagnose early, in a precise and timely fashion, the state of the group.

This will demand an ability to tap into group behavior at several of the levels described earlier (verbal, nonverbal, environmental), and to develop some standard of "correct" behavior on the dimensions proposed above. This is not a simple task. Unfortunately, the conduct of research of the magnitude proposed here is expensive and time consuming and does not seem in the offing in the near future. Furthermore, the strategy proposed calls for a multidimensional study of group functioning cast within a general theoretical framework. Typically, research on group processes operates out of conceptual frameworks but is not multidimensional in nature. Single behaviors are generally studied in basic research situations, whereas in more goal oriented or applied settings one typically studies extant people and groups. Furthermore, in basic settings there is more of a theoretical orientation guiding the research, whereas in applied settings the work is generally eclectic or atheoretical.

What has been called for in this chapter, especially with regard to socially isolated groups, is a style of research that is both theoretically oriented and group-as-system oriented. Only with such a strategy can the behavioral sciences make problem oriented and conceptually significant contributions to the understanding of interpersonal relationships.

REFERENCES

Altman, I. 1970. Territorial behavior in humans: Analysis of the concept. In *Spatial behavior of older people,* ed. L. Pastalan & D. H. Carson, pp. 1–24. Ann Arbor, Mich.: University of Michigan–Wayne State University Press.
——. 1971. Ecological aspects of interpersonal functioning. In *Behavior and environment: Proceedings of the International Symposium on the use of space by animals and men,* ed. A. H. Esser, pp. 291–306. New York: Plenum Press.
Altman, I., & Haythorn, W. W. 1965. Interpersonal exchange in isolation. *Sociometry* 23(4):411–26.
——. 1967a. The ecology of isolated groups. *Behav. Sci.* 12(3):169–82.
——. 1967b. The effects of social isolation and group composition on performance. *Human Relations* 20:313–40.
Altman, I., & Lett, E. E. 1970. The ecology of interpersonal relationships: A classification system and conceptual model. In *Social and psychological factors in stress,* ed. J. E. McGrath, pp. 177–201. New York: Holt, Rinehart and Winston.

Altman, I., & Taylor, D. A. 1968. Disclosure as a measure of social penetration. Paper presented at a symposium on Self-disclosure and the interpersonal relationship. APA, San Francisco, Calif., September.

Altman, I., Taylor, D. A., & Sorrentino, R. 1968. Ecological implications of interpersonal compatibility and incompatibility. (Mimeo.)

Altman, I., Taylor, D. A., & Wheeler, L. 1971. Ecological aspects of group behavior in social isolation. *J. appl. soc. Psychol.* 1:76–100.

Argyle, M., & Dean, J. 1965. Eye-contact and affiliation. *Sociometry* 28:289–304.

Argyle, M., & Kendon, A. 1967. The experimental analysis of social performance. In *Advances in experimental social psychology*, ed. L. Berkowitz, pp. 55–91. New York: Academic Press.

Barker, R. G., ed. 1963. *The stream of behavior*. New York: Appleton-Century-Crofts.

Barker, R. G. 1968. *Ecological psychology*. Palo Alto: Stanford University Press.

Barker, R. G., & Gump, P. 1964. *Big school, small school*. Stanford, Calif.: Stanford University Press.

Barker, R. G., & Wright, H. F. 1955. *Midwest and its children*. New York: Harper & Row.

Blake, R. R., Rhead, C. C., Wedge, B., & Mouton, J. S. 1956. Housing architecture and social interaction. *Sociometry* 19:133–39.

Byrne, D. 1961. The influence of propinquity and opportunities for interaction on classroom relationships. *Human Relations* 14:63–69.

Byrne, D., & Buehler, J. A. 1955. A note on the influence of propinquity upon acquaintanceships. *J. abnorm. soc. Psychol.* 51:147–48.

Caplow, T., & Forman, R. 1950. Neighborhood interaction in a homogeneous community. *Amer. Soc. Review* 15:357–66.

Cole, J., Machir, D., Altman, I., Haythorn, W. W., & Wagner, C. M. 1967. Perceptual changes in social isolation. *J. clin. Psychol.* 23 (3):330–33.

Colson, W. N. 1968. Self-disclosure as a function of social approval. M.A. thesis, Howard University, Washington, D.C.

Davitz, J. R., ed. 1964. *The communication of emotional meaning*. New York: McGraw-Hill.

Deutsch, M., & Collins, M. E. 1951. *Interracial housing: A psychological evaluation of a social experiment*. Minneapolis: University of Minnesota Press.

Ekman, P., & Friesen, W. V. 1967a. Head and body cues in the judgment of emotion: A reformation. *Percep. mot. Skills* 24:711–24.

———. 1967b. Nonverbal behavior in psychotherapy research. In *Research in psychotherapy*, ed. J. Shlien, Vol. 3, pp. 1–76. APA, Washington, D.C.

———. 1967c. Origin, usage, and coding: The basis for five categories of nonverbal behavior. Paper presented at symposium on Communication theory and linguistic models in the social sciences, Torquato Di Tella Institute, Buenos Aires, Argentina, October.

Exline, R. 1963. Explorations in the process of person perception: Visual interaction relation to competition, sex and need for affiliation. *J. Personality* 31:1–20.

Exline, R., & Eldridge, C. 1967. Effects of two patterns of a speaker's visual behavior upon the perception of the authenticity of his verbal message. Paper presented at meeting of Eastern Psychological Association, Boston. April.

Exline, R., Gray, D., & Schuette, D. 1965. Visual behavior in a dyad as affected by interview content and sex of respondent. *J. person, soc. Psychol.* 1:201–9.

Exline, R. V., & Winters, L. C. 1965. Affective relations and mutual glances in dyads. In *Affect, cognition and personality*, ed. S. Tomkins & C. Izard, pp. 319–51. New York: Springer.

Festinger, L., Schachter, S., & Back, K. 1950. *Social pressures in informal groups: A study of human factors in housing.* New York: Harper.

Frankfurt, L. P. 1965. The role of some individual and interpersonal factors on acquaintance process. Ph.D. dissertation, American University, Washington, D.C.

Goffman, E. 1959. *Presentation of self in everyday life.* New York: Doubleday.

———. 1961. *Asylums.* Chicago: Aldine-Atherton.

Goldberg, G. N., Kiesler, C. A., & Collins, B. D. 1969. Visual behavior and face-to-face distance during interaction. *Sociometry* 32 (1):43–53.

Hall, E. T. 1966. *The hidden dimension.* New York: Doubleday.

Haythorn, W. W., & Altman, I. 1967. Together in isolation. *Trans-action* 4: 18–22.

Haythorn, W. W., Altman, I., & Myers, T. I. 1966. Emotional symptomatology and subjective stress in isolated pairs of men. *J. Exper. Research Person.* 1 (4):290–306.

Jourard, S. M. 1964. *The transparent self.* Princeton, N.J.: Van Nostrand.

Kendon, A. 1967. Some functions of gaze direction in social interaction. *Acta Psychological* 26:22–63.

Lett, E. E., Clark, W., & Altman, I. 1969. A propositional inventory of research on interpersonal distance. Technical Rept. #1, Naval Medical Research Institute, Bethesda, Md.

Mehrabian, A. 1968a. Inference of attitudes from the posture, orientation and distance of a communicator. *J. cons. clin. Psychol.* 32:296–308.

———. 1968b. Relationships of attitude to seated posture, orientation and distance. *J. person. soc. Psychol.* 10:26–30.

———. 1969. Significance of posture and position in the communication of attitude and status relationships. *Psycholog. Bull.* 71(5):359–73.

Page, J. 1968. Social penetration processes: The effects of interpersonal reward and cost factors on the stability of dyadic relationships. Ph.D. dissertation, American University, Washington, D.C.

Patterson, M. 1968. Spatial factors in social interactions. *Human Relations* 21 (4):351–61.

Polansky, N. 1965. The concept of verbal accessibility. *Smith College Studies in Social Work* 26:1–48.

Rosenfeld, H. M. 1965. Effects of an approval-seeking induction on interpersonal proximity. *Psycholog. Reports* 17:120–22.

Rosenfeld, H. M. 1966a. Approval-seeking and approval-inducing functions of verbal and nonverbal responses in the dyad. *J. person. Soc. Psychol.* 4:597–605.

———. 1966b. Instrumental affiliative functions of facial and gestural expressions. *J. person. soc. Psychol.* 4:65–72.

Scheflen, A. E. 1964. The significance of posture in communication systems. *Psychiatry* 27:316–31.

———. 1965. Quasi-courtship behavior in psychotherapy. *Psychiatry* 28:245–57.

———. 1968. Human communication: Behavioral programs and their integration in interaction. *Behav. Sci.* 13(1):44–55.

Sommer, R. 1967. Small group ecology. *Psycholog. Bull.* 67 (2):145–152.

———. 1969. *Personal space: The behavioral basis of design.* Englewood Cliffs, N.J.: Prentice-Hall.

Taylor, D. A. 1968. Some aspects of the development of interpersonal relationships: Social penetration processes. *J. soc. Psychol.* 75:79–90.

Taylor, D. A., Altman, I., & Frankfurt, L. 1966. Personality correlates of self-disclosure. (Mimeo.)

Taylor, D. A., Altman, I., & Sorrentino, R. 1969. Interpersonal exchange as a function of rewards and costs and situational factors: Expectancy confirmation-disconfirmation *J. exper. soc. Psychol.* 5(3):324–39.

Taylor, D. A., Altman, I., Wheeler, L., & Kushner, E. 1969. Personality factors related to response to social isolation and confinement. *J. cons. clin. Psychol.* 33 (4):411–19.

Taylor, D. A., & Oberlander, L. 1969. Person-perception and self-disclosure: Motivational mechanisms in interpersonal processes. *J. exper. Research Person.* 4:1, 14–28.

Taylor, D. A., Wheeler, L., & Altman, I. 1968. Stress reactions in socially isolated groups. *J. person. soc. Psychol.* 9:369–76.

Tuckman, B. W. 1966. Interpersonal probing and revealing and systems of integrative complexity. *J. person. soc. Psychol.* 3:655–64.

Germaine de Montmollin, *Professor of Social Psychology at the University René Descartes in Paris, received her Ph.D. from the University of Paris. In 1951 she was appointed by the National Center for Scientific Research (C.N.R.S.) to the staff of the Laboratory of Experimental Psychology at the Sorbonne. Here she devoted many years to research in experimental social psychology. During that time she also taught social psychology at the Paris Institute of Psychology. In 1969 she joined the University of Paris, Vincennes, as a Professor and in 1972 the René Descartes University. Her research interests have focused on the problems of communication and working in groups, influence processes, and social perception. She has written many papers on these topics, the greater part of which were published in* Année Psychologique, *and she has collaborated on several works in psychology. From 1966 to 1971 she was Chief Editor of the* International Journal of Psychology.

G. de Montmollin *comments on Altman's theoretical model and experimental investigations and asks questions about the legitimacy of applying a general model to particular groups. She stresses the specificity of isolated small groups and contends that physical and social confinement implies not only changes in parameters and quantitative relationships between variables, but also changes in the structure of the relationship between space, time, and persons. She emphasizes the importance of group tasks and the effects of interpersonal relationships on task efficiency. Thus, it is necessary to consider the problems of isolated small groups not only in terms of individual adjustment and conflict resolution, but also at the level of interdependence within a group. Finally, she proposes a practical and short-term strategy to manage interpersonal relationships in isolated small groups through special training in simulated conditions of physical and social environment and task.*

10

Concepts and Strategies of Research on Groups in Isolation: Comments on Altman's Approach

GERMAINE DE MONTMOLLIN

Because Professor Altman's chapter is very rich, his views intellectually exciting and new, and his theoretical and empirical work very good, it is impossible to comment on all the points of his analysis. This chapter will center, therefore, on the discussion of the following questions: (1) Can a general model of interpersonal behavior be applied to isolated groups? What unique properties do isolated groups have that could make the application of a general model appropriate or not? (2) For what purpose should interpersonal relationships be efficient? What are the links between interpersonal relationships and group tasks? (3) Must the problem of interpersonal relationships within an isolated group be centered on individual personality and individual abilities of adjustment to social environment, or on the group as a whole and the interdependence of its members? (4) As isolated groups are a very complex and immediate problem, would a research strategy centered on group task not be more useful?

CAN A GENERAL MODEL OF INTERPERSONAL BEHAVIOR BE APPLIED TO ISOLATED SMALL GROUPS?

In the preceding chapter, Altman emphasizes that his aim is "to seek out principles and strategies applicable to the functioning of any small social group." The small isolated group is a vehicle for understanding generic

Editor's note: Professor de Montmollin went well beyond the question of commenting on Professor Altman's NATO paper. Her ideas point to some penetrating issues on research in the field as a whole, and have considerable importance for future work. For this reason, we have asked her to expand on views she presented at the Rome Conference, so as to incorporate her material as a chapter in this volume.

group processes and for building a general strategy and theory that can be adapted to particular situations.

It is well known that nothing is more useful than a good theory, that true scientific knowledge never will be achieved solely by accumulating empirical studies. It is rational, economical, and elegant to develop a general model and then to adjust it to particular situations by slightly "tailoring." But in what cases is this strategy rewarding and in what cases is it not; this is what first must be asked. It is undoubtedly desirable when particular situations differ from the model only because of absence or presence of some parameters and/or because of some quantitative variations along pertinent dimensions of the model. But is such a strategy still successful when the structure or the relationships between the dimensions of the particular situations are different from that of the model? Let us develop Altman's metaphor: the pattern of a dress well may be fitted to a fat woman by enlarging the size of the pattern here and there; it may be adjusted to one's own taste by adding some details, such as buttons and belt; but will the pattern be tailored just the same to fit a fish or an octopus, whose morphology is so different?

How could one possibly know whether a general model can be applied to isolated small groups before having first precisely stated the "unique properties" of those groups? Are the interpersonal events merely more salient and drastic when they occur within a small isolated group than within a nonisolated group? Or to the contrary, are there some psychological events specific of the situation of an isolated small group? In Altman's experiments, the subjects who are isolated in groups seem to be in a situation of conflict inducing anxiety. It would appear that within an isolated small group the conflict results from the specific relationships between *space, time* and *people*, which are not structurally balanced for participants, so that their behavior may be interpreted as conflict resolution toward balance restoration.

Under normal conditions, a small group face to face can be described as a sample of specific interactions in the defined limits of *small space-short time*. For instance, a small work group meets, for a special task, every day from 2:00 to 6:00 P.M. in a particular place, room, or office; a group of friends meets every Saturday from 8:00 to 12:00 P.M. in the living room of one of them or at their club. But, outside of this short time, each member enjoys a *physical space* that is far more extended and differentiated according to his various activities and functions, and a *social space,* differentiated according to his roles and needs—he meets other people, participates in other groups for other activities, and so forth; so the total *time of life* of each individual is "distributed" between many different places, different activities, and different people.

It can be assumed that the equilibrium of an individual results from the multiplicity of differentiated social exchanges and membership groups, which implies that the borders of each of these groups are not so strong as to make contacts with the outside impossible or threatening for his membership. Under normal conditions, a small group, in a small space, is never isolated for a long time.

What happens when a small group is isolated in a small space for a long time? First, the small space leads to *physical confinement*. The space is almost undifferentiated for the various activities, and borders are strong between in-group and out-group. Second, the social isolation from outside—a counterpart of physical isolation—becomes *social confinement* inside. The sample of people to live with, and of groups in which to participate, is restricted. The links between activities and persons are undifferentiated. Third, there is *unreduced time*. The members of the group do not spend a short period of time together, but a long one; the time is no longer distributed nor differentiated.

Thus, the equilibrium of the individual, formerly secured by the range of differentiated links between space, time, and people, is threatened by this unusual structure of same persons–small space–long time—and by life conditions so homogeneous that the individual can feel a sort of "deindividuation," in Festinger's terms. There is a threat to personal identity that can be discarded only by creating a new frame of life; the participants differentiate their space (Altman's "territoriality") and their time (Altman's "synchrony"). To divide and organize space and time, as we know, are two ways of resolving interpersonal conflicts.

In an isolated small group, as is particularly obvious in Altman's experiments, there is an additional disharmony in the correlations between the order of physical distances and the order of emotional relationships. In normal space-time conditions, space is structured so that if affective relationships are positive, physical distances tend to be short; if affective relationships are neutral or negative, physical distances tend to be great. But in an isolated small group this is reversed; the participants are strangers and their physical distances are short. Hence the situation is perceived as unbalanced. When a social situation is unbalanced, there are two major ways to resolve the conflict: either strangers become friends, or interpersonal distances are enlarged. As it is impossible to really enlarge distances, however, they must be changed *symbolically*. Hence one finds "territorialities" whose function is to isolate the individual from the others.

Under normal space-time conditions, time also is correlated with affective relationships. If affective relationships are positive, the time spent together tends to be long; if affective relationships are neutral or negative, the time spent together tends to be short. In Alman's isolated small groups, the relation is reversed: the participants are strangers, and the lapse of time spent together is long. Hence, the relation is perceived as unbalanced and the conflict must be resolved; the strangers must become friends or the time spent together must be shorter. As it is impossible to really decrease shared time, the reduction could be only *symbolic*. The participants slept a lot, lay on their beds and engaged in solitary activities, all of which are ways to isolate oneself from others.

Under Altman's experimental conditions, the probability of the second solution (symbolic changes in space and time) seems to be high because it is more difficult for strangers to become friends. We must wonder why and inquire about the conditions that would lead to the first alternative, that is, a change from neutral to positive relationships. This mode of resolution would be more stable, because the structure of relationships would then become truly balanced rather than symbolically. It also would be more rewarding for the participants.

The experimental situation likewise involves conflict because, in an isolated small group, an unrewarding interpersonal relationship cannot be suppressed. In normal conditions, when an individual meets unrewarding interpersonal relationships, he can leave the group. With the strong limits of an isolated small group, the individual must stay in the group. He can only "symbolize" his departure, by isolating himself. In addition, because of physical and social confinement over a long period of time, and the lack of differentiation, the probability for personal relationships to lead to both satisfactions *and* dissatisfactions is high; hence, the unstable state of relationships, even for good relationships. Finally, because there are few participants in a small space and over a long time period, each individual can quickly achieve good predictions of the reactions of the others; hence, the "routine" condition is established. This condition is such that the situation lacks novelty and surprise, which are, as Berlyne says, stimulating and agreeable to the individuals.

It follows from the above that the "social penetration" processes, such as Altman has investigated, and the development of interpersonal relationships in conditions of confinement immediately appear as *individual* processes of *conflict* resolution. The question then may be raised as to whether the rupture of interpersonal relationships by individual voluntary isolation in space and time (interpersonal "unefficient" relationships, for Altman), as well as the management of interpersonal relationships through "synchronies" (interpersonal "efficient" relationships for Altman) are not adaptations to others at an inferior level. If interpersonal relationships and individual motivations could be managed *before* experimental (or real) isolation, could this passive adjustment be changed into active adaptation, as in cooperative *problem* solving?

Support of the above position is found in Kelley and Thibaut's (1969) description of mixed cooperation–competition situations: "The second mode of coping with problems under conditions of inadequate information or restricted communication consists primarily in the adoption or emergence of various types of rules specifying response sequences" (p. 48). Kelley et al. (1962) show that this implicit mutual adaptation is impossible within a relationship of mutual fate control only when the responses of the members occur in proper synchrony. "The external-locus-of control types . . . might be especially likely to avoid a problem-solving orientation and to rely heavily on methods incorporating the use of simple rules. Furthermore, since many (if not most) of these simple rules are concerned wholly with response distribution (with alternation, coordination, queuing, matching, and sequencing routines) and not with stabilizing causal attributions, it is quite possible that prolonged and constrained dependence on such rules could contribute to the process of alienation described by sociologists" (p. 51).

Describing conditions in which individuals are led to a problem solving orientaton, Kelley and Thibaut (1969) say:

> In an important class of groups which we have elsewhere called unvoluntary relationships, problem-solving sets are likely to be adopted only minimally or transiently. These groups . . . are defined as being constrained to a relationship that provides outcomes below the comparison level. In these groups, as in any group exercising a low degree of control over an improvident environment, the members may perceive no way of altering their situation and have little alternative but to adapt to their poor outcomes by lowering their comparison levels. . . . In fact, only in a group with resources capable of developing and distributing task-relevant information will the members be able to set and maintain comparison levels sufficiently high to prevent this kind of apathetic adaptation. Hence, an implicit condition for adoption of an orientation of group problem solving is the perception of the members that they possess sufficient informational and behavioral resources and are able to organize for their effective use in sufficient degree to enable them to solve common problems. (p. 33)

Finally, commenting on Torrance's (1954) research on air crews downed over enemy territory during World War II or over Korea, Kelley and Thibaut say: "Crew survival appeared to depend critically on a stable group structure and good communication procedures. Factors inimical to survival included the failure of affectional linkages, resulting in competition . . . and an obfuscation of path-goal relationships resulting in immobilization of group action and an *excessive concern with individual welfare*" (p. 32, emphasis added)

FOR WHAT PURPOSES SHOULD INTERPERSONAL RELATIONSHIPS BE EFFICIENT?

Neither in his experiments nor in his model does Altman emphasize the task (or tasks) the subjects have to perform together. Hence the following questions: (1) On what criteria can interpersonal relationships be assessed as "efficient"? What does "efficiency" of interpersonal relationships mean? (2) What relationships are there (or must there be) between interpersonal relationships and task efficiency?

In their book, *Small group research, A synthesis and critique of the field*, McGrath and Altman (1966), reviewing studies on this topic, have shown how results are ambiguous; in some cases "good" interpersonal relationships lead to a good group performance in the task, and in some others there is no relation.

In fact, the underlying theoretical ideas are relatively biased on two points. First, we believe, or would like to observe, that there is a simple and unequivocal correlation between "good" performance and "good" social relationships, as well as between "bad" performance and "bad" social relationships. This is a view not based on empirical evidence; in fact, it is a belief, an ideological point of view. Second, the problem is thought of in terms of causality, whereas nothing but empirical correlations have occasionally been observed until now. In this field, researchers are not concerned enough with processes underlying the group task and with influence of good or bad relationships on task processes. Moreover, the problem is thought of in static terms; interpersonal relations are conceived as preexisting task operations. On the contrary, we must think of the problem in dialectical terms; interpersonal relationships are both means and outcomes of task performing.

A question also arises as to whether the process of "social penetration," to use Altman's words, deals only with information relative to "persons." If one conceives of social behavior as a system, does this system not imply interrelated subsystems, person-person and person-task? It would appear that social situations demand the development and management of *functional* interpersonal relationships, as well as *effective* interpersonal relationships. For isolated small groups, which is our topic here, "task" means several things: the group *mission*, to which isolation and social confinement are contingent; the collective or individual *operations* within the frame of the mission; and collective or individual *operations* for the biological and psychological survival of the group. It is necessary to define and rank these tasks in order to possibly understand the influence of interpersonal relationships on the quality of task performance and the influence of the different tasks on the quality of interpersonal relationships.

In Altman's experiments, the subjects have to perform tasks (personal or collective) that are a part of the life-program imposed by the experimenter. But the results obtained in these tasks are not explicitly and precisely related to the development of interpersonal relationships. Furthermore, these tasks are neither related to a group "mission" nor to the group survival. They have the character of games, or are pedagogical, and thus not functional. These tasks, controlled by the experimenter, are repetitive, not rewarded, and, seemingly, without feedback, whereas the time and choice of leisure are controlled by the participants. The life-program of the participants, therefore, consists of a sequence of separate activities, which are not significant for the *group* and cannot be a basis for a real shared field. It is not surprising that the observed behaviors are consistently centered on the individual, concerned with personal comfort, and not really cooperative.

Must the Problem of Interpersonal Relationships in a Small Group, Isolated or Not, Be Focused on Individual Personality and Adjustment, or on the Group as a Whole and the Interdependence of Its Members?

Altman presented a model of *individual* personality as related to social environment and exchanges with the others; but, however rich it may be, it is not a model of the *group*. To be more precise, as is shown by the table of dimensions along which the actual level of interpersonal relationships could be assessed in comparison with the necessary level, it is a model for interpersonal communication. It is irrelevant, however, to assume that a positive and active adaptation in a small group, that is in group cohesion, common goals and a "shared psychological field" (Asch, 1957) may be developed. Hence, Altman's experiments are no longer experiments on groups. The participants are put together and confronted with the same conditions of environment. They can mutually interact, but the conditions are not appropriate to develop any kind of *interdependence* between the participants. The subjects have no *common* goal (no mission, no survival to secure) for the success or failure of which they would depend on one another; they only have individual goals that can only be harmonized so as to avoid interferences.

Many previous studies have shown that to maintain interpersonal relationships in a group, and face difficult conditions, stress, or crisis, the major factor is group *organization*. This includes the product of the members' previous interdependences, their skills and abilities, their training to deal with the demands of the environment, and the prominence of the common goals over the individual interests. French (1941), to take one example, demonstrated that organized groups composed of previously unacquainted undergraduates and working over particularly difficult problems "showed intense frustration, which they expressed in intermember aggression and a general disorganization of group activity . . . many of them were unable to remain intact under frustration: in some instances, opposing factions formed, and in other cases, members abandoned the group permanently to work on irrelevant tasks." On the other hand, the organized groups, which are "highly cohesive athletic teams from Harvard houses and established clubs . . . resisted disruption, maintained high levels of we-feeling, great social freedom among the members, and a strong sense of common purpose" (quoted by Kelley and Thibaut, 1969, p. 31.)

In his studies on adolescent groups in tension, Sherif (1953) demonstrated that one way of getting out of strong intergroup competition is to give the groups high-order common goals. However difficult achieving such a program may be, it is considered that this perspective of working will be rewarding.

On Research Strategy in the Isolated Small Group Field

Altman is correct to say that studies on isolated small groups must be integrated within a very large theoretical and methodological framework. But if the aim is to manage the biological and psychological survival of isolated teams, one should perhaps define shorter term objectives of research. As isolated small groups are in a situation of mixed cooperation-competition, with a high probability of interpersonal conflicts, and their mission is important and their survival difficult and essential, it is necessary to help them quickly achieve a hierarchical order of common goals and interpersonal relationships.

In view of the above, it is considered that the problem is not to understand but to *manage* the psychological life environment of actual and present groups. In this perspective, it would be better to test experimentally the efficiency of various programs of training for confinement-isolation on interpersonal relationships and performances in prescribed tasks. Among other things, it would be necessary to develop and to test programs of training in interpersonal relationships; programs of individual and collective training to social confinement; programs of selection of participants on the basis of experienced relations in simulated conditions; programs of life in isolated groups in simulated conditions; and programs of common goal sharing with subjects who already have strong individual motivations for the mission. These short-term trial and error studies would imply a coordination between specialists. In order to state the coordinates of the simulated situations in which the participants would be trained in living in social confinement, it would be necessary to describe precisely the life conditions (lack of gravity, for example) and the tasks to be performed by a given small group in isolation.

References

Asch, S. 1957. *Social psychology*. Englewood Cliffs, N.J.: Prentice-Hall.
French, J. R. P. Jr. 1941. The disruption and cohesion of groups. *J. abnorm. soc. Psychol.* 36:361–77.

Kelley, H. H., & Thibaut, J. W. 1969. Group problem-solving. In *Handbook of social psychology*, ed. G. Lindzey & E. Aronson, Vol. 4, pp. 1–101. 2d ed. Reading, Mass.: Addison-Wesley.

Kelley, H. H., Thibaut, J. W., Radloff, R. & Mundy, D. 1962. The development of cooperation in the 'minimal social situation.' *Psychol. Monogr.*, 76: No. 19 (whole No. 538).

McGrath, J. E., & Altman, I. 1966. *Small group research: A synthesis and critique of the field.* New York: Holt, Rinehart and Winston.

Sherif, M. & Sherif, Carolyn W. 1953. *Group in harmony and tension.* New York: Harper.

Torrance, E. P. 1954. The behavior of small groups under the stress of conditions of "survival." *Amer. Soc. Review* 19:751–55.

S. B. Sells *received his Ph.D. from Columbia University in 1936 and from 1948 to 1958 was Professor and Head of the Department, Medical Psychology at the U.S.A.F. School of Aviation Medicine. He joined the faculty of Texas Christian University in 1958, and established the Institute of Behavioral Research there in 1962. He was named Research Professor (Psychology) in 1968. He is Associate and Managing Editor of* Multivariate Behavioral Research *and Editor of T.C.U. Press's Behavioral Science Monographs. He is a consultant to the Navy Neuropsychiatric Research Unit, San Diego, the National Center for Health Statistics, and the National Institute for Mental Health. His long-time interests in personality and social psychology have extended to applications in industrial personnel and management research, aerospace and military problems, and research on program evaluation involving educational and health services.*

Sells *proposes the thesis that a taxonomy of man in isolation or of man in enclosed space requires analysis of isolated and confined situations in the context of a social system model. He maintains that while the effects of social isolation, confinement, and sensory restriction appear to be salient, they cannot be disentangled from the highly interdependent social system contexts in which they occur, and that it is also strongly indicated they vary significantly among classes of social systems. An original social system model is presented and Sells points out both ways in which it requires further development and the power that is provided by even this primitive version in taxonomic analysis which uses multivariate methods of profile and hierarchical grouping analysis. An example is presented comparing system profiles of the prototypic space ship with profiles computed for Sealab, Tektite, and other small, isolated systems.*

11

The Taxonomy of Man
in Enclosed Space

S. B. SELLS

The record of achievement in space and undersea exploration has generated the highest expectations in relation to further plans to extend the human frontier. New programs may present the most difficult scientific and technological problems, as outlined by Perkins in his 1969 Bauer Lecture to the Aerospace Medical Association (Perkins, 1969), but the spirit of these times reflects a remarkable faith in the ingenuity and power of man to overcome nature. The casual acceptance of new materials, designs, and concepts applied to structures, propulsion, communication, tools, and life support systems by those who watch lunar walks on television should not, however, obscure this important aspect of contemporary scientific posture. Regrettably, more systematic effort has been devoted to the study of materiel than to man, at least in respect to understanding the nature and effects of prolonged social isolation and environmental restriction. Until this imbalance is restored, the limiting factor in man's further exploration of the universe may be man himself.

The importance of research on behavioral effects of isolation has been widely appreciated since the early days of the space effort. However, progress has been slow, partly as a result of constraints imposed by prevailing ethical attitudes regarding human experimentation. Major problems have been encountered in efforts to simulate realistic conditions in the laboratory, with the result that a number of responsible workers have shifted their emphasis to field situations in which people have experienced isolation. These include naturalistic observation and field experiments. Reports in the former category reflect extremely diverse sources, including patients in "iron lung" respirators, elderly persons in nursing homes, incarcerated prisoners and prisoners of war, hospital patients, mental hospital inmates, lone sailors on solo voyages, survivors of exploration, and expeditions. Examples of field experiments include the Sealab studies (Radloff & Helmreich, 1968) and Operation Tektite (Radloff, 1969), and the McDonnell-Douglas 60- and 90-day manned tests of spacecraft life support systems (Arndt & Jackson, 1968; Jackson & Houghton, 1969).

Unfortunately, interpretation of field observational studies presents other problems. As expected, the behavior of individuals in field isolation situations reflects the complex interaction with isolation variables of numerous other variables such as personality, other stresses, social relations among the members of the isolated party, and duration of exposure, which define specific situations. Efforts to draw conclusions from this literature are frustrated by the problem of distinguishing effects attributable to isolation and confinement per se from those accounted for by such confounding factors as danger, discomfort, illness, deprivation, and social disorganization among widely different groups in widely different circumstances.

This problem is not eliminated in the field experiment; the advantage of the field experiment lies primarily in increased opportunity to control significant aspects of the experience on which conclusions will be based, and the introduction of planned, quantitative measurement. Selection of field isolation situations on the basis of relevance to the problem of interest is frequently feasible and may enhance the value of such sources. This is illustrated by observations based on the performance of remote task groups in submarines, Arctic and Antarctic duty stations, and other isolated situations, which have generally confirmed the occurrence among even these personnel of a wide range of subjective symptoms. However, the nature of the social system makes a difference. Among the most common complaints of individuals are sleep disturbance, restlessness, inability to concentrate, fatigue, muscular weakness and soreness, boredom, monotony, feelings of dirtyness, headaches, dizzyness, psychosomatic reactions, apathy, low morale, time disorientation, frustrations, anxiety, irritability, hostility, depression, and withdrawal. But in each situation involving organized and professionally led groups, with trained, disciplined personnel and in the absence of major disorganizing forces of disaster, the occurrence of serious overt interpersonal conflict, deterioration of interpersonal behavior, and group disorganization, frequently mentioned in the anecdotal literature, has been rare (Sells & Rawls, 1969).

Although of interest in the broad spectrum of stress behavior, isolation associated with disaster, as in shipwrecks and marooned expeditions, has only marginal relevance to the problem of organized, diciplined, trained groups. The former represent accidental isolation and have almost always involved participants unprepared for the rigors encountered. Whether many of these would have ended in the disaster experienced if adequate planning and preparation had been made is problematic. It is of course impossible to foresee every contingency and to eliminate risk entirely, but it is important to recognize that, in the design of hazardous programs, such as long-duration space missions, one does not plan for disaster, but rather attempts to minimize risk by controlling all known factors through appropriate design and management. Effects of isolation associated with disaster can be considered academic in this framework. The pertinent question concerns the effects that may be expected under optimal operational conditions.

More particularly, managers of space and undersea programs need to know what effects may be expected for an optimally qualified, well-organized, and trained crew, functioning under effective leadership, in an optimally designed vehicle or habitat, but locked in the isolated environment and confined for the duration of a long mission. Such specification is necessary to guide relevant critical research and the formulation of useful hypotheses that can be tested and revised as successive missions proceed to longer and more isolated mission profiles.

Three major dimensions of isolation have ben identified by most investigators, including Fraser (1966), Gunderson and Nelson (1966), Haythorn (1966), Lilly (1956), Schultz (1965), Sells (1956), Wheaton (1958), Zubek (1969), and others. These are: first, *social isolation*, which emphasizes separation from significant people, groups, activities, and social situations; second, *confinement*, which involves principally restraint and restricted mobility; and finally, *sensory restriction*, in which the variation of environmental stimulation is reduced. Basically, all combinations of these factors involve *states* in which individuals or groups are in some sense cut off from significant and subjectively important elements of the environment, producing experiences of aloneness or apartness, with consequent effects on behavior. However, although these dimensions illuminate the nature of the isolated situation, by themselves they are too general to account for behavioral effects, except perhaps in extreme cases. Such effects depend on the complex interaction of many factors, including the characteristics of persons involved, of the social circumstances, and of the physical conditions. A taxonomy of man in isolated and enclosed space requires identification of the significant variables and processes related to each set and multivariate classification within the domain represented by these sets.

The proposals presented here are concerned primarily with identification of appropriate variables for the taxonomic analysis. Some preliminary efforts to develop a social system model for isolated microsocieties will be reviewed and interpreted in relation to needed future research.

Identification of Relevant Variables

A complete accounting of variables related to behavior in isolation would
be too ambitious a goal at this time. The present discussion outlines three
sets of variables believed to account for major portions of variance and to
specify effects associated with them. These represent the situation, the
social system, and the individual personality. As the discussion proceeds
it will be apparent that both the situational dimensions and the personality process dimensions should properly be represented as subsets of the
social system. One of the most interesting properties of the system concepts is the interdependency of its parts. As a result, most real-life social
systems have highly specific environmental characteristics and personnel
requirements. For the purpose of the present discussion it is sufficient to
point this out. The salience of situation and personality dimensions can
then be treated in more detail and the discussion of social system can be
focused on system characteristics, which require a holistic emphasis.

CHARACTERISTICS OF THE SITUATION

The following analysis outlines 10 situational dimensions that are believed to have significant implications for behavior in isolation. Although
there is some experimental basis for the conclusions drawn in relation to
these variables, much of the position taken is based on observations reported in field situations. Despite the apparent confidence reflected in the
discussion, further research is needed to obtain critical support or to
modify these interpretations.

1. *Voluntary vs Involuntary.* Tolerance of discomfort, deprivation,
and of danger are increased when the expected reward is high in relation
to psychological costs. Although perhaps not invariable, it is assumed
that the reward-cost ratio is highly favorable for voluntary participants
and unfavorable for involuntary participants. Voluntary participation is
assumed to represent self-initiated inclusion, open choice among equally
available alternatives, and informed consent without direct or indirect
coercion. Astronauts and aquanauts, as in the Sealab and Tektite projects,
are examples of voluntary participants in isolation, as are monks, nuns,
and religious recluses. Prisoners, shut-ins, trapped miners, impressed sea-
men, slaves, and castaways are isolated involuntarily. Inasmuch as this
dimension is generally confounded with preparation, preselection, and
training, it is extremely difficult to test the motivational factors independently.

2. *Instrumental vs Obstructive.* Tolerance of isolation is believed to be
greater when the isolation is instrumental to an important goal (as in

space missions) and reduced when it obstructs goal attainment (as in most involuntary situations). Involuntary isolation, such as the assignment of military personnel to remote stations, is better endured when the mission is accepted as plausible, important, and necessary. Involuntary isolation that obstructs personal goal attainment, and for which the goal served is rejected, as in the case of many draftees assigned overseas in Vietnam, is doubly frustrating.

3. *Planned vs Unplanned.* When isolation is entered knowledgeably, with purposeful and productive planning, preparation, training, and equipment, the likelihood of successful outcomes is increased in comparison with unplanned, unprepared, accidental experiences. Even in the case of wartime bombing of cities and natural disasters, advance knowledge of possible occurrences and of procedures to follow has materially reduced casualties.

4. *Duration.* Isolation may extend from brief exposures, as in many experiments, to extremely long periods, as in certain classical cases of imprisonment. The stress of isolation is believed to increase as a function of duration. Long before the voyage of Columbus and many times since, ships' crews functioned effectively in isolation for periods comparable to those currently estimated for a Mars mission. The critical importance of duration increases, however, as the effects of close confinement and other stresses are compounded.

5. *Individual vs Group.* As noted earlier, the evidence from extensive field observations indicates that individuals tolerate isolation and other stresses better as members of organized groups than alone. The influence of the group is undoubtedly mediated by group structure and dynamics, including acceptance of role expectations and requirements, reciprocal role relations, leadership, discipline, and mutual support characteristic of military units, space and ship crews, and organized expeditions. The disorganization and panic often observed in civilian disasters reflects the reactions of the unorganized collective aggregation.

6. *Space Restriction.* Human space requirements are not absolute. Norms for individual space have increased historically and are known to vary culturally as a function of industrialization and social affluence. A characteristic human tendency has been for luxuries to become necessities, and this has been true in the case of normal and minimum standards for individual space. In addition to this cultural relativity, many personal and situational factors affect space requirements (Hall, 1966; Sommer, 1969; Trego & McGaffey, 1969). A particularly interesting interaction

exists between this factor and the preceding one. In group situations, the significant aspects of space restriction include, in proportion to the degree of crowding, loss of privacy, enforced intimacy, restraint, and restriction of movement. Restraint and restriction of movement also occur in the alone situation. Although space requirements vary, crowding and confinement to close quarters are significant sources of stress, and they increase as a function of duration.

7. *Threat.* Subjectively, isolation may involve varying degrees of threat derived from objective assessment of known dangers, as well as fear of the unknown and problems related to separation. In space and undersea operations, the capsule exists as a safe shelter in a hostile environment and is protective as long as it functions adequately, although at the same time its confined internal accommodations may be a source of stress. Threat related to separation will reflect individual differences in personality, status, and personal situations, but the reward component of the reward-cost ratio will also depend on aspects of the mission.

8. *Social Conditions.* Important considerations here are the number and nature of the persons present, communications, interpersonal, and role relations. The pattern of social conditions may contribute to the support or degradation of the adjustive capabilities of the individual or individuals involved.

9. *Support Conditions.* Variations of support include supplies, equipment, and other logistic aspects that may determine how long the party can hold out under existent conditions of isolation.

10. *Environmental Variability.* Variability of the isolated environment is related to the phenomenon of *sensory deprivation,* and affects level of arousal and compensatory functions when sensory input variation is minimal, producing monotony, boredom, and even hallucinatory experiences in rare cases, as discussed by Dr. Zubek in this volume. Even when monotony is only moderate, however, social and behavioral effects may be heightened by the combined effects of other stresses.

SOCIAL SYSTEM CHARACTERISTICS

The social system concept is a relatively new but important development in the study of human groups and organizations and their influences on individual behavior. Group concepts have focused primarily on organizational structure and various aspects of intra- and intergroup interaction. The social group is, however, a subsystem of the larger unit, the social system. The social system is a more inclusive concept that identifies the functioning human and environmental components as a holistic unity with distinctive purposes. It relates in the system concept all of the highly interdependent elements that have significant effects on system behavior. Examples of microsocial systems in which isolation is in some manner a significant problem include not only spacecraft and submersibles, but also exploration parties and expeditions, naval ships, bomber crews, remote duty organizations (such as radar outposts), traveling professional athletic teams, various remote duty industrial work groups, shipwreck and disaster situations, prisoner of war groups, prison society, hospital wards, and other shut-in situations.

Elsewhere (Sells 1966, 1967a) I have proposed a structural model for such social systems, described by 55 quantifiable system characteristics representing seven major component categories. These are enumerated briefly below; the detailed specifications and rationales are available in the original papers.

I. OBJECTIVES AND GOALS

As incorporated in the model, objectives and goals are viewed as critical elements of system structure rather than in terms of specific task objectives, which are implied in other sections. Each of the following seven characteristics (as well as those discussed in subsequent categories) is believed to be capable of being expressed on a quantitative scale: (1) degree of *formal prescription* of objectives and goals, (2) extent to which they are *mandatory*, (3) endorsement by *formal authority*, (4) degree of *polarization* toward a major specific goal, (5) degree of *remoteness of the goal* or goals, (6) clarity of the *criteria of success*, and (7) degree of *uncertainty of success* of accomplishment.

II. PHILOSOPHY AND VALUE SYSTEMS

The philosophy and value systems of an organization generally reflect the attitudes of its governing center with respect to considerations of ethics, concern for human values, designation of priorities in decision making, and other fundamental policies critical to system operation. In relation to the "capsule society" of the spaceship, six characteristics were prescribed, but these might be modified to fit other types of systems or to achieve greater generality (Sells, 1968). The spaceship characteristics included were (1) obedience to command, (2) emphasis on mission as a supreme priority, (3) respect for individual lives, (4) extent to which the program reflects a high national priority, (5) acceptance of the military tradition in norms for personal attitudes, and (6) acceptance of traditional national values (the American Way of Life).

III. PERSONNEL COMPOSITION

The high interdependence of system components is exemplified by the fact that optimal personnel selection tends to be guided by compatibility with goals, values, technology (see below), and other system characteristics. A comprehensive set of descriptors of individual members includes: (1) intellectual factors, (2) education, (3) extent of relevant training, (4) extent of relevant life experience, (5) personality factors, (6) character and moral factors, (7) physical factors, (8) skill factors, (9) motivation to participate, (10) sex, (11) age, and (12) social level, socioeconomic status, and rank. In addition to individual descriptors, two group (crew) description items were included in the original model. Listed under number 13, homogeneity of the personnel complement, these were (a) the presence of noncrew members (passengers or scientist passengers) in the complement, and (b) the rank distribution, particularly with reference to subgrouping and the issue of whether the crew is composed of officer-types only, as in Gemini and Apollo, or of officer and enlisted types, as in naval ships and submarines.

IV. ORGANIZATION

Eleven organizational factors were cited in the spaceship model. These include: (1) degree of formal structure, (2) degree of formal role prescription, (3) existence of a command structure, (4) existence of a centralized authority, (5) existence of a chain of command with provision for succession, (6) extent of provisions of back-up and support organization, (7) degree of group autonomy with respect to goals, (8) extent to which discipline is prescribed, (9) extent of prescribed social distance among crew, and (10) congruence of rank and crew status. The overlap among several of these items serves to emphasize salient facets and could easily be accommodated in a working model. The eleventh factor is group size, which in the spaceship would probably not exceed 12 persons, but might reach a larger number in a space station. In a generalized model for isolated microsocieties, this section might well undergo revision in the statement of descriptors.

V. TECHNOLOGY

Space and undersea technology are advancing at such a rate that planners must be ready to forecast expected developments that are not yet perfected in consideration of projects scheduled even 5 years ahead. As space technologists think now about Mars missions in the 1980s, it is urgent that the effects of possible new propellants such as nuclear power, new means of communication such as lasers, improved life support systems, and the like, be taken into consideration in conceptualizing the tasks, equipment, quarters, and other aspects of the spaceship social system. The characteristics related to technology in the original spaceship system model are: (1) degree of technological complexity, (2) relation to the aviation tradition, (3) use of simulators and other technical training devices, (4) extent of required preparation for missions, (5) extent of dependence on technical communication procedures, (6) degree of required physical preconditioning, and (7) scientific principles involved in operations.

VI. PHYSICAL ENVIRONMENT

The rationale of each of the eight environment factors is clear enough. In addition to these, listed below, a category representing the social environment is included later. The physical environment factors are: (1) extent of required physiological protection and life support, (2) degree of remoteness from (home) base, (3) extent of environmental hazards (including the likelihood of unknown factors), (4) degree of space restriction and confinement, (5) endurance demands, (6) provisions for mobility, including the extent to which the situation is static (as in Tektite) or maneuvering (as in spaceflight) and the amount of intra- and extravehicular mobility permitted, and (7) amount of communication permitted within the system and with external persons (official and personal).

VII. TEMPORAL CHARACTERISTICS

A very important aspect of every social system is its temporal character. For the spaceship system model, three temporal factors were mentioned. The first relates to the duration of exposure to isolation and confinement in a continuous mission. Second is the total time involved, including preparation and postmission quarantine. Finally, the extent to which each daily cycle is fully occupied is important; on a spaceship this is total, in contrast to work situations while living at home, which provide many relaxing discontinuities and respites from sameness and boredom.

These 7 categories of social system descriptors were used effectively (Sells, 1966) in discriminating a conceptual model of the Gemini-Apollo era spaceship from 11 other identifiable systems, as shown in Table 11.1. The results of this analysis are summarized in Table 11.2, which lists the 11 comparison systems in rank order and by score, where the maximum score is 110. Although the comparisons are of considerable substantive interest, the main purpose of the two tables in the present context is to demonstrate the possibility of quantitive assessment of social system profiles as a basis of similarity analysis. Further comparisons are presented subsequently.

The social system model explicated here was published in 1966. Largely as a result of a penetrating analysis by Warren (1966), it became clear that more specific attention needed to be devoted to the *social-cultural environment*, both of the society which the isolated social system represents and of the parent organization of which it is a part. A later, more general version of the model (Sells, 1968) included additional factors representing this category. While this section overlaps in part with the items on philosophy and value systems, the additional descriptors, listed below, would be of greatest importance in studies involving transcultural analysis. These items are derived from the comprehensive study of sociocultural characteristics of human populations by Murdock et al. (1961).

1. geography
2. human biology
3. behavior process and personality
4. demography
5. history and cultural change
6. total culture
7. language
8. communication
9. records
10. food quest
11. animal husbandry
12. agriculture
13. food processing
14. food consumption
15. drink, drugs, indulgence
16. leather, textiles, fabrics
17. clothing
18. adornment
19. exploitative activities
20. processing of basic materials
21. building and construction
22. structures
23. equipment and maintenance of buildings
24. settlements
25. energy and power
26. chemical industries
27. capital goods and industries
28. machines
29. tools and appliances
30. property
31. exchange
32. marketing
33. finance
34. labor

35. business and industrial organization
36. travel and transportation
37. land transport
38. water and air transport
39. living standards and routines
40. recreation
41. fine arts
42. entertainment
43. individuation and mobility
44. social stratification
45. interpersonal relations
46. marriage
47. family
48. kinship
49. kin groups
50. community
51. territorial organization
52. state
53. government activities
54. political behavior
55. law
56. offenses and sanctions
57. justice
58. armed forces
59. military technology
60. war
61. social problems
62. health and welfare
63. sickness
64. death
65. religious beliefs
66. religious practices
67. ecclesiastical organization
68. numbers and measures
69. exact knowledge

70. ideas about man and nature
71. sex
72. reproduction
73. infancy and childhood

74. socialization
75. education
76. adolescence, adulthood, old age

Although many of these items apply to social systems and culture viewed in "macroperspective," it seems advisable to include them in the complete list. Furthermore, examination of the list suggests that many of these have significant analogs in a "microperspective," as well.

PERSONALITY PROCESSES

The interaction principle emphasized throughout this paper assumes contingent relations between personality and behavior in isolation. The contingencies are reflected in the social system profiles as implied above. The extent to which such contingent relations have been investigated is extremely limited. However, some important examples are discussed below, using the salient factors of social isolation, confinement, and sensory restriction as keys to the system profiles.

Social Deprivation. Social deprivation is an effect of the *state of isolation* rather than of *remoteness per se,* and often occurs even in the midst of the "lonely crowd." Indeed, throughout the world there are many men and women who, although their entire lives are spent in remote, out-of-the-way existence, nevertheless show no evidence of social deprivation, because their hamlets are their homes. On the other hand, "homesickness" is common among individuals cut off from their familiar surrounds. Apparently, familiarity and dependence on the familiar for support are essential for adjustment, and remoteness is involved only as it is associated with deprivation. Individual differences in dependency and choice of dependency objects account for variations in experienced deprivation.

Social deprivation as a general concept involves separation from any significant supports. These may include significant persons and role partners in family, work, and social relationships, as well as statuses, activities, objects, and surrounds on which the individual has learned to depend for feelings of well-being and security. The general hypothesis is that such separation is a source of stress to the individual to the extent that the isolated situation calls for modes of personal problem-solving that are not available and for which suitable alternatives cannot be found.

To the extent that social deprivation, as defined, leaves the individual deprived of effective and previously depended upon modes of coping with problems, it is related to the concepts of alienation and anomie (Durkheim, 1951; Merton, 1957; Srole, 1956) that have received extensive attention by sociologists, and which Jessor et al. (1968) consider conducive to deviance in the sense of absence or lessening of effective (normative) control of behavior.

For men entering long-duration expeditions requiring extended absence from home base, social deprivation is a potential problem. Individuals without family ties might appear to be best suited for such activities because of their lack of encumbrances. However, this is doubtful inasmuch as the lonely state frequently reflects other problems. On the other hand, men whose professional identifications and career goals take precedence over wife, family, and home may be better adapted to endure extended isolation than those who depend heavily on family ties for their sense of well-being. It has been suggested (Sells, 1967b) that the practice of early sailing ship captains to bring their wives on voyages may have developed as a means of compensating for deprivation. Then, at least the captain would remain sane.

At the present state of knowledge, assessment of dependency is an uncertain process. In practical selection situations, some of the problems in this area could be minimized by the practice of using volunteers. In this respect, informal procedures of self-selection in choice of crew members and in crew assembly may still be the most reliable approach. There is at least some basis for expecting that men dedicated to goals of supreme importance to them could endure deprivation of sexual gratification and other personal satisfactions in the course of participation in a great adventure of overwhelming historical significance.

At the same time, the need for continuing research must be emphasized. In view of the gravity of the unprecedented situation implied by space missions of possibly 2 years duration, prudence demands that no possible sources of future problems be overlooked. Haythorn (1966) has emphasized the importance of compatible personalities in the limited social situation and has made a significant start in the quantitative study of this problem. Both Cowan and Strickland (1965) and Dunlap (undated) have reported that compatibility had a favorable effect on experimental isolated groups. Wheaton (1958) has noted instances in which participation in group activities was a significant source of support for group members.

Several writers have commented on dependencies related to various personality traits. Gunderson (1965) reported that men with high affectional needs experienced problems in wintering-over situations in the Antarctic. Miller (1959), in a study of Arctic Aircraft Control and Warning site personnel, reported comparable problems in relation to individuals high in dominance and high in dependency. Mullin (1960), who interviewed scientists and naval personnel in the Antarctic, reported that neither physical danger, nor hardship, nor extreme cold were the most serious stresses mentioned, but that individual adjustments to the group, the sameness of the environment, and the absence of many usual sources of gratification were more important.

Confinement. The term confinement refers both to the physical arrangements of the isolated situation and to the implications of close physical confinement for the social system existing in the enclosed space. Both have extremely important effects on behavior.

Physical confinement implies restraint, restriction of freedom of movement and action, enforced closeness with other crew members, and reduced social variation. For men of action, such as aggressive combat and test pilots, from whose ranks most of the present astronauts have been drawn, extended confinement in the space capsule may be regarded as a challenge to develop effective compensatory modes of behavior. The close quarters, with incident status leveling, familiarity, reduction of privacy, enforced intimacy, absence of shelter from interpersonal conflict, and limited opportunity for recreational pursuits, present numerous problems in relation to personal conduct, interpersonal interaction, leadership, organization, and group management.

Haythorn (1966) has observed, in experimental studies of small groups in confinement, a speeding up of the acquaintance process, marked by an accelerated rate of interpersonal information exchange. The depth and breadth of exchange of confidences under such enforced closeness is impressive. A difficulty resulting from such speeded acquaintanceship among experimental subjects was that information acquisition frequently exceeded the rate at which an individual could learn to accept idiosyncracies of another person or to cope with values markedly different from his own.

Under such circumstances, among individuals capable of controlling extrapunitive, aggressive impulses, the tendency to withdraw is a reasonable alternative and leads to breakdown of communication, guarding of personal possessions and prerogatives, and territoriality, in the sense of establishment of propriety in respect to use of personal items and areas of space not to be intruded upon by others. Experimental work in this area is discussed elsewhere in this volume by Professor Altman.

Observations of these phenomena are common in the literature and have even been translated into formal provisions against the forces toward intimacy on ships, which have evolved designated areas for high rank officers, noncommissioned officers, and rank and file crew. The "captain's territory" is a sanctuary within which he can attempt to function impartially and defend his authority against informal, personal influences in the closeness of the ship environment. Both Altman and Haythorn (1967) and Cowan and Strickland (1965) have reported that

territoriality occurred earlier and more extensively among their isolated experimental subjects than among controls, and that it increased with time.
It began with the claiming of fixed geographic areas and highly personal
objects and extended later to more mobile areas (personal distance) and
less personal objects. Cowan and Strickland mentioned that their isolated
subjects in the UCLA Penthouse Experiment actually staked out areas of
exclusion of others and acted with marked hostility toward trespassers.

Such reactions can apparently be reduced by selection of members of
isolated groups who are compatible with each other, as reported by the
investigators already mentioned. Knowledge of the basis for such selection is presently grossly insufficient, although Altman and Haythorn have
shown that positive results can be attained using personality measures.

The general effects of the enforced intimacy of confined groups are
multifaceted. Not only are personal rights and privileges vulnerable to vio-
lation, giving rise to the defense of privacy and territoriality, and the need
for greater personal space, but strong forces toward informality and intimacy are generated which threaten formal command structure. The process of status leveling (Rohrer, 1959; Sells, 1963, 1967a; Torrance, 1957;
Wilkins, 1967) makes it difficult and sometimes impossible to achieve
and maintain the social distance between superior and subordinate in a
command relationship needed to support the authority of the superior.
Many questions concerning the basis of social power and leadership style
appropriate to such situations can presently be answered only by educat-
ed guesses, and without hard data.

Mullin (1960) recorded an observation frequently mentioned in the
literature, that group and individual tensions and irritations are ever present, but that the most important lesson a member of such a group could
learn was that he could not afford to alienate himself from the support of
the group. In such microsocieties, each individual is highly dependent on
the good will of the others and of the group as a whole for his feelings of
acceptance, worth, and security.

A mechanism of displacement of hostility frequently observed among
isolated groups is the tendency to direct anger, scorn, and even ridicule,
with intensity often out of proportion to the focal issue, on external com-
petitors and superior authorities. The naval literature, as well as reports
of expeditions and military operations, reveals repeated instances of an-
tagonism toward headquarters by field parties, and of complaints about
"excessive demands" by outside persons who are said to be "unaware" of
the ongoing realities. Some occurrences of this type have been suspected
in the space program and may be expected with greater vehemence as
time and distances increase. Such observations have been made by Cowan and Strickland (1965), David (1963), Farrell and Smith (1964),
Hanna (1962), McGrath et al. (1962), Rodgin and Hartman (1966),

and Smith (1966). While the effects may be hygienic, insofar as they furnish a common target for the venting of repressed hostility, the positive values for group mental health may be more than offset by disruption of significant communications with base support groups.

Confined Social Systems. Goffman, whose book *Asylums* (1961) has become a classic of sociological research, has developed the concept of the "total group," which is cut off from society and leads a closed existence. While Goffman's basic formulation is focused on hospitals and custodial institutions, in which the staff-inmate distinction is critical, there are, nevertheless, several aspects that have important implications for confinement in other situations as well. According to Goffman, one effect of a total institution is that it places many human needs under bureaucratic control. In a hospital, the staff are the managers and the patients, the managed. Staff surveillance of patients encourages conformity to staff desires, but engenders hostility, with the result that each group develops stereotypes, misunderstanding, and mistrust in relation to the other. Communication is restricted and inmates are commonly excluded from information and decisions concerning their fates. The closed society has no opportunities for discontinuity or escape, such as in open societies, in which individuals routinely move from home to office, to coffee break, to lunch, to clubs, and the like, with consequent release from tension. Instead, tensions boil up, as in a pressure cooker.

The absence of discontinuities in hospitals and prisons is equally apparent in spaceships and may be equally significant. In addition, despite the obvious social differences between the capsule and institutional societies, there are analogues of more than academic interest with reference to the perceived relations between commander and crew, and between astronaut and scientist crew members in relation to maintenance of discipline, control of significant information, decision making, and influence by example. There is great need for the capsule community to be truly a therapeutic community rather than a pressure cooker.

Reduced Sensory Variation. As in all confined situations, life in an isolated capsule must necessarily involve extended sameness, monotony of social stimulation, reduced opportunities for social comparison, and minimal diversion in work and recreational activity. Although such situations are on a continuum with those involving the classical sensory deprivation cubicles, reviewed definitively by Zubek (1969), the monotony of the space capsule does not even approach the extremity of restriction obtained by Heron, Bexton, and Hebb (1953), Lilly (1956), Zubek, and other sensory deprivation investigators. The problem appears rather to involve the same faces, the same personalities, the same surrounds, the same routine over and over, accompanied by minimal physical mobility and activity; that is, restriction of the amount and variety of meaningful sensory stimulation over a prolonged period.

Fraser (1966) concluded, after reviewing a number of studies of confined groups, that perceptual aberrations are related to reduced or distorted sensory input and do not occur in the presence of good consensual validation. This is at least in part related to the fact that fewer problems have been observed for small groups in isolation and confinement than for individuals, as reported by Fraser (1966), Smith (1966), and others. The presence of at least one other person tends to enrich the environment and make it more tolerable. In pronounced contrast to the profusion of symptoms described for individuals experiencing sensory deprivation, studies of groups in isolation have reported few incidents of unusual visual and auditory sensations, perceptual distortions, difficulties in distinguishing between sleep and waking states, unusual dreams, and other distorted experiences.

Most writers on isolation have noted the prevalence of monotony and boredom as pervasive problems. As a result, much interest has been focused upon effects on intellectual functioning, on performance and on morale, as well as on arrangements for leisure and recreation. Mullin (1960) noted a widespread lack of intellectual energy among Antarctic personnel despite the fact that most of the men had planned to engage in intellectual pursuits such as learning a language, correspondence courses, and the like. However, it is important to note that this may simply reflect the effects of new surrounds and not of restricted environmental input, as such. Indeed, evidence of performance deterioration based on objective data is hard to find among isolated groups, while many reports make specific mention that deterioration did not occur. Reports by Burns and Kimura (1963), Eilbert and Glaser (1959), Gunderson and Nelson (1966), Mullin (1960), and Rohrer (1959), have included descriptive accounts of morale problems affecting performance. Other studies of both short-term and moderate exposure have revealed no clear evidence of decrement of intellectual performance in isolation over time (Agadzhanian et al., 1963; Alluisi et al., 1963; Faucett & Newman, 1964; Hammes, 1964; Hanna & Gaito, 1960; Hartman et al., 1964; McGrath et al., 1962; Rodgin and Hartman, 1966; Zubek et al., 1962).

Comparison of Social Systems

The study of social systems, using models such as that presented above, is recent, and further experience is needed to develop an optimal set of characteristics for various purposes. For taxonomic analysis, which has the goal of classification into homogeneous groupings in order to facili-

TABLE 11.1 *Comparison of spaceship social system with 11 other isolated microsocieties, by category of social system model. (The maximum comparison score for each category is shown at the head of each column.)*

System Description Category Total

Comparison System	objectives and goals	philosophy and value systems	personal composition	organization	technology	physical environment	temporal characteristics
Max. score	14	12	26	22	14	16	6
Submarines	10	11	13	18	9	8	4
Exploration parties	13	4	17	13	7	11	4
Naval ships	12	11	6	17	7	4	2
Bomber crews	12	9	6	17	7	4	2
Remote duty stations	10	9	6	19	6	3	4
POW situations	9	4	4	6	10	2	6
Prof. athletic teams	11	2	10	5	3	2	1
Mental hosp. wards	4	1	0	1	6	1	6
Prison society	4	0	1	2	5	1	6
Indust. work groups	8	3	3	3	0	0	0
Shipwrecks, disasters	2	0	0	0	0	7	0

TABLE 11.2   *Rank order and comparison scores, showing similarity of 11 social systems to that of the spaceship system*

Rank	Comparison System	Total Score	Per cent of Maximum
1	Submarines	73	67
2	Exploration parties	69	63
3	Naval ships	59	54
4	Bomber crews	57	52
5	Remote duty stations	57	52
6	POW situations	41	37
7	Prof. athletic teams	34	31
8	Mental hosp. wards	19	17
9	Prison society	19	17
10	Indust. work groups	17	15
11	Shipwrecks, disasters	9	8

tate meaningful functional analyses, comprehensive coverage of all relevant system characteristics is important. This requires detailed familiarity with a range of specific social systems as a basis for judgment. Characteristics selected for inclusion should have generality across systems and be measurable. At present measurement scales are available for a large number of the characteristics cited; some can be recorded only dichotomously, while quantification of others remains to be developed. In many cases, the judicious use of rating scales may be more efficient than any other approach. Other purposes, such as studies of behavior contingencies (including research on isolation effects), may require the inclusion of additional information, such as evaluation of role performance, interpersonal interactions, and performance effectiveness, that are related less to the identification of classes of social systems and more to variations of functioning within homogeneous classes.

Even the crude model presented, however, has much promise for meaningful classification. The data presented in Tables 11.1 and 11.2 were regarded as consistent with subjective appraisal by almost every colleague with whom they were discussed. Such consensual consistency is increased by the extensive interdependence among the major categories of the model and makes the omission of specific items that should be included less conspicuous. For purposes of efficient measurement and classification it may be possible to shorten the list, where reliable dependencies are found by correlational analysis, as between personnel characteristics and technology characteristics.

At present, however, it may be more productive to specify at length rather than to seek shortcuts. Indeed, experience in comparing the results of detailed profile analysis with global judgment has shown that the detailed enumeration of characteristics may reveal features of particular

TABLE 11.3 *Comparison of Sealab, Tektite, and McDonnell-Douglas simulator social system profiles with that of the spaceship. (Maximum score for each category is shown by the number in parenthesis after the category title.)*

	Sealab			Tektite			McDonnell-Douglas		
	score	%	rank	score	%	rank	score	%	rank
1. Objectives and goals (14)	13	93	2	12	86	2	10	71	4
2. Philos. and value syst. (12)	11	92	3	7	58	7	5	42	7
3. Personnel composition (26)	20	77	6	26	100	1	24	92	1
4. Organization (22)	21	96	1	16	73	4	16	73	3
5. Technology (14)	11	79	5	10	72	5	8	57	5
6. Physical environment (16)	12	75	7	11	69	6	8	50	6
7. Temporal chars. (6)	5	83	4	5	83	3	5	83	2
Total	93	85		87	80		76	69	

systems that are easily overlooked. For example, I was interested in comparing the social system profiles of the Sealab, Tektite, and McDonnell-Douglas simulator systems with that of the spaceship, used in Tables 11.1 and 11.2. These results are shown in Table 11.3.

It was hypothesized that the McDonnell-Douglas simulation system would have greatest resemblance to the spaceship system, among these three, principally because the spaceship had been used as a reference model in its construction, while Sealab and Tektite, being underwater habitats with extensive extravehicular diving activity, would suffer by comparison. However, the results of the comparison, based on the judgment of one individual, appear to reject this hypothesis. To the extent that these data may be used, even for illustration, both underwater systems were found to have high similarity to the spaceship (Sealab 85 per cent and Tektite 80 per cent), while the spaceship simulator fell closer to, but still higher than, the rating of submarines. Its rated similarity was 69 per cent.

Table 11.3 shows the areas of greater and less similarity of all these comparison systems to the social system of the spacecraft, both by percentage of maximum possible score and by rank order of categories within each system. The high similarity of Sealab to the spaceship social system reflects the extent to which it simulates that type of system in respect to objectives and goals, philosophy and value systems, and organization, principally as a function of its military frame of reference. Tektite and the McDonnell simulator are more similar in personnel composition, but achieve low similarity scores in a number of other categories, particularly philosophy and value systems, reflecting essentially less formal, nonmilitary approaches to organization and operation.

Concluding Remarks

The thesis presented in this chapter is that a taxonomy of man in isolation or of man in enclosed space requires analysis of isolated and confined situations in terms of a social system model. While the effects of social isolation, confinement, and sensory restriction appear to be salient, they cannot be disentangled from the highly interdependent social system contexts in which they occur, and it is strongly indicated that they vary significantly among classes of social systems.

The social system model presented here requires further development, but even in the primitive form of the current model it lends itself to taxonomic analysis by multivariate methods of profile and hierarchical grouping analysis.

REFERENCES

Agadzhanian, N. A., Bizin, I. P., Doronin, G. P., & Kuznetsov, A. G. 1963. (Change in higher nervous activity and some vegetative reactions under prolonged conditions of adynami and isolation). *Zhurnal vysshei nervoni Deiatelnosti, Pavlov* 13:953–62. (In Russian.)

Alluisi, E. A., Chiles, W. D., Hall, T. J., & Hawkes, G. R. 1963. Human group performance during confinement. Technical Rept. No. AMRL–TDR–63–87. Contract no. AF 33(616)–7607, 7570th Aerospace Medical Research Laboratory, Wright-Patterson AFB, Ohio. Lockheed-Georgia Co., November.

Altman, I., & Haythorn, W. W. 1967. The ecology of isolated groups. *Behav. Sci.* 12:169–82.

Arndt, W. F. Jr., & Jackson, J. K. 1968. Life support system tests in a manned space cabin simulator. McDonnell-Douglas Astronautics Co., Santa Monica, Calif.

Burns, N., & Kimura, D. 1963. Isolation and sensory deprivation. In *Unusual environments and human behavior*, ed. N. Burns, R. Chambers, & E. Hendler, pp. 167–92. New York: Macmillan.

Cowan, E. H., & Strickland, D. A. 1965. The legal structure of a confined microsociety (A report on the cases of Penthouse II and III). Internal working paper No. 34, Space Sciences Laboratory, Social Sciences Project, University of California, Berkeley, Calif., August.

David, H. M. 1963. Prolonged space flight poses monotony problem. *Missiles and Rockets* 13:31–32.

Dunlap, R. D. n. d. The selection and training of crewmen for an isolation and confinement study in the Douglas space cabin simulator. Douglas Paper No. 3446, Man-system Integration Branch, Advance Biotechnology Department, Douglas Missile and Space Systems Division, Douglas Aircraft Co., Inc.

Durkheim, E. 1951. *Suicide*. Trans. J. A. Spaulding & G. Simpson. New York: Free Press.

Eilbert, L. R., & Glaser, R. 1959. Differences between well and poorly adjusted groups in an isolated environment. *J. appl. Psychol.* 43:271–74.

Farrell, R. J., & Smith, S. 1969. Behavior of five men confined for 30 days: Psychological assessment during project MESA. Contract No. NASW–658, no. D2–90586. The Boeing Co., Seattle, Wash.

Faucett, R. E., & Newman, P. P. 1953. Operation hideout: Preliminary report. Medical Research Laboratory, U.S. Naval Submarine Base, New London, Conn. Report No. 228, July.

Fraser, T. M. 1966. The effects of confinement as a factor in manned space flight. NASA Contractor Report, NASA CR–511, July.

Goffman, E. 1961. *Asylums.* Chicago: Aldine-Atherton.

Gunderson, E. K. E. 1965. Biographical predictors of performance in an environment. *J. Psychol.* 61:59–67.

Gunderson, E. K. E., & Nelson, P. D. 1966. Criterion measures for extremely isolated groups. *Personnel Psychol.* 19:67–80.

Hall, E. T. 1966. *The hidden dimension.* New York: Doubleday.

Hammes, J. A. 1964. Shelter occupancy studies at the University of Georgia. Final Report, Athens, Ga.: Civil Defense Research.

Hanna, T. D. 1962. A physiologic study of human subjects confined in a simulated space vehicle. *Aerospace Med.* 33:175–82.

Hanna, T. D., & Gaito, J. 1960. Performance and habitability aspects of extended confinement in sealed cabins. *Aerospace Med.* 31:399–406.

Hartman, B. O., Flinn, D. E., Edmunds, A. B., Brown, F. C., & Schubert, J. E. 1964. Human factors aspects of a 30-day extended survivability test of the minuteman missile. USAF School of Aerospace Medicine, Aerospace Medicine Division (AFSC), Brooks AFB, Tex., Technical Documentary Rept. No. 64–62, October.

Haythorn, W. W. 1966. Social emotional considerations in confined groups. In *The effects of confinement on long duration manned space flights,* Proceedings of the NASA Symposium: 8–15.

Heron, W., Bexton, W. H., & Hebb, D. O. 1953. Cognitive effects of a decreased variation in the sensory environment. *Amer. Psychologist* 8:366.

Jackson, J. K., & Houghton, K. H. 1969. Test plan and procedure. Operational ninety-day manned test of a regenerative life support system. NASA-LRC Contract NAS 1–8997. McDonnell-Douglas Astronautics Co., Santa Monica, Calif.

Jessor, R., Graves, T. D., Hanson, R. C., & Jessor, S. L. 1968. *Society, personality, and deviant behavior.* New York: Holt, Rinehart and Winston.

Lilly, J. C. 1956. Mental effects of reduction of ordinary levels of physical stimuli on intact healthy persons. *Psychiatric Research Reports* 5:1–9.

McGrath, J., Maag, C., Hatcher, J., & Brewer, W. 1962. Human performance during five days confinement. Technical Memo 206–14. Human Factors Research, Los Angeles, Calif., January.

Merton, R. K. 1957. *Social theory and social structure.* New York: Free Press.

Miller, D. C. 1959. A brief review of salient specific findings on morale and human behavior of young men living under the isolation and relative deprivation of a radar base habitability—Working paper. Washington, D.C.: Disaster Research Group, Division of Anthropology and Psychology, National Academy of Sciences—National Research Council.

Mullin, C. S. 1960. Some psychological aspects of isolated Antarctic living. *Amer. J. Psychiatry* 117:323–25.

Murdock, G. P., Ford, C. S., Hudson, A. E., Kennedy, R., Simmons, L. W., & Whiting, J. W. M. 1961. *Outline of cultural materials.* 4th rev. ed. New Haven, Conn.: Human Relations Area Files, Inc.

Perkins, C. D. 1969. Beyond Apollo. *Aerospace Med.* 40:815–19.

Radloff, R. W. 1969. Artificial groups under controlled or direct observation, NATO Symposium on Man in Enclosed Space, Rome, October.

Radloff, R., & Helmreich, R. 1968. *Groups under stress: Psychological research in Sealab II.* New York: Appleton-Century-Crofts.

Rodgin, D. W., & Hartman, B. O. 1966. Study of man during a 56-day exposure to an oxygen-helium atmosphere at 258 mm Hg total pressure: XIII. Behavioral factors. *Aerospace Med.* 37:605–8.

Rohrer, J. H. 1959. Studies of human adjustment to submarine isolation and implications of those studies for living in fallout shelters—Working paper. Washington, D.C.: Disaster Research Group, Division of Anthropology and Psychology, National Academy of Sciences—National Research Council.

Schultz, D. P. 1965. *Sensory restriction effects on behavior.* New York: Academic Press.

Sells, S. B. 1956. Emerging problems of human adaptability to military flying missions. Paper presented at the Human Factors Technical Symposium, Chicago, 5–6 June.

———. 1963. Tapescript to accompany tape recording of research report on leadership and organizational factors at effective AC&W sites. Institute of Behavioral Research, Texas Christian University, October. AF Contract no. 41(657)–323.

———. 1966. A model for the social system for the multiman extended duration space ship. Paper presented at the AIAA/AAS Conference, Stepping Stone to Mars, Baltimore, Md., March.

———. 1967a. Capsule society. New problems for men in space on long-duration missions. Paper presented at the Conference on Bioastronautics, Virginia Polytechnic Institute, Blacksburg, Va., August.

———. ed. 1967b. Conference on social-behavioral problems of long-duration space missions. Institute of Behavioral Research, Texas Christian University, September. Report of NASA Grant NGR 44–009–008.

———. 1968. *People, groups, and organizations.* General Theoretical Problems Related to Organizational Taxonomy: A Model Solution, pp. 27–47. New York: Teachers College Press.

Sells, S. B., & Rawls, James R. 1968. Effects of isolation on man's performance. Institute of Behavioral Research, Texas Christian University. Report of NASA Grant NGR 44–009–008.

———. 1969. Bioengineering and Cabin Ecology. Science and Technology Series. Tarzana, Calif.: American Astronautical Society. pp. 89–116.

Smith, W. M. 1966. Observations over the lifetime of a small isolated group: Structure, danger, boredom, and vision. *Psycholog. Reports.* 19:475–514. (Monogr. Supp. 3–V19.)

Sommer, R. 1969. *Personal space: A behavioral basis of design.* Englewood Cliffs, N.J.: Prentice-Hall.

Srole, L. 1956. Social integration and certain corollaries: An exploratory study. *Amer. Soc. Review* 21:709–16.

Torrance, E. P. 1957. What happens to the sociometric structure of small groups in emergencies and extreme conditions? *Group Psychotherapy.* 10:212–20.

Trego, R., & McGaffey, C. N. 1969. Personal space: A critical review. Institute of Behavioral Research, Texas Christian University, September. Unpublished report of NASA Grant NGR 44–009–008.

Warren, Donald I. 1966. The subculture and organizational setting of space-flight: Some preliminary applications of sociological theory in the prediction of future multi-man missions. Institute of Behavioral Research, Texas Christian University, December. Report of NASA Grant NGR 44–009–008.

Wheaton, J. L. 1958. Fact and fancy in isolation and sensory deprivation. School of Aviation Medicine, USAF, Randolph AFB, Tex., June.

Wilkins, W. L. 1967. Group behavior in long-term isolation. *Psychological stress: Issues in research*, ed. M. Appley & R. Trumbull. New York: Appleton-Century-Crofts.

Zubek, J. P. 1969. *Sensory deprivation: Fifteen years of research*. New York: Appleton-Century-Crofts.

Zubek, J. P., Aftanas, M., Hasek, J., Sandom, W., Schludermann, E., Wilgosh, L., & Winocur, G. 1962. Intellectual and perceptual changes during prolonged perceptual deprivation: Low illumination and noise level. *Percep. mot. Skills* 15:171–98.

Walter L. Wilkins, *Scientific Director of the Navy Medical Neuropsychiatric Research Unit in San Diego since 1959, received his Ph.D. from Northwestern University. Before and after World War II he taught psychology at the University of Notre Dame and then for ten years headed the psychology department at St. Louis University.*

Wilkins *provides an overview of the research presented at the NATO Symposium on Man In Isolation and Confinement, held in Rome, Italy. The papers considered range from the detailed, meticulous study of the individual volunteer in a university laboratory who is systematically deprived of every possible stimulating input to the study of the behavior of groups of men who find themselves in socially isolating situations. He finds encouraging signs of validity in the ways investigators using different methods and different populations are developing general principles applicable to the understanding of men in isolation. In addition, he looks for a sharpening of research focus in the field as researchers from psychology, anthropology, sociology, medicine, and human engineering all contribute their methods and insights.*

12

Isolation Research: The Methodological Context

WALTER L. WILKINS

In man's constant study of the behavior of man the student may wonder where man *should* be studied so that his behavior is most deeply understood and perhaps even most accurately predicted. Where *should* the psychologist study man? Already in the literature, and easy to find, are comments (sometimes biased, sometimes not) on the relative importance of meticulously controlled laboratory experiments, of less rigidly controlled field situations, and of virtually uncontrolled natural situations where only an acute observer is present. Not so well discussed in the literature is how generalizations from the different approaches used in the laboratory and outside of it can be used to help each other's validity.

The common sense answer to the question would seem to be that the psychologist should study man wherever man is behaving in a way that might throw light on his abilities and how they function, on his motives and his aspirations, on his hopes and fears, on his life style. So psychologists must study man the poet, man the mathematician, man the architect, the bridge builder, the sculptor, the creator. As we know, these behaviors of man have been stubborn to reveal their secrets—of ability as well as of motivation—to the scientist.

The psychologist must study man the worker, the consumer, the child and the parent, the lover. Psychology has been a little more successful here than in the study of man's artistic or mathematical or scientific creativity. Psychology must also study man the patient, the learner, the teacher, the healer, the counselor. Here the psychologist has been fairly successful.

At the same time, psychology must study man as he acts in other than his typical daily rounds. It must address itself to the question: What do men do when, by design or fortune, they find themselves in situations far different from their usual lives? There has always been a considerable interest in man in isolation, and accounts of his adjustment have been contributed by biographers, historians, and others. Men have isolated themselves alone or in groups for religious, adventurous, scientific, and military purposes.

This book has not concerned itself with the isolation of prisoners in jails, of monks in monasteries or hermits, of remote tribes isolated by geography or by politics, but has looked more on isolation and modern civilized man. The volume provides up-to-date and comprehensive summaries of the present state of knowledge in this difficult and challenging topic. It includes exhaustive reviews of what has been done, of what has been learned from the experiences of men as individuals or in groups who have been isolated, physically or socially, or confined by force of circumstances or act of God. We can see how they survived, how they accomplished their tasks, how they kept their sanity, and what effects their experiences had on their later lives, their characters, and on their relations with fellow men.

Seeking to test the hypotheses developed from such experiences, ingenious experimenters, including the authors of several preceding chapters, have set up situations in which objective and subjective measures of effects of isolation in natural settings could be made. Professor Haggard's sympathetic account of the Norwegian isolated single farm showed us that there are isolation situations in which man, with his surprising resiliency of physique and of personality, can adapt. The developmental approach to the understanding of human behavior is reinforced by Haggard's data. If one wants to find out, really, how a psychological attitude functions in the life of an individual, one must study how it developed. Haggard observes that some of these isolated families, by their use of communications among themselves and by the subtle induction of attitudes and frames of reference, actually prepare their children for an existence that city folk would describe as lonely and would certainly find intolerable. This provides a useful model for study of the ways families structure attitudes toward life.

I am reminded of another isolated society that it would be interesting to know more about, but which for the present I hope the social scientists can leave alone. Niihau, one of the most western of the central islands of the State of Hawaii, is a place where the original language, customs, means of living, growing of food, and nurture and training of children are preserved, and are unaffected by all the clangor, bustle, and civilization of the other nearby islands. Niihau has no TV, no newspaper, and has only one emergency radio for calling for medical or other help. It will be interesting to see how long the family that owns the small island will be able to keep it unsullied from this world, and, as it were, a living historical account of idyllic mid-Pacific life. Haggard's research illustrates the use of unobstrusive measures with a population accustomed to isolation for generations and more or less adequately adapted to their isolation as a way of life, either preferring it or being unfamiliar with alternative modes of existence.

He was interested in finding out whether such isolated persons, accustomed to low levels of social stimulation, had much in common with persons in urban cultures who were somewhat withdrawn in personality or whose skills at interpersonal affairs were perhaps simply undeveloped. Isolates who grow up in remote areas tend to be nonverbal, and also seem to be able to tolerate monotony and perceptual deprivation with relative ease.

One of the characteristics Haggard noted was a less well-developed sense of time. It is known from the French cave experiments carried on by Jouvet and Fraisse that a sense of the passage of time can be affected by prolonged absence—in this case weeks—from the usual *Zeitgeber*, such as night and day. It may turn out that for the native farmer in a less time-constrained society that the social time-givers, being less regularly enforced or even attended to, bring about a general disregard for the imperatives of time that are so potent in urban cultures. Haggard addressed himself to the question of how individuals growing up in extremely isolated families developed the character structure, the philosophy of life, and the interpersonal skills (or the lack of them if one regards them from the point of view of the ordinary city dweller) that enabled them to adapt to the monotony, the routines of limited variation, and the lack of people. Gunderson turned to another question. How does the person from a more urban environment, accustomed to the stimulation of many people, of variability in demands of job and of living, adapt when he finds himself away from the civilization to which he is accustomed and a member of a group isolated from the usual comforts and rewards?

Gunderson, studying for a decade the adjustment of men wintering in the Antarctic, has very patiently attacked the complex problem of what constitutes good or acceptable performance in isolation situations, and what in the situation—physical, mental, social—may contribute to degradation of performance. Accomplishment in a strange and isolated environment, especially where there may be an added element of peril, may be markedly different from accomplishment in routine jobs. Thus, Gunderson (1963) analyzed carefully what each man's job demanded from the man in terms of both competence and motivation. He and his colleagues also were able to show how, in a situation in which men have to cooperate to get a mission accomplished, they get along with each other —how personality factors and job factors interact with sociability to produce acceptability among peers. And, paying attention to the sorts of things Haggard alluded to, he looked into the matter of emotionality. Gunderson's classical paper on the waxing and waning of emotional symptoms over a year's time in an isolated group lies at the background of this analysis. Again, personality factors and job factors show some relationship with the sort of emotional composure Gunderson and Nelson have described as critical in the adjustment of men to such situations.

Prolonged confinement of the sort described by Zubek for volunteers in a perceptual deprivation experiment in the Manitoba psychological laboratories brought about some effects distinguishable from those of deprivation itself. Prolonged confinement in the enforced socialization of the group isolated by the Antarctic weather had a tendency to produce emotional and motivational problems. Sometimes the behavior was rather childish; some expedition member would sulk or have a minor temper tantrum. Sometimes it involved some hours or days of self-imposed or group-imposed withdrawal from the group activities, perhaps motivated by a need for solitude and at other times resulting from a sort of Coventry imposed by peers.

A methodological contribution from Gunderson's work that should be emphasized is the way in which he used factor analyses of trait ratings made by peers and by supervisors in the isolation situation. Emerging from these analyses were salient dimensions of emotional control, along with acceptance of authority, industriousness, and motivation toward achievement, and being likable in the eyes of supervisors and friendly in the eyes of one's peers. The congruence with the results of analyses of the behaviors needed in such situations could hardly be more tidy nor more appropriate. There have not been many examples of the Campbell-Fiske (1959) convergent and discriminant validation of psychological measures using real-life situations. The use of the Antarctic stations as real-life experimental situations has produced a validated picture of the personality-task interactions in a situation of social isolation. The most important sort of validity in life or in laboratory situations is predictive validity. The measures developed by Gunderson possess this commendable feature.

A most interesting question raised by Gunderson in relation to the Antarctic data is this: Is it really true that the best predictor of future adjustment is past adjustment? Can one do better in predicting human behavior than to say that it will be about the same tomorrow as it was yesterday? Gunderson's answer is qualified. The prediction of performance in individuals in naturally isolated groups is very difficult because of the complexity of the situation. If one can achieve some specificity in the identification of appropriate predictors and of job roles, however, one can relate these characteristics to valid parts of the general criterion situation.

Common sense would tell us that past experience helps predict adjustment, if the past experience be in some demonstrable way related to the experience being predicted to. But Gunderson shows us that *just* past experience will not do. If past experience is combined with some evidence of competence, the prediction will be better. For instance, in his groups, men who had shown their competence by being promoted in Navy rates or technical proficiency levels were more likely to do well than were unpromoted men. But his analyses of the actual competencies needed and the personality factors—emotional composure—focus attention on the really useful predictors.

Another step takes us to the sorts of situations described by Nelson, in which he focused attention upon certain phenomenological features of the problems. Environmental restriction may be physical (resulting from confinement or constraints of environment), social, or only mental. In his poem "The Locomotive God," Professor William Ellery Leonard of the English Department at the University of Wisconsin some years ago described how his physical universe became constricted geographically to just a few square blocks, although his intellectual and cultural universe remained rich and varied.

Nelson also, wisely, called our attention to the culture of the group—the values held in common by the members, the norms, the attitudes, even the humor—and how the developed culture is relevant to goals, to morale, and to accomplishment. These considerations are just as true of isolated groups as of any other groups. Group cohesiveness is related to the group goals. Nelson reminds us of how, in the prisoner-of-war situation, men lose their drive and their sense of responsibility, or are induced to do so by the conduct of their captors, and thus lessen any chances of their achieving any goals, either group or individual.

Attention turns, naturally, to the purposeful small group, specifically in the case of the experiment reported by Radloff, to men living for 60 days or so in an underwater environment. In the Sealab and Tektite experiments it was possible, because of both the technology and methods available and the acquiescence of the participants, to set up almost continuous monitoring and recording of the behavior of the men isolated. During the day the TV and the other monitors described by Dr. Radloff allowed the collection of great amounts of data and at night the men even had their sleep recorded.

The isolation of the deep-sea saturation diver, as he describes it, may not seem to be as serious as that of the Antarctic scientist who must wait for the following spring to return, nor as that of the astronaut, geographically so remote from his base. But the inexorable demands of human physiology make the aquanaut, only a few hundred feet away, many days from rescue if something should go awry. While isolated, he is still observable. So Radloff asks what we can learn about isolation and man's behavior in isolation from noninterfering, unobtrusive observation.

The chief gains in knowledge seem to be in the area of social interaction among the members of the isolated group, especially in the way they work together. As Radloff says, the work a man does not only helps him and his group to survive and to accomplish the goals of the group's mission. It also is an important contributor to the man's status within the group, and it is a consumer of time. This last point is of considerable significance to healthy adjustment in isolation.

How shall work and its accomplishments be measured? Obviously by multiple measures of various sorts of productivity over time. There is a suggestion in Radloff's chapter that deviation scores of some sort can be profitably used. The man who seriously deviates from the group norms, especially the one who falls below the norms quite noticeably, is not contributing to the mission and may even be endangering it. It is possible that Berg's deviation hypothesis (see Berg & Bass, 1961) might have more utility in the selection of men for exotic assignments than had been assumed.

A step further brings us to Dr. Haythorn's meticulously designed studies of the interactions of two-man groups under conditions of considerable restriction of personal space, of things to do, and of reduction or elimination of the routine rewards of social living. He introduces Myers's concepts of tedium stress, unreality stress up to claustrophobic reactions, and positive contemplation. Attention is drawn to the possible rewarding, perhaps even the therapeutic, effects of social isolation for some people under some conditions. At one time it was popular in both Western and Eastern religions for the committed to retreat for a few days from the stresses of daily concerns. The positive contemplation factor identified by Thomas Myers and confirmed by Zuckerman and Zubek is worthy of further study.

Men in isolation have social needs. Haythorn shows that some of these needs are affiliative, some are for achievement, and so on. His work demonstrates how pairs of men with compatible needs exhibit less tendency to establish territories to be defended, while those with incompatible or incongruent needs show the opposite. Again, men with equally strong needs to dominate a social situation tend to be unable to continue in experimental isolation experiments, while men with complementary dominance needs show less hostility and can persist in isolation.

Discussions of hierarchies of needs center on those advanced by A. Maslow. Should men in isolated groups be guaranteed that all their needs will be gratified? In point of fact, some of the needs at the apex of the Maslow scheme are such that for most people they are never satisfied at all. Self-actualization must be, even for creative people, relatively infrequent in its fullest flower. Haythorn's chart provides a useful checklist to call attention to important areas systems designers might neglect, but it contains no assertion that every such need must be fulfilled.

Altman goes further, and in his thoughtful remarks about the dynamics of social penetration brings out some implications for learning and training as well as for consideration of the personality structure. He is properly concerned about the communication process in isolated groups and how communication relates to the dimensions of an effective interpersonal system. Obliquely, he raises the question of whether all human relationships need richer and fuller communication. The answer seems to be that they probably do not, but some important ones surely do. The interesting studies of Ekman and Friesen (1969) of the California State Department of Mental Hygiene Institute at San Francisco, and of Mario von Cranach at the Max Planck Institut für Psychiatrie at Munich are relevant to these considerations. They have been photographing interpersonal behavior and analyzing components frame by frame, and thus discovering the basic means of social communication of nonverbal sorts. Altman's placing of his data and his theory in an ecological framework, and his emphasis on the demands of time are positive contributions.

In her response to Altman, de Montmollin inquires whether it might not be interesting to utilize the research strategy we could obtain from ergonomics. If one conceives of ergonomics as involving the range of study of man working, from psychological, physiological, and industrial engineering points of view, this is certainly a sound suggestion. She also asks whether training people for isolation might not be an extremely effective way of improving performance in isolation. We know of course in the field of child development that informing a child about an imminent danger or problem goes a long way toward allaying his anxiety about it; the classic example is the child entering the pediatric hospital for serious surgery. If he be told, calmly and positively, about the up-coming event, his postoperative recovery is both physiologically and psychologically improved.

The thought of anxiety and surgery should also remind us of the fact that a little anxiety may be a very good thing indeed when a critical situation is coming up—in sports, in education, or in battle. Irving Janis's book *Psychological Stress* (1958), a study of reactions to surgery, gives cogent evidence on the effect of reasonable anxiety on postoperative recovery times and readjustment.

Sells also mentions, in addition to thorough training, the effects of anticipations on reactions and how prudent order can help control undesired reactions. In an unpublished experiment a few years ago, John Rasmussen and Richard Trumbull found a group of naval reserve officers ordered to Washington for 2 weeks of active duty for training. The group was a mixed bag of university professors, scientists, and engineers. On the first day, while the group was being shown the spaces for the study of isolation (a tunnel dug into a hillside), the door clanged shut on them, leaving Trumbull inside as an expert observer. In this experiment the fact that the men were all military officers and had ranks that defined their authority and their responsibility helped their organization for living for 2 weeks in an uncomfortable, crowded place. They were disconcerted, but before long settled down, thus corroborating the validity of Sells's generalization. Leadership, whether assigned as in military situations, or assumed as in disaster situations, is a really critical aspect of adjustment to novel or unusual situations. We really should know more about leadership styles in isolated groups. Nelson's early study of Antarctic stations should be greatly expanded.

Nelson is interested in the self-sustaining character of most groups, in or out of isolation. Here the study of why groups break up is relevant. Sometimes, instead of breaking up when things do not work out, groups change their original goals when the old goals are deemed to be no longer appropriate. There is, however, Sells's example of a goal almost impossible to modify: the space capsule whose path cannot be changed because of the inexorable constraints of physical laws. Part of the self-sustaining feature of groups, including isolated ones, is the culture of the group—its values, its signs, its humor, its life style.

The precise measurement of effects of prolonged deprivation, so necessary to check the hypotheses of the naturalistic and the empirical situations, is copiously described by Zubek. The work initiated at McGill and carried on so comprehensively at Manitoba has answered a whole range of questions about psychophysiological, perceptual, and cognitive effects of sensory deprivation and of perceptual deprivation. Noteworthy in Zubek's chapter are his emphases on the possible existence of critical periods—for instance, the critical period of deprivation for perceptual effects seems to be 2 days—and his discussion of the sensation seeking needs. Just as we need quiet after too much noise, we need stimulation (activity) after too much quietude.

We need more research, probably cross-cultural, on the differences between quitters and endurers. Zubek shows us that personality tests are disappointing in identifying those who persist and those who drop out. Are there national or characterological differences? Rural-urban? Haggard's data suggest that the rural farmers might be more persistent than urban dwellers. A device to identify persisters would be most useful to academic, industrial, and military selection systems.

Not only in isolation experiments, but also in many industrial situations there is not enough attention paid to sleep and its hygiene, for there *is* a hygiene of sleep. The capsule designers, when they get to designing vehicles for periods longer than 2 or 3 weeks, will have to plan carefully. In the Antarctic, Gunderson says, men can, during periods of reduced work load in the depth of winter, do without quite a bit of sleep. But a situation in which vigilance is required cannot tolerate a man whose sleep has been critically reduced or interfered with. My colleague, Paul Naitch, has published some admonitions on this problem (Naitch & Townsend, 1970) and on the degradation of performance resulting from sleep loss.

In the San Diego laboratory we are very attentive to physical condition and its relation to stamina and performance. After all, as the physiologists remind us, man was made to work. He needs a certain amount of work to be fit. Planning for fitness in isolation ranks with planning for sleep in isolation among the neglected concerns.

A topic mentioned in every chapter of this volume is time. The duration of the isolation experience itself is important, and so is the perception of the duration. Gunderson and Nelson some years ago wrote about the significance of midwinter day, June 21, at the South Pole. On this day there is a great celebration, for the long 6-month night is half over. June 21 is an annual *Zeitgeber* for the ice-bound scientists and sailors. Now what is the result of the loss of the usual time givers? In Fraisse's cave experiments, where the sun was eliminated and where noise and work were reduced or manipulated so that the subject's perception of time was considerably affected, the effects were so great that, at least in one instance, weight loss resulted from the subject's not taking enough food. The misperception of time also influenced sleep so that a considerable sleep deficit was earned. Exercise was also affected, with results that might be expected in lowered muscle tone and other effects.

Another thing about time is its function as a healer. We all know the benison of a poor memory. Life is kind in allowing us to forget a large proportion of the situations in which we, as both children and adults, were traumatized. We develop some sort of emotional overlay that enables us to go on after life crises, even though it seemed at first as though we could not live through the embarrassment or the grief. Some of the time compressions and other time phenomena noted in this book may be related to some fundamental relationship between adjustment and the time parameter. Time is an important feature of man's capacity to adapt, and complements his remarkable resiliency in stressful situations.

Let us remind ourselves of the goals involved in having men in isolation—and since we are planning, let us confine our attention to groups of men who are in isolation of some sort, spatial, oceanic, remote, or what not, on purpose. As Sells and others have pointed out, the purpose may be their own, with its associated motivational system, or the purpose may be that of some higher organization.

At the present time, there can be little doubt that one of the principal motivations for men to enter into situations that involve isolation is that of research. In astronauts, aquanauts, people in laboratory experiments, and Antarctic wintering-over situations, the need to learn more about man's reaction to stress is the overriding motivation. Man, of course, lives under a more or less constant condition of stress, and the strains he experiences have been of interest to medical science for many, many years and, more recently perhaps, to behavioral science. When we reflect, however, on the fact that life is stressful and that everybody experiences strains, we have not touched the motivation of the researcher—and of his subject or his volunteer—who desires to know the limits of human tolerance to stress. The underwater divers who go deeper and stay longer, the astronauts who venture even farther from earth, are testing the limits of human capability, of human ingenuity, of human engineering.

A fundamental feature of research is a spirit of adventure, and it is a commendable feature. Now it happens that while all research worth the effort has venturesome features, even though these be mostly intellectual, the research area discussed in this book happens to enjoy the venturesomeness of the intellect that is the hallmark of all great, and of much good, research. It also has a marked venturesomeness in other aspects of human striving. The natural situations and the laboratory experiments described therein put men into conditions of inconvenience, of pain, of cold and hunger, indeed, of real peril. I feel sure that the extra attraction of research in the area of human isolation is partially the result of this fillip of danger, the feeling of something previously not really hazarded. It is true, as Gunderson pointed out, that because of extraordinary care and uncommon prudence and superb technology there have been very few men lost in the Antarctic, or in space, or in underwater research. There have been some, though—enough to remind us that we are experimenting with human life, and that sheer survival must be kept at the top of the list of things to be accomplished in any mission where men are isolated.

Research in the area of human stress through isolation has a good bit of the motivation of the old-fashioned explorer who was determined to set foot where no man before him had. It may also have, as Radloff suggests, much of the motivational pull that religion had in the great cathedral-building age in Europe.

Next in any list of goals for the study of man in isolation, we should put the economic and the military. There are economic reasons for the conquest of the ocean floor and these are often identified as metallurgical and agricultural. There are military reasons, too, for such interest and for interest in many remote areas of the world. If economic gain can be realized from isolation research, it will probably be adequately funded.

A review of goals reinforces the conclusion that when we send men into an organized, planned situation where they will be isolated geographically or in any other way from their routine ways of living and from their source of support—support in energy, in food, in solace, in belongingness —we must give absolute primacy to the importance of the *mission* they are embarked upon. This primacy carries with it some important implications. For instance, if accomplishment of the goals comes first—you will recall that we have already mentioned survival—then selection of the members of the group must be made after a careful analysis of the technical or other requirements. Where health is a matter of concern over a long-duration mission, one would assume that a physician, and one with a broad range of skills from orthopedics to psychiatry, would be included. Where a mission may involve some manipulation of equipment with consummate skill and daring, as with Neil Armstrong's last moments before setting the capsule on the moon, then one would assume that a person possessing the required skill would be included.

So as we analyze what must be accomplished, we make compromises with space and with comfort, but not with safety. We count up what must be done and we count the people needed to do it. At the South Pole, a given station may require a physician, a cook, an electrician, a radioman, and technicians, to monitor the scientific gear. In a space capsule a different set of competencies is required, but they also are tailored to the mission and the insurance of its achievement.

A proper guide for making judgments about the mission and the tolerance limit of isolation is Sells's list. His chapter shows that missions which are planned, are instrumental, and are voluntary will involve less stress than those that are not. He also emphasizes mission duration; threat (real and perceived); the important interaction between lack of space and lack of privacy and the size of the group embarked; and variability of the environment, which may involve even sensory deprivation.

When man enters a new and unfamiliar environment he carries big pieces of his environment, and not just nuts and bolts, along with him. Nelson gives some illustrations of this in his comments on life style and humor as a needed factor. All too often, I am afraid, we think of air, food, water, warmth, and such life support systems only when we think of man's taking along his environment. But the astronauts carried along also their style of life—one that has been highly publicized—and their particular culture as well. And so will all groups of men entering an isolation situation.[1]

There is a pertinent example of a wider principle, of course. When

---

1. What different missions need may well differ. There is, in a Stockholm museum, a copy of a letter from Sir Ernest Shackleton to his whisky supplier in Scotland, ordering 472 cases of whisky to be delivered dockside to his ship before his last expedition. We must conclude from this, I presume, that some of the glamour has gone out of exploration. I doubt that NASA or the equivalent Russian space authorities would order up such a morale builder. Indeed, perhaps not even the National Geographic Society would.

people move from one culture to another and suffer culture shock, they bring along as much of their culture as they can. The Italian immigrants coming to New York 70 years ago settled near each other for comfort and familiarity and held tightly to the language and the religion that were a part of their lives. I quote from Haggard's chapter: ". . . the individual's adaptation patterns will be stressed or even break down if the isolation situation in question is sufficiently long, especially if it is very different from those to which that individual is accustomed." So when men are sent into isolation we must remember the supports that keep them fit. These supports are technical and physical, but they are also social and emotional, and probably spiritual in a wide sense.

It is gratifying that the researches of Gunderson and Radloff, done so many miles apart on such different samples and with different missions, should have agreed on the factors of emotional stability and composure and of social compatibility. Of course, as Sells points out in his taxonomy, these concepts are too broad to provide a basis for specific action—either research action or real-life situations. There have been other instances of the sort of convergence that Altman pleads for. Certainly his own laboratory experiments and those of his longtime colleague, Haythorn, provide illuminating examples of concepts developed in the laboratory and tested with people, and of concepts developed in the natural situations and put to a rigorous test in the laboratory.

Nelson asks two most difficult questions. Is it possible, now, to construct a general system of isolation? And, does the study of isolation have any peculiar quality that makes it more important to study than any of a hundred other social phenomena? The first question deserves a hesitant no. To the second Fraisse responds cogently and appropriately, in my view. The study of men in isolation is both practical and scientific. Man is a social animal and we should study him in social situations in which he finds real and meaningful tasks, and perhaps some possibility of social conflict. Moreover, man in isolation is, as Radloff reminds us, man in stress.

Does the study of men under these exotic or abnormal conditions have implications for understanding behavior generally—that is, for psychology as a science, or perhaps for anthropology and for sociology? As Haythorn points out and as Altman stresses, too, the generalizations we can make about man's behavior in isolation are worthy of confidence to the extent that we *can* put them in generalizable terms. This is not to say that all of our studies will need large populations. Science learns a great deal sometimes from just a few examples, or from even one. For instance, we may recall that two men in the history of medical science had wounds or conditions that allowed surgeons to observe directly the movements and reactions of the stomach and associated organs. These volunteers provided for Dr. William Beaumont and for Dr. Harold Wolff data of inestimable value. When the experiment allows generalization, the single case may well be enough. So far we have visited the moon only a few times, but we have learned much from it. To learn some of the lessons isolation research may teach us we may not need hundreds of experiments; perhaps dozens will do if properly designed to give us the basic information.

We may also ask if research on man in isolation will provide us with models of behavior. In this sense, I refer not to models in the scientific sense, but to models that men can learn from. I feel that all too often men imitate behavior for reasons other than demonstrable statistical validity. If statistical validity were sufficient to convince men of the appropriateness of an action, then smoking would be an historical event instead of a common habit, and automobile drivers would act quite differently toward other motorists and pedestrians. When one visits the great churches of Italy and France one sees the monuments to the lives of the saints who through individual sacrifice or galvanizing of faithful opinion changed social and moral conditions in their time. Nobody now, nor then, imitates sanctity because it is statistically good. The conduct itself on the part of the individual hero was worthy of our doing the same. The lessons for man from the study of isolation may come as much from the conduct of certain persons or of certain traits in those persons. The men who spent months and years in isolation and then described their reactions were also men of heroic conduct.

One might compare here the field of abnormal psychology, and what it can and cannot tell us about normal behavior. Surely the study of men behaving neurotically or psychopathically can tell us much about the motivations of people in normal conditions, whatever they may be. Of course we have to be careful about generalizing from insights in abnormal psychology to those in general psychology. Isolation, in like manner, allows us to focus our scientific microscopes, if you will, on behavior in a real, challenging, and dramatic area of life.

Finally, who should mount, who should support a research effort of this significance, this expense, this challenge? There are sufficient challenges for many laboratories—but not for all. One or two laboratories or field research stations in each country that has a viable capacity for research in medicine, in anthropology and psychology, in industrial engineering, and so on, would be enough. Yet, one never knows when or where a breakthrough may come, so many should be encouraged.

This volume can help sort out the directions—there is no use doing research that has already been done. Still, we must never blithely assume that somebody else's research, just because it is not ours, is inferior. We should encourage crossnational comparisons in these matters, for this book provides evidence of some characterological differences that may prove significant. Perhaps research on the effects of isolation on man, through the different approaches of different scientists from different countries and trained in different disciplines, could set an example of an imitable transnational research effort.

REFERENCES

Berg, I. A., & Bass, B. M. 1961. *Conformity and deviation.* New York: Harper.

Campbell, D. T., & Fisk, D. W. 1959. Convergent and discriminate validation by the multitrait-multimethod matrix. *Psycholog. Bull.* 56:81–105.

Ekman, P., & Friesen, W. V. 1969. The repertoire of non-verbal behavior: Categories, origin, usage, and coding. *Semiotica* 2:49–98.

Gunderson, E. K. E. 1963. Emotional symptoms in extremely isolated groups. *Arch. gen. Psychiatry* 9:362–68.

Janis, I. 1958. *Psychological stress: Psychoanalytic and behavioral studies of surgical patients.* New York: Wiley.

Naitch, P., & Townsend, R. 1970. The role of sleep deprivation research in human factors. *Human Factors* 12:575–585.

Index